PHILOSOPHICAL
WRITINGS

Simone de Beauvoir

PHILOSOPHICAL
WRITINGS

Edited by Margaret A. Simons

with Marybeth Timmermann and Mary Beth Mader

Foreword by Sylvie Le Bon de Beauvoir

University of Illinois Press

Urbana and Chicago

⊗ This book is printed on acid-free paper.
c 6 5 4 3 2

Library of Congress Cataloging-in-Publication Data
Beauvoir, Simone de, 1908–
Philosophical writings / Simone de Beauvoir ; edited by
Margaret A. Simons with the assistance of Marybeth Timmermann and
Mary Beth Mader.
p.   cm. — (Beauvoir series)
Includes bibliographical references and index.
ISBN 0-252-02982-8 (cloth : alk. paper)/ISBN 978-0-252-02982-0
1. Beauvoir, Simone de, 1908—Philosophy. I. Simons, Margaret A. II.
Timmermann, Marybeth. III. Mader, Mary Beth. IV. Title.
PQ2603.E362A6   2004
844'.914—dc22   2004011785

The editors gratefully acknowledge the support of a grant from the
National Endowment for the Humanities, an independent federal
agency, and a Matching Funds grant from the Illinois Board of Higher
Education. This volume also received a translation grant from the
French Ministry of Culture.

IN MEMORY OF KATE FULLBROOK

Contents

Foreword to the Beauvoir Series

Sylvie Le Bon de Beauvoir

TRANSLATED BY MARYBETH TIMMERMANN

It is my pleasure to honor the monumental work of research and publication that the Beauvoir Series represents, which was undertaken and brought to fruition by Margaret A. Simons and her team. These volumes of Simone de Beauvoir's writings, concerning literature as well as philosophy and feminism, stretch from 1926 to 1979, that is to say, throughout almost her entire life. Some of them have been published before and are known, but they remain dispersed throughout time and space, in diverse editions, newspapers, or reviews. Others were read by Beauvoir during conferences or radio programs and then lost from view. Some had been left completely unpublished. What gives all of them force and meaning is precisely having them gathered together, closely, as a whole. Nothing of the sort has yet been realized, except, on a much smaller scale, *Les écrits de Simone de Beauvoir* (The Writings of Simone de Beauvoir), published in France in 1979. Here, the aim is an exhaustive corpus, as much as that is possible.

Because they cover more than fifty years, these volumes faithfully reflect the thoughts of their author, the early manifestation and permanence of certain of her preoccupations as a writer and philosopher, as a woman and feminist. What will be immediately striking, I think, is their extraordinary *coherence.*

Obviously, from this point of view, *Les cahiers de jeunesse* (The Student Diaries), previously unpublished, constitute the star document. The very young eighteen-, nineteen-, or twenty-year-old Simone de Beauvoir who writes them is clearly already the future great Simone de Beavoir, author of *L'invitée* (She Came to Stay), *Pour une morale de l'ambiguïté* (The Ethics of Ambiguity), *Le deuxième sexe* (The Second Sex), *Les Mandarins* (The Mandarins), and *Mémoires* (Memoirs). Her vocation as a writer is energetically affirmed in these diaries, but one also discovers in them the roots of her later reflections. It is particularly touching to see the birth, often with hesitations, doubt, and anguish, of the fundamental choices of thought and existence that would have such an impact on so many future readers, women and men. Beauvoir expresses torments, doubt, and anguish, but also exultation and confidence in her strength and in the future. The foresight of certain passages is impressive. Take the one from June 25, 1929, for example: "Strange certitude that these riches will be welcomed, that some words will be said and heard, that this life will be a fountainhead from which many others will draw. Certitude of a vocation."

These precious *Cahiers* will cut short the unproductive and recurrent debate about the "influence" that Sartre supposedly had on Simone de Beauvoir, since they incontestably reveal to us Simone de Beauvoir *before* Sartre. Thus, the relationship of Beauvoir and Sartre will take on its true sense, and one will understand to what point Beauvoir was even more herself when she agreed with some of Sartre's themes, because all those lonely years of apprenticeship and training were leading her to a definite path and not just any path. Therefore, it is not a matter of influence but an encounter in the strong sense of the term. Beauvoir and Sartre *recognized themselves* in one another because each already existed independently and intensely. One can all the better discern the originality of Simone de Beauvoir in her ethical preoccupations, her own conception of concrete freedom, and her dramatic consciousness of the essential role of the Other, for example, because they are prefigured in the feverish meditations that occupied her youth. *Les cahiers* constitute a priceless testimony.

I will conclude by thanking Margaret A. Simons and her associates again for their magnificent series, which will constitute an irreplaceable contribution to the study and the true understanding of the thoughts and works of Simone de Beauvoir.

Acknowledgments

Simone de Beauvoir's *Philosophical Writings* is dedicated to Kate Fullbrook, whose discoveries with Edward Fullbrook inspired the Beauvoir Series project. This volume would not have been possible without the generous support of a Collaborative Research Grant from the National Endowment for the Humanities (NEH), an independent federal agency; a Matching Funds grant from the Illinois Board of Higher Education allocated by the Graduate School of Southern Illinois University Edwardsville (SIUE); and a translation grant from the French Ministry of Culture. I am very grateful to the following persons for their encouragement and assistance: Margot Backas and Michael Hall, of NEH; Anne Solange Noble and Florence Giry, of Éditions Gallimard; Joan Catapano, editor in chief of the University of Illinois Press; and Dean Steve Hansen, Provost Sharon Hahs, Dean Kent Neely, David Steinberg, Tom Paxson, and Bill Hamrick, all of SIUE. This volume and the Beauvoir Series project as a whole have benefited from the guidance of the members of the Beauvoir Series Editorial Board: Kristana Arp, Debra Bergoffen, Anne Deing Cordero, Elizabeth Fallaize, and Eleanore Holveck. For their assistance in identifying quotations, I thank Bill Hamrick, Carol Keene, Henry W. Pickford, Matthew Schmitz, Carl Springer, Julie Ward, and Edwin Lawrence. The many transcribers, translators, and authors of introductions, listed with the individual texts, have taught me so much about Beauvoir's philosophy, and I am grateful to them. I would like to give special thanks to Jo Barnes and Janette Johnson for their assistance with administering the grants; Bessie Richards and Hope Myers for tracking down Beauvoir's elusive texts; Marybeth Timmermann and Mary Beth Mader for their help in editing the translations; and my coeditor of the Beauvoir Series, Sylvie Le Bon de Beauvoir, for her warm encouragement and steadfast support.

PHILOSOPHICAL
WRITINGS

,

Introduction

Margaret A. Simons

Simone de Beauvoir's death in 1986 awakened a renaissance of scholarly interest in her philosophical work,[1] a renaissance encouraged by Sylvie Le Bon de Beauvoir's publication in 1990 of her adoptive mother's war diary and letters and her donation of several manuscripts, including handwritten diaries and the typescript of *The Second Sex* (1949),[2] to the Bibliothèque Nationale. The heightened interest has extended to the general public as well, with discussions of research on Beauvoir's philosophy appearing in the *Chronicle of Higher Education* (September 4, 1998), the *New York Times* (September 26, 1998), and the *Chicago Tribune* (March 31, 1999). When *Time* magazine selected the top ten nonfiction books of the twentieth century, the list included *The Second Sex*, "Simone de Beauvoir's philosophical treatise on the condition of women in modern life" (June 8, 1998). *Life* magazine named Simone de Beauvoir one of the one hundred most influential people of the millennium: "She developed existentialist philosophy in novels and nonfiction, . . . and wrote the most influential feminist book of the twentieth century."[3]

But despite the scholarly research and wide public interest, Beauvoir's philosophy remains relatively unanalyzed and widely misunderstood. One reason may be Beauvoir's highly original philosophical methodology. Beauvoir

1

rejects traditional philosophical system building, which she characterizes as "a concerted delirium" requiring that philosophers stubbornly give their "insights the value of universal keys."[4] Instead, Beauvoir argues that philosophy should reflect the ambiguities of actual life. "In truth, there is no divorce between philosophy and life," Beauvoir writes in the preface to a 1948 collection of her essays. "Every living step is a philosophical choice and the ambition of a philosophy worthy of the name is to be a way of life that brings its justification with itself."[5] In order to present the opacity, ambiguity, and temporality of lived experience, Beauvoir began her career by writing philosophy in literary form, confronting the problem of the Other in her metaphysical novel *She Came to Stay* (1943).[6] Even later, when she began writing philosophical essays as well, she focused on concrete problems, pioneering the phenomenological description of oppression in *The Second Sex*.

Another reason, in addition to her original methodology, that Beauvoir's philosophical work has remained unanalyzed and misunderstood is that it has been overshadowed by that of her companion, Jean-Paul Sartre, whose relationship with Beauvoir was chronicled in her multivolume autobiography. Beauvoir was a trained philosopher with a graduate *diplôme* on Leibniz and an *agrégation* degree in philosophy. But from the beginning, she was assumed to be Sartre's philosophical follower and her work merely an application of his philosophy. The postwar French popular press ridiculed Beauvoir as "la grande Sartreuse" and "Notre-Dame de Sartre."[7] Even serious critics subsumed her work under his. Maurice Blanchot's 1945 critical discussion of Beauvoir's philosophical novels, for example, appears in an article entitled "Les romans de Sartre" (Sartre's Novels).[8] By the mid-1950s, when Beauvoir was beginning her memoirs, the sexist assumption that she was merely Sartre's philosophical disciple was deeply embedded in the scholarly literature.[9] Beauvoir's memoirs only compounded the problem, since in them, and in later interviews, Beauvoir paradoxically disavows her work in philosophy, deleting references to philosophy from diaries and letters excerpted in her memoirs and describing herself as never "tempted to try my hand at philosophy."[10] In our 1979 interview, for example, Beauvoir declares adamantly: "Sartre was a philosopher, and I, I am not; and I never really wanted to be a philosopher. I like philosophy very much, but I have not constructed a philosophical work. I constructed a literary work."[11]

It was not until 1994, after both of their deaths, that this account of their work was effectively challenged. A study by Edward Fullbrook of their posthumously published letters and diaries found that Sartre had read a second draft of Beauvoir's *She Came to Stay*, just as he was beginning work on *Being and*

Nothingness (1943). Thus Beauvoir's novel, long assumed to be an application of Sartre's philosophy in his essay, was instead discovered to be one of its sources.[12] My analysis of Beauvoir's 1927 diary, written while she was a philosophy student at the Sorbonne, two years before her first meeting with Sartre, confirms her early determination to become a philosopher: "Oh! tired, irritated, sure of arriving at nothing through this desperate appeal to philosophy—and yet I *want* it, I owe it to myself to do it. . . . To reason coldly. Ah! there's a lot to do to make myself a philosopher!" The diary also reveals her passionate commitment to philosophy: "I didn't know that every system is an ardent, tormented thing, an effort of life, of being, a drama in the full sense of the word and that it does not engage only the abstract intelligence. But I know it now, and that I can no longer do anything else."[13]

That Beauvoir saw herself as constructing a philosophical work in the following decades is also clear. In a 1945 interview, for example, Beauvoir describes herself as having constructed an original existentialist ethics: "No ethics is implied in existentialism. I have sought, for my part, to extract one from it. I expounded it in *Pyrrhus and Cineas,* which is an essay, then I tried to express the solution that I found in a novel and a play, that is to say in forms at once more concrete and more ambiguous."[14] Beauvoir's commitment to philosophy also seems clear in her defense of her methodology in "Literature and Metaphysics" and in the 1948 preface cited above. Not even the critical failure of her philosophical novels, *Le sang des autres* (The Blood of Others) in 1945 and *Tous les hommes sont mortels* (All Men Are Mortal) in 1946, lessens her commitment. In a 1948 letter to Nelson Algren, Beauvoir declares her intention to "find an answer to this problem" of writing philosophy in literary form, an effort that would eventually find success in her award-winning 1954 novel, *Les Mandarins* (The Mandarins).[15]

Why Beauvoir should have denied her work in philosophy remains something of a mystery, but one possible explanation is suggested by the timing of the disavowals, which apparently began in 1958 with the publication of *Mémoires d'une jeune fille rangée* (Memoirs of a Dutiful Daughter). When asked in a 1960 interview why she was writing her memoirs, Beauvoir replies that she wanted to show her readers who she was, in order to counter the dismissive reading of *The Second Sex* as a work of "feminine resentment": "I would like it to be known that the woman who wrote *The Second Sex* did not do it at forty years of age in order to avenge a life that would have been totally unhappy and that would have embittered her. If one interprets the book in that way, one might as well say that one repudiates it."[16]

Had Beauvoir recounted in her autobiographies the full story of her early philosophical ambitions, as well as her failure to win recognition for her achievements that followed, including her formulation of the problem of the Other and her construction of an existentialist ethics, which were both credited to Sartre, it would have seemed a bitter tale indeed and a painful reminder of Sartre's failure to come publicly to her defense and acknowledge his philosophical debt to her. The story would have thus stirred up painful memories and fueled the dismissive reading of *The Second Sex* as a work of resentment that she sought to counter. Whatever the reason, the suppression of the full story has contributed to the misunderstanding of her philosophical work.

A third factor contributing to the misunderstanding, at least in English-speaking countries, is that much of her work has not been readily available in full, accurate English translations. In the 1960s, when the popularity of French existential phenomenology was at its height and scholars were writing its history, Americans read English translations of essays by Sartre and Maurice Merleau-Ponty, Beauvoir's colleagues first as philosophy students and then as coeditors of the journal *Les temps modernes*.[17] But most of Beauvoir's essays from the same period remain untranslated even now and her contributions to *Les temps modernes* and, more generally, to the development of French existential phenomenology, largely overlooked. Furthermore, when Beauvoir's texts have been translated by commercial publishers the accurate and consistent translation of philosophical terms has not been a priority.

Indeed, this problem is already apparent in the first text by Beauvoir to appear in English translation, an article entitled (by the editors of *Harper's Bazaar*) "Jean-Paul Sartre: Strictly Personal," which was published in the January 1946 issue of the magazine. Karen Vintges found, in comparing that version with the recently discovered French typescript of Beauvoir's article, that the magazine had deleted fifty-five lines of Beauvoir's discussion of Sartre's philosophy, retaining only a biographical sketch. This obscured the deeper implications of Beauvoir's approach, which presents philosophy not as timeless, abstract reasoning but as a way of life. It also misled critics who read the article's exclusive focus on Sartre's life as part of a publicity campaign designed to make him a celebrity.

The English edition of Beauvoir's most historically important text, *The Second Sex,* is also marred by deletions and mistranslations. The translator, H. M. Parshley, a zoologist and authority on sex and reproduction, deleted more than 10 percent of the French text and mistranslated key philosophical terms. He justified his disregard for philosophy in the preface: "Mlle de Beauvoir's book is, after all, on woman, not philosophy."[18] Unfortunately this trend of providing popular editions at the expense of the integrity and accurate translation of Beauvoir's texts has continued. The 1991 English translation of Beauvoir's *Letters to Sartre* (1990) deleted one-third of the French text. Despite the translator's claim to have preserved "all discussion of De Beauvoir's own or Sartre's work," thirty-eight references to Beauvoir's work on *She Came to Stay* have been deleted from letters in November and December 1939 alone. There are also mistranslations, such as the translation of "the central subject" of *She Came to Stay,* "Françoise's problem with consciousnesses," as the "problem with consciousness," which misconstrues a social problem as an individual one.[19] Such mistakes are all too typical of translations of Beauvoir's texts by translators lacking the requisite philosophical background and required by commercial publishers to make substantial cuts.

A determination to change this situation has brought together an international team of scholars in philosophy and French language and literature united in the goal of providing scholarly and complete English translations of all of Beauvoir's available texts with introductions explaining their philosophical significance. Supported by a Collaborative Research Grant from the National Endowment for the Humanities and a Matching Funds Grant from the Illinois Board of Higher Education, we are translating seven volumes of Beauvoir's texts. In addition to the present volume of philosophical writings, we are translating student diaries recounting her struggle against despair and her early dedication to philosophy; a war diary recording the writing of *She Came to Stay* and her developing sense of social responsibility during the Nazi occupation; works of fiction; and essays on literature, politics, and feminism.

Our goal of providing complete and accurate translations of Beauvoir's texts has guided our translation of Beauvoir's philosophical writings. We have, for example, included the original French terms, within brackets, when necessary for clarity or to highlight a French term whose English translation varies depending upon the context. We have also retained Beauvoir's practice of using the male pronoun to refer to individual humans, since she wrote before the day of gender-neutral usage. Finally, we have retained her capitalization of terms meant in an absolute sense; for example, "the Other" is another person who is treated not as a peer but as an absolute object with no possibility of reciprocity.

Given our interest in Beauvoir's philosophy, one might ask why we have decided to provide scholarly translations of all of her available texts. Our decision has been guided by Beauvoir's own unique philosophical methodology, which produces not only formal essays on existentialist ethics but also works of fiction and articles on political affairs. Our selection of texts has thus been limited solely by practical considerations, which necessitate giving priority first to previously untranslated texts and then to shorter texts requiring retranslation.

Beauvoir's methodological focus on the exploration of concrete, lived experience has also posed a dilemma for the organization of the volumes. Assigning some texts to a volume of "philosophical writings" and others to volumes of "literary" or "political" writings imposes problematic distinctions that run counter to Beauvoir's philosophy. But the alternative of publishing all of her texts in a chronologically ordered "Collected Works" is, we decided, more problematic. While such a publication would highlight the historical connections between the texts and avoid the misleading division of texts into topics, it would be too expensive and unwieldy for classroom use. Since one of our goals is to introduce a historically important woman philosopher into the philosophical curriculum where women's voices are currently underrepresented, we have chosen to organize the volumes by topic, retaining a chronological organization for the individual texts within each volume and providing introductions pointing out connections with other texts.

The present volume of philosophical writings obviously does not include all of what might be defined as Beauvoir's philosophical work in the narrow sense, since it does not include such important and lengthy essays as *Ethics of Ambiguity* (1947) and *The Second Sex*. But the volume does bring together diverse elements of Beauvoir's philosophical work, ranging from metaphysical literature to essays on existentialist ethics, and highlights continuities in the development of her thought. It includes some of Beauvoir's most important essays, including *Pyrrhus and Cineas* (1944), an essay in existential ethics, translated here for the first time, which lays the groundwork for her *Ethics of Ambiguity*. Framed as a confrontation between the man of action and the cynic, for whom every action seems absurd, *Pyrrhus and Cineas* provides a historic precedent for the contemporary problem of postmodern disengagement and argues for the fundamental intersubjectivity of human reality.

Also included in the volume are four essays in existentialist ethics and aesthetics originally published in *Les temps modernes* in 1945–46 and later reprinted in a volume entitled *L'existentialisme et la sagesse des nations* (Existentialism and Popular Wisdom) (1948): "Moral Idealism and Political Realism," which posits existentialism as an alternative to the dilemma of moral purity and political cynicism; "Existentialism and Popular Wisdom," a defense of existentialism against the charge that it is a philosophy of despair; "An Eye for an Eye," Beauvoir's response to the treason trial of the collaborationist newspaper editor Robert Brasillach, where she confronted the life-

and-death consequences of being a politically engaged writer; and "Literature and Metaphysics," where Beauvoir defends her methodology of writing philosophy in literary form.

The volume begins with a recently discovered 1924 essay in the philosophy of science written for a senior-level high school philosophy class, the only surviving text from Beauvoir's years as a philosophy student, her *diplôme* on Leibniz having apparently been lost. The student essay is followed by two unpublished chapters of *She Came to Stay*, which tell the story of the novel's protagonist, Françoise, in her youthful confrontations with being. Beauvoir's 1945 review of Merleau-Ponty's *The Phenomenology of Perception*, published in the second issue of *Les temps modernes*, is also included, as is the article on Sartre discussed above and Beauvoir's 1946 article "Introduction to an Ethics of Ambiguity," which was later revised and incorporated into the first chapter of *The Ethics of Ambiguity*.

The volume ends with two articles published in American newspapers at the end of Beauvoir's extended visit to the States in 1947. "An Existentialist Looks at Americans," originally published in English in the *New York Times*, is the only text in the volume for which we were unable to find the original French typescript, and thus the only one reprinted without retranslation. The final text in the volume, "What Is Existentialism?" is a defense of existentialism published in the American French-language newspaper *France-Amérique*. Spanning the first twenty-five years of Beauvoir's work in philosophy, the texts assembled in this volume provide an introduction to Beauvoir's early philosophical work and thus a useful context for reading not only other early texts, such as *When Things of the Spirit Come First, She Came to Stay, The Blood of Others, Les bouches inutiles* (Useless Mouths) (1945), *All Men Are Mortal*, and *The Second Sex* (1949), but her later work as well.[20]

The introductions to the texts in this volume together highlight several interesting and surprising themes. The biggest surprise may be the early date of the appearance of key elements in Beauvoir's philosophical methodology. Her rejection of philosophical absolutes and turn to the "disclosure" of concrete reality, traditionally assumed to reflect the influence of Bergson's philosophy and Husserlian phenomenology, are already suggested in her 1924 student essay on the philosopher of science Claude Bernard. Scientific discoveries, according to Bernard, require the rejection of philosophical absolutes and the assumption of one's freedom. Beauvoir's later concept of philosophy as a way of life, with its call to reject the quest for being, embrace the exhilarating if uncomfortable reality of one's freedom, and pursue the disclosure of being, seems to reflect Bernard's philosophy.

Another interesting theme in this collection is Beauvoir's turn to the philosophical novel for a methodological alternative to philosophical absolutes and system building. As she later explains in "Literature and Metaphysics," the author of a metaphysical novel is able to disclose the reality of human experience in its opacity, ambiguity, and temporality, which is not possible in an abstract philosophical essay. The struggle between the desire to be and the desire to disclose being is a subject of her first published philosophical work, the metaphysical novel *She Came to Stay.* The novel's two unpublished chapters included in this volume form a short story chronicling the temptations of solipsism and conventional identity for a young girl who eventually rejects the quest of being for the joys of embodied experience and friendship with a resolutely separate other.

Perhaps the most important theme in this collection is Beauvoir's development of an existentialist ethics, a development that is framed, surprisingly often, by a discussion of violence. *She Came to Stay* concludes with an act of murder that highlights Beauvoir's early, solipsistic ethics of radical freedom, an ethics undermined by the Nazi occupation, which gave her a new awareness of her connection with others. In the texts that followed, several of which are included in this volume, Beauvoir seeks to construct an alternative to the moral solipsism of *She Came to Stay,* initiating what she later termed the "moral period" in her literary life. A key theme is the development of an ethics based on the concept of ambiguity.

Beauvoir already explores the ambiguities of self and other, present and future, and consciousness and embodiment in *She Came to Stay.* But her early philosophy ignores the full ambiguity of social and historical existence. *Pyrrhus and Cineas,* a tragic vision of the inevitably violent human condition written during the occupation, retains from *She Came to Stay* a concept of inner freedom as immune from the other's power, but it moves beyond moral solipsism in its ethical attentiveness to the singular other, an awareness that our actions produce the conditions in which the other acts, and an exploration of the notion of "appeal."

In "Moral Idealism and Political Realism," Beauvoir emphasizes the social and temporal ambiguities of human reality as she takes up the question from her 1945 novel *The Blood of Others* of whether moral action is possible in the ambiguous and violent world of politics. In "Eye for an Eye," Beauvoir seems to abandon her earlier claim of an inner freedom immune from the power of the Other. She condemns Brasillach's exposure of Jews to murder by the Nazis, as the degrading of a man to a thing. Such a degradation, which touches a person's inner depths, is made possible by the tragic ambiguity of our human condition as consciousness and material thing. But, Beauvoir argues, we can found an ethics on the reciprocal affirmation of this ambiguity, which I experience differently in relation to myself and to others. Beauvoir's project of constructing an ethics founded on a metaphysical account of the fundamental ambiguity of the human condition culminates in *The Ethics of Ambiguity*, which lays the groundwork for her later account of freedom in situation in *The Second Sex*.

A fourth theme in the introductions to the texts in this volume highlights the influences that Beauvoir drew upon in constructing her philosophy. There is, first of all, the surprising evidence of Beauvoir's early interest in Claude Bernard and the intriguing references in her philosophy school textbook to Hegel and Fouillée. Hegel's influence is evident in many of the texts, from *Pyrrhus and Cineas* to "What Is Existentialism?" Bergson's influence is evident in *Pyrrhus and Cineas* as well, as it is in "Literature and Metaphysics" and in Beauvoir's review of Merleau-Ponty's text with its appreciation of the flow of experience underlying theory.

The introductions identify phenomenology as another important influence. Beauvoir first read Husserl in 1934–35, before writing the two unpublished chapters of *She Came to Stay*, and as we know from a letter to Sartre, she first read Heidegger in July 1939.[21] Heidegger's influence is evident in several works, including *Pyrrhus and Cineas*, "Literature and Metaphysics," and "Existentialism and Popular Wisdom." And there is evidence of Husserl's influence as well. In her introduction to Beauvoir's "Review of *The Phenomenology of Perception* by Maurice Merleau-Ponty," Heinämaa notes Beauvoir's reference to the ethical implications of the phenomenological notion of intentionality. In "Introduction to an Ethics of Ambiguity," Beauvoir makes the Husserlian distinction between the desire for being and the desire to disclose being a centerpiece of her ethics, through the concept of an existential conversion, a concept modeled on Husserl's notion of *epoché*, as Holveck notes in her introduction to "Existentialism and Popular Wisdom."

These texts also clarify and complicate our understanding of Beauvoir's intellectual relationship with Sartre, as several of the introductions point out. For example, Heinämaa argues that Beauvoir, in her review of Merleau-Ponty's book, takes distance from Sartre's ontology and describes Merleau-Ponty's non-dualist notion of subjectivity based on the experience of temporality as a fruitful alternative. Heinämaa asks whether Beauvoir's discussion of subjectivity is really similar to Sartre's or nearer to that of Merleau-Ponty or Heidegger.

The questions for further research raised by these texts form a final theme in this volume. How does Beauvoir's later work respond, for example, to the question raised by Bernard of the role and method of philosophy in the absence of absolutes and system building? How do Beauvoir's works of philosophical literature written during her "moral period" develop themes evident in these essays? What evidence is there of the influence of Heidegger's concept of temporality in Beauvoir's novel *All Men Are Mortal*? Many of these essays are framed in terms of dilemmas, that is, Pyrrhus versus Cineas or Antigone versus Creon, an approach that seems to characterize Beauvoir's discussion of race in *America Day by Day*, which is constructed as a search for an alternative to nominalist and essentialist views. Is this a method that characterizes Beauvoir's work in general?

Bergoffen, in her introduction to *Pyrrhus and Cineas*, asks whether Beauvoir's later works mute the tragedy of the human condition so starkly delineated in *Pyrrhus and Cineas*. What happens to the focus on violence in her later work? How does Beauvoir, in *The Second Sex* and *The Mandarins*, address the shortcomings that she saw in the work of her "moral period," that is, its excessive individualism, ahistorical perspective, and abstraction from a social context? How does she develop the concept of freedom in her later work, particularly in reference to new concepts such as "situation"? What role does the concept of "ambiguity" play in her later work?

NOTES

1. Recent books on Beauvoir include: Kristana Arp, *The Bonds of Freedom: Simone de Beauvoir's Existentialist Ethics* (Peru, Ill.: Open Court, 2001); Deirdre Bair, *Simone de Beauvoir: A Biography* (New York: Summit, 1990); Nancy Bauer, *Simone de Beauvoir, Philosophy, and Feminism* (New York: Columbia University Press, 2001); Joy Bennett and Gabriela Hochmann, *Simone de Beauvoir: An Annotated Bibliography* (New York: Garland, 1988); Debra B. Bergoffen, *The Philosophy of Simone de Beauvoir* (Albany: State University of New York Press, 1997); Catharine Brosman, *Simone de Beauvoir Revisited* (Boston: Twayne, 1991); Claudia Card, *The Cambridge Companion to Simone de Beauvoir* (Cambridge: Cambridge University Press, 2003); Margaret Crosland, *Simone de Beauvoir: The Woman and Her Work* (London: Heinemann, 1992); Christine Delphy and Sylvie Chaperon, *Cinquantenaire du deuxième sexe* (Paris: Syllepse, 2002); Elizabeth Fallaize, *The Novels of Simone de Beauvoir* (London: Routledge, 1988) and *Simone de Beauvoir: A Critical Reader* (London: Routledge, 1998); Penny Forster and Imogen Sutton, eds., *Daughters of de Beauvoir* (London: Women's Press, 1989); Claude Francis and Fernande Gontier, *Simone de Beauvoir*, trans. L. Nesselson (New York: St. Martin's, 1989); Kate Fullbrook and Edward Fullbrook, *Simone de Beauvoir and Jean-Paul Sartre* (New York: Basic, 1993) and *Simone de Beauvoir: A Critical Introduction* (Cambridge: Polity, 1998); Sara Heinämaa, *Toward a Phenomenology of Sexual Difference: Husserl, Merleau-Ponty, Beauvoir* (Lanham, Md.: Rowman and Littlefield, 2003); Eleanore Holveck, *Simone de*

Beauvoir's Philosophy of Lived Experience: Literature and Metaphysics (Lanham, Md.: Rowman and Littlefield, 2002); Barbara Klaw, *Le Paris de Simone de Beauvoir: Beauvoir's Paris* (Paris: Syllepse, 1999); Michèle Le Dœuff, *Hipparchia's Choice: An Essay Concerning Women, Philosophy, etc.*, trans. T. Selous (Cambridge, Mass.: Blackwell, 1991); Eva Lundgren-Gothlin, *Sex and Existence: Simone de Beauvoir's "The Second Sex,"* trans. L. Schenck (Hanover, N.H.: University Press of New England, 1996); Toril Moi, *Simone de Beauvoir: The Making of an Intellectual Woman* (Cambridge, Mass.: Blackwell, 1994); Wendy O'Brien and Lester Embree, eds., *The Existential Phenomenology of Simone de Beauvoir* (Dordrecht, The Netherlands: Kluwer, 2001); Jo-Ann Pilardi, *Writing the Self: Philosophy Becomes Autobiography* (Westport, Conn.: Praeger, 1999); Margaret A. Simons, ed., *Feminist Interpretations of Simone de Beauvoir* (University Park, Pa.: Penn State University Press, 1995) and "The Philosophy of Simone de Beauvoir," special issue, *Hypatia* 14, no. 4 (Fall 1999); Margaret A. Simons, *Beauvoir and "The Second Sex": Feminism, Race, and the Origins of Existentialism* (Lanham, Md.: Rowman and Littlefield, 1999) and "Présences de Simone de Beauvoir," *Les temps modernes,* June–July 2002; Ursula Tidd, *Simone de Beauvoir, Gender and Testimony* (Cambridge: Cambridge University Press, 1999); and Karen Vintges, *Philosophy as Passion: The Thinking of Simone de Beauvoir,* trans. A. Lavelle (Bloomington: Indiana University Press, 1996).

2. Simone de Beauvoir, *Le deuxième sexe* (Paris: Gallimard, 1949), trans. H. M. Parshley as *The Second Sex* (New York: Knopf, 1952).

3. See ‹http://www.life.com/Life/millennium/people/71.html›, accessed March 25, 2004, where Beauvoir is listed as number 72.

4. Simone de Beauvoir, *La force de l'âge* (Paris: Gallimard, 1960), 254.

5. Simone de Beauvoir, "Préface," *L'existentialisme et la sagesse des nations* (1948; Paris: Nagel, 1963), 11. The book contains four of Beauvoir's articles reprinted from *Les temps modernes:* "L'existentialisme et la sagesse des nations," "Idéalisme moral et réalisme politique," "Littérature et métaphysique," and "Oeil pour oeil." Translations of Beauvoir's preface and all four articles are included in the present volume.

6. See Simone de Beauvoir, *L'invitée* (Paris: Gallimard, 1943), trans. Yvonne Moyse and Roger Senhouser as *She Came to Stay* (Cleveland: World, 1954).

7. Simone de Beauvoir, *La force des choses,* folio ed., 2 vols. (Paris: Gallimard, 1963), 1:71.

8. Maurice Blanchot, "Les romans de Sartre," *L'Arche* 10 (October 1945), reprinted in *La part du feu* (Paris: Gallimard, 1949), 200, 203–4; Beauvoir erases this slight in her reference to Blanchot's essay in her autobiography ("Blanchot, dans son essai sur 'le roman à thèse,'" in *La force de l'âge,* 622).

9. See my "Sexism and the Philosophical Canon: On Reading Beauvoir's *The Second Sex,*" in Simons, *Beauvoir and "The Second Sex,"* 101–14.

10. Beauvoir, *La force de l'âge,* 253.

11. "Beauvoir Interview," in Simons, *Beauvoir and "The Second Sex,"* 9.

12. See Fullbrook and Fullbrook, *Simone de Beauvoir and Jean-Paul Sartre,* and Edward Fullbrook, "*She Came to Stay* and *Being and Nothingness,*" *Hypatia* 14, no. 4: 50–69.

13. Simone de Beauvoir, fourth notebook, holograph manuscript, 1927, Paris, Bibliothèque Nationale, transcription by Barbara Klaw, Sylvie Le Bon de Beauvoir, and Margaret A. Simons, 116, 133–34 (my translation).

14. Dominique Aury, "Qu'est-ce que l'existentialisme? Escarmouches et patrouilles," *Les lettres françaises,* December 1, 1945, 4.

15. Simone de Beauvoir, *A Transatlantic Love Affair: Letters to Nelson Algren,* ed. Sylvie Le

Bon de Beauvoir, trans. E. G. Reeves (New York: Norton, 1998), 212–13. Thanks to Evangelia Romoudi at St. Louis University for referring me to this letter.

16. "Une interview de Simone de Beauvoir par Madeleine Chapsal," in *Les écrivains en personne* (Paris: Julliard, 1960), 17–37, reprinted in *Les écrits de Simone de Beauvoir,* ed. Claude Francis and Fernande Gontier (Paris: Gallimard, 1979), 381–96; the quotation is from page 396.

17. See Jean-Paul Sartre, *Literary and Philosophical Essays,* trans. Annette Michelson (New York: Criterion Books, 1955), and Maurice Merleau-Ponty, *Sense and Non-Sense,* trans. Hubert L. Dreyfus and Patricia A. Dreyfus (Evanston, Ill.: Northwestern University Press, 1964).

18. See my "The Silencing of Simone de Beauvoir: Guess What's Missing from *The Second Sex,*" in Simons, *Beauvoir and "The Second Sex,"* 61–71.

19. Simone de Beauvoir, *Lettres à Sartre,* ed. Sylvie Le Bon de Beauvoir, 2 vols. (Paris: Gallimard, 1990), 1:178; *Letters to Sartre,* trans. Quintin Hoare (New York, Arcade, 1992), 111.

20. Written from 1935 to 1937, *Quand prime le spirituel,* Beauvoir's ironically titled study of bad faith, remained unpublished until 1979. See Simone de Beauvoir, *Quand prime le spirituel* (Paris: Gallimard, 1979), trans. Patrick O'Brian as *When Things of the Spirit Come First* (New York: Pantheon, 1982).

21. See Beauvoir's *Lettres à Sartre,* 1:77, and Sartre's *Lettres à Castor,* ed. Simone de Beauvoir, 2 vols. (Paris: Gallimard, 1983), 1:235 ("Enfin, vous avez lu Heidegger").

Analysis of Claude Bernard's
Introduction to the Study of Experimental Medicine

INTRODUCTION
by *Margaret A. Simons and*
Hélène N. Peters

In December 1924, when Simone de Beauvoir almost certainly wrote her essay analyzing Claude Bernard's *Introduction à l'étude de la médecine expérimentale* (Introduction to the Study of Experimental Medicine), part 1 (1865),[1] a classic text in the philosophy of science, she was a sixteen-year-old student in a senior-level philosophy class at the Institut Adeline-Désir, or Cours Désir, a private Catholic girls' school that she had attended since the age of five. The year-long class prepared the students for the philosophy exam, the second stage of the two-year program required to pass the difficult *baccalauréat* exam, which also offered a mathematics track (called *mathématiques élémentaires*) for the scientifically minded student. Completion of this exam assured access to the university and entrance to the professions.[2]

Thanks to a French governmental decree in May 1924, courses in Latin and advanced philosophy were offered for the first time that fall to girls in the public secondary schools. The decree, which marked an important turning point for the education of French women, was shaped largely by economic necessity. The economic losses suffered by many bourgeois families, including Beauvoir's, in the aftermath of World War I meant that they would be unable to provide a dowry and arrange a marriage for their daughters, who would have to prepare for a career instead. Private girls' schools, such as the Cours Désir, seeking an advantage in the competition for students, led the curricular reform, offering the necessary courses in Latin and philosophy despite the fears of parents in the Catholic schools that the study of secular philosophy would undermine the religious faith of their daughters.[3]

Beauvoir's philosophy class was taught by an elderly, kindly priest, l'Abbé Trésal.[4] Beauvoir writes in her *Mémoires* that psychology, logic, ethics, and metaphysics (the four subject areas of the philosophy syllabus) were "disposed of . . . at the rate of four hours of classes per week" (*Mémoires*, 219), half of the standard eight hours of class offered weekly in the boys' *lycées*.[5] According to Beauvoir, the textbook for the philosophy course, *Manuel de philosophie* (Philosophy Manual) by Father Charles Lahr, was no more "encumbered with subtleties" than was their instructor: "regarding each problem, the Reverend Father Lahr made a rapid inventory of human errors and taught us the truth according to Saint Thomas" (*Mémoires*, 219). Despite its weaknesses, Lahr's textbook did introduce Beauvoir to Hegel's theory of the opposition of the self and the nonself, and to Alfred Fouillée's (1838–1912) conclusion: "l'homme ne naît pas libre, il le devient" (man is not born but becomes free), which is surely the model for the famous line from *Le deuxième sexe* (The Second Sex) (1949): "On ne naît pas femme: on le devient" (One is not born but becomes a woman).[6]

The inadequacies of her philosophy course may have contributed to Beauvoir's poor performance on the philosophy exam the following spring. Having passed the first part of the *bac* with distinction the previous year, despite having taken exams in both the science and Latin–modern languages tracks, Beauvoir barely passed the philosophy *bac* in July 1925.[7] Fortunately she once again took the exceptional step of preparing for exams in two tracks: philosophy and elementary math (which included several more hours of examination in physics, chemistry, and math than required on the philosophy track). She was able to make up "in the sciences" the points lost in the philosophy exam.[8]

Given the popular conception of existentialism as antiscience, Simone de Beauvoir's early interest in science, reflected in her *baccalauréat* successes as well as in her paper on Claude Bernard, may be surprising. But it was quite extensive. Her study of science apparently began in the fall of 1922 when an extra teacher was hired by the Cours Désir to teach math and physics in response to a request by the father of one of Beauvoir's classmates. Beauvoir was charmed by the young and enthusiastic teacher, who wasted no time on "silliness" or "the interminable discussions of morality" found in her other classes (*Mémoires,* 209). In her autobiographical account of her early "passion" for philosophy, Beauvoir refers to philosophers of science, including Henri Poincaré and his work on relativity, although not to Claude Bernard (*Mémoires,* 220). Beauvoir's interest in math and science continued after graduation, when, since her mother opposed her plan to study philosophy at the Sorbonne, she decided to pursue a certificate in math, along with certificates in literature and classics.[9]

Beauvoir's essay on Claude Bernard was probably not a regular assignment but an extra paper, since it bears instructor's comments but no numerical grade.[10] Largely expository, it summarizes and paraphrases Bernard's *Introduction à l'étude de la médecine expérimentale,* part 1, for decades a standard text on the reading list for the philosophy *bac.*[11] Despite its elementary nature, Beauvoir's essay is important, since it is the only formal essay known to exist from Beauvoir's years as a philosophy student, her graduate thesis on "the concept according to Leibniz" for her *diplôme* having apparently been lost along with other papers written while she was a philosophy student at the Sorbonne from 1927 to 1929. Beauvoir's essay on Bernard's *Introduction* might have survived by chance while more important papers were lost. But her enthusiasm for Bernard is both unmistakable and significant. In her autobiography, Beauvoir tells of the way philosophy affected her as a student: "I did not meet [*accueillais*] it passively; . . . if a theory convinced me, it did not remain exterior to me; it changed my relation with the world; it colored my experience."[12] The essay on Claude Bernard provides unique evidence of one of Beauvoir's early philosophical awakenings, while also shedding light, as we shall argue, on the development of her philosophical methodology, subjects that receive a cursory and sometimes misleading treatment in her *Mémoires.*

Claude Bernard (1813–78), an eminent French physiologist, may be best known for his concept of the *milieu intérieur,* the internal environment of blood plasma and lymph that provides higher animals with protection, and thus independence, from changes in the external environment. Bernard, who has been credited with founding the science of experimental physiology, wrote his *Introduction* to argue for the application of the scientific method to medicine. He rejected the reduction of physiology to chemistry and challenged the then dominant theory of vitalism, the view that human life is subject to unpredictable forces that defy natural law and that doctors must rely more on personality than on science. He sought to free medicine from both dogmatism, that is, theorizing without testing or observation, and crude empiricism, that is, observation not directed by a research idea or hypothesis.[13]

We have identified three themes in Beauvoir's essay that reappear in her later work. The theme that Beauvoir calls "the most interesting part of [Bernard's] interesting work" is the valuing of philosophical doubt. In his *Introduction,* Bernard writes: "The great experimental principle, then, is doubt, that philosophical doubt which leaves to the mind its freedom and initiative" (*ISEM,* 37). He contrasts the skeptic, who "believes only in himself," with the scientist, who "doubts only himself and his interpretations, but believes in science [and in] the determinism of phenomena, which is as absolute in the phenomena of living bodies as in those of inorganic matter" (*ISEM,* 52). The result of the scientist's "fertile" doubt is a sense of both mastery and ignorance: "[T]rue experimental science gives [man] power only in showing him his ignorance. . . . Indeed, our mind is so limited that we can know neither the beginning nor the end of things; but we can grasp the middle, i.e., what surrounds us closely" (*ISEM,* 50; *IEME,* 85).

Lahr's *Manuel de philosophie* discusses philosophical doubt and cites Bernard's essay, but it warns against an "excess" of doubt as eroding religious faith and recommends that one turn to Aquinas, that is, theology and scholasticism, instead of science for its proper use.[14] In such an atmosphere, Bernard's characterization of doubt as a virtue rather than a source of despair must have appealed to Beauvoir, who had earlier lost her faith in God.

A second theme in Beauvoir's essay, one related to the valuing of philosophical doubt, is the rejection of "scholasticism," "immutable truths," and philosophical system-building (*ISEM,* 42). In his *Introduction,* Bernard warns that an "exaggerated belief in theories . . . enslaves the mind, by taking away its freedom, smothering its originality and infecting it with the taste for systems" (*ISEM,* 39; *IEME,* 73). Lahr's *Manuel* omits Bernard's criticism of the "theological yoke" and defends philosophical system-building: "After having refuted skepticism and relativism, it remains for us to conclude in favor of dogmatism."[15] But Beauvoir, whose later philosophy rejects philosophical system-building, repeats Bernard's criticism of "systematizers" and his praise of experimenters who reject every "philosophical and theological yoke" (*ISEM,* 43; *IEME,* 77).[16]

In her later work, Beauvoir often sought to expose the harmful reality hidden by myths and ideals. In *America Day by Day,* for example, Beauvoir exposes the mystification of race in the American system of racist segregation; in *The Second Sex,* she lays open the mystification of sexual difference; and in her 1970 study of old age, Beauvoir seeks to expose the sordid treatment of old people hidden behind "myths of expansion and affluence."[17]

A third theme in Beauvoir's essay is the valuing of the discovery of the external world. In Beauvoir's celebration of the "marvelous discoveries" and unlimited "power" of experimental science we see an early expression of an important theme in her philosophy that is often traced to the later influence of phenomenology, that is, the disclosure of the world offered as a positive alternative to mythical thinking. Bernard's account of scientific discovery, where he argues that discoveries are engendered not by reason but by "[a] feeling for the complexity of natural phenomena" (*ISEM*, 37; *IEME*, 70), anticipates the phenomenological focus on embodiment and the subjective element in disclosure of the world. Bernard calls upon the scientist to "submit his idea to nature," breaking with the traditional view of science as dominating nature: "It has been said that the experimenter must force nature to disclose herself." "Yes," Bernard writes, the experimenter does "attack nature with all manner of questions." But the experimenter "must never answer for her nor listen partially to her answers by taking, from the results of an experiment, only those which support or confirm his hypothesis" (*ISEM*, 23; *IEME*, 53).

Beauvoir's early enthusiasm for scientific discovery and for Bernard's call to "go down into the objective reality of things" is evident in her later works. Even in the mid-1930s, when Beauvoir was working most intensely with Husserlian phenomenology, an idealist metaphysics and subjectivist methodology that arose in opposition to scientific naturalism, there is evidence of her enduring respect for scientific discoveries and the scientific method. Many of Beauvoir's early philosophical novels, including *When Things of the Spirit Come First*, written during 1935–37, offer the disclosure of the external world as an alternative to the mystifications of bad faith.[18] In her 1946 essay "Literature and Metaphysics," Beauvoir describes her method of writing philosophy in literature as an experiment, analogous to a scientific experiment.

Beauvoir's attempt to integrate science and phenomenology, an attempt assisted by her earlier familiarity with Bernard's account of the subjective elements in scientific discovery, is more evident in her post–World War II writings on racism and feminism. These writings are regarded, somewhat paradoxically in this context, as antinaturalist.[19] The explanation may lie with the definition of naturalism by those who appeal to a narrow biological reductionism in justifying racist and sexist oppression. Beauvoir's naturalism, in the broader sense of a reliance on scientific explanation, is evident in her appeal to science in support of political change.

For example, in *America Day by Day*, an account of her trip to the United States in 1947, Beauvoir first offers a phenomenological description of her initial encounter with racial segregation in the South, describing her skin as having "become heavy and stifling" with a color that "burns" her.[20] But she follows this phenomenological description of her own "meager" experience with detailed references to an "authoritative" scientific study by Gunnar Myrdal, *An American Dilemma*, "an experience whose extent, depth, and value are officially recognized in America."[21]

In *The Second Sex*, Beauvoir strikes several Bernardian chords. She describes her project as a "search for truth" (*DS*, 1:29), an effort at lucidity (*DS*, 1:30), and an attempt to get out of the "ruts" of political polemics (*DS*, 1:28) and dogmatic absolutes. Elsewhere she describes writing the book as the "sudden discovery" of "an aspect of the world that is staring you in the face and that you did not see."[22] Beauvoir asserts, following Bernard, that discoveries can be furthered by one's situation, arguing that "certain women are best placed to elucidate woman's situation," because they "grasp more immediately what the fact of being feminine signifies for a human being" (*DS*, 1:29). Finally, while Beauvoir, in *The Second Sex*, rejects a biological determinist account of women's inferior position, she incorporates "physiological givens" into her analysis of femininity as "neither an essence nor a nature: it is a situation created by civilizations from certain physiological givens."[23]

NOTES

1. Claude Bernard, *Introduction à l'étude de la médecine expérimentale*, preface by François Dagognet (Paris: Garnier-Flammarion, 1966) (hereafter referred to as *IEME*), trans. H. C. Green as *An Introduction to the Study of Experimental Medicine*, foreword by I. Bernard Cohen (New York: Dover, 1957) (hereafter referred to as *ISEM*).

2. See Frederick E. Farrington, *French Secondary Schools*, 2nd ed. (1910; New York: Longmans, Green, 1915), on the unique role of the philosophy class (292) and the difficulty of the *bac* exam (143–45). According to Farrington, an average of only 54 percent of those students who took both parts of the exam in 1902–8 passed.

3. See Karen Offen, "The Second Sex and the Baccalauréat in Republican France, 1880–1924," *French Historical Studies* 13, no. 2 (Fall 1983): 252–86. Note that Offen mistakenly claims that the decision to send Simone to a private Catholic school reflects the "antisecular" attitude of her father (265). In fact, Beauvoir reports in her *Mémoires d'une jeune fille rangée* [Memoirs of a Dutiful Daughter] (Paris: Gallimard, 1958) that her father, a nonbeliever, wanted her to attend a public *lycée*, but that she successfully resisted the change with the support of her pious mother (170–71). Subsequent citations from the *Mémoires* appear parenthetically in the text.

4. Referred to as Abbé Trécourt in Beauvoir's *Mémoires*, he is identified as "M. l'abbé Trésal, professeur de philosophie du cours Désir" in *Zaza: Correspondance et carnets d'Elisabeth Lacoin, 1914–1929* (Paris: Seuil, 1991), 46 n. 1.

5. See Farrington, *French Secondary Schools*, 134, on the eight-hours-per-week standard philosophy class.

6. Le Père Charles Lahr, S.J., *Manuel de philosophie résumé du Cours de philosophie*, 2nd ed. (Paris: G. Beauchesne, 1926), 252, 789. The passage on Hegel begins: "According to Hegel,

everything starts from the self, which creates itself in positing itself, and in that very instant creates the nonself. The self *posits itself,* that is the thesis, but at the same time it *opposes* the nonself, this is the *antithesis,* and in that very way he *identifies* with it, this is the *synthesis*" (789). (Unless noted otherwise, translations are by the authors.) Beauvoir writes in her *Mémoires* that Fouillée's *Idées-forces* was an assigned reading in her philosophy class (219).

7. The program of study followed by Beauvoir during 1922–24 in preparation for the first part of the *bac* (*baccalauréat*) exam was established in 1902. It presented four alternative tracks: (a) Latin-Greek, (b) Latin–modern languages, (c) Latin-science, and (d) Science–modern languages; see Farrington, *French Secondary Schools,* 143, on the program of *bac* exams established in 1902. Our conclusion that Beauvoir took the first part of the *bac* exams in one of the two science tracks (c or d) as well as the Latin–modern language track (b) is based on four facts: first, she and her best friend, Zaza Lacoin, took courses in both tracks in preparation for the first part of the *bac* ("L'institut ne préparait que latin-langues [M. Lacoin] voulait que sa fille eût une formation scientifique; moi, j'aimais ce qui résistait: les mathématiques me plaisaient. On fit venir une extra qui à partir de la seconde nous enseigna l'algèbra, la trigonométrie, la physique" [*Mémoires,* 209]); second, the first part of the *bac* is based on the previous two years of course work (see Farrington, *French Secondary Schools,* 141); third, Zaza took the first part of the *bac* in both areas ("Zaza est reçue aux deux sections, scientifique et littéraire" [*Zaza,* 52 n. 1]); and fourth, one of her examiners at the first *bac* greeted Beauvoir with the wry comment: "So, Mademoiselle! You're collecting diplomas!" (*Mémoires,* 217). In May 1923, the *baccalauréat* program was revised to include only two tracks, one modern and one classical, eliminating the Latin–modern languages track (b); see John Talbott, *The Politics of Educational Reform in France, 1918–1940* (Princeton: Princeton University Press, 1969), 84. But the examination administered to Beauvoir, in the spring of 1924, would have followed the 1902 program, since it governed her course of study.

8. "In July [1925], I passed the exams in elementary mathematics and philosophy. The Abbé's teaching was so weak that my essay, which he would have given a 16 [out of 20], earned me only an 11. I made up for it in the sciences" (*Mémoires,* 223). See Offen, "Second Sex and the Baccalauréat," 280–81, on the 1924 reforms. See Simone Pétrement, *La vie de Simone Weil,* vol. 1 (Paris: Fayard, 1973), 53, on Simone Weil's brother's taking both *bac* exams in two tracks in the early 1920s.

9. "My science teacher pushed me to try general mathematics and the idea pleased me. I would prepare this certificate at the Institut Catholique" (*Mémoires,* 233).

10. The practice of giving numerical grades only to assigned papers or exams is standard throughout secondary school. See Pétrement, *Vie de Simone Weil,* 78, for an example of numerical grades' being given only to assigned papers in a philosophy class.

11. On the presence of Bernard's text on the 1923 program for the philosophy *bac,* see Lahr, *Manuel,* vii, x. On the presence of Bernard's text on the philosophy *bac* in the 1950s, see I. Bernard Cohen, "Foreword," *ISEM,* n.p.

12. Simone de Beauvoir, *La force de l'âge* (Paris: Gallimard, 1960), 254 (hereafter referred to as *FA*).

13. See François Dagognet, "Préface," *IEME.*

14. Lahr, *Manuel,* 681.

15. Ibid., 400, 691.

16. See Beauvoir, *FA,* 254, where she describes philosophical systems as a "concerted delirium" whose creators require a "kind of obstinacy" to see their insights "as universal keys."

17. Simone de Beauvoir, *L'Amérique au jour le jour* (Paris: Gallimard, 1948), trans. Carol Cosman as *America Day by Day* (Berkeley: University of California Press, 1999). Simone de Beauvoir, *Le deuxième sexe*, 2 vols. (Paris: Gallimard, 1949), trans. H. M. Parshley as *The Second Sex* (New York: Knopf, 1952) (hereafter referred to as *DS*). Simone de Beauvoir, *La vieillesse* (Paris: Gallimard, 1970), trans. Patrick O'Brian as *The Coming of Age* (New York: Putnam, 1972), 2 (quote).

18. *Quand prime le spirituel* (Paris: Gallimard, 1979), trans. Patrick O'Brian as *When Things of the Spirit Come First* (New York: Random House, 1982). Beauvoir concludes *Spirit,* as she later explains, with the autobiographical story of a young woman who initially "fell into the traps" of surrealist fantasies, but then "her eyes were opened, she threw overboard all mysteries, mirages and myths, and decided to look the world in the face" (*FA*, 258).

19. See Michel Kail, "Pour un antinaturalisme authentique, donc matérialiste," and Françoise Armengaud, "Le matérialisme beauvoirien et la critique du naturalisme: une 'rupture épistémologique inachevée'?" in C. Delphy et al., *Cinquantenaire du deuxième sexe* (Paris: Éditions Syllepse, 2002).

20. Beauvoir, *America Day by Day,* 203.

21. Ibid., 236 (quote). See Gunnar Myrdal, *An American Dilemma: The Negro Problem and Modern Democracy* (New York: Harper, 1944).

22. Simone de Beauvoir, *La force des choses,* folio ed., 2 vols. (Paris: Gallimard, 1963), 1:258. Bernard describes how a scientist can suddenly see a familiar fact in a new light, which shows that "the discovery inheres in a feeling about things which is not only individual, but which is even connected with a transcient condition of the mind" (*ISEM*, 34).

23. Beauvoir, *FA,* 417.

TRANSCRIPTION BY JUSTINE SARROT

TRANSLATION BY MARYBETH TIMMERMANN

NOTES BY TRICIA WALL

Analysis of Claude Bernard's *Introduction to the Study of Experimental Medicine*

Saturday, December 13, [1924]

The "introduction to the study of experimental medicine" is defined by Claude Bernard himself in the beginning of his work.[1] "I deem it useful," he says, "to give a few explanations in this introduction in relation to the theoretic and philosophic side of the method which this book, after all, treats merely on its practical side."[2]

In the first part of this introduction that we are going to study, he proposes considering the difficulties of experimental reasoning,[3] and for that, he tries to study the role played by observation and experiments in experimentation, and then the importance of preconceived ideas and doubt.

Observation and Experiment

Observation and experiments are the only means that man possesses for gaining knowledge of phenomena. The first reveals their existence, and the second uncovers their signification.

This manuscript was found in the collection of Sylvie Le Bon de Beauvoir. © Sylvie Le Bon de Beauvoir. A note written in another handwriting, presumably that of Beauvoir's philosophy professor, Abbé Trésal, diagonally across the top margin reads: "Insofar as I could read your work, this essay is complete and personal."

Sometimes people seem to confuse the two. Most often, arbitrary distinctions between them have been established. The observer is said to be passive in the production of the phenomena while the experimenter is said to take an active part in it. This is the opinion of Zimmermann and Cuvier.[4] But Claude Bernard shows by examples that this separation, which is so clear in theory, is difficult or impossible in practice. In fact, there are active as well as passive observations since some are made randomly and others are made in order to verify the accuracy of what has been hypothesized. Likewise, certain experiments are passive; the activity of the experimenter does not always intervene.

Another theory claims that observation consists of noting what is normal while experiments imply the idea of a disturbance intentionally brought on by the investigator.

Consequently, like the first one, this theory considers an element as necessary that is not: intentional activity. In addition, if it is really true that "in an experiment one must make a judgment by comparing two facts,"[5] nothing indicates that one of these two facts must be abnormal.

These two definitions are false because the meanings of the two words "observation" and "experiment" are too restricted, and they are not recognized as the opposite extremes in experimental reasoning.

Indeed, one must not confuse the expressions "to conduct experiments" and "to make observations,"[6] which mean conducting an investigation in order to gain knowledge from it, with the expressions "to rely on observations" and "to gain experience," which mean using observation as a starting point for reasoning and using experience as a point of support. Experience here is instruction given by life.[7] One can acquire it nonempirically, without conducting experiments, as well as experimentally, by studying the exact facts and putting them to use. Taken in this general sense, observation and experience are practically inseparable; they serve as starting point and conclusion for experimental reasoning, outside of which there are only concrete facts.

Knowledge of these facts is essential and obtained by investigation. Investigation, which is extremely important, brings facts to light and notes them as rigorously as possible. The means differ according to each science, but the more they are improved, the more progress that particular science makes. "The greatest scientific truths," says Claude Bernard, "are rooted in details of experimental investigation, which form, as it were, the soil in which these truths develop."[8]

From a philosophical point of view, observation and experiment cannot be distinguished within the art of investigation, both being merely facts brought to light by the investigation. Practically, the difference is considerable. The sciences of observation concern phenomena that one records without the possibility of modifying them. On the contrary, the experimental sciences allow the scientist [*savant*] to vary the objects of study and obtain them under determined conditions. The judgment yielded by the first will be a comparison of two observations, while the second will be able to compare two experiments or one observation and one experiment. Experimental reasoning thus remains the same in both cases, but varies in its applications, because the science of observation is practically sterile, whereas "thanks to experimental science, the power that man may acquire over nature can no longer be limited."[9]

We finally arrive at the veritable definition of experiment: it is a provoked observation; that is to say that the experimenter produced or invoked it, which means he made use of a natural phenomenon with the aim of verifying an idea or, on the contrary, to suggest an idea if the object to be studied is completely unknown. "The experimenter, then, invokes or provokes the [*sic*] observed facts in determined conditions in order to draw from them the teaching he desires. The observer obtains facts from observation and judges whether they are well established and recorded with the help of suitable means."[10] Other than that, the observer is not different than the experimenter. The observer "listens to nature and writes at nature's dictation,"[11] but he must then interpret, while the experimenter "asks nature a question,"[12] but as soon as nature speaks, he must remain quiet and be satisfied to listen.

So here is the process of experimental reasoning such as it is described in the first chapter of this introduction: First, a fact is noted. Second, an idea is born in the mind concerning this fact. Third, with this idea in view, the scientist reasons, sets up an experiment, and executes it. Fourth, this experiment reveals a new fact and so forth.[13]

"All the parts of the experimental method are interdependent. The facts are the necessary materials; making use of them with experimental reasoning is what truly constitutes and edifies science. The idea formulated by the facts represents science. The hypothesis is only the preconceived and anticipated scientific idea."[14] Claude Bernard studies this idea, its role, and its importance in the second chapter.

The a priori idea and doubt in experimental reasoning.
At first glance, man comes up with ideas about what he sees;[15] the experimental method transforms this a priori conception into an a posteriori interpretation founded on the study of the phenomena. The idea is engendered by feeling, and reason develops it by using an experiment.

But one must notice that the experimental method is concerned only with objective truths. The truth appears to us only as relative since we do not know the primary causes and the essence of things, but truth is absolute for the subjective sciences that follow from principles of which the mind is conscious. On the contrary, in the objective sciences, the principle of things is unknown to us, and even if we want to determine it subjectively, we must rely on an experimental and relative criterion, instead of on a criterion that is interior and absolute.[16] One can sometimes apply this to the objective sciences simplified in such a way that the mind can embrace them in their entirety, but here again experimental verification is necessary.

The starting point in experimental reasoning is always an idea, without which fixed knowledge cannot be gained. It is not innate, but is a result of observation that, by showing us an effect, brings us to research its cause. It is by no means arbitrary, and in order to have value, it must be subject to verification. It is essentially individual.

The experimental method adds nothing to this idea; it can only direct and develop the idea, which is the basis of science, science itself. A fact or a discovery has value only insofar as it suggests an idea. The sole purpose of the scientific method is to develop the idea and encourage its birth.

In order to attain this result, the scientist must conserve a great freedom of mind founded in philosophic doubt. Claude Bernard thoroughly develops this very fertile idea in pages so rich that they lend themselves more to an exposition than an analysis and in my opinion are the most interesting part of his interesting work. One must believe in science, which is the absolute and necessary relation of things, yet be convinced that we have only an imperfect knowledge of this relation. When the starting point of a reasoning is absolute, one must accept its conclusions, but here the starting point is always doubtful, and consequently reasoning guides us but does not impose its consequences upon us. If we discover a new fact, we must never reject it under the pretext that it contradicts an accepted theory. "Theories are but relative principles to which only a temporary value must be accorded."[17] Progress consists precisely of constantly changing the theory because the more facts we know, the more we must widen the theory in order for all the facts to fit within it. Regarding this, and with an admirable clarity, Claude Bernard defines the role of scientific geniuses, to whom he pays the highest homage without according them any personal authority. The experimental method draws upon an impersonal authority within itself that dominates everything. The scientist believes only in the results of his experiments; therefore he conducts them without bias and without rejecting results that do not agree with his opinions; he will model his opinions on the observed facts, not the facts on his opinions. Just as he rejects any scientific authority as pure superstition, the experimenter also rejects every philosophical and theological yoke.[18] Only under these conditions can science make real and certain progress without engaging itself down false paths.

There is really something very noble in this humility of the scientist in the face of truth, in his abdication of all personality before science. One also appreciates this breadth of ideas that rejects biases and systems, and this consciousness that wants to base everything on facts.

Next, Claude Bernard examines "how the method ought to direct reasoning in the search for truth more surely by always imposing a [sic] dubitable form upon that reasoning."[19] They say there are two sorts of reasoning: first, by investigation, which is inductive reasoning that goes from the particular to the general, and second, by demonstration, which is reasoning that goes from the general to the particular. The first is useful when one wants to gain knowledge, and the second for proving what one already knows. They say that the first is proper to the experimental sciences. In reality, it is difficult to distinguish them since in all science there is something known and something unknown, and naturally one is always initially ignorant of where one should begin to induce, and likewise, once the principle has been posited, one always applies deduction. Therefore, there is but one form of reasoning: deduction by syllogism.[20]

Claude Bernard then reviews the importance of philosophic doubt: the conclusion of our reasoning must always remain dubitable, he says, whenever the starting point is not an absolute truth.[21] The greatest error of the experimenter would be to take truths that are merely relative as absolutes. Contrary to systematizers, who build a theory upon a fixed starting point, the experimenter will doubt his starting point and modify it according to the observed facts.

But one must not confuse this fertile doubt with sterile skepticism. The scientist doubts himself and his interpretations but believes in science and, even in the experimental sciences, accepts a scientific criterion or principle that is absolute.[22]

And what is the basis of this criterion? Reason and not mere facts; the [sic] fact is nothing by itself. It takes on value only by the idea attached to it and the proof it furnishes.[23] There is in fact an absolute principle in science: the necessary determinism in the conditions of the phenomenon, which does not vary without a change being produced in the conditions to which it is subject, and, in addition, these variations are rigorously linked together. The criterion is therefore the same as in the science of mathematics, only it is more complex and can be isolated only through analysis.

Thus, the fact, before which all theories must give way [*s'effacer*], must in turn give way before this supreme principle: in the presence of a fact without cause, the fact must be denied, not the science that the fact contradicts. These two fundamental laws are contradictory only in appearance; the first prevents science from enclosing itself within the narrowness of a system, while the second assures a fixed foundation for science.

When the experimenter has proven with facts the preconceived idea suggested to him by an observation, there remains only one operation to accomplish in order to make up all the parts of experimental reasoning: the counterproof. In order to establish that a given condition is in fact the cause of a phenomenon, one must prove not only that it always accompanies the phenomenon, but that the phenomenon disappears if the condition is eliminated. The counterproof consists of the elimination of this phenomenon. "That is what proves the necessary determinism of phenomena, and reason will be satisfied by nothing else."[24]

Claude Bernard himself, Pasteur,[25] and all the great scientists of the last century have made their marvelous discoveries by applying the principles put forth in this work. It is thanks to the experimental method that science has made such remarkable progress in these last fifty years. These facts show the soundness and depth of Claude Bernard's theories more eloquently than any critique or praise.

NOTES

1. Claude Bernard (1813–78) was a French physiologist and founder of experimental medicine.

2. Claude Bernard, *Introduction à l'étude de la médecine expérimentale* (Paris: Garnier-Flammarion, 1966), 27 (hereafter referred to as *IEME*), trans. H. C. Green as *An Introduction to the Study of Experimental Medicine* (New York: Dover, 1957), 3 (hereafter referred to as *ISEM*).

3. "D'envisager" (considering) is underlined in the text, and "illisible" (illegible) is written in the margin in the handwriting presumably of Abbé Trésal.

4. Jean-George Zimmermann (1725–95), a medical doctor and philosopher, was the author of *Traité sur l'expérience en médecine* [Treatise on the Experiment in Medicine] (Paris, 1774). Baron Georges Cuvier (1769–1832) was a French naturalist and pioneer in the sciences of comparative anatomy and paleontology.

5. Beauvoir quotes Bernard's *IEME*: "dans l'expérience il faut porter un jugement par comparaison de deux faits" (38), which Green translates as "in experimentation, we make judgments by comparing two facts, one normal, the other abnormal" (*ISEM*, 9).

6. The phrase "les expressions" (the expressions), is underlined in the text; the word "illisible" (illegible) is written in the margin.

7. This clarification is necessary because in French the word *expérience* means the knowledge gained in the practice of life, both in the concrete sense of learning facts from experi-

mental information (experiment) and in the abstract sense of interpreting facts or observations in relation to life (experience).

8. Bernard, *IEME*, 44; Green, *ISEM*, 15.

9. Beauvoir, paraphrasing Bernard (although using quotation marks), writes, "grâce aux sciences expérimentales, on ne saurait assigner de limites à la puissance que l'homme peut acquérir sur la nature." Bernard's *IEME* reads "A l'aide de ces *sciences expérimentales actives*, l'homme devient un inventeur de phénomènes, un véritable contremaître de la création; et l'on ne saurait, sous ce rapport, assigner de limites à la puissance qu'il peut acquérir sur la nature, par les progrès futurs des sciences expérimentales" (48). Green translates this as follows: "With the help of these active experimental sciences, man becomes an inventor of phenomena, a real foreman of creation; and under this head we cannot set limits to the power that he may gain over nature through future progress in the experimental sciences" (*ISEM*, 18).

10. Beauvoir quotes Bernard's *IEME*: "L'expérimentateur est donc celui qui invoque ou provoque dans des conditions déterminées des faits d'observation pour en tirer l'enseignement qu'il désire. L'observateur est celui qui obtient les faits d'observation et qui juge s'ils sont bien établis et constatés à l'aide de moyens convenables" (51). Green translates this as follows: "An experimenter, then, is a man who produces or induces, in definite conditions, observed facts, to derive from them the instruction which he wishes,—that is, experience. An observer is a man who gathers observed facts and who decides whether they have been ascertained by the help of appropriate means" (*ISEM*, 21).

11. Bernard, *IEME*, 52; Green, *ISEM*, 22.

12. Beauvoir quotes Bernard as "pose une question à la nature," but Bernard's *IEME* reads "pose des questions à la nature" (53), which Green translates as "puts questions to nature" (*ISEM*, 22).

13. Beauvoir closely paraphrases page 54 of Bernard's *IEME*.

14. Beauvoir quotes Bernard's *IEME*: "Tous les termes de la méthode expérimentale sont solidaires les uns des autres. Les faits sont les matériaux nécessaires; c'est leur mise en oeuvre par le raisonnement expérimental qui constitue et édifie véritablement la science. L'idée formulée par les faits représente la science. L'hypothèse n'est que l'idée scientifique, préconçue et anticipée" (53). Green translates this as follows: "We see, then, that the elements of the scientific method are interrelated. Facts are necessary materials; but their working up by experimental reasoning, i.e. by theory, is what establishes and really builds up science. Ideas, given form by facts, embody science. A scientific hypothesis is merely a scientific idea, preconceived or previsioned" (*ISEM*, 26).

15. Beauvoir writes, "L'homme se fait de prime abord des idées sur ce qu'il voit," and Bernard's *IEME* reads "[c]haque homme se fait de prime abord des idées sur ce qu'il voit" (59), which Green translates as follows: "Everyone first works out his own ideas about what he sees" (*ISEM*, 27).

16. Beauvoir's manuscript reads "il faut nous appuyer sur un critérium expérimental et relatif au lieu que le critérium intérieur est [*sic*] absolu," paraphrasing Bernard's *IEME*: "l'homme peut rapporter tous ses raisonnements à deux critériums, l'un intérieur et conscient, qui est certain et absolu; l'autre extérieur et inconscient, qui est expérimental et relatif" (63).

17. Beauvoir, paraphrasing Bernard, writes, "les théories ne sont que des principes relatifs auxquels il ne faut accorder qu'une valeur provisoire." Bernard in *IEME* writes of "les théories qui ne sont que des principes relatifs auxquels on ne doit accorder qu'une valeur provisoire

dans la recherche de la vérité" (73), which Green translates as "theories which are only relative principles to which we should assign but temporary value in the search for truth" (*ISEM*, 39).

18. Beauvoir, paraphrasing Bernard's *IEME*, writes, "De même qu'il rejette toute autorité scientifique, pure superstition, l'expérimentateur rejette tout joug philosophique et théologique." Bernard's text reads "[l]a methode expérimentale est la methode scientifique qui proclame la libérté de l'esprit et de la pensée. Elle secoue non seulement le joug philosophique et théologique, mais elle n'admet pas non plus d'autorité scientifique personnelle" (77), which Green translates as "[t]he experimental method is the scientific method which proclaims the freedom of the mind and of thought. It not only shakes off the philosophical and theological yoke; it does not even accept any personal scientific authority" (*ISEM*, 43).

19. Beauvoir quotes Bernard's *IEME*: "comment la méthode doit, en imposant toujours au raisonnement la forme dubitative, le diriger d'une manière plus sûre dans la recherche de la vérité" (78). Green translates this as follows: "Let us now consider how the method, while always forcing upon reason the dubitative form, may guide it more safely in the search for truth" (*ISEM*, 44).

20. Beauvoir paraphrases Bernard's *IEME* (78–79 and 83) throughout this paragraph.

21. Beauvoir writes, "la conclusion de notre raisonnement doit toujours rester dubitative, dit-il, quand le point de départ n'est pas une vérité absolue," paraphrasing Bernard's *IEME*, which reads "la conclusion de notre raisonnement doit toujours rester dubitative quand le point de départ ou le principe n'est pas une vérité absolue" (83–84) and is translated by Green as "the conclusion of our reasoning must always remain dubitative when the starting point or the principle is not an absolute truth" (*ISEM*, 49).

22. Beauvoir writes, "le savant doute de lui-même et de ses interprétations mais croit à la science et admet, même dans les sciences expérimentales, un critérium ou principe scientifique absolu," paraphrasing Bernard's *IEME*: "Le douteur est le vrai savant; il ne doute que de lui-même et de ses interprétations, mais il croit à la science; il admet même dans les sciences expérimentales un critérium ou un principe scientifique absolu" (87), which Green translates as "[t]he doubter is a man of science; he doubts only himself and his interpretations, but he believes in science; in the experimental sciences, he even accepts a criterion or absolute scientific principle. This principle is the determinism of phenomena" (*ISEM*, 52).

23. Beauvoir quotes Bernard's *IEME*: "Un fait n'est rien par lui-même. Il ne vaut que par l'idée qui s'y rattache ou par la preuve qu'il fournit" (88), which Green translates as "[a] fact is nothing in itself, it has value only through the idea connected with it or through the proof it supplies" (*ISEM*, 53).

24. Beauvoir writes, "C'est elle qui prouve le déterminisme nécessaire des phénomènes, elle seule est capable de satisfaire la raison," which is nearly a direct (yet incomplete) quote of Bernard's *IEME*: "C'est la contre-épreuve qui prouve le déterminisme nécessaire des phénomènes, et en cela elle est seule capable de satisfaire la raison à laquelle, ainsi que nous l'avons dit, il faut toujours faire remonter le véritable critérium scientifique" (92), which Green translates as "[c]ounterproof establishes the necessary determinism of phenomena; and thus alone can satisfy reason to which, as we have said, we must always bring back any true scientific criterion" (*ISEM*, 57).

25. Louis Pasteur (1822–95), the French chemist and microbiologist, formulated vaccines for rabies, anthrax, and chicken cholera and originated the pasteurization process, which removes pathogens by heat.

Two Unpublished Chapters

from *She Came to Stay*

INTRODUCTION
by Edward Fullbrook

The degree of formative philosophical influence that Simone de Beauvoir had on Jean-Paul Sartre and vice versa has long been a subject of scholarly inquiry and debate.[1] This open question is important in terms of the history of twentieth-century philosophy and of women's part therein. In the 1990s this particular inquiry became centered on the relation between two texts, Beauvoir's *She Came to Stay* and Sartre's *Being and Nothingness*.[2] The investigation revolves around two questions: Which book was conceived and written first? and Is Beauvoir's novel a philosophical text in the sense that it intentionally expounds, develops, and tests philosophical ideas?[3] Beginning in the mid-1980s, researchers gained access to Beauvoir's and Sartre's letters and journals, and these showed beyond doubt that *She Came to Stay* was conceived and written first. But for some scholars the second question remains open to contention. The text that this essay introduces is highly relevant for resolving, once and for all, this lingering dispute. "Two Unpublished Chapters" was Beauvoir's original beginning to *She Came to Stay*. Although the two beginnings to her novel are totally distinct in terms of the places and events described, close reading reveals a startling similarity. This introduction will explain how and why this is so.

The ambiguity of language permits the construction of texts that are readable at more than one level of meaning. Showing people how to access different levels of meaning of sophisticated texts is the daily business of literature teachers. But willingness to acknowledge such sophistication in a particular text often depends on the social category to which its author belongs. This is so because social prejudices do not magically vanish when reading, teaching, or writing about books. When a society withholds recognition of an existing level of meaning in a text, it imposes on that text a form of censorship.

Until quite recently, getting anyone to read a Beauvoir text for its philosophical content was nearly impossible. And reading one with a view to finding in it philosophical originality was deemed laughable.[4] Beauvoir the philosopher had been erased from existence.

"Two Chapters" is easily censored contextually. These, remember, were the original first two chapters of *She Came to Stay,* and this book, Beauvoir's first novel, has become the most contextually censored of all of her works. I say "has become" because in the beginning *She Came to Stay* was not censored. Initially it was reviewed as a philosophical text by her good friend and fellow philosopher Merleau-Ponty. Also, in 1959 Hazel Barnes, the English translator of *Being and Nothingness* and a Sartrean, not only saw fit to introduce Beauvoir's novel to English audiences as a philosophical work, but also demonstrated that some of its philosophical content was identical to that found in key parts of *Being and Nothingness.*[5] But willingness to acknowledge the philosophical dimension of *She Came to Stay* remained the exception, even after a momentous interview with Beauvoir in 1979.[6] Responding to penetrating questions from Margaret A. Simons and Jessica Benjamin, Beauvoir denied categorically that Sartre had any input into *She Came to Stay.* If Beauvoir was not lying—and there was no prima facie evidence that she was—then it followed that it was her book that was the primary text and Sartre's *Being and Nothingness,* at least in significant part, the secondary one.[7]

Censoring contextually *She Came to Stay,* however, was made easy by two cultural differences between analytical and continental philosophy. The first concerns the unit of work. The most famous "continental" philosophers have constructed "systems" designed to encompass solutions to many of philosophy's perennial problems. Kant, Hegel, Marx, Heidegger, and Sartre are examples. These system builders took other philosophers' solutions along with some of their own and combined them in novel ways. But system builders in the analytical tradition are virtually unknown. Here the focus of work and the basis of reputation is almost exclusively problem-solution.

In the English-speaking world the continental philosopher has been cruelly and crudely stereotyped as someone unconcerned with philosophical problems, so much so that, as Simon Critchley has observed, "Continental philosophy has been reduced to a list of proper names."[8] This prejudice works very strongly against the recognition of Beauvoir, who was a problem-oriented philosopher, and in favor of Sartre, who was a system-oriented philosopher. As evidenced in her student diaries,[9] Beauvoir was from the beginning self-consciously problem oriented in her approach to philosophy, and she remained so. But Beauvoir and Sartre scholars who have been infected with the prejudice described above do not look for solutions to philosophical problems in Beauvoir's work and, if called to their attention, dismiss them as unimportant because she has not made them part of a philosophical system.

The second cultural difference facilitating the contextual censorship of *She Came to Stay* concerns phenomenological and existential philosophy in particular. Whereas rationalist philosophers begin with supposed universal truths and analytical philosophers with the presumed universal subject and then proceed to truths of diminishing generality, philosophers in the phenomenological-existential tradition begin with concrete individual experiences and then, if possible, proceed to generalizations. This diametrical opposition of perspectives makes it easy to sabotage understanding between the two traditions. But some philosophers in the analytical tradition have worked hard to break down these barriers to cross-cultural understanding.

One of these is the Cambridge philosopher Mary Warnock. "The methodology of Existentialism," she says, "consists in a perfectly deliberate and intentional use of the *concrete* as a way of approaching the abstract, the *particular* as a way of approaching the general." She adds: "The existential philosopher, then, must above all *describe* the world in such a way that its meanings emerge. He cannot, obviously, describe the world as a whole. He must take examples in as much detail as he can, and from these examples his intuition of significance will become clear. It is plain how close such a method is to the methods of the novelist, the short-story writer."[10]

Close, indeed: Sartre's novel *Nausea* has long occupied a central place in the phenomenological-existentialist canon.[11] The eminent American philosopher Arthur Danto begins his book on Sartre's philosophy as follows: "Sartre's great philosophical novel, *Nausea,* is a sustained reflection on the relationships and ultimately the discrepancies between the world and our ways of representing it."[12] Like Warnock, Danto is an analytical philosopher, and yet he treats *Nausea* as Sartre's second-most important philosophical work and devotes a fifth of his book to explicating *Nausea*'s philosophical content.

35

Following Beauvoir's death, her and Sartre's letters and diaries gradually became available to researchers. These documents showed beyond all doubt that not only was *She Came to Stay* written before *Being and Nothingness* but also that Sartre first began to compile notes for his philosophical masterpiece in the days immediately following his reading of the second draft of *She Came to Stay.* These documents, once in the public domain, redefined, as had the Simons-Benjamin interview earlier, the possible terms of the debate. This time the redefinition was definitive: to save the traditional narrative regarding the development of French existentialism, and to preserve Sartre's status as the sole provider of the philosophical ideas that he and Beauvoir shared, it now was imperative not to read *She Came to Stay* as a philosophical text. Obviously, given the phenomenological-existentialist philosophical tradition and *Nausea*'s status as part of its canon, this censorship appeared problematic. Either henceforth *Nausea* should no longer be read as a philosophical text, or the ancient principle of a male-female double standard should be allowed to prevail once again.

"Two Unpublished Chapters" poses still a further threat to the traditional patriarchal exclusion of *She Came to Stay* (scs) from the phenomenological-existentialist philosophical canon. As suggested earlier, even the best teacher cannot force a reader to engage with a textual level or even to acknowledge its existence, especially when a cultural gestalt obscures a level of meaning or when self-interest would be ill-served by acknowledgement of its existence. This is so because the very nature of multiple levels of meaning is that they are not all easily discernible for all readers. And such circumstances create pedagogical impasses. But for the reading of *She Came to Stay,* "Two Unpublished Chapters" comes to the rescue. It is hard to imagine how anyone who compares these two texts could thereafter *in good faith* deny that both works, no less than Sartre's *Nausea,* are philosophical texts. Let me explain.

"Two Unpublished Chapters" (TUC) traces the childhood and adolescence of Françoise, the novel's central character. In 1938 Beauvoir abandoned these chapters, begun in 1937, after showing them to Sartre and to Brice Parain, the editor at Gallimard. Instead of beginning with an account of Françoise's childhood, Beauvoir now began her novel with Françoise as a young woman. Whereas most of the first chapter of TUC takes place in and around a country house, the entire first chapter of scs takes place in a Paris theater and its courtyard. Thus on the level of simple storytelling the two beginnings to Beauvoir's novel are totally dissimilar. Nevertheless when one compares the two texts one is struck by the fact that large parts of both are centered on very similar, but otherwise highly idiosyncratic, descriptions. Some examples, all drawn from the opening pages of the two beginnings to the novel, will show what I mean.

* * *

TUC: There was a scent of scrub, there were pine needles, a taste of apple . . . and Françoise no longer existed anywhere. . . . She spent a long time lying there, her mind blank. She no longer even felt her body: she could feel the warm air, she could smell the scent of the grass; in the valley wrapped in mist, two red spots shone. Suddenly, Françoise was no more than this mist, these bright spots, and there was nothing else left in the world.

SCS: She leaned back against the hard wood of the bench. A quick step echoed on the asphalt of the pavement; a motor lorry rumbled along the avenue. There was nothing but this passing sound, the sky, the quivering foliage of the trees, and the one rose-colored window in a black façade. There was no Françoise any longer, no one existed any longer, anywhere.[13]

* * *

TUC: She . . . had the mission to make as many, as beautiful and varied things as possible come into existence.

SCS: It was as if she had been entrusted with a mission: she had to bring life to this forsaken theatre (2). . . . but for me this square exists and that moving train . . . all Paris, and all the world (4).

* * *

TUC: If she looked away, it had no more existence for anyone.

SCS: When she was not there, . . . [they] did not exist for anyone; they did not exist at all (1).

* * *

TUC: Until today, nobody smelt the scent of charcoal and scrub; nobody knew that these white rocks and the black bare remains of the trees existed; they did not know it themselves; it was as if they had not existed at all. But now, I am here.

SCS: When she was not there [in "the dark corridors"], the smell of dust, the half-light, and their forlorn solitude did not exist for anyone; they did not exist at all. And now she was there (1).

* * *

TUC: In her absence, the scents, the light were plunged in a torpor that could not be conceived of; one might as well try and imagine oneself dead.

37

SCS: She exercised that power: her presence snatched things from their unconsciousness; she gave them their color, their smell (1–2).

* * *

TUC: Françoise's heart swelled: the people on the street, the people in the
houses, all the people needed her; when she abandoned them, their movements and their faces disintegrated like a deserted landscape.

SCS: I feel that things that don't exist for me simply do not exist at all (6).

* * *

TUC: When she stood up to leave, she felt as if she was committing a betrayal. . . . From the moment she pushed open the stained-glass door, the
shadows and the scents were swallowed in impassive night.

SCS: She put her hand on the door-knob, then turned back with a qualm
of conscience. This was desertion, an act of treason. The night would once
more swallow the small provincial square (3).

* * *

TUC: She felt she was the center of the world.

SCS: Wherever I may go, the rest of the world will move with me (5).

* * *

TUC: A brief anguish wrenched her heart; she could not be everywhere at
once.

SCS: She would have had to be everywhere at the same time (2).

* * *

TUC: Françoise knew perfectly well who she was; sometimes at night, she
could hear her parents talk about her when they thought that she was asleep.

SCS: We get the impression of no longer being anything but a figment of
someone else's mind (7).

* * *

Clearly then—and this is not a difficult matter to see—in these two beginnings to her novel, Beauvoir is telling us more than just, in the one, about a
child's mundane experiences in the woods and, in the other, about a thirty-
year-old woman's mundane experiences in a theater. It also is abundantly
clear that this something extra, this other stream of meaning that Beauvoir
delivers to us, is approximately the same in both texts. She has constructed

these otherwise dissimilar narratives as vehicles for introducing the same or similar sets of philosophical ideas. Both narratives serve Beauvoir the philosopher as means to an end. The philosophical and argumentative shape of the novel as a whole required her to introduce certain ideas and positions at or near the beginning. She especially wants to settle at the outset some basic ontological questions, that is, what kinds of being exist and the broad nature of the relations between them. Being a phenomenologist, she can do this through her characters' perceptions. Indeed, for Beauvoir only phenomenological evidence, not abstract reason, is admissible.

A distinctive thesis of Beauvoir is that consciousness is not just the desire to be but also the desire to reveal being, of taking delight in the pure witnessing of the world around oneself, of confronting the mere existence of the world in pure and selfless and, sometimes, joyous wonderment. The first seven groups of quotations above catch Françoise in this mode of intentionality. The eighth relates to Beauvoir's concept of embodiment (that one's experiential world is centered on one's body moving in physical space), the ninth to her theory of appearances by which she demonstrates phenomenologically the existence of a world independent of consciousness, and the tenth to her theory of the Other.

But the important thing for us here is not so much the ideas themselves but rather that the two texts, despite their dissimilarity on the level of simple storytelling, convey similar content on another level of meaning, namely, that of phenomenological philosophy. The only rational explanation for this similarity is that Beauvoir's "Two Unpublished Chapters" and *She Came to Stay,* no less than Sartre's *Nausea* and *Being and Nothingness,* are philosophical texts.

NOTES

1. See Margaret A. Simons, "Beauvoir and Sartre: The Question of Influence," *Eros* 8, no. 1 (1981): 25–42.

2. See Simone de Beauvoir, *She Came to Stay* (London: Flamingo, 1984), and Jean-Paul Sartre, *Being and Nothingness* (New York: Philosophical Library, 1956).

3. These and other questions are taken up at greater length in Kate Fullbrook and Edward Fullbrook, *Simone de Beauvoir and Jean-Paul Sartre: The Remaking of a Twentieth-Century Legend* (London: Harvester, 1993).

4. *The Ethics of Ambiguity* might appear as an exception, but in fact it was generally read as the ethics that Sartre had promised at the end of *Being and Nothingness,* with Beauvoir acting as his intermediary.

5. See Hazel Barnes, *The Literature of Possibility: A Study in Humanistic Existentialism* (London: Tavistock, 1961).

6. See Margaret A. Simons and Jessica Benjamin, "Simone de Beauvoir: An Interview," *Feminist Studies* 5 (Summer 1979, part 2): 330–45.

7. See the discussion in Edward Fullbrook, "*She Came to Stay* and *Being and Nothingness*," *Hypatia* 14, no. 4 (1999): 50–69.

8. Simon Critchley, *Continental Philosophy: A Very Short Introduction* (Oxford: Oxford University Press, 2001), 125.

9. For discussion of these diaries, see Margaret A. Simons, "Beauvoir's Early Philosophy: The 1927 Diary," in *Beauvoir and "The Second Sex": Feminism, Race, and the Origins of Existentialism* (Lanham, Md.: Rowman and Littlefield, 1999), 185–243.

10. Mary Warnock, *Existentialism* (Oxford: Oxford University Press, 1970), 133, 136.

11. See Jean-Paul Sartre, *Nausea,* trans. Robert Baldick (Harmondsworth, Eng.: Penguin, 1965).

12. Arthur Danto, *Sartre* (London: Fontana, 1991), 5.

13. Beauvoir, *She Came to Stay,* 2. Subsequent page references to this work in this introduction are cited parenthetically in the text.

Two Unpublished Chapters from *She Came To Stay*

Chapter 1

The house was empty; the shutters had been closed to shut out the sun and it was dark. On the first-floor landing, Françoise was standing close up against the wall, holding her breath. Earlier on, the steps of the staircase, then the old floorboards, had been creaking, and the glass panels of the bookcase had been shaking slightly; now there was not a sound to be heard. The door to my bedroom, the door to the bathroom, Grandma's bedroom, Papa and Mama's bedroom. It was funny to be there all alone when everyone else was in the garden; it was funny and frightening. The furniture looked as it always did, but at the same time it was completely changed: thick and heavy and secret; under the bookcase and under the marble console lurked a deep shadow. It was not that you wanted to run away, but it felt creepy.

The old jacket was hanging over the back of a chair; Anna had probably cleaned it with petrol, or else she had just taken it out of camphor-balls and put it there to air. It was very old and it looked very worn out. It was old and

"Deux chapitres inédits de *L'Invitée*," in *Les écrits de Simone de Beauvoir,* ed. Claude Francis and Fernande Gontier (Paris: Gallimard, 1979), 275–331. © Éditions Gallimard, 1979.

worn, but it could not complain as Françoise complained when she had hurt herself; it had no soul; it could not say to itself: "I'm an old worn jacket." It was strange. Françoise tried to imagine what she would feel like if she could not say: "I am Françoise, I am six years old, I am in Grandma's house"; if she could not say anything at all to herself. She closed her eyes. It was as if you did not exist, and yet other people could come here; they could see me and talk about me. She opened her eyes; she could see the jacket; it did exist but it was not aware of it: this was both irritating and slightly frightening. What is the use of existing if it doesn't know it? She thought about it; "Maybe there is a way out of it. Since I can say 'I,' what if I said it for it?" This was rather disappointing; no matter how long she looked at the jacket, seeing nothing else while saying very fast: "I am old, I am worn," nothing new happened; the jacket was lying there, indifferent, completely foreign, while she was still Françoise. Anyway, if she became the jacket for a moment, then she, Françoise, would no longer know about it. Everything began to spin in her head, as when she went into a rage and ended up lying on the floor, having cried and screamed until she dropped. She went into her mother's bedroom, took the book she had come to get, and rushed back into the garden.

On the following days, while playing under her mother's guard, she often felt a bit uneasy. There she was, making mud cakes or flower rings; was she not also somewhere else, or did she not also exist somewhere else without knowing it, like the old jacket? This was like a pitch-dark night that was terrible to imagine. I cannot remember anything from before I was born; this is exactly what it must have been like; it is the same for the little children who have not been born yet: they do not know, they will not remember anything; what if one of them happened to be myself? She stood stock-still in the middle of the lawn, trying to catch one of these opaque little souls as they flew by in the air in order to illumine it from inside briefly, so that it might at least remember something later on. There was no use; all she could do was say "I am Françoise" and that was all; she could say "I" for no one else.

She could play at being another. She could say: I am in a hovel, I am hungry, I have got to beg for a few coins, and she felt very sad and stunted; she had turned into a poor, starving orphan. But it was only a game; for real, she always remained Françoise.

Françoise knew perfectly well who she was; sometimes at night, she could hear her parents talk about her when they thought that she was asleep. "She is a precocious child," her father said, satisfied; her mother replied: "Yes, she has a good nature, is very upright, and she tells me everything." Françoise flushed with pleasure and turned over in her bed. She told her mother everything, never lied, liked reading, did well at school, and went into terrible spells of rage when she was denied a treat, but she was never disobedient. She had beautiful chestnut brown and naturally curly hair. She was proud of her curls, her good marks, being a precocious child and having a good nature. She would not have liked to have a mother with rings on every finger like Madame Malin, nor a mother always dressed in black like Madame Lemoine; no flat looked as pretty as hers did, with its beautiful carpets, its bay windows, its huge mirrors; and above all, it would have been terrible to be stupid like Jacqueline and Marthe, or grumpy like Jeannette, or again timorous and sickly-sweet like Mireille. She was really lucky to be this very little girl and no other.

This little girl was Françoise; she looked at her in the mirror in contentment and she said to herself "it's me!" But she was not always this little girl; when she is alone, there sometimes happen strange things, and she is not too sure whom they happen to; they are nonsense. To be troubled by an old jacket is nonsense; to tickle oneself at length in that place where the skin is so soft and sticky when in bed at night is nonsense. Françoise told her mother everything, but nonsense does not exist; it is nothing, and there are no words to talk about it; these moments counted for nothing in Françoise's life.

At other moments, on the contrary, she felt very strongly that she was Françoise. This was the case one morning when Françoise was ten, sitting in the garden at a metal table with round, club-shaped and diamond-shaped holes in it. She was doing a problem, and while thinking about it, she was running a finger along one of the bars of the table, scraping small soft lumps of brown paint from it. It was one of her fascinations that year; she would scratch the trickles of congealed wax on the smooth surface of candles, the rough bits of straw that wrinkled the pages of old books, the scabs from her scrapes, and the small pimples on the back of her neck and on her forehead. She looked up; she could see the blue cedar, the huge terra-cotta pots, the sandy paths; she looked down again and traced a few words in her notebook. As she would every year, Françoise, the studious little girl, was doing her summer homework in the garden. She was writing neatly—it was fun; she could feel every single movement of her hand, she could hear the pen creaking, the garden was present all around her, and there she was, very zealous, infinitely studious, willing, attentive . . . She stopped suddenly; it was like a story one tells oneself, when one says: "I am a poor orphan" and one feels very sad and starved inside; the garden was truly a garden, the nib a real nib, and there was the real Françoise; and yet she felt as if she was playing; just as she would sometimes play at being another, she was playing at being herself. She remained puzzled for a moment. What am I, for real? There were still the blue cedar, the roses, and the brown table with its pattern of clubs and diamonds; but she felt she was no longer anything at all.

Suddenly she saw her mother next to her: "You aren't doing anything, Françoise. Are you daydreaming?" Madame Miquel was smiling slightly reproachfully, under her flowery bonnet. "I'm almost finished, Mama," Françoise said hurriedly, and she dipped the nib in the inkpot. Françoise was never idle and she was never daydreaming; it was not like her to let her mind wander, like a scatterbrain; she resumed her work zealously.

After lunch, Françoise went for a walk in the woods; she took a slice of bread and cheese and a volume of the *Petite Illustration* with her; her father had marked the titles of the plays she was allowed to read: *Les bouffons* by Zamacois, *Barbe-Bleue* by Madame Rosemonde Gérard.[1] As soon as she had pushed the white gate open, she started running toward the woods with a beating heart. In the shade of the tall pines, she was going to feel that joy again, that anguish which she never experienced in the garden that was open to the broad daylight for everybody to see.

There was a path disappearing under the trees and she slowed down the pace of her walk; at the end of the path, there was a sort of glade where she came to sit every day. The bushes and the pines had been burnt down in a fire four years earlier, and a large circular clearing was left in the middle of the wood. Françoise wished to sneak in there one day, silently, as she had done once in the deserted house. When she was not there, the white rocks, the burnt stumps, the bushes with pointed leaves, everything must look different; but the clearing could never be caught by surprise. She stood motionless for a moment, holding her breath, behind a clump of ilexes; then she moved the branches aside; she had missed it once again.

She sat at the place she had chosen at the beginning of the summer, in the shade of a rock; she swept away some pine needles and uncovered a heap of apples. Françoise was not allowed to eat in between meals, and Françoise was obedient, but here, rules no longer counted; she bit into an apple and opened the book on an unmarked page. When she had eaten the apple and finished reading the first act of *Maman Colibri*, she stripped a small branch of its bark and gently rubbed this sticky sprig between her thighs: she found it disgusting to touch the damp flesh with her fingers. The image of her mother came to her and she dismissed it without shame; it was like another existence where one had no more parents, no future, no longer even a name. There was a scent of scrub; there were pine needles, a taste of apple, a gentle and mysterious sensation that turned the whole body, from head to toe, into a shivering piece of tissue paper; and all this was neither good nor bad. It existed, indifferent, and Françoise no longer existed anywhere.

The evening bell rang, and Françoise jumped to her feet. Spots of sunlight were shining on the stones of the path, but at the end of the pine border, the grass was thick and black. She stepped forward cautiously; a branch snapped and she leaned close to a tree trunk. Silent, invisible, she looked in the distance, as far as the end of the path, trying to make out these surroundings for which she was still absent. She could see only indistinct and dark shapes. She resumed her walk; she stepped forward on tiptoe, and yet, as she went along, spots of sunlight appeared on the sparse grass, the leaves rustled as birds fluttered away, the rocks and the clumps of myrtle quickly took on their familiar aspect. The secret was receding further and further away in front of her. At the end of the path she turned around: at the back of the pine border, the grass was thick and black; the bushes and the rocks had returned to their solitude and had become themselves again.

Françoise shuddered; if she remained all her life in the wood, she thought, she would end up being no one; it was a bit frightening. She started running. What am I for real? The house was closer and the afternoon spent in the wood was beginning to seem like a dream. She went through the park and slipped into the dining room. The light was on, the table was set; she saw her china plate with a big blue butterfly painted on it, the egg cup bearing her initials; from the drawing-room, her father called: "Is that you, Françoise?" So she smiled, reassured.

In the streets in Paris, and on the lawns of the Ranelagh, nothing reminded Françoise of the burnt clearing; she never happened to lose herself in it. In Paris, Françoise had only one existence, and each of her actions left a mark that could either tarnish or enhance her image; she carefully controlled all her moves and when she happened to act carelessly, she at once begged forgiveness from her mother, who erased it with a kiss. She did not make any fuss anymore, she came first in all the school tests, she read all the books that her father recommended to her, and she was admired by her friends for inventing new games. To make her image more dazzling day by day was an absorbing task, and she had time for nothing else.

At thirteen, Françoise was an accomplished young lady; even Maurice, her cousin who was two years older and such a remarkable young man, said that she was brilliant. Maurice had no parents, and he often came to the house after dinner to chat with his uncle about Edmond Rostand, or Victor Hugo, and sometimes Françoise took part in the conversation.[2] She liked her cousin very much and her heart would beat with emotion when she recognized his ring at the door. One evening, she was already in bed when she heard his voice and rushed into the study, wearing her nightgown; Madame Miquel blushed and said she was too old to make an appearance dressed like that; she sent her back to her room with an angry look. Upon reflection, Françoise felt embarrassed too and thought proudly and anxiously that she was no longer a child; she wore tights, her pretty curls had been cut, and her chest was swollen by two little hard stones that were a bit painful. She never slipped her hand beneath her nightgown anymore; she had read from a book that it was an unhealthy habit that bore an awful name.

Three months later Françoise had her first period; as her mother had not forewarned her, she thought that she was suffering from a disgusting infirmity and she spent part of the night trying to clean off the brownish stains from her underpants. But in the morning her mother told her that all women went through this slight inconvenience every month, and she took from the wardrobe a rubber belt and a towel that were specially meant to deal with it. She looked vaguely gratified, and in the afternoon, while her mother was serving tea, it seemed to Françoise that Madame Miquel's friends were looking at her in a funny way. From then on, Françoise's feelings toward her mother were never quite the same anymore.

At the end of the school year, Françoise got the prize for being first in her class as well as twelve nominations. There was a round of applause as she went to the dais, stiff in her new raspberry-colored silk dress adorned with golden embroideries. Her father gave her a wristwatch as a present, and her mother gave her a fountain pen made of pink enamel with silver rims. In the afternoon, there was a big tea party in her honor, and she drank a little champagne, Aunt Louise sat at the piano, and Françoise danced with Maurice and also with M. Perrier, who looked so young although he had a twelve-year-old son, and who treated her exactly like a grownup. Uncle Charles asked Papa: "What are you going to make of this young lady?" and Monsieur Miquel put his hand on Françoise's shoulder and said that she would go to college like a boy and maybe she would become his assistant. That very evening, Françoise left for the South with Anna, and on the train she was completely sullen. Leaning her head on the blue cushions, she remembered the afternoon party; at these times, it was as if other people no longer counted, even in their own eyes. She was more important to them than themselves, something that should never end. When I get married, this will last for days on end, but that is a long time from now, she thought with a sigh.

She felt no joy showing her Grandma the pink fountain pen, the wrist-

46

watch, the brand-new books, and she went for a stroll in the park. She felt completely stunted; neither Maurice, nor M. Perrier, nor Uncle Charles were thinking anymore of the little girl in the raspberry-colored dress who danced so gracefully after receiving all the prizes. Everyone was thinking of themselves again and she did not count for anybody anymore but herself. The two months that she was to spend in the country seemed endless to her.

Carrying a book, Françoise made her way to the woods. The glade was bathing in the sun, and the pointed leaves of asphodels cast sharp black shadows onto the dry white ground. Françoise was overcome by the hot smell of the junipers and the myrtles and she slumped, overwhelmed, at the bottom of a rock. The fountain pen, the wristwatch, the raspberry-colored dress, and all the people were suddenly of no importance any longer. She crushed a sprig of lavender between her fingers, she leaned her cheek against the warm ground, and her eyes brimmed with tears. Nothing had changed: the craggy stones, the burnt and contorted trunks. Had they not missed me during all this time when there was nobody to look at them?

She propped herself up on her elbow. Until today, nobody smelt the scent of charcoal and scrub; nobody knew that these white rocks and the black bare remains of the trees existed; they did not know it themselves; it was as if they had not existed at all. But now, I am here, and I will come every day, she whispered passionately.

She came back every day. She ran through the wood and perched on the flat top of a rock; the white ridge of a hill stood out against the sky. Her gaze made the scrubland undulate gently, and the dark spot of a pine forest appear among the clumps of ilex. Françoise was exhilarated by the feeling that she was necessary to this countryside that she loved; in her absence, the scents, the light were plunged in a torpor that could not be conceived of; one might as well try and imagine oneself dead. Françoise smiled at the thought of her childish attempts to take the solitary glade by surprise; it was ridiculous. There could be no secret since the black stumps and the white stones could neither see themselves nor talk to themselves; each was lying there, huddled upon itself, inert and shapeless.

Françoise was sitting still in her rocky retreat, and, her book open in her lap, she looked at the shadows spread and darken on the ground. If one was distracted for just a moment, one suddenly saw that the horizon had become mauve: the grays and pinks had crossed the sky in vain. Smitten with remorse, Françoise stared at the hills as they were turning pale, and when she stood up to leave, she felt as if she was committing a betrayal; only she could alleviate the secluded sadness of these woods. From the moment she pushed open the

47

stained-glass door, the shadows and the scents were swallowed in impassive night.

Françoise spent whole days lying on the stone, while the scorching heat of the sun devoured her bare legs and arms. Sometimes, however, she got to her feet and started running; she ran through the thickets, where the thorns of the brambles and the sharp branches of cystus and gorse scratched her legs; she climbed rocks, and she rolled down to the bottom of gullies; her gaze wrenched dry riverbeds, walls of rock, and bare plateaus bristling with straight and sharp blades of grass, from their unconsciousness. "When I'm grown up, I'll be an explorer," she decided, tumbling to the ground, exhausted and overcome with her sense of potency. Behind her, the thicket and steep gullies could go back to sleep; it would never be the same again.

One evening, Françoise stopped, exhausted, on the side of a hill; the ruins of a deserted village were lying at her feet; the big red disc of the sun was sinking behind the mountains. She paused: if she went a bit further up, she would discover the whole valley; on the other hand, the deserted streets of the village in the dusk were full of mystery. A brief anguish wrenched her heart; she could not be everywhere at once. She threw herself down and stretched out on the dry grass. The world was so wide that she could never live long enough to travel through all of it.

She spent a long time lying there, her mind blank. She no longer even felt her body: she could feel the warm air, she could smell the scent of the grass; in the valley wrapped in mist, two red spots shone. Suddenly, Françoise was no more than this mist, these bright spots, and there was nothing else left in the world. A pure and bright joy was shining without beginning or end. Time had stopped.

An image went through her mind; a dining room, some faces; it went by, tranquil at first, like the mist and the grass; then it suddenly pinched her heart and stirred her body. Françoise found herself on the edge of a valley over which constellations were glimmering; nine o'clock, dinner. She started running.

"What time do you call this?" said her father harshly. She just stood silent in the middle of the drawing room. A few moments ago, she was a deserted village, a black sky, and that extraordinary joy; now, she was a little girl who was being scolded. At that minute, there were thousands of little girls in houses.

"You could at least apologize," Madame Miquel said. "We've finished dinner. Where have you been? Did you get lost?"

Other houses, other furniture, other people; why was she in this precise drawing room? These faces were strangers to her and, for the first time in her life, reproaches had no effect on her. It seemed to Françoise that she might equally have been anywhere else.

"Answer me," Monsieur Miquel said angrily, "have you lost your tongue?" "I lost track of time," she said vaguely. All the villages in the valley had lit up, crickets were droning in the dilapidated houses, and there she was, playing out this absurd scene. The lamp, Monsieur Miquel, the workbasket, nothing seemed real.

Words still reached Françoise's ears and from time to time, her lips uttered an answer; she had no idea why she lent herself to this ridiculous game. Then she heard her mother's voice: "you won't set a foot outside the park again." She gave a start; these words were truly addressed to her and they made her wince.

"But Mama . . ." she said; her voice faltered. She wished she could scream: "Let's start again; I didn't know it was for real." But there was no excuse. Madame Miquel had a closed and obdurate expression. Françoise had not responded to the reproaches, she had refused to give any explanation, and she had to be punished. That was what had truly happened, and there was no way of effacing it. The whole scene was reality itself.

Françoise did not go beyond the park the next day; she strolled around the sandy paths, boiling with anger. Monsieur and Madame Miquel were chatting peacefully outside the house, unaware that their blind commands had annihilated all the scents of the scrubland. Françoise cast a hateful look at them; they never went to lie down under the pines; they feared the coolness of the evening, the noonday sun, fatigue, and dust. Their whole life was spent in surroundings that were made just for them, and they were always exactly themselves. Françoise was their daughter, but she also had a life that depended on no one; that this life might be affected by thoughtless words was monstrous.

In the evening, Françoise was so tense that, when her mother kissed her, telling her that her punishment was lifted, she shed a few tears; she felt shame for it, but Madame Miquel was very touched and said that they should be real friends to each other. From that day on, she told her some childhood memories, asked her questions about all the books that she saw her read, and when school started again, she often took her with her to go shopping. Françoise did not like it very much when her mother asked her questions in a confidential tone, but on the other hand, she was proud of having tea like a young lady at the Marquise de Sévigné's or at Colombin's. She started taking dancing lessons and some evenings her father took her to ice-skate at the

Palais de Glace; he said jokingly that she was not too ugly for a girl entering the awkward age. He told her a bit about his work and about the advance of science. He was a great and very famous doctor who was doing cancer research, and Françoise began venerating her father.

She was very busy and very happy; yet, in the evening, she often felt miserably dejected. She recalled the wide white desert of Provence and it seemed horrible to her that she should be a mere imperceptible spot in a city swarming with people, where she was not needed; she thought with anguish that, one day, she would die and nothing would be changed.

One evening, her parents were out to dinner in town, and, sitting in a leather armchair in the study, she was tired of reading and bored; she took a few steps across the room, opened the drawers of the desk, and closed them again without disturbing anything. Then she took the field glasses from their hook next to the mantelpiece and went onto the balcony. It was mild, and yet all the windows along the avenue Mozart were closed. There were few people on the street, and they walked by quickly, heads lowered. She amused herself looking at them though the magnifying glasses; she explored the black fronts of the buildings, and she spied on young people dancing behind a lit-up bay window. Suddenly, facing these houses full of people, she felt as alone as in the burnt glade. No one saw the chimney pots standing out against the sky, no one was looking at the trees, the lit-up windows, the reddish mist above the roofs. Behind one of the windows, a maid was patting the cushions of a sofa flat; the maid could see the pillows and the sofa, but only Françoise could see her movement. Through the circular magnifying glasses, this stood out as on the stage of a theater; if she looked away, it had no more existence for anyone. Two young people went by in an embrace; each could see the other's face, but only Françoise could see them both. "They are lovers," she thought, and their tentative gait took on a romantic grace and disappeared around the street corner. Françoise's heart swelled: the people on the street, the people in the houses, all the people needed her; when she abandoned them, their movements and their faces disintegrated like a deserted landscape.

From then on, Françoise spent hours leaning her forehead against her bedroom window, and in the evening, she often watched through the field glasses until the dead of night. In these moments, she felt she was the center of the world; she and nobody else had the mission to make as many, as beautiful and varied things as possible come into existence. Her parents never raised the curtains from the windows; her friends never lingered around the streets, and their attention was never caught by anything around them; when they described a theater set, a place in Paris, a shop display, Françoise felt that they had not seen it; she had to look at them with her own eyes.

As Françoise grew up, her mission became more pressing, and soon she considered it her only duty. There were rules, however, in her life as a brilliant pupil and as an accomplished young lady; it was a matter of winning the game, and even cheating was allowed provided no one noticed. Françoise seldom cheated and would not have tolerated accomplices. She never let any dancing partner kiss her, nor her friends engage in dubious conversation. It was only in solitude that she read forbidden books; in solitude, no action was of any importance.

One Sunday afternoon, she copied her Greek translation without any qualms from a Guillaume Budé edition of Monsieur Miquel's.[3] She always got the best mark at translation from Greek, but this kind of work took her a lot of time and she wanted to have the afternoon to herself to read *Chéri*.[4] Within half an hour, the work was finished; it was not a slavish copy, and she had scattered a few words and phrases of her own in it. With a light heart, she returned to the study to lie down on the carpet in front of the crackling fire. She breathed in with delight the smell of the leather armchair against which she was leaning her head and the smell of burnt wood that was reminiscent of Provence. "How can anyone be unhappy?" she wondered with surprise. If one was poor, or ill, one was unhappy, but these were accidents; people who were unhappy through love, boredom, or unsatisfied ambition, that was inconceivable. To read a novel by the fire would always be possible; what more was needed?

The week went by, and on Friday evening, Françoise came across her Greek teacher in a corridor. Mademoiselle Vaisson often praised her translations in class for their style, but she never talked to her outside the classroom; she stopped, however.

"Françoise Miquel, you have given me an excellent Greek translation," she said. She looked at her in the face, with a singular expression. "Did you do it on your own?"

Françoise felt her cheeks redden. "Yes, Mademoiselle, on my own," she said firmly.

Mademoiselle Vaisson stared at her. "That's fine, then. I'll tell you about it tomorrow in class."

She went away and Françoise stood petrified; her heart was beating hard: Mademoiselle Vaisson knew. For a moment, Françoise stood stiff, repeating with all her strength: it is impossible; such disasters could happen, but not to her. She could not survive it, yet she knew that she was not going to die. Then she went off and wandered around the streets. The next day, Mademoiselle Vaisson would put the papers on her desk and say: "Françoise Miquel has plagiarized her translation."

Françoise wrung her handkerchief. It was awful; it was unfair; she did not mean to plagiarize, she just wanted to gain two hours. It was merely a small personal arrangement, a harmless action that lasted only a few moments. Suddenly it had become a hideous flaw that would remain attached to her person for years to come; it existed forever and it was still going to amplify: the next day the whole class would know, as would the headmistress, Papa and Mama. Françoise leant over the bridge over the Seine; it would be easier to destroy oneself than to erase this fleeting act that had not really been committed. She rushed into a broad black avenue; in a detective novel she had read, a man suddenly vanished at a dark street corner; but it was a novel, and anyway, he was back at the end. Even if she walked along the barracks all night, there would come the time when the school bell would ring on the playground at eight o'clock; and she would hear it. There was no way of stopping time, nor of taking a detour to avoid the fateful moment.

Françoise managed to control herself at dinner, but she had a dreadful night. She dreamt that her father caught her in the act of reading *Nana;*[5] then she found herself in her nightgown sitting on her cousin Maurice's lap, and Madame Miquel arrived, snickering, arm in arm with Mademoiselle Vaisson. She woke up, covered in sweat. Dawn was coming, and there was no chance of salvation unless Mademoiselle Vaisson got run over by a car; Françoise imagined the crash against the big truck, and the small crushed body; the chief supervisor would come into the classroom. "Children, there's been a terrible accident," and Françoise would weep a bit because she liked her teacher. She repeatedly imagined the scene so intensely that she almost came to believe in it. Mademoiselle Vaisson *could* die; but that Françoise should be humiliated in front of the whole class in a few hours' time was impossible.

As she went through the school main door, she felt her knees give way beneath her. She considered for a minute going to tell Mademoiselle everything and beg her to keep the secret, then she rejected the idea with horror; if she admitted, the unfair nightmare would irreparably become real; she must deny at all costs. She sat at her desk. Mademoiselle Vaisson came in and put the papers on the desk.

"Françoise Miquel, you've handed in the best translation," she said, and the corners of her mouth went down. "But the thing is that you did not do it; you shamelessly plagiarized. I did not expect this from you," she added in an infinitely sad tone.

Françoise stood up and exclaimed violently: "It isn't true, I did my homework on my own." She stifled a sob: "Ask Mama, I spent the whole Sunday afternoon on it."

"Unfortunately, I use the Guillaume Budé translation," Mademoiselle Vaisson said dryly. "At first, I didn't want to believe my eyes, but then, I had to bow to facts."

In the second row, Jacqueline Hézard and her friends were snickering.

"Translations may happen to be very similar," Françoise said desperately. "Why should I plagiarize? I give you my word of honor."

"She is always first in the class; she doesn't need to plagiarize," Marthe Sabran said, and some other voices agreed. Mademoiselle Vaisson hesitated for a minute. "Go through the word-for-word translation," she said.

Françoise blew her nose and started translating; before going to bed, she had learnt the text almost by heart and her translation was excellent. Some murmurs could be heard.

"I've made my decision," Mademoiselle Vaisson said, "however, you've given your word of honor, and I don't want to run the least risk of injustice. I will just not give this homework a grade."

The class came to an end in complete silence; Françoise was thinking very hard. This was not sufficient, she could not stand the fact that Mademoiselle Vaisson believed she could lie or take a false oath. She wanted to convince her; and whatever she wanted, she would generally get. At the end of the class, she went up to the desk: "Mademoiselle, I beg you to believe me; I am not a liar," she said with emotion. Mademoiselle Vaisson looked at her coldly: "This is now a matter between you and your conscience," she said, and she walked out purposefully. Françoise's eyes followed her with astonished hatred as she went away; she went along the school corridors and tranquilly went on with her life, harboring this hostile and stubborn thought over which there was no hold from the outside; it was frightening and nearly monstrous.

Over the following weeks, school was distasteful to Françoise; she avoided Mademoiselle Vaisson's gaze; she felt ill at ease with her friends. Her mother had advised her not to frequent the girls who did not belong to her social circle, and she was intimate only with Marthe Sabran. They both went out a lot that winter. Marthe told her dancing partners that Françoise was very intelligent and quoted her opinions on shows and books; but she said that, as for emotional life, Françoise was still a child and she advised her on her outfits. Françoise let her mother choose her clothes for her and did not spend much time looking at herself in mirrors; she did not envy the magnificent dresses that Marthe, Rosine Guerdan, or Lucette Porteret wore. They were all very coquettish and very jealous of one another. They often teased Françoise for her shyness with boys; Françoise danced well and she was often invited out, but she had no regular admirers, whereas her friends competed over many a boyfriend. Françoise looked amusedly at their little games; they were elegant and beautiful, and when they danced, their eyes sparkled with passion; yet, as she looked at them, Françoise was overwhelmed with a peaceful and powerful joy. She would not have let herself be enclosed like the others in little personal affairs; she successively lived all the affairs of other people, Rosine's and Marthe's, as well as those of the tired musicians who waited for the end of the night to come, those of the shy high-school boys, those of the weary mothers; and sometimes, while all the people around her were engrossed in their triumphs and their worries, she had the exhilarating impression that the lights, the jazz, the sparkling dresses created these revels only for her.

Never to hear Françoise's little secrets in exchange for her own sometimes annoyed Marthe.

"You never dream about the future, do you?" she said impatiently. Françoise smiled. On many occasions, when she strode around the lakes, she thought about the future, but she dreamt neither of a handsome young man, nor of little fair heads, nor of precious jewels. She never worried about what would become of her. For her, the future was an ever wider world: it was Venice and Athens, the cure for cancer, the life of the stars in the sky, and the complete works of Shakespeare and Dostoevsky; to possess such a world equaled happiness.

Chapter 2

When Françoise started the senior-year philosophy class,[6] Madame Miquel thought it was time she introduced her to the realities of life, and, one morning, she came and sat down with a slightly pompous air in her daughter's bedroom. She blushed before opening her mouth, and so did Françoise. Madame Miquel finally stated that Françoise was no child anymore, and Françoise hurriedly said that she was aware of a great many things. Her mother looked relieved but, scolding her gently, said that she should have started asking her questions a long time ago, and that these conversations were perfectly natural between mother and daughter. She left quickly, and the subject was never broached again.

Françoise went back to school with pleasure. Everybody had been charming with her when she had passed her *baccalauréat* with honors, and Mademoiselle Vaisson, patting her arm, said that it was a deserved success. Françoise looked at her slightly embarrassed, but Mademoiselle Vaisson seemed to have completely forgotten the little incident in the first term. Françoise felt somehow disappointed by this.

Marthe Sabran had failed her exam, and she did not take it again; she was almost engaged. There were a few new faces in the class, but none of them looked nice. Françoise decided not to join any group and sat down at the end of a table, next to Marguerite Georges, a good and completely nondescript friend. A week after school started, Françoise's curiosity was aroused by a tall red-headed girl wearing a black silk dress with huge leg-of-mutton sleeves. Monsieur Borgeaud mispronounced her name. "Mademoiselle Labrousse," he called.

The red-headed girl stood up: "Labroux, Élisabeth Labroux," she said, with a broad smile revealing all of her teeth.[7]

"Are you a new student?" Monsieur Borgeaud said.

She nodded her head. "Yes, I'm sorry for being a week late, but I've been in Paris for only a few days, I couldn't come earlier."

Her voice was as odd as the words she uttered; it was too resonant, too vibrant. It was an undisciplined voice, Françoise thought reproachfully. She felt embarrassed, the other pupils were snickering, and Monsieur Borgeaud looked a bit puzzled. "Fine. Try and catch up," he said quickly.

Élisabeth Labroux sat down and Françoise observed her at length; her hair, which tumbled in disorder across her shoulders, was opulent, almost indiscreet. Françoise was satisfied with this adjective; the voice was indiscreet too, as was that strange dress. The new student took a big child's nib-holder, which looked exactly like a stick of barley sugar, from a black pencil box with a painted lid. Françoise took her pink enamel fountain pen out of her bag; all her friends had fountain pens, and hers was the most beautiful.

Monsieur Borgeaud was talking about introspection, "These are the objections that Auguste Comte has summed up in a pleasant formula: whoever wishes to look within himself is like a man who would look out of the window in order to see himself walk by in the street."[8] Françoise wrote the quotation down and wondered for a moment: how unpleasant, to think that, concealed behind their windows, other people could see you while you could not see yourself.

The lesson finished at noon, and all the pupils headed for the cloakroom. Élisabeth Labroux went straight to Françoise.

"You're the best student in the class, aren't you?" she said politely. Françoise laughed self-consciously. "I don't know, why do you ask?"

"Could you let me have your notes? I was told you were the best student." Holding the first page of her notebook, she dangled it from her fingertips.

55

"Look," she said smiling. The pages were blank except for a few scribblings here and there. "I don't know how you manage," she said, sullen. "I'll let you have them, but not until Sunday," Françoise said. She looked, amused, at this odd face: above the green eyes, the thick golden eyebrows almost joined; the mouth was too big, and the line of the heavy cheeks was indistinct. Peasant hands with nails the color of dark blood emerged out of the huge sleeves. "She's quite a character," Françoise thought, and she decided that she deserved further examination. Élisabeth slipped a yellow jacket on and put a tiny black cap with gold studs on it on her shock of hair.

"What about this gentleman? Is he a good teacher?" she said. "He looks a bit of an old dotard to me. Who's your favorite philosopher?"

"I haven't read anything yet" Françoise said.

"I love Nietzsche," Élisabeth said in a kind of languishing way. "I also like Lucretius. Are you a materialist or a deist?"[9]

"I've got no definite opinion," Françoise said, slightly perplexed; she added cautiously: "I'll wait until I know more about it."

"You will, will you?" Élisabeth said surprised. "It seems to me one can't wait!" She held out her hand, smiling. "See you later; thanks in advance for the notebook."

Françoise followed her with her eyes and shrugged her shoulders slightly. Of course, she could have replied that she did not believe in God, but to talk about these things was indecent. The existence of God, or materialism, could be discussed in the classroom, but as for what was said in class, no one took it to heart; it would have been snobbish. What one took to heart, one kept for oneself. "The idea of painting one's nails red! Especially with hands like hers!" she finally thought, nettled.

In the afternoon, in history class, Élisabeth intentionally sat down next to Françoise. "I'm going to try and see how you go about it," she said, examining the open notebook that was covered with a neat handwriting. She opened hers at the first page; in wide and round letters, she had written: "History notebook, Élisabeth Labroux"—an illiterate person's handwriting. At the bottom of the page, in very small print, there could be read:

> But the green paradise of childhood loves,
> with its romps and songs, its kisses and bouquets.[10]

Françoise put her finger on the last words and looked at Élisabeth inquisitively.

"Baudelaire," Élisabeth said. "You aren't familiar with him?"[11] Her milky complexion had turned slightly red.

"I know 'The Invitation to the Voyage,'" Françoise said.

—My child, my sister,
just imagine the happiness
of voyaging there to spend our lives together ... [12]

Élisabeth whispered; she leant her chin on her hand and looked straight ahead of her. What was she thinking about, with this big stubborn face? "The green paradise of childhood loves, it must be symbolic," Françoise thought. Why had she written this verse rather than any other in her notebook? What would I write? Anything, nothing, there's no point. She looked at Élisabeth surreptitiously; she did not change her behavior, she ignored the fact that Mademoiselle Castin had just come in, she ignored her fellow students, she ignored Françoise. What link was there between these harsh eyes, Baudelaire's verse, and the dress with leg-of-mutton sleeves? All the other girls' faces, clothes, and tastes seemed interchangeable.

"Which way are you going?" said Françoise when they got out of school; there was a funny little lump in her throat that would not go down.

"I live on the rue de la Tour," said Élisabeth. "And you?" she asked engagingly.

"On the avenue Mozart. I'll go with you; I like going for a walk at this time. Where did you live, before coming to Paris?"

"Near Privas. Do you know the place?"

Françoise shook her head. "Is there a high school in Privas?"

"No, there isn't. It's the first time I've been to high school. I wonder if I'll stay the whole year; I don't like it too much. But to study philosophy, there's hardly any other way."

She spoke as if she was free to live her life as she wanted, and yet, she was not much older than Françoise. Eighteen years old, maybe.

"Did you take the first part of the exam on your own?" Françoise said, slightly skeptical.

"I had a few lessons." She looked at Françoise in the face with shameless curiosity. "What do you want to do, when you're grown up?"

"Medicine; or history, I don't know yet. What about you?"

"I'll be a painter," Élisabeth said, "but first, I need to pass my *baccalauréat;* it could help me find a job."

They went around the corner and Élisabeth stopped in front of a modest-looking building. "Good-bye, see you tomorrow," she said. Françoise remained standing on the pavement. Through the glass door, she could see Élisabeth, who stood looking at the mirror in the entry hall: she had taken her cap off and was combing her hair. The comb went down the red locks, and the heavy shock of hair swelled and shivered on the back of her neck. Once, twice, ten times; with a regular movement, the hand with red nails ran the comb through the copper-colored mane; the comb went again and again along the heaving wisps; once again; once again. It was fascinating. Françoise did not feel her body anymore; hair was brushing against the back of a neck, a cheek; she felt only the silky caress brushing against a flesh that was not hers. The comb was gliding slowly; the silky hair was brushing against the white, delicious and cruel flesh, caressing it. Élisabeth pushed the second door open and started walking up the stairs. There existed the stairs, the carpet, and the railing on which the hand with painted nails rested. Françoise had ceased existing.

"Well!" Françoise said loudly. She suddenly found herself standing on the curb. Something had just happened; she was not sure what, but it had been rather painful. Slowly, she walked off and went up the rue de Passy; under her eyes were displayed crates of oranges and grapefruits, crispy croissants, scrubbed meat stuck with green and red rosettes. She stopped in front of the large butcher's shop; with a blank mind, she gazed at the black and white tiles that were covered with sawdust, the brass scales, and bunches of raw chops in their frilly ruffs on the wooden block. These were here, but somewhere else, where she was not, there were other things. A white skin felt the touch of a silky dress against it, the back of the neck felt the shiver of red hair. One could no longer say: all this does not know that it exists, it is as if it did not exist. It knew. It felt itself existing from inside; it had no need of Françoise in order to be felt; she could only go around it like a stranger. She went on her way. She no longer looked at anything. Things felt themselves existing without her; another thought, other eyes than hers cast a melancholy shadow onto the surface of the sky. It was almost intolerable. "Of course," she murmured, irritated, "I'm aware that I'm not the only person in the world." But with other people, it was so different! When one parted with Marthe at a street corner, she faded into nothingness. Élisabeth was real.

Françoise went up the stairs, opened the door to the study and slumped into the leather armchair; she did not turn the light on, she did not pull the curtains. The yellow light of a streetlight filtered through the tulle blinds, shining dimly into the room. At this minute, in a flat in the rue de la Tour, Élisabeth had opened a book, or she was dreaming, wallowing on a sofa and smoking a cigarette. As she brought this book, this dream, the taste of this cigarette to life, she deprived Françoise of them. Françoise stuck her nails into the fragrant leather of the armchair. How could she have imagined that the world amounted to what she grasped of it? It was there in front her, like a forbidden immensity; she had just been given a tiny part of it, which had lost its taste for her. A supple body in a tight silk dress was lying down onto the cushions of a sofa and thick lips were blowing wisps of blue smoke. Each to his own body, each to his little patch of land, his memories and his pleasures. Deep in the leather armchair, there remained just a seventeen-year-old girl called Françoise Miquel, a few pounds of healthy flesh, a series of images and sensations brought together under the same label. This could die, nothing would change around her.

The front door of the flat banged; there were light steps, a scent, and the study was flooded with light.

"What's the matter, dear, are you tired?"

Françoise jumped to her feet; she hated the understanding expression that her mother took on toward her that year—an understanding and eager expression: head forward, eyes bright.

"I was resting for a minute; the streets are so crowded, it's exhausting." She examined the shelves of the bookcase.

"Has Papa got Nietzsche's works? They're worth reading, I heard."

"You're working too hard, dear, you've got dark circles under your eyes. Go to bed early tonight, do it for me. I want my daughter to look beautiful tomorrow evening. Did you give José a call to make an appointment?"

"Yes, I did, Mama," Françoise said, "I'm going tomorrow at half past five, I'll be back at seven." She had at last found *Thus Spake Zarathustra* and took both volumes under her arm.

"Tight ringlets, that is, and the forehead completely bare, exactly the same style as last time; it was perfect."

"Yes, Mama," Françoise repeated while fiddling with the door knob.

"Good, go and do your work," Madame Miquel said in a slightly disappointed tone.

The next morning, when Françoise was sitting next to Élisabeth in philosophy class, she looked her up and down, slightly surprised. She could see an eighteen-year-old girl who was neither plain nor beautiful, rather badly dressed, a high-school student among others, with two eyes and a nose in the middle of the face like everybody. Exactly like Françoise's, her eyes reflected the walls of the classroom, the bent necks, Monsieur Borgeaud's pince-nez. There was nothing worrying in this. In the cloakroom, they exchanged a few words: "This is a funny little garment," Françoise said, smiling amicably, as Élisabeth threw a black cape across her shoulders.

"Do you like it? With all this ridiculous hair, it's quite in Marie Bashkircheff's style, isn't it?[13] I'd like to make a portrait of myself dressed like this; it could be delightful."

Françoise looked at her in astonishment. In the evening, she repeated Élisabeth's words to Marthe, and they both had a good laugh. Yet Françoise was sullen all evening. Élisabeth simply seemed to think she was the center of the world, and it was time that things were made quite clear. Françoise decided to become close with her and show her who she was.

When Élisabeth invited her over for tea the following Sunday, Françoise gladly accepted and made plans straight away. She would dazzle Élisabeth with her vast knowledge and her sharp mind; she need not fear she would come across as pedantic, as Élisabeth was not sensitive to such nuances. Then, she would ask her questions and make her tell her secrets. As yet, she knew nothing about Élisabeth, except that she had a brother in Paris, that her parents stayed in Privas, and that she lived with her grandmother; but Élisabeth would certainly talk. Marthe said that Françoise had a knack of making people talk. When she knew about her life, Françoise would no longer have this irritating feeling of mystery when facing Élisabeth; she could at last turn her mind to other things.

As she went up the stairs, Françoise felt very confident; she had read one Nietzsche volume, as well as a long article critiquing Baudelaire, whose poems she had read through. Yet, she remained standing on the fifth-floor landing for a long time before she rang the bell. Élisabeth was in there, behind the wood flap, absorbed in unimaginable thoughts and activities, and her face had an unknown expression to it: no sharing of secrets could dispel this mystery. One would have to glimpse Élisabeth through the keyhole, before the bell's ring would change her face; but nothing could be seen through the keyhole. Françoise rang. Élisabeth came and opened the door with her ordinary face. She still wore the same black silk dress and Françoise noticed that the fabric was worn, and there were some shiny stains on the skirt.

"I made some chocolate," Élisabeth said. "Go through to the dining room, I'm getting the pan."

Françoise went through and her throat tightened at the strong smell of smoke. She looked around with curiosity; she had often tried to imagine Élisabeth's flat, and now suddenly, it was obvious: she must live exactly here, between the black stove with its glowing glass panels, the table covered with a green plush cloth, and the large sideboard full of tarnished silverware. It was dark; the silk lampshade with its ribbed fabric and pearl fringes cast a round spot of yellow light on the table.

Élisabeth came in, holding the pan handle wrapped in a cloth.

"I'll see if there are cookies," she said. "My grandmother must have hidden them." She knelt by a chest of drawers and rummaged through bundles of rags and balls of string for a moment. "She's locked them away, the old bitch," she said, opening a tin box, which proved empty. She suddenly said exultantly: "Well, I had almost given up on them!"

Françoise bent forward and saw a big cardboard box full of pictures and toys. Élisabeth put the box onto the table.

"Do you like chocolate, at least?"

"I love chocolate," Françoise said passionately; she held out her hand. "Oh! what a nice spinning top!" she said, taking hold of a big red and golden metal spinning top. "Where is its little china base?" Élisabeth said. "It must have been lost. We used to make it spin on that little base, which looked as if it was meant for it; and while it was spinning, we'd stick cardboard circles of all colors onto it, you could make a thousand patterns." She smiled. "I never got tired of it," she added on a kind of reproachful tone.

She poured the chocolate and Françoise put the beautiful and shiny toy delicately on the table. "Father Bellyache," she read on the lid of a small box. "What can that be?" Out of the box, she got a doll made of lead, with a cotton hat on its head and a hole in its bottom.

"Ah! Father Bellyache! That was a naughty game!" Élisabeth said. You'd stick in a little white cap, Grandma'd lift a match up to it . . ."; she tossed the tiny doll in her hand. "It's incredible the number of memories that have come back to me since I've been here. Sometimes I can hardly believe that the little girl I used to be is really completely dead. Do you ever feel like that?"

"No," Françoise said. She cast a searching look at the old tapestries so laden with memories, but she saw nothing but dusty colors.

"So you've lived in Paris before?" she said.

"I did, until the age of ten." Élisabeth brusquely pushed away the lead doll, which rolled on the table. "From one day to the next, one doesn't realize how much things have changed," she said sadly.

"Do you think things change? I think it's rather always the same," Françoise said. "I can't wait to leave high school and see new things. I'd like to be older by a few years."

"Well, I don't," Élisabeth said angrily. "When I think of all the time I've wasted back there, it shouldn't count!"

"Is it because of your parents that you didn't come over to Paris earlier?"

Élisabeth laughed scornfully. "They'd never have let me go; I was the one who left; in the end, I was fed up, you see."

"You left just like that?"

61

"I stole the money for the trip from my father. I took the train, and once I was here, I wrote to my mother. She was swell; she asked Grandma to put me up and to enroll me in school. It made my father blow his top; he loves no one but me; he's a sad boor."

"You left, without telling anyone?" Françoise repeated, astounded. It was too hot in the room; it was difficult to collect one's mind: these toys, this red-haired girl, the stories she was telling, it all sounded like a novel. Only in novels do people leave because they are fed up; in life, one's moods do not count.

"Why not? If one doesn't do as one likes, there's no point in living," Élisabeth said definitively; her face brightened up: "What a trip that was! I spent the whole night leaning out of the window, with the wind lashing at my face. On arrival, I looked like a lunatic!" She plunged her hand through her hair: "What about you? Have you always lived in Paris?"

"Always," Françoise said bitterly. "I've never even moved houses, and I've been going to Molière School for ten years." What else could she have added? Nothing had ever happened to her.

"Tell me about you, instead" she said.

"My father really got screwed," Élisabeth said with a nasty look, "he thought he'd got a great deal when he joined the Morin family—an old bourgeois family, which impressed him no end. Grandpapa offered no dowry, but he promised great returns and an important position in the stained-glass window business. Poor fellow! He got the position and a twelve-hour-day's work, but, as for money, he never set his eyes on it. The business was going bankrupt, and when my uncle refloated it, he got rid of all the former staff. So, we were told not to set foot in the firm building, but the old caretaker liked us and she let us sneak into the attic. I was terrified, but I followed Pierre; Pierre was never afraid of anything."

Élisabeth talked at length about her brother. He was some kind of genius; he had always done as he liked. As a boy, he had decided to become a great man, and now he was an actor in an avant-garde theater; his parts were still small ones, but he would soon be a great actor, a great director, and a great playwright, like Shakespeare or Molière.[14]

Françoise shook off her torpor: "What about you, don't you want to be a theater actress?"

"No, I don't. I want to paint," Élisabeth said a bit sharply; there was a silent pause. "Do you like Van Gogh," she added.[15] "He's my favorite painter."

"I like him very much," Françoise said; she wondered, slightly worried, who her favorite painter was. The idea of choosing one had never occurred to her.

"I also like Gauguin," Élisabeth said.[16] She jumped to her feet and went to open the window; the atmosphere was stifling and Françoise noticed that her head was buzzing.

"Thank you very much for letting me have your notebook," Élisabeth said. "Since you're so kind, I'm going to ask you for another favor. Would you explain some things about consciousness for me? I'm not very good at abstract ideas. How do you manage?" she added, slightly mockingly. "You seem to understand everything."

She left the dining room to get her philosophy notebook and Françoise cast a slightly anguished look around her. She understood everything; she liked anything. She envied so much the strong resistance that she felt Élisabeth could show!

"You know, I'm happy to have found a friend," Élisabeth said graciously. She paused for a minute. "All the other girls look like such fools." Françoise opened the notebook without answering; as for her, it was not a matter of friendship.

An hour later, Françoise was back in her room and looked around her with disgust. It was the room of anybody, her dress was imposed on her by the seamstress, and her hairdo had been chosen by her mother. "What am *I?*"

My favorite painter. I want to paint. I left. Françoise took her head in her hands. What am I worth? What do I like best? Nothing. There was nothing in her that could decide or choose. It was like a formless swamp where ideas and images sunk in without any obstacle. There was no story—just a jumble of swarming memories. If the memories and the images were put aside, only nothingness remained. She closed her eyes. Nothing existed any longer, either around her or inside her—nothing but the sharp consciousness of this nothingness.

Françoise hardly opened her mouth over the whole dinner, and she was extremely sullen the following days. Her mother kept asking her what she was thinking about, but she took a sudden dislike of Madame Miquel's smooth voice, her distinguished manners and sober elegance, and she was disappointed by her father: he was ignorant of Nietzsche, Baudelaire, and Van Gogh. The easy and orderly life that was led there, on the avenue Mozart—a life without any quarrels, without any creditors, without any tears—seemed horribly dull to her. She had no pleasure anymore at dancing or skating, and she told Marthe Sabran that she was going through an awful fit of the blues.

The only times of her life that remained remotely worthwhile in her eyes were when she was with her cousin Maurice. Maurice was studying law and

political sciences, he was interested in literature, in the arts, and in social issues, and Monsieur Miquel said jokingly that he had very progressive ideas.
Maurice was not superficial like other young men and, unlike them, he did
not behave stupidly with Françoise. He treated her like a friend, he called her
"buddy," and he put his hand on her shoulder in a familiar way; he often
took her for a drive to the Bois de Boulogne. They only talked about trivial
matters, but there was a particular feel in his voice or in his handshake that
showed that he and Françoise were truly friends. One evening, as Françoise
was coming back from school, the sight of Maurice's car parked outside the
door set her heart beating, and she realized that she was in love with him;
they were so well suited for one another that she was immediately sure that
one day she would be his wife. They would live in the little townhouse on the
rue de la Pompe, they would entertain lots of friends, and there would be a
bar in the American style in the sitting room; the decoration would be very
original and Françoise would dress in her very own way; she would write
books. She confided to Marthe that she was starting to crave independence
and that her mother did not understand her at all. Marthe said that the style
of the clothes Madame Miquel bought her was too classic and that Françoise
should try to bring out her own physical personality. Françoise agreed that
these matters had their importance, and they spent a whole afternoon looking in fashion magazines for the style that defined Françoise's type. It was
agreed that, from then on, she would wear dark tube sweaters and coil her
hair in a net at the back of her neck. Marthe advised her not to wear blusher
on her cheeks, but to use a dark powder, and they agreed that one could var-
nish one's nails but not lacquer them. Françoise went straight to Guerlain's
and bought a compact of dark-rachel face powder with geranium scent, and
she decided that geranium would be her perfume; she also decided that she
would smoke only Cravens and that her letter-writing paper would always
be cream colored with untrimmed sides.

Madame Miquel was very angry when Françoise came back from the hair-
dresser's; she took her in front of the mirror and begged her to look at herself impartially. Françoise thought that she looked interesting and said she did
not so much want to look pretty as to be truly herself. Madame Miquel got
irritated; she told her she did not approve of Élisabeth's style at all, that
Françoise had not gone to play tennis for a month, that she was becoming
horribly withdrawn, and that she was losing all her charm. Françoise held her
ground ironically, but once alone in her bedroom, she shed a few tears; things
were no longer as easy as when she was a child, and she did not know why.
Previously, there was a secret life and a public life, and in the latter there were

clear hierarchies where she had to come in first; in the former she could do exactly as she wished because she was completely alone in the world. But now, Françoise was no longer alone in the world, and there was no position that was indisputably first; every choice was also a sacrifice: one could not have both Élisabeth's striking originality and the discrete balance that Madame Miquel liked. Françoise saw it as an outrage [*scandale*] that she should have to give up one or the other of these attractive images that she felt capable of embodying.

Élisabeth congratulated Françoise on her new hairdo.

"It suits you, and, at least, it looks less bourgeois than your rolls," she said; she inspected Françoise from head to toe and started laughing. "You always look immaculate; it's quite something!"

"I don't like sloppy-looking women," Françoise retorted sharply.

"Yes, you like what Pierre and I call tissue-paper women; I find it sad: I always feel like scratching to see if blood will come out."

She negligently coiled a wisp of hair around her finger and Françoise cast a vindictive look at her. "Your nails are too red; they aren't pretty," she said.

Élisabeth looked at her hand and had a charmed and mysterious smile; she was not put off by mocking or critical remarks; on the contrary, she looked pleased to be the only one who knew and loved herself. This delighted complicity with oneself sometimes brought Françoise to the verge of tears; she could find nothing in herself that she could love as deeply.

Françoise was desperately jealous of Élisabeth. She did not take her father's field glasses off their hook anymore; she did not lean her forehead against the window anymore; it was Élisabeth's privilege to make things truly exist. Françoise read Baudelaire and Nietzsche's complete works; she asked Élisabeth about her brother, her childhood, her paintings; she needed to know everything Élisabeth knew. When she rang the doorbell of the flat on the rue de la Tour, she felt such keen and painful curiosity that her hands were shaking.

Élisabeth's voice or the smell of coal made envy and vindictiveness fade away. Sitting in the tapestry armchair, near the stove, Françoise gave up her pride, her past, and any desire at once. She looked at Élisabeth's red hair, and as she listened, she forgot her own existence. Then everything became easy; there was no obstacle left between Élisabeth and herself; she had no other story than Élisabeth's story; and Élisabeth was nothing else but the story she was telling.

There was an attic with high windows; the sun filtered through lead-rimmed medallions, and Saint Radegonde's and Saint Odile's dresses cast blue and pink spots of light onto the dusty floor;[17] sitting on stairs, a small

65

red-headed girl and a little boy without a face were listening intently to any noise from the first floor. They slipped through the corridors; they ran across a street; some doors banged in the small badly heated flat; a hurried pace shook the floorboards, and, huddled against the stove inlet, a little girl was crying. Monsieur Labroux had a yellow face with a black moustache across it; a wide overall was flapping around his ankles; he was dipping a wide brush into a pail of paint and he was daubing the garden fence with paint; his face was distorted and a horsewhip lashed against the cheek of a tall, impassive young man; among the yews, which were clipped into animal shapes and the laurel bushes, some shirts and underpants were hanging in the wind from a line . . .

"It's getting late," Élisabeth said suddenly. "I've got to go; Pierre is expecting me at the theater at seven." Françoise tried to imagine a dark young man with a scar across his face; but Élisabeth did not say anything else, and words had suddenly lost their power; they evoked a pale indefinite face and in a moment, Élisabeth would shake a warm hand that was alive; she would step onto floorboards that were hard. Françoise got up. "See you tomorrow," she said. "See you tomorrow," Élisabeth said, smiling kindly. She had stopped playing; she was leaving Françoise behind as one leaves an inanimate doll aside and was hurriedly putting on her coat and her gloves before getting back to her real life. Françoise went down the stairs with a heavy heart; her mind went again through the tales Élisabeth had just told her and she realized disappointedly that they had taught her nothing. Élisabeth kept talking about her childhood; she shamelessly described her father's bouts of anger, her mother crying, but what counted for her was something else about which she said nothing. While talking, she often stared at the stove, and her voice took on a regretful tone. Françoise wondered what kind of lost happiness she was evoking when she described the slaps in the face, the poverty, the chilblain. This was the secret that she would have liked to take by surprise; Françoise felt that once she had come to know Élisabeth completely, she would feel either scorn or love for her, and in any case, she would be relieved. She tried stubbornly to penetrate to the heart of this life that was barred to her. One day, she arrived early at the flat on the rue de la Tour; Madame Morin let her into Élisabeth's bedroom; it was a small, bare, and untidy room; a pair of stockings, a hat, some brushes, and a bottle of cologne were lying on the mantelpiece; the desk was covered with notebooks; the pencil box was lying next to an ink bottle. Françoise looked around, agitated; this was where Élisabeth spent her hours of solitude, where she was truly herself: all these objects bore her mark; when she had got up, she had pushed the armchair away from the desk, she had opened Sophocles's plays, which she had been reading; she had brusquely flung the yellow woolen jacket that was lying across the bed. Françoise sat down in the armchair; she skimmed through the scene from Antigone that Élisabeth had just stopped reading; she examined the pictures on the wall at length; she thought hard about Élisabeth while looking at Van Gogh's *Sunflowers*. Staring at the *Sunflowers,* she called Élisabeth's face to her mind, and it seemed to her that, looking at the yellow flowers, she would grasp the vision Élisabeth had had of them; she did it time and time again, and time and time again she was on the verge of a discovery that never came to completion. Then, she opened the drawers of the desk; she found a notebook of excerpts and a kind of diary; but the quotations that Élisabeth had written down, her reflections on painting and feminism, were again only indecipherable clues; beyond the words written in blue ink, Élisabeth's real thought escaped.

Soon afterward, Françoise tried again; she came to tea at her friend's, but after an hour's talk, Élisabeth got up from her armchair. "I'm afraid I've got to leave you," she said importantly. "Pierre's asked me to come to a rehearsal; it's an adaptation of Sophocles's *Philoctetes* that he wrote himself."[18] She pouted. "I proposed a project for the set that I find charming, but they haven't made up their minds yet."

"To think that I haven't seen a single of your paintings," Françoise said. "You always say that you'll show me some."

"The thing is that I fear your judgment," Élisabeth said in a soft tone. "I fear you might feel disconcerted. You see, I haven't found my technique yet, and because I want to convey all my sensibility in each painting, the finished works are so dense that it is difficult to detect my abilities." She closed the entrance door and put on her silk mittens. "I'll bring one or two of the most restrained of my sketches for you to see; for the moment, everything is on the rue de la Grande-Chaumière."

"Can't you even tell me what they look like?"

"It's difficult. In any case, it isn't feminine painting." Élisabeth scornfully stressed the word. "I'd hate to be a Marie Laurencin.[19] I can't understand how talented women, intelligent women, can debase themselves because of their sex."

"I've often resented not being a boy," Françoise said; "they are free."

"Oh! a woman can have exactly the same life as a man, nowadays," Élisabeth retorted briskly; "the thing is that nine out of ten of them are just drips. As far as I'm concerned, I see no difference whatsoever between my brother and myself, for instance."

She went down the stairs to the Passy metro station, and Françoise leant her forehead against the iron grillwork. The show was over, Élisabeth had taken on her real face again, and she was rushing toward this life that Françoise would never enter. Françoise took a few steps; where could she go now? Dolls that have been left behind become mere pieces of wood again, but in Françoise, there was left a kind of empty consciousness that vainly sought something to grasp. She went along a street and through the Trocadéro gardens. There was nothing; the houses, the trees, the Seine were mere shadows. Françoise held up her hand; "Taxi!" she shouted, and the taxi stopped. "Place d'Italie." Élisabeth had gotten off the metro; she was crossing the square; she was going into the theater. Françoise could not go in, but she could at least walk around and watch. The taxi stopped around the corner of a wide avenue, and Françoise slipped along the houses with a beating heart; she feared she might come upon Élisabeth. The trees, the streetlights, the green trailers parked along the pavement looked hostile. Suddenly Françoise saw a wooden shed of a blue-gray color just ahead of her; there was a black and red farandole on the wall, and above the door large white letters read: THE TRESTLES. It was all there, so simply, so evidently that Françoise stood in a daze for a moment. The white letters were slightly faded; to the right, a red light of a window was shining. She slowly went around the shed; she pressed her hand against the painted wood and she stripped a splinter of wood, which she split into small pieces; then she stopped, hesitating outside the door. She thought: "Élisabeth is in there, with her real face, among her real friends, and between her and me there is only this blue partition of rough wood"; but the images that she had so often tried to evoke did not become any clearer or more lively. She went around the theater again; there it was; but it was of no avail.

Françoise went off straight ahead of her. She had better give up the battle; she would never know anything about Élisabeth's life but the outside, the reverse side of it; she felt very sorry for herself.

Suddenly, as she went by a general store, she stopped and bought a notebook covered with oilcloth; she pushed open the door of a cafe, sat at a table and ordered a cassis.[20] Onto the first page of the notebook, she wrote decisively: "My thoughts."

The waiter brought a glass full of a shaky and sticky liqueur. Françoise was holding her pink enamel fountain pen and looking at the blank page with emotion; it seemed to her that a great change had just been accomplished within her. On the back of the cover, she wrote: "You must become what you are," and underneath, in smaller print, she wrote the name of Nietzsche. Then, holding her pen in the air, she tried to put her view on life, on the world, into words. It was not easy; her mind went suddenly blank. She thought that the seats were red, that these men sitting behind their Pernods laughed in a vulgar way:[21] these were not thoughts; she concentrated. During the day, what had she been thinking? That she would like to have a job and money problems; that Élisabeth sometimes reasoned without any logic; that there was an abyss between the image one had of an object and the real presence of it. These were not truly thoughts either; they were truths that suddenly occurred and were then forgotten. What she wanted to put down in this notebook were *her* ideas, ideas that she would draw only from herself. She could not find anything. She closed the notebook angrily and got up.

In the evening, before going to bed, Françoise opened her notebook again. "I spent the early afternoon at Élisabeth's," she wrote. "When she left me, I got a taxi to the Place d'Italie, and I saw The Trestles theater; it was a nice little theater. Then I walked around; and suddenly, as I walked around those streets, it seemed to me I found myself again, I, who had abandoned myself for so long. Élisabeth loves herself more than anyone else, but if I don't love myself more than anyone else, nobody will."

Françoise paused; it was nice; as the blue letters appeared on the paper, a story was born, which was her story. She started describing in detail the cafe where she had stopped, the cashier with a purple shawl, who was dunking a croissant in her *café crème,* and the streetlights that were reflected by the red tables. Rereading the description, what appeared was not the cafe, but, in the middle of the cafe, a touching figure that was the figure of Françoise.

Every evening, Françoise wrote in her diary; she looked for details that she could add to it, from Paris streets, from dancing parties, from books: every new page made the image that it reflected more qualified and complex. Françoise wanted a notebook for excerpts too; she chose the first ones haphazardly: a few lines of Verlaine, some sentences by Dostoevsky that sounded good;[22] the next ones she chose because they expressed the same tastes and the same concerns as the first ones. When she read through her notes, she was pleasantly surprised to discover the sign of a strong and coherent personality.

Around that time, Françoise began to like recalling childhood memories. She told Élisabeth about the bouts of anger she went through when she was little: she would roll onto the carpet and scream for hours, and she had to be given a cold bath to calm down. She also told her about her walks in the scrubland, and the stir she caused when she was late for dinner. This social life was so vain; she had always hated all constraints. Élisabeth listened to her talking with polite condescension, but Maurice and Marthe did not care for it at all.

Madame Miquel often reproached Françoise for her infatuation for Élisabeth, and of course, Françoise could not tell her the truth. Françoise patiently searched for futile and convincing arguments. "She is so intelligent," she said, "she likes philosophy so much; and she has very good manners, you know"; but Madame Miquel made no secret that she did not approve of this friendship. When Françoise asked for permission to go to the dress rehearsal of *Philoctetes* with Élisabeth, her mother flatly said no.

"If you were going with somebody else, I'd let you go," she said. "I'm not so narrow-minded. But I'm not at all eager for Élisabeth to introduce you into that circle. You have no reason to adopt her way of life."

"It isn't a question of getting into any circle or adopting any way of life," Françoise said. "It's a question of going to the dress rehearsal of *Philoctetes*."

"That's not the only thing," Madame Miquel said. She stopped Françoise with a gesture. "Don't insist; there's absolutely no use."

When she happened to take on this definitive tone, it was not decent to argue. Françoise looked at her slightly amused; she did not care about the image her parents had of her anymore: an image that was very hollow compared to all the pleasures they wanted to deprive her of. "I'd better warn you that I'll go at any cost," she said calmly. "You're only giving me vague reasons on principle, and that's not enough."

"My decision should be enough," Madame Miquel said; suddenly her face flushed. "Is it you talking like this? Ask your father; you'll see what he'll say to you. Lucien, have you got a minute?" she cried, trying to steady her voice.

Her lips were trembling; there was nothing but a void in her head, and yet, her lips were trembling, and blood was flowing to her cheeks. Monsieur Miquel's voice rose, harsh and sharp, like in a debate about politics; he was all empty inside too. Françoise looked at the tips of her shoes absentmindedly; how heavy was the little bluish gray theater on the surface of the earth!

Monsieur Miquel's voice became louder; Madame Miquel had tears in her eyes. The next day, Françoise could say: there was a scene at home, Mama cried, Papa shouted, and I was standing in the sitting room, without answering a word. And yet, it was not a real scene, like those that Élisabeth had experienced. There was no strength, no depth to it; it was only a bit of vain agitation.

Nothing that happened to Françoise was quite true. Sometimes, when she looked back, she could see something that looked like an act or an idea, and other people could be mistaken about it; but she never caught herself in the process of acting or thinking. On Friday at five, when leaving school, she called home: "Could you tell Mama that I won't be back," she said to the maid. "I'm going to the theater with Élisabeth Labroux." She hung up. Presently, Élisabeth would say to her: "That's good, you've been forceful," and she would let her talk, but it would be a lie: she was never anything at all; she had simply said some words into a telephone.

It was a beautiful May day; Françoise went across the Champ-de-Mars and along the boulevard Montparnasse. She had been in a bar with Marthe and her fiancé one evening, and she had promised herself to go back alone to that room with its low ceiling lit up by some kind of circular windows. She sat down in a leather armchair, at a varnished barrel, and she lit up a Craven; her hand was shaking a bit; she had never disobeyed her parents so seriously. "What will this evening bring me?" she wondered with a heavy heart. She felt that, when she set her eyes on Pierre Labroux in the flesh, the whole of Élisabeth's life would be revealed. Would he have a liking for her, or would he be scornful? Fear and hope made her throat dry.

Françoise sucked with a straw the golden drink that filled her glass: the bottom was sweet and a bit viscous: at the surface, it tasted acid and sharp. The varnished wood of the tables and the copper staves of the barrels flashed in the sunlight. Françoise had put her jacket on the back of the armchair and the silk blouse was caressing her breasts gently; she was comfortable. She leant her head against the leather cushions; after all, what were Madame Miquel's anger, Pierre Labroux's esteem, and even Maurice's love, to her? Anger, esteem, love, words could be exchanged one for the other, this made no difference to the shine of the copper staves, or to this taste of lemon and honey. One should always remain enclosed in the present moment, Françoise thought. She straightened up; comfort was already turning into boredom; she was already waiting for this evening that did not yet exist but made her palms perspire slightly. It seemed as if the instants were not sufficient unto themselves.

It was half past eight when Françoise arrived at the place d'Italie. The door of the theater was wide open; a yellow poster read: "*Philoctetes:* A one act play based on Sophocles. Adaptation by Pierre Labroux." Pierre Labroux had his name printed in large black letters; it was because of him that a smartly dressed crowd was gathering in the illuminated lobby; men were freshly shaven, women had artistically applied shadings of red and ocher on their cheeks. The next day, there would be a report on the play in the newspapers. "I'll never be somebody," Françoise thought despondently.

"Hello," Élisabeth said smiling; she was wearing a dark dress cinched at the waist with a golden cord; under her too-thick eyebrows, her eyelids were blue and her eyelashes were overcovered with mascara. "Pierre's wound up, Ulysses's terribly nervous, and, believe it or not, the prompter hasn't arrived yet," she said very loud. Françoise followed her into an iron-gray room separated from the stage by a heavy blue curtain.

"I wonder how the audience is going to react," Élisabeth said importantly; she cast a glance at the rows of seats. "The guy who's sucking licorice, over to the right, is a critic. These critics! They have colds even in August. Ah, there are my cousins, the Sabrans—the tall blonde with a black hat on." She had blushed lightly. Françoise turned around curiously. The stained-glass window business belonged to the Sabrans now, and Pierre lived with them.

"She's awfully well dressed," Françoise said.

"She's got nothing else to do!" Élisabeth said. "The terrible thing about it is that she sees herself as an intellectual and an artist. After all, they're useful to Pierre, that's the main thing."

She took a mirror out of her bag and powdered her face. The lights went off and three strikes on a gong were heard. The stage was empty, and wide lemon, orange, and mauve panels stood out against a harsh blue background. Two men with bare legs and wearing sulfur yellow tunics slowly came on stage and scrutinized the distance; a discordant music punctuated their walk. The music stopped.

"Ulysses, this must be his lair," said one of the men. Françoise was a bit surprised; the actors acted like ordinary actors, their clothes were made of fabric, the sets were made of cardboard; she had expected something more startling. "This way of evoking Greek landscapes with merely a few bright colors is ingenious," she decided. She looked at Élisabeth, whose face expressed avid interest. One of the panels slid along and revealed a huge plaster head.

"This is the chorus," Élisabeth whispered. "A clever idea, isn't it?" The music started again, punctuating the recitative that seemed to be coming out of the still lips. Philoctetes appeared, wearing black rags with bloodstains on them. "He lacks grandeur," Élisabeth said. "If Pierre had been given the part, he would have struck a terrific character."

Françoise was waiting for Pierre's appearance with anguished impatience; the moment was coming; she kept staring at the back of the stage, nervously holding her handkerchief tight in her sweaty hands.

"Two men are coming toward us," the plaster head shouted. "One is a sailor and the other is a stranger; who has sent them here?"

At first Françoise could not make out the features of the face, under the curly wig and the makeup; she only knew that he was there. Then she could see black eyes, and a slightly heavy mouth; from now on, she would have to introduce this heavy mouth, these full cheeks, into the garden planted with yews where Monsieur Labroux lashed his whip and into the attic with stained-glass windows, but it was not easy. Monsieur Labroux's movement, the stained-glass windows, the garden had been tailored for the dark, haughty and romantic hero who had just vanished forever. He swept them away in his death. What was left was this man with a red cloak on, standing against a harsh yellow wall; and he was already going off stage.

"He's incredibly talented, isn't he?" Élisabeth whispered.

"Incredibly," Françoise said; inaccessible to Philoctetes' sufferings, she remained despondent until the end of the show. She had never grasped anything from Élisabeth's past; she had made up its images out of her own past.

"You'll see how fun it is in the foyer," Élisabeth said, clapping enthusiastically. "The building is so small that the actors haven't even got a dressing room. Did you enjoy it?"

"Yes, I did!" Françoise said. "Everything is so beautiful, the play, the music, the sets."

Élisabeth took on a childish and sulking expression: "As for the sets, mine were much prettier." She took Françoise to the exit. "Will you excuse me for a minute? I'm going to say hello to my cousins and I'll be back." She walked to the blond young woman and Françoise noticed that she was twisting the fringes of her cord nervously; the young woman held out her hand in a very kind way, but Élisabeth's smile looked constrained.

"They don't like the music," she said as she got back to Françoise. "They're so irritating."

She pushed open a small door and Françoise found herself on the stage. "Let me introduce you to my brother Pierre; this is my friend Françoise Miquel. It worked terribly well, Pierre," she added with a quavering voice.

Pierre bowed slightly; he had put on his town clothes again and Françoise found him properly dressed, but looking a bit poor.

"I hope you had good seats," he said with a zealous smile.

"Very good," Françoise said, "right next to a critic who kept sucking licorice."

"You know, Pierre, it's really . . . terrific," Élisabeth said; her face winced. "It's got such rhythm, and then, the quality of the adaptation is . . . extraordinary." She was not talking as easily as usual. Françoise felt ill at ease.

"What are people saying?" Pierre asked.

"The old fossil next to us never stopped grumbling, an old hairless dotard."

"It must be Gauthier," Pierre said.

"I don't think it was Gauthier," Élisabeth said.

"Why not? You've never met Gauthier."

Élisabeth blushed. "I thought he was more . . . I didn't think he looked like that."

73

"After all, maybe it wasn't Gauthier," Pierre said.

Françoise was obviously out of place [*de trop*] here; Élisabeth and Pierre looked embarrassed by her presence and were just talking hot air to allay suspicion. Françoise looked around her; behind their sequined veils, the women looked like any other women, and their laughter, their affected voices, would not have been out of place in Madame Miquel's sitting room; it looked as if everyone was waiting for Françoise to leave before taking on their ordinary voices and resuming their ordinary movements.

"I've got to go," she said, "don't let me disturb you; I'll find my way out."

She pushed open the door. Pierre suddenly smiled; his friends were gathering around him and they started talking about all kinds of profound things. Élisabeth had her decisive tone again; women were laughing in bursts, and all their movements became unexpected and charming. It was a beautiful dress rehearsal evening, and the next day, Élisabeth would tell Françoise about it. Françoise had gone into the theater, but again, she had seen nothing. It was as before, along the paths lined with pines; the secret was receding ever further away.

NOTES

1. *La petite illustration* was a French performing arts journal; *Les bouffons: pièce en quartre actes en verse* (1910) was written by Miguel Zamacois (1866–1955); *Barbe-Bleue,* by Rosamonde Gérard (1866–1953).

2. Edmund Rostand (1869–1918), poet and playwright, was the author of *Cyrano de Bergerac;* the novelist Victor Hugo (1802–85) is best remembered for *Les miserables.*

3. Guillaume Bude (1467–1540), a French classical scholar and translator, was credited with reviving classical studies in France after his *Commentarii linguae Graecae* (Commentaries in the Greek Language) was published in 1529.

4. *Chéri,* a novel by Sidonie-Gabrielle Colette (1873–1954), details the love affair between an older woman and a younger man.

5. *Nana,* a controversial novel by Émile Zola (1840–1902), tells of a woman forced, through economic necessity, to become an actress and courtesan.

6. The final year of the *lycée* prepared students for the second part of the *baccalauréat* exam in philosophy or, for those students following a science track, in mathematics.

7. In *She Came to Stay,* Elizabeth's surname has been changed to Labrousse.

8. August Comte (1798–1857) was a French philosopher and founder of "Positivism."

9. Friedrich Nietzsche (1798–1857) was a German philosopher whose works include *Thus Spake Zarathustra;* Lucretius (c. 99–c. 55 B.C.E.), Latin poet and philosopher, was the author of *On the Nature of Things,* a lengthy poem outlining the philosophy of Epicurus.

10. *The Complete Verse of Baudelaire,* trans. Francis Scarfe (London: Anvil Press Poetry, 1986), vol. 1, 141.

11. Charles-Pierre Baudelaire (1821–67), experimental poet and anarchist, wrote *Les fleurs*

de mal (The Flowers of Evil), which was banned for obscenity in 1857. The book influenced the later Symbolist movement, the Surrealists, and the "Beat" poets of the 1950s and 1960s.

12. *The Complete Verse of Baudelaire,* vol. 1, 125.

13. Marie Bashkircheff (1858–84) was a diarist and painter.

14. Molière, pseud. Jean-Baptiste Poquelin (1622–73), actor and playwright, was the author of *Tartuffe* and *The Misanthrope.*

15. Vincent Van Gogh (1853–90) was a Dutch postimpressionist painter.

16. Paul Gauguin (1848–1903), the French postimpressionist painter, was also a sculptor and printmaker.

17. Saint Radegonde (520?–587), founder of the abbey at Poitiers, was known also as Radegonde, Queen of the Franks; Saint Odile (6??–720), or Odila, patroness of Alsace, is said to have been born blind and to have miraculously regained her sight when baptized.

18. Sophocles (496–406 B.C.E.) was the Athenian author of many tragedies, including *Oedipus the King, Antigone,* and *Philoctetes,* the latter a play about a man who is made lame by a snakebite and abandoned by the Greeks on their way to Troy, only to be commanded back by Odysseus through a third party.

19. Marie Laurencin (1883–1956), a watercolorist, printmaker, and set designer, was known for a pretty, simple, and distinctly "feminine" style.

20. Cassis is a black-currant liqueur.

21. Pernod is an aromatic French liqueur.

22. Verlaine (1844–96) was a lyric poet known as the leader of the Symbolist movement; Feodor Mikhailovich Dostoevsky (1821–81), a Russian psychological, philosophical novelist, was the author of *The Brothers Karamazov* and *Crime and Punishment.*

3

Pyrrhus and Cineas

INTRODUCTION

by Debra Bergoffen

In *The Prime of Life,* Simone de Beauvoir identifies 1943 as the beginning of what she calls the moral period of her literary career.[1] This is the year Jean Grenier asked her to contribute something to an anthology he was editing. Understanding that he was interested in essays that reflected contemporary ideological trends and that he identified her as having something to contribute as an existentialist, Beauvoir was at first reluctant. She did not think she was qualified to write an existential philosophical essay. Sartre encouraged her to accept, and upon reflection, she says, she realized that she had something more to say about problems she had recently tackled in *The Blood of Others.* Beauvoir also determined that writing this essay would give her the chance to reconcile Sartre's views of freedom with her distinct ideas, "upheld against him in various conversations" (434), concerning the significance of the situation. The text of *Pyrrhus and Cineas* seems almost to have written itself. Perhaps we should not be surprised that it was finished in three months (July 1943), for Beauvoir tells us that the dialogue between Pyrrhus and Cineas is very much like the conversation she had with herself (recorded in her private diary) on her twentieth birthday (435).

Written during the Nazi occupation, *Pyrrhus and Cineas* was published in

September 1944, after the liberation. Looking back, in volume 1 of *Force of Circumstance,* Simone de Beauvoir speaks of her pleasure in writing *Pyrrhus and Cineas.* She describes herself as both surprised and delighted with its reception in postwar France. However, Beauvoir does not give the text high intellectual marks. Finding it too abstract, she attributes its success to a French public starved for philosophy.

The fate of *Pyrrhus and Cineas* echoes Beauvoir's judgment. It is a largely neglected work. Unlike *The Ethics of Ambiguity,* which appeared in English shortly after its publication in France, *Pyrrhus and Cineas* was not deemed worthy of an English edition until now, more than fifty years after its original publication. This translation should change all that. It comes at an auspicious moment in Beauvoir studies: a moment when Beauvoir's refusal to identify herself as a philosopher in her own right is itself refused; a moment when her work is being studied for its unique insights and contributions to philosophical and feminist thought; a moment when the questions of violence and justice, crucial issues in *Pyrrhus and Cineas,* are pressing political and ethical concerns.

Once we take Beauvoir as a serious philosopher, we cannot ignore *Pyrrhus and Cineas.* It addresses critical, fundamental ethical and political issues: What are the criteria of ethical action? How can I distinguish ethical from unethical political projects? What are the principles of ethical relationships? Can violence ever be justified? It examines these questions from an existential-phenomenological perspective. Beginning from the situation of the concrete existing individual, it provides an analysis of our human condition that takes account of our unique and particular subjectivity, our embeddedness in the world, and our essential relatedness to each other. Though not feminist in any identifiable sense, *Pyrrhus and Cineas* directs us to the compelling feminist question, Under what conditions, if any, may I speak for/in the name of another?

Reading *Pyrrhus and Cineas* today, it is difficult to come to it with fresh eyes. Knowing that the author of this text is also the author of *The Second Sex,* we are hard pressed to read *Pyrrhus and Cineas* for what it was then, the writing of a largely unknown author, rather than for what it is now, the early work of Simone de Beauvoir, a woman identified as one of the most important authors of the twentieth century. Reading *Pyrrhus and Cineas* with an eye toward *The Second Sex,* we cannot help but look for the ways in which concepts fully operative in the later, more famous text are already fully in play here, visible in their absence, or present in seedling form.

Reading in this way we will look for what has remained constant in Beauvoir's thought and for what has changed. We will look for the ways in which ideas pursued in *Pyrrhus and Cineas* are transformed, pushed in unexpected directions, abandoned or embraced in *The Second Sex*. We will, in short, look for the continuities and discontinuities in Beauvoir's thinking and methods. In pursuing a reading of this sort we will be assuming a certain constancy in Beauvoir's intellectual project; for even if we speak of discontinuities, we measure these against a certain sense of an identifiable intellectual trajectory. This type of reading, a reading that might be called historical-philosophical, is valuable for tracing the lines of Beauvoir's thought. Ironically, however, it goes against a central thesis of *Pyrrhus and Cineas*—the thesis that there is no progress, continuity, or steady development in the life of either the individual or the species.

This thesis suggests another approach to the text, one that could be called phenomenological-philosophical. Here we would bracket what we now know about Beauvoir to take up the text for itself and in its relationship to the horizon of its times. This horizon would be both political-existential and intellectual-existential. Addressing the political-existential horizon, we would delineate the situation of occupied France and postwar France. We would look at the ways in which that situation provoked the questions of *Pyrrhus and Cineas* and at the ways in which the analyses of *Pyrrhus and Cineas* spoke to the lived realities of these wartime circumstances and their aftermath. Addressing the intellectual-existential horizon, we would look at the ways in which Beauvoir took up ideas and positions circulating in the philosophical field of her era. Here Beauvoir herself is a reliable guide. She refers us to Hegel, Heidegger, Nietzsche, Kierkegaard, and Descartes among others, as she situates herself among those influencing her thinking. The value of reading *Pyrrhus and Cineas* in this way is that we capture its originality and freshness. By not reading it as an immature text, or as a mere precursor to *The Second Sex*, we discover the ways in which it stands on its own, the ways in which the arguments do or do not work per se, and the ways in which Beauvoir was creating a unique philosophical style and space that she could call her own.

Though *Pyrrhus and Cineas* is a text that is focused on ethical and political questions, it begins in a surprisingly apolitical and amoral way. Instead of opening with a distinctly ethical or political issue, or with an analysis of the principles and precepts of justice or morality, it begins with a staged conversation between Pyrrhus, the king of Epirus, born in 318 B.C.E., and Cineas, his adviser. They are discussing Pyrrhus's plan to conquer the world. The issue between them does not concern the morality or justice of this particular action but the rationality of action itself. Agreeing that once the conquest is completed Pyrrhus will retire to his home, Cineas protests. If at the end of all this activity Pyrrhus will return to where he is now, why not just stay put? Action, Cineas concludes, is always irrational, ultimately unproductive, and essentially futile. Our goals are never realized. We are never satisfied.

Between the cynic, Cineas, and the king, Pyrrhus, Beauvoir aligns herself with Pyrrhus. Her decision does not concern the details of the king's project. It concerns the ontological truth of his position: to be human is to act. The cynic has reason on his side: there are neither absolute ends of, nor guaranteed justifications for, our projects. From a rational point of view, action is perverse. From an existential point of view, however, it is inevitable. We cannot not act. We must therefore analyze the reality of this fact of our condition.

The opening dialogue of *Pyrrhus and Cineas* is no mere theatrical device. The man of action must account for himself before the tribunal of reason. Beauvoir will be his advocate. Her advocacy appeals to the logical impossibility of establishing an absolute justification of/for action (thereby taking the argument directly to the cynic) and to the existential reality of our particularity (thereby marking her philosophical territory). This structure of *Pyrrhus and Cineas* reflects Beauvoir's existential commitments. She will not take up the ethical question, How ought I act? until she answers the existential question, Why act? Within the context of *Pyrrhus and Cineas* the matter of ethical action cannot be separated from the matter of action itself; for it is within the context of determining the distinct structures of human activity that Beauvoir discovers the parameters of moral and just action.

Part 1 of *Pyrrhus and Cineas* is addressed to the particular, finite, existing individual. Addressing this individual, Beauvoir determines that spontaneity, the drive to engage the world and make it ours, is the truth of our humanity. Using Candide's "cultivate your garden" as her foil, Beauvoir sets the scene for part 1. Candide does not urge me to cultivate any garden. The injunction directs me to cultivate my own garden. In this it speaks a certain truth and raises basic questions. The truth concerns the basic structure of action. I take up projects in the world to make the world mine, to make myself essential. This truth, however, raises unsettling questions: Where is my garden? What is it? How do I mark the boundaries between my garden and yours? Can there be such a thing as our garden? What goals ought I set for this garden? What hopes may I have for it?

These questions direct us to the phenomenon of situated freedom. A garden becomes my garden through my free choice. This choice, however, is not arbitrary. It is factually conditioned by my past and present circumstances and ontologically conditioned by the structures of time and transcendence. When Beauvoir identifies us with freedom, she is not using the term to designate the process by which we decide to do one thing rather than another. She is using it to designate the transcending nature of our being. As human I am perpetually transcending myself toward a yet to be defined future in which I seek to establish myself in my concrete particularity. I am a way of being that makes myself be by reaching beyond myself toward something other than myself. I am a transcending transcendence, a going beyond without end. Today's tomorrow becomes a yesterday. A new future calls me to new ends.

Existential freedom as structured by time renders my identity unstable. As structured by finitude this freedom is the source of my insatiability. Each goal reached satisfies me insofar as it constitutes the fulfillment of a particular project. Given the necessary particularity of every project, however, I soon become dissatisfied. The reached goal is limited. Something else is required. I take up a new project. It is a never ending story. As finite I necessarily fail to bring closure to myself or my projects. This inevitable failure lies at the heart of the meaning of our condition as finite and existentially free beings. Any action that calls its goal an ultimate end in itself must be rejected as antihuman. Today's utopian vision is tomorrow's reign of terror.

Given these existential commitments, we expect Beauvoir to reject God as a possible source of moral justification. We might not, however, expect her to reject the idea of humanity as a proper object of our ethical and political projects; but the idea of humanity, when subjected to the logic of finitude, shares the fate of the idea of God. Distinguishing what she calls the cult of humanity from the truth of the human, Beauvoir rejects the idea of a universal human identity, goal, or good. As particular existing human beings we form our singular identities by choosing particular goals and goods. Our choices, by affirming some things and people, inevitably reject others. Humanity as a whole cannot be embraced.

As a particular existing individual I am not an individuated particular who shares a common destiny with others of my species. I am an isolated particular separated by/in my freedom from the freedom of others. This separateness is the source of conflict, which Beauvoir finds inevitable, and solidarity, which Beauvoir finds necessary. The argument from finitude to separateness to conflict seems pretty straightforward. The argument from finitude to separateness to solidarity seems counterintuitive. It depends on acknowledging our ambiguous condition as both a subject for the world and an object in it. As a subject for the world, my actions create the realities of the world. These realities however, escape me. They cease to be mine as soon as they come into existence. They become objects in, conditions of, the world and those who inhabit it. As objects in the world, my projects may or may not be taken up by others. The fate of my desire depends on the other. If no one adopts my goals, they vanish. Without the support of others my projects come to nothing.

These conflicting dimensions of intersubjective life reflect the ambiguity of our humanness (I am always both subject and object) and establish the problematic of ethics and politics. Given that others exist for me as objects in the world whose instrumentality is necessary for the success of my projects, how can I get them to support my cause without violating their status as human subjects who, like me, perpetually escape their worldly objective givenness? Kant is useless here. Our ambiguity cannot be subsumed by the categorical imperative. The other is never a pure subject. It is not necessarily immoral to see the other as a means to my ends. It may be immoral to treat the other as an end in itself. In taking up the ethical problem from the site of the ethical act (the site of the existing individual), Beauvoir determines that abstract ethical formulas are unhelpful at best and destructive at worst.

Moving from the ontological truth: I am a finite freedom whose endings are always and necessarily beginnings; *Pyrrhus and Cineas* raises the existential questions, How can I desire to be what I am? How can I live my finitude with passion? These questions are posed in order to turn to the moral and political issues, What actions express the truth and passion of our condition? How can I act in such a way as to create the conditions that sustain and support the humanity of human beings? Part 1 concludes with the observation that "[a] man alone in the world would be paralyzed by . . . the vanity of all his goals. He would undoubtedly not be able to stand living. But man is not alone in the world." Part 2 opens by taking up the ethical questions raised by our communal existence. What is my relation to the other? What can I expect from the other? What obligations do I have toward the other?

The sections of part 2, headed "Others," "Devotion," "Communication," and "Action," pursue the logic of transcendence, singularity, and finitude to distinguish immoral attention to false idols/ideals from an ethical attentiveness to the singular other and the forever elusive goal of our desire. The analysis is dominated by the problem created by Beauvoir's insistence on the radical nature of our freedom. According to Beauvoir, the other, as free, is immune to my power. Whatever we do, if as masters we exploit slaves, or as executioners we hang murderers, we cannot violate others in the inner depths of their free subjectivity. Substituting the inner-outer difference for the Cartesian mind-body distinction, Beauvoir argues that we can never directly touch others in the heart of their freedom. Our relationships are either superficial, engaging only the outer surface of each other's being, or mediated through our common commitment to a shared goal or value. As free we are saved from the dangers of intimacy.

This line of argument would seem to lead either to benign Stoic conclusions of mutual indifference or to finding tyrants and reigns of terror no threat to individual freedom. Beauvoir does not let it drift in these directions. Instead she uses the inner-outer distinction, and the idea that I need others to take up my projects if those projects are to have a future, to introduce the ideas of the appeal and risk. Developing the concept of freedom as transcendence, Beauvoir identifies the essence of freedom as the uncertainty and risk of our actions. She writes: "To be free is to throw oneself into the world without weighing the consequences or stakes; it is to define any stake or any step oneself." To be free is to be radically contingent. As free, I bring value and meaning to a world without value and meaning of its own. I cannot, however, support these values alone. They will find a home in the world only if others embrace them; only if I persuade others to make my values theirs.

As radically free, I need the other. I need to be able to appeal to others to join me in my projects. Here lies the knot of the ethical problem: How can I, a radically free being who is existentially severed from all other human freedoms, transcend the isolations of freedom to create a community of allies? Given the necessity of appealing to another's freedom, under what conditions is an appeal possible?

In answering these questions Beauvoir turns the inner-outer distinction to her advantage as she develops the concept of situated freedom. Though I can neither act for another nor directly influence another's freedom, I must, Beauvoir argues, accept responsibility for the fact that my actions produce the conditions within which the other acts. However irrelevant my conduct may be for the other's inner freedom, it concerns mine. I am, Beauvoir writes, "the face" of the other's misery. "I am the facticity of his situation." Pursuing this difference between my power to effect the other's freedom and my responsibility for the other's situation, and exploring the conditions under which my appeal to the other can/will be heard, Beauvoir determines that there are two conditions of the appeal. First, I must be allowed to call to the other and must struggle against those who would silence me. Second, there must be others who can respond to my call. The first condition is political-civic. The second is political-material. Only equals, Beauvoir argues, can hear or respond to my call. Only those who are not consumed by the struggle for survival, only those who exist in the material conditions of freedom, health, leisure, and security, can become my allies in the struggle against injustice.

The first rule of justice, therefore, is to work for a world where the civic and material conditions of the appeal are secured.

Violence is not ruled out. Given that Beauvoir has argued that we can never reach others in the depths of their freedom, she cannot call violence evil. She does not, however, endorse it. She does not accept the proposition that the ends justify the means. Neither does she envision a future without conflict. The logic of her ethics of particularity determines that violence is inevitable. The fact that we are differently situated and engage in the work of transcendence from different historical, economic, sexed, and race positions ensures that some of us will always be an obstacle to another's freedom. We are, Beauvoir writes, "condemned to violence." As neither evil nor avoidable, violence, Beauvoir argues, is "the mark of a failure that nothing can offset." It is the tragedy of the human condition.

Thus the argument ends on an uneasy note. As ethical we are obliged to work for the conditions of material and political equality. In calling on others to take up our projects and give our projects a future, we are precluded from forcing others to become our allies. We are enjoined to appeal to their freedom. Where persuasion fails, however, we are permitted the recourse to violence. The ambiguity of our being as subjects of and objects in the world is lived in this dilemma of violence and justice. Becoming lucid about the meaning of freedom, we learn to live our freedom by accepting its finitude and contingency, its risks and its failures.

And so we come full circle. Having established in part 1 that the logic of passivity, however compelling, must submit to the facticity of transcendence and freedom, Beauvoir concludes in part 2 that the logic of the appeal must acknowledge the facticity of violence. In each case the clean lines of deductive reason must defer to the messy contingencies of existence. The abstract Cartesian method and the universal optimistic Hegelian dialectic are rejected. In their place, Beauvoir develops a method of reflective description that appeals to concrete examples and focuses on the particulars of the existential singular to delineate the paradigms and ambiguities of the ethical injunctions of our existential freedom.

The meaning of our situated freedom, the material conditions of justice, the possibilities of the appeal, and the risks of violence are issues that will concern Beauvoir throughout her life. In *The Ethics of Ambiguity* (1944) she returns to the questions of violence and freedom. In *All Men Are Mortal* (1946) she plays with the idea of finitude to fully explode the folly of Cineas's injunction to not act. In *The Second Sex* she pierces the democratic myths of liberty, equality, and fraternity by exposing the violence that separates women from the possibilities of their existential freedom. More phenomenological in their attention to our embodiment, these works abandon the inner-outer split of *Pyrrhus and Cineas,* speak of the ways in which our freedoms touch each other, reconsider the matrix of violence and evil, and provide more nuanced accounts of the material conditions of the possibility of freedom.

With this fluid and crisp translation of *Pyrrhus and Cineas* we can determine whether or not Beauvoir's work is woven of one cloth. We can determine whether the trajectory of her thought mutes the tragedy of the human condition so starkly delineated here, or whether it finds credible alternatives to the dilemmas depicted in *Pyrrhus and Cineas.* In asking the question, What can we hope? *Pyrrhus and Cineas* provides a chilling answer. It may be that Beauvoir's later works are propelled by this question and the desire to answer it in ways that bring us closer to the possibilities of justice while remaining cognizant of the risks of freedom and the dangers of utopian dreams.

NOTE

1. *The Prime of Life,* trans. Peter Green, intro. Toril Moi (New York: Paragon, 1992), 433; hereafter, all page numbers given parenthetically in this introduction refer to this text unless otherwise indicated.

TRANSLATION BY MARYBETH TIMMERMANN

NOTES BY MARYBETH TIMMERMANN AND STACY KELTNER

Pyrrhus and Cineas

A Cette Dame

Table of Contents

Pyrrhus et Cinéas (Paris: Gallimard, 1944) © Éditions Gallimard, 1944. This translation is based on the original 1944 edition. The folio paperback edition of *Pyrrhus et Cinéas,* first published in 2003, contains corrections and additions to the text by Sylvie Le Bon de Beauvoir.

Plutarch tells us that one day Pyrrhus was devising projects of conquest. "We are going to subjugate Greece first," he was saying. "And after that?" said Cineas.¹ "We will vanquish Africa."—"After Africa?"—"We will go on to Asia, we will conquer Asia Minor, Arabia."—"And after that?"—"We will go on as far as India."—"After India?"—"Ah!" said Pyrrhus, "I will rest."—"Why not rest right away?" said Cineas.

Cineas seems wise. What's the use of leaving if it is to return home? What's the use of starting if you must stop? And yet, if I don't first decide to stop, it seems to me to be even more pointless to leave. "I will not say A," says the schoolboy stubbornly. "But why?"—"Because, after that, I will have to say B." He knows that if he starts, he will never be finished with it: after B, it will be the entire alphabet, syllables, words, books, tests, and a career. Each minute a new task will throw him forward toward a new task, without rest. If it is never to be finished, what's the use of starting? Even the architect of the Tower of Babel thought that the sky was a ceiling and that someone would reach it one day. If Pyrrhus could push the limits of his conquests back beyond the earth, beyond the stars and the furthest nebulae, to an infinity that would be constantly fleeing before him, his undertaking would only be more foolish because of it. His efforts would be dispersed without ever coming together for any goal. Viewed by reflection, all human projects therefore seem absurd because they exist only by setting limits for themselves, and one can always overstep these limits, asking oneself derisively, "Why as far as this? Why not further? What's the use?"

"I found that no goal was worth the trouble of any effort," said Benjamin Constant's hero.² Such are often the thoughts of the adolescent when the voice of reflection awakens in him. As a child, he was like Pyrrhus: he ran, he played without asking himself questions, and the objects that he created seemed to him endowed with an absolute existence. They carried within themselves their rea-

son for being. But he discovered one day that he had the power to surpass [dé-passer] his own ends. There are no longer ends; only pointless occupations still exist for him; he rejects them. "The dice are loaded," he says. He looks at his elders with scorn: how is it possible for them to believe in their undertakings? They are dupes. Some have killed themselves in order to put an end to this ridiculous illusion. And it was indeed the only way to end it, because as long as I remain alive, Cineas harasses me in vain, saying: "And after that? What's the use?" In spite of everything, my heart beats, my hand reaches out, new projects are born and push me forward. Wise men have wanted to see the sign of man's incurable folly in this stubbornness. But can a perversion so essential still be called perversion? Where will we find the truth about man if it is not in him? Reflection cannot stop the élan of our spontaneity.[3]

But reflection is also spontaneous. Man plants, builds, conquers; he wants, he loves: there is always an "after that?" It could be that from moment to moment he throws himself into new undertakings with an ardor that is always new, like Don Juan deserting one woman only to seduce another.[4] But even Don Juan gets tired one fine day.

Between Pyrrhus and Cineas the dialogue starts over with no end.

And yet, Pyrrhus must decide. He stays or he leaves. If he stays, what will he do? If he leaves, how far will he go?

"We must cultivate our garden," says Candide.[5] This advice will not be of much help to us because what is my garden? There are men who claim to work the entire earth, and others will find a pot of flowers too vast. Some say carelessly, "What happens when we're gone is none of our concern," while the dying Charlemagne cried at the sight of the Normans' ships.[6] A young woman gets irritated because she has leaky shoes that take in water. If I say to her: "What does that matter? Think of the millions of men who are dying of hunger in the middle of China," she answers me angrily: "They are in China. And it's my shoe that has a hole." However, another woman may cry about the horror of the Chinese famine. If I say to her: "What does that matter to you? You are not hungry," she would look at me with scorn: "What does my own comfort matter?" So how to know what is mine? The disciples of Christ asked: who is my neighbor?

What, then, is the measure of a man?[7] What goals can he set for himself, and what hopes are permitted him?

Part 1

Candide's Garden

I knew a child who cried because his concierge's son had died. His parents let him cry, and then they got annoyed. "After all, that little boy was not your brother." The child dried his tears. But that was a dangerous thing to teach. Useless to cry over a little boy who is a stranger: so be it. But why cry over one's brother? "It's none of your business," says the woman holding back her husband who wants to join in a fight. The husband goes away, docile. But if the woman asks for his help a few minutes later, saying: "I'm tired, I'm cold," he looks at her with surprise from the heart of the solitude where he has withdrawn, thinking: "Is that *my* business?" What does India matter? And what does Epirus matter? Why call this soil, this woman, these children *mine?* I brought these children into the world; they are here. The woman is next to me; the soil is under my feet. No tie exists between them and me. Mr. Camus's Stranger thinks like this;[8] he feels foreign to the whole world, which is completely foreign to him. Often during hardship man thus denies all his attachments. He does not want hardship; he looks for a way to flee from it. He looks within himself: he sees an indifferent body, a heart that beats to a steady rhythm. A voice says: "I exist." The hardship is not there. It is in the deserted house, on this dead face, in these streets. If I go within myself, I look at those inert streets with astonishment,[9] saying: "But what does it matter to me? All this is nothing to me." I find myself indifferent, peaceful. "But what has changed?" asked the sedentary petit bourgeois in September 1940,[10] sitting in the midst of his belongings, "We still eat the same steaks." The changes only existed outside: what did they concern him?

If I myself were only a thing, nothing indeed would concern me. If I withdraw into myself, the other is also closed for me. The inert existence of things is separation and solitude. There exists no ready-made attachment between the world and me. And as long as I am a simple given in the midst of nature, nothing is mine. A country is not mine if I only grew there like a plant. What is built up upon me, without me, is not mine. The rock that passively supports a house cannot claim that the house is its own. Mr. Camus's Stranger is right to reject all those ties that others want to impose upon him from the outside; no tie is given at first. If a man is satisfied with a completely exterior relationship with the object, saying, "My painting, my park, my workers" because a contract bestowed him with certain rights over these objects, it is because he is choosing to delude himself. He would like to spread out his place on earth, to expand his being beyond the limits of his body and his memory, yet without running the risk of any action. But the object facing him remains, indifferent, foreign. Social, organic, economic relationships are only external relationships and cannot be the foundation of any true possession.

In order to appropriate safely goods that are not our own, we can still resort to other ruses. Seated by his fire and reading in his newspaper the tale of someone who climbed the Himalayas, the contented bourgeois cries out proudly: "Now there's what a man can do!" He feels like he climbed the Himalayas himself. By identifying himself with his sex, his country, his class, with the whole of humanity, a man can increase his garden, but he increases it only in words. This identification is but an empty pretension.

Only that in which I recognize my being is mine, and I can only recognize it where it is engaged. In order for an object to belong to me, it must have been founded by me. It is totally mine only if I founded it in its totality. The only reality that belongs entirely to me is, therefore, my act; even a work fashioned out of materials that are not mine escapes me in certain ways. What is mine is first the accomplishment of my project; a victory is mine if I fought for it. If the weary conqueror can rejoice in the victories of his son, it is because he wanted a son precisely in order to prolong his work; it is really the accomplishment of his own project that he salutes. It is because my subjectivity is not inertia, folding in upon itself, separation, but, on the contrary, movement toward the other that the difference between me and the other is abolished, and I can call the other mine. Only I can create the tie that unites me to the other. I create it from the fact that I am not a thing, but a project of self toward the other, a transcendence. And it is this power that Camus's Stranger is unaware of: no possession is given, but the foreign indifference of the world is not given either. I am not first a thing but a spontaneity that desires, that loves, that wants, that acts. "That little boy *is* not my brother." But if I cry over him, he is no longer a stranger to me. It's my tears that decide. Nothing is decided before me. When the disciples asked Christ: who is my neighbor? Christ didn't respond by an enumeration. He told the parable of the good Samaritan. The latter was the neighbor of the man abandoned on the road; he covered him with his cloak and came to his aid. One *is* not the neighbor of anyone; one makes the other a neighbor by making oneself [*se faisant*] his neighbor through an act.[11]

What is mine is therefore first what I do. But as soon as I have done it, the object goes and separates itself from me; it escapes me. The thought that I expressed a moment ago, is it still my thought? In order for the past to be mine, I must make it mine again each instant by taking it toward my future. Even the objects that were not mine in the past because I didn't found them can be made into mine if I found something on them. I can rejoice in a victory in which I did not participate if I take it as a point of departure for my own conquests. The house that I did not build becomes my house if I live in it, and the earth my earth if I work it. My relationships with things are not given, are not fixed; I create them minute by minute. Some die, some are born, and others are revived. They are constantly changing. Each new act of surpassing [*dépassement*] gives me anew the thing surpassed, and that's why technologies are ways of appropriating the world: the sky belongs to those who know how to fly; the sea belongs to those who know how to swim and navigate.

Thus our relationship with the world is not decided from the onset; it is we who decide. But we do not arbitrarily decide just anything. What I surpass is always my past and the object such as it exists within that past. My future envelops that past; the former cannot build itself without the latter. The Chinese are my brothers from the moment I cry over their hardships, but one does not cry over the Chinese as he pleases. If I have never worried about Babylon, I cannot suddenly choose to be interested in the latest theories about the location of Babylon. I cannot suffer a defeat if I was not engaged in the vanquished country. I will suffer defeat in accordance with my engagements. A man who has fused his destiny with that of his country, its leader for example, could say "*my* defeat" in the face of the disaster. A man who has lived in a certain country without doing anything but eating and sleeping there will see the event only as a change of habits. It can happen that, in light of a new fact, one suddenly becomes aware of engagements that have been lived without being thought. But at least they had to have existed. As distinct from me, things never affect me; I am never affected except in my own possibilities.

We are therefore surrounded by forbidden wealth, and we often get irritated with these limits. We would like the entire world to become ours; we covet the goods of others. I knew, among others, one young student who wanted first to make the world of the athlete hers, then that of the gambler, the flirt, the adventurer, the politician, one after another. She tried her hand in each of these domains, without understanding that she remained a student hungry for experience. She believed that she was "varying her life," but the unity of her life unified all of its diverse moments. An intellectual who takes the side of the proletariat does not become proletarian; he is an intellectual taking the side of the proletariat. The painting that Van Gogh paints is a new and free creation, but it is still a Van Gogh. If he claimed to paint a Gauguin, he would only make an imitation of Gauguin by Van Gogh.[12] And that's why Candide's advice is superfluous: it's always *my* garden that I will cultivate. I am enclosed within it until death because that garden becomes mine from the moment I cultivate it.

In order for this piece of universe to belong to me, however, I must truly cultivate it. Man's activity is often lazy.[13] Instead of accomplishing true acts he contents himself with pretenses: the fly on the stage coach claims that he is the one who led the carriage to the top of the hill. To walk around talking about it, taking photographs of it, is not to participate in a war, in an expedition. There are even behaviors that contradict the ends that they claim to aim for: by establishing institutions that allow a sort of equilibrium in the midst of misery, the charitable lady tends to perpetuate the misery that she wants to alleviate. In order to know what is mine, I must know what I am really doing.

We see then that one can assign no dimension to the garden in which Candide wants to enclose me. It is not drawn out in advance; it is I who choose its location and limits.

And since, in any case, these limits are ridiculous compared to the infinity that surrounds me, wouldn't it be wise to reduce them as much as possible? The smaller it is, the less hold destiny will have over it. Let man therefore renounce all projects; let him imitate that judicious schoolboy who cried in order to not say A. Let him be like the god Indra,[14] who, after having exhausted his strength in his victory over a fearsome demon, reduced himself to the dimensions of an atom and chose to live outside the world, under silent and indifferent waters, at the heart of a lotus stem.

The Instant

If I am no longer anything but a body, barely a place in the sun and the instant that measures my breath, then I am released from all worries, fears, as well as regrets. Nothing moves me, nothing matters to me. I attach myself only to this minute that my life is filling up, that alone is a tangible prey, a presence. Only the impression of the moment exists. There are empty moments that are only a sort of connecting fabric between the full moments; we patiently let them roll by. And in the instants of fullness, we will find ourselves satisfied, fulfilled. It's the moral of Aristippus, that of Horace's "*Carpe diem,*" and Gide's *Nourritures terrestres* [The Fruits of the Earth].[15] Let us turn away from the world, from undertakings and conquests; let us devise no more projects; let us remain at home, at rest at the heart of our enjoyment.

But is enjoyment rest? Will we find it in us, and can it ever fulfill us?

"Enough, no more, 'Tis not so sweet now as it was before," says the duke of Mantua to the musicians at the beginning of *Twelfth Night.*[16] The sweetest melody, repeated indefinitely, becomes an annoying refrain.[17] The taste at first delicious soon sickens me. An unchanging enjoyment that stays the same for too long is no longer felt as a plenitude; in the end it merges with a perfect absence. For enjoyment is the presence of an object to which I feel present.[18] It is presence of the object and of myself in the heart of their difference. But as soon as the object is handed over to me, the difference dissolves. There is no longer an object, but once again a single, empty existence that is but vapidity and ennui. As soon as I eliminate the distance that, in separating me from the object, allows me to throw myself toward it, to be movement and transcendence, this fixed union of the object and me no longer exists except in the way a thing does. The Stoic can rightly put pleasure as well as pain among those realities that are foreign and indifferent to me since he defines them as a simple state that I can passively allow to continue within me.[19]

But in reality, enjoyment is not a given fixed in the narrow envelope of the instant. Gide tells us that each pleasure envelops the entire world; the instant implies eternity; God is present in the sensation.[20] Enjoyment is not a separation from the world; it assumes my existence in the world. And first of all it assumes the world's past, my past. A pleasure is even more precious if it is newer, if it stands out more intensely against the uniform background of time. But the instant limited to itself alone is not new; it is only new in its relationship with the past. That figure [*forme*] that just appeared is only distinct if the ground that supports it is itself distinct as ground. At the side of the sunny road the coolness of the shade is most precious, and a break is relaxing after tiring exercise. From the top of the hill I look at the path traveled, and the entire path is present in the joy of my success. The walk gives the rest its worth, and my thirst gives the glass of water its worth. A whole past comes together in the moment of enjoyment. And I don't just contemplate it. To enjoy a good thing is to use it, to throw oneself with it toward the future. To enjoy the sun or the shade is to feel its presence as a slow enrichment. I feel my strength being reborn in my relaxed body; I rest in order to leave again. While looking at the path traveled, I look at those valleys toward which I am going; I look at my future. All enjoyment is project. It surpasses the past toward the future, toward the world that is the fixed image of the future. To drink cinnamon-flavored chocolate, says Gide in *Incidences,* is to drink Spain.[21] Any perfume, any countryside that charms us throws us beyond itself, outside of ourselves. Reduced to itself, it would only be an inert and foreign existence. As soon as it falls back onto itself, enjoyment becomes ennui again. There is no enjoyment except when I leave myself and engage my being in the world through the object that I am enjoying. The psychasthenics that Janet describes only experience a feeling of indifference before the most beautiful sights because no action forms within them.[22] Flowers are no longer made to be plucked and smelled, paths no longer to be followed. The flowers seem made of painted metal; the countryside is no longer anything but a facade. There is no longer any future, no longer any surpassing, no longer any enjoyment. The world has lost all of its depth.

If man wants to rest in himself and tear himself away from the world, then he must renounce even enjoyment. The Epicureans knew this well; they scorned the pleasure of movement in order to preach only the pleasure of repose, pure ataraxia.[23] And even better, the Stoics demanded that the wise man renounce even his body.[24] Nothing is mine, they thought, but my pure interiority. I no longer have an exterior; I am but a naked presence that even pain cannot touch, an intangible upspringing [*jaillissement*],[25] gathered in the instant, and knowing only that it exists. So there is no longer good nor evil facing me, nor anxiety within me. I am, and nothing means anything to me anymore.

In this way the pouting child withdraws into a corner and says: "I don't care about anything." But soon he looks around, he fidgets, he gets bored. When life withdraws into itself, it is not peaceful ataraxia but the anxiety of indifference that flees from itself, that tears itself away from itself, that appeals to the other. "All the unhappiness of men arises from one single fact, that they cannot stay quietly in their own chamber," says Pascal.[26] But what if he cannot remain there? If he avoided all diversions, man would then find himself at the heart of what Valéry calls "the pure ennui of living," and, as Valéry says, this purity "instantly stops the heart."[27]

But is it then fitting to talk about "diversions" and to say along with Valéry that it is "reality in its pure state" that would be discovered at the heart of ennui? Hegel has shown convincingly that reality should never be conceived as an interiority hidden in the depths of appearance.[28] Appearance hides nothing; it expresses. Interiority is not different from exteriority; appearance is itself reality.[29] If man was only an atom of immobile presence, how would the illusion that the world is his and the appearance of desires and worries be born within him? If he is conscious of desiring and fearing, man desires and fears. If Pyrrhus's being was a being "at rest," he wouldn't even be able to think about leaving. But he does think about it. As soon as he thinks about it, he has already left. "Man is a being of faraway places," says Heidegger;[30] he is always *somewhere else*. There exists no privileged spot in the world about which he can safely say, "This is me." He is constitutively oriented toward something other than himself. He is himself only through relationships with something other than himself. "Man is always infinitely more than he would be if he were reduced to what he is in the instant," says Heidegger.[31] Every thought, every look, every tendency is transcendence. This is what we have seen by considering enjoyment. It envelops the past, the future, the entire world. The man lying in the shade at the top of the hill is not only there, on that piece of earth that his body embraces. He is present to those hills that he perceives. He is also in the faraway cities, as someone who is absent. He rejoices in this absence. Even if he closes his eyes and tries to think about nothing, he feels like himself in contrast with the background of immobile and unconscious heat in which he bathes. He cannot suddenly spring forth into the world in the pure ipseity [selfness] of his being without the world suddenly springing forth in front of him.

It is because man is transcendence that it is so difficult for him ever to imagine any paradise. Paradise is rest; it is transcendence abolished, a state of things that is given and does not have to be surpassed. But then, what shall we do there? In order for the air there to be breathable, it must leave room for actions and desires; we must have to surpass it in its turn; it must not be a paradise. The beauty of the promised land is that it promised new promises. Immobile paradises promise us nothing but an eternal ennui. Pyrrhus speaks of resting only because he lacks imagination. Once returned home, he will hunt, he will legislate, he will go to war again. If he tries to stay truly at rest, he will only yawn. Literature has often described the disappointment of the man who has just attained the ardently desired goal: and after that? One cannot fulfill a man; he is not a vessel that docilely allows itself to be filled up. His condition is to surpass everything given. Once attained, his plenitude falls into the past, leaving that "constant emptiness of the future" [*creux toujours futur*] of which Valéry speaks gaping open.[32] Such are the passionate lovers described by Marcel Arland or Jacques Chardonne.[33] They wish to settle down forever at the heart of their love, and soon, enclosed in their solitary retreat, without having stopped loving each other, they get desperately bored. "Happiness is nothing more than this then!" says the heroine of *Terres étrangères* [Foreign Lands].[34] Each object, each instant, reduced to its immediate presence, is not enough for a man. He is himself not enough for himself since he is always infinitely more than he would be if he were only that. To live a love is to throw oneself through that love toward new goals: a home, a job, a common future. Since man is project, his happiness, like his pleasures, can only be projects. The man who has made a fortune immediately dreams of making another. Pascal said it perfectly: it is not the hare that interests the hunter, it's the hunt.[35] One is wrong to reproach a man for struggling for a paradise in which he would not wish to live. The goal is a goal only at the end of the path. As soon as it is attained, it becomes a new starting point. The socialist wants the advent of the socialist State, but if that State were given to him at the outset, he would desire something else. From within the State, he would invent other goals. A goal is always the meaning and the result of an effort. Separated from that effort, no reality is a goal but only a given, made to be surpassed. This does not mean that only the struggle counts, that the stakes do not matter, as is sometimes said, because the struggle is a struggle for the stakes. If the stakes are taken away from it, the struggle loses all meaning and all truth. It is no longer a struggle but a stupid marching in place [*piétinement*].

The serious mind claims to separate the end from the project that defines it and to recognize in it an intrinsic value. He believes that values are in the world, before man, without him. Man would only have to pick them. But Spinoza, and Hegel, more definitively, have already dissipated this illusion of false objectivity.[36] There is a false subjectivity that, in a symmetrical movement, claims to separate the project from the end and to reduce it to a simple game, a diversion. It denies that any value exists in the world because it denies man's transcendence and wants to reduce him to his immanence alone. A man who desires and who lucidly starts an undertaking is sincere in his desires. He wants an end; he wants it at the exclusion of any other end, but he does not want it in order to stop there, to enjoy it. He wants it in order for it to be surpassed. The notion of end is ambiguous since every end is a point of departure at the same time. But this does not prevent it from being seen as an end. Man's freedom resides in this power.

This very ambiguity seems to authorize the irony of the humorist.[37] Isn't Pyrrhus absurd to leave in order to return home? Isn't the tennis player absurd to hit a ball in order for someone to send it back to him and the skier absurd to climb a slope in order to immediately come back down? Not only does the goal conceal itself, but the successive goals contradict each other, and the undertaking is completed only in destroying itself.

But here the humorist uses a sophism. He decomposes all human activity into elementary acts whose juxtaposition appears contradictory. If he completed the decomposition to recover the pure instant, then all contradiction would disappear. Only a shapeless incoherence would remain, a pure contingency that would neither outrage [*scandaliser*] nor astonish.[38] But he is cheating. He maintains the existence of partial meanings that oppose each other at the heart of the ensemble whose global meaning he rejects. One says that the skier only climbs up in order to come down. Then one is admitting that he climbs, that he comes down, that his movements do not follow each

99

other randomly but aim for the top of the hill or the bottom of the valley. One therefore grants the existence of synthetic significations toward which every element transcends itself. But it is then a purely arbitrary decision to reject the idea of a greater ensemble where the ascent and the descent surpass themselves toward a walk or an exercise. It is not up to the humorist to decide; it is up to the skier. Pyrrhus would be absurd if he left in order to return home, but it is the humorist who introduces this finality here. He does not have the right to extend Pyrrhus's project farther than Pyrrhus has settled upon. Pyrrhus is not leaving in order to return; he is leaving in order to conquer. That undertaking is not contradictory. A project is exactly what it decides to be. It has the meaning that it gives itself. One cannot define it from the outside. It is not contradictory; it is possible and coherent as soon as it exists, and it exists as soon as a man makes it exist.

In this way, wisdom for man does not consist of withdrawing into oneself. The wise man himself who advises the immobility of rest to his disciples contradicts this advice by giving it; he should not say anything. He should not find himself disciples. Epicurus preaches ataraxia, but he preaches, and he preaches that it is necessary to preach; he preaches friendship. Neither does the Stoic remain stiffly in an indifferent freedom resting uselessly upon itself. He teaches all men the power of their freedom. And even when the wise man avoids loudly proclaiming the value of silence, he never succeeds in maintaining himself at the heart of himself and maintaining the world around him in an equal indifference. It doesn't matter to him whether he eats or fasts, governs an empire or lives in a barrel, but he still must choose: he eats or fasts, he rules or abdicates. Here lies the disappointing character of every conversion. I judge the movement of my transcendence to be futile [*vain*], but I cannot prevent it. Time continues to flow by; the instants push me forward. So I am wise, and what will I do now? I live, even if I judge that life is absurd, like Achilles always catching up with the tortoise despite Zeno.[39]

Each man decides on the place he occupies in the world, but he must occupy one. He can never withdraw from it. The wise man is a man among men, and his very wisdom is a project of himself.

Infinity

Why then would Candide choose to assign no limit to his garden? If man is always somewhere else, then why isn't he everywhere? Expanded to the borders of the world, would he experience that rest he was looking for by contracting into himself? If I am everywhere, where will I go? Movement disappears here as surely as if I were nowhere. "That little boy was not your brother," said the parents to their oversensitive son. They added, "You are not going to cry your whole life. Each day there are thousands of children across the earth who die." Not all our life, so why five minutes? Not over all children; why over this one? If all men are my brothers, no particular man is my brother any longer. Multiplying the ties that bind me to the world by infinity is a way of denying those that unite me to this singular minute, to this singular corner of the earth. I no longer have a homeland, nor friends, nor parents. All figures disappear; they are reduced to the universal ground whose presence cannot be distinguished from absolute absence. Here also, there is no longer desire, nor fear, nor hardship, nor joy. Nothing is mine. Eternity joins with the instant; it's the same naked facticity, the same empty interiority. It is undoubtedly not by chance if the psychasthenic who denies himself the world and who renounces his transcendence is so often haunted by the idea of the impersonal infinity of this world. A needle, a subway ticket makes him dream about all needles, about all subway tickets in the world, and, stunned by this dizzying multiplicity, he remains immobile, using neither his needle nor his ticket.

Stoicism shows us how these two paths join together. If the wise man reduces himself to a pure upspringing of being falling back upon himself, he merges with the universal harmony at the same time. Destiny can have no hold on me since there is no longer anything that is outside of me. My own self is abolished within the universal. Spread out to infinity, my place in the world is erased just as if I had succeeded in containing it in one dimensionless point.

But this effort to identify myself with the universal immediately receives a denial. It is impossible for me to assert that it is the universal that is since I am asserting it. By asserting, I make myself be; it is I who am. As I distinguish myself from my pure presence by reaching out toward something other than me, I also distinguish myself from this other toward which I reach by the very fact that I reach toward it. My presence is. It breaks up the unity and the continuity of that mass of indifference into which I wanted it to be absorbed. Spinoza's existence sharply contradicts the truth of Spinozism. Hegel declares in vain that individuality is only a moment of the universal becoming.[40] If this moment, as unsurpassed, had no reality, then it should not even exist in appearance; it should not even be named. If there is a question about it, the question gives it a truth that asserts itself against any surpassing. Whatever the truth of the sun and of man in the heart of the all, the appearance of the sun for man exists in an irreducible manner. Man cannot escape his own presence or that of the singular world that his presence reveals around him. His very effort to tear himself away from the earth only carves out his place there. Spinozism defines Spinoza, and Hegelianism defines Hegel. Flaubert believes he has rejoined the universal when he writes in substance: "Why concern myself with the proletariat of today rather than the slaves of antiquity?"[41] But by saying so he escapes neither his era nor his class. On the contrary, he behaves like a nineteenth-century bourgeois whose fortune, pastimes, and vanity mask his solidarity with his time.

Man can neither indefinitely reduce his being, nor expand it to infinity. He cannot find rest, and yet what is this movement that leads him nowhere? One finds the same antinomy in the realm of action as in that of speculation. Any stopping is impossible because transcendence is a perpetual surpassing. But an indefinite project is absurd since it leads to nothing. Here man dreams of an ideal symmetrical to that of the unconditioned God called for by speculative thought. He demands an unconditioned end for his acts such that it could not be surpassed, a term at once infinite and complete in which his transcendence would grasp itself anew without limiting itself. He cannot identify himself with infinity. But within his singular situation can he destine himself to it?

God

"God wills it." This saying sheltered the Crusaders from the questions of Cineas. The conquests of the Christian warriors were not a vain pursuit, like those of Pyrrhus, if they were willed by God. One does not surpass the will of God. Man meets an absolute end of his efforts in God because there is nothing outside of him. The necessity of the divine being extends over those actions that end with him and saves them for eternity. But what does God will?

If God is infinity and the plenitude of being, there is in him no distance between his project and his reality. What he wills is; he wills what is. His will is only the immobile foundation of being; one can barely still call it a will. Such a God is not a singular person. He is the universal, the unchangeable and eternal everything. And the universal is silence. He demands nothing; he promises nothing; he requires no sacrifice; he dispenses no punishment or reward; he can justify nothing, nor condemn anything. One can found neither optimism nor despair on him. He is; one can say nothing more. The perfection of his being leaves no place for man. To transcend oneself in an object is to found it, but how can one found what already *is*? Man cannot transcend himself in God if God is completely given. Man is then nothing but an indifferent accident on the surface of being. He is on earth like the explorer lost in a desert. He can go to the right, to the left; he can go where he wants, but he will never go anywhere, and the sand will cover up his tracks. If he wants to give meaning to his behavior, he should not address himself to this impersonal, indifferent, and complete God. His motto would be the one proposed on the pediment of the abbey of Thélème: "Do what thou wilt."[42] If God wills all that is, man has only to act however he wants. "When one is in God's hands, one need not worry about what one has to do; one has no remorse about what one has done," said the heretical sect of Amalricians in the twelfth century. And they squandered their lives in joyous orgies.

The Church burned the Amalricians with great pomp.[43] There exists, however, a Catholic naturalism that extends the benediction of God over the entire earth. We find an echo of this, for example, in Claudel.[44] Everything comes from God, therefore everything is good. Man does not have to turn away from the earth, and he even has a lot of trouble corrupting this original destination within him because he is a creature of God. It is difficult to do evil because what is, is the good. But an orthodox Christian avoids taking such a thought to the extreme. "Well, dear ma'am," says the worldly and gourmand priest as he sits down at the table, "Would God have invented all these good things if he did not want us to eat them?" But he is carefully forgetting that God also invented woman. There was an old woman who, outraged, refused to put butter in her soft-boiled egg. "I eat it like the dear Lord made it," she said. And she reached for the salt shaker.

"We shall pray to God with his entire oeuvre! Nothing that he does is in vain; nothing is foreign to our salvation!" cries Claudel. If God's oeuvre is completely good, it is because it is completely useful to the salvation of man. It is therefore not an end in itself, but a means that gets its justification from how we use it. But then how do we know if the melon was really invented to be eaten with our family? Maybe it was invented to not be eaten; maybe the goods of this world are good only because man can refuse them. This is why Saint Francis of Assisi smiled at the world but did not partake of it.[45] "For all things, you have but praise," says the archeologist to the viceroy of Naples, in the *Soulier de satin* [The Satin Slipper] [1929] by Claudel. "But it angers me to see that you use none of it."[46] However, the viceroy gives away the riches that he does not use, and to give something away is a way of using it. Asceticism is another form of pleasure. Whatever he does, man makes use of earthly goods because through them he accomplishes his redemption or his ruin. He must therefore decide how to make use of them. His decision is not written in the object because any use is surpassing, and the surpassing is not given anywhere. It is not; it has to be [*a à être*]. What does it have to be?

It has to be in accordance with the will of God, says the Christian.

So one renounces all naturalism. Nothing is good except virtue; evil is sin, and virtue is the submission to divine exigencies. There are, therefore, exigencies in God. He waits for man to destine himself to him. He created man so that there exists a being who is not a given but who accomplishes his being according to his creator's desire. The will of God then seems like an appeal to man's freedom; it demands something that has to be, that is not yet. It is thus project; it is the transcendence of a being who has to be its being, who is not. So a relationship between God and man is conceivable. As long as God is not all that he has to be, man can found him; he finds his place in the world. He is in situation with respect to God. And this is how God seems to be in situation with respect to man. This is what the German mystic Angelus Silésius means when he writes, "God needs me as I need him."[47] The Christian then finds himself in front of a personal and living God *for* whom he can act. But in this case, God is no longer the absolute, the universal. He is that false infinity about which Hegel speaks who allows the finite facing him to subsist as separate from him. He is for man a neighbor.

This definite, singular God could satisfy the aspirations of human transcendence. He would indeed be a concrete being, complete and closed in upon himself, because he would exist and at the same time be indefinitely open because his existence would be an endless transcendence. He could not be surpassed, because he would himself be a perpetual surpassing. Man could only accompany his transcendence without ever transcending it. When I have accomplished the will of God, a new will will grab me; there will never be any "after that?"

But the will of this God is no longer written in things, because it is no longer the will of what is, but of what has to be. It is no longer the will of everything, and man must discover its singular shape. To want the will of God: this entirely formal decision is not sufficient to dictate any actions to man. Does God want the believer to massacre the unfaithful, burn the heretics, or tolerate their faith? Does he want him to go off to war or to make peace? Does he want capitalism or socialism? What is the temporal and human side of the eternal will? Man claims to transcend himself in God, but he never transcends himself except in the heart of immanence. He must accomplish his redemption on earth. Which of the earthly undertakings will raise him up to heaven?

"Let us listen to the voice of God," says the believer. "He will tell us himself what he expects of us." But such a hope is naïve. God could manifest himself only through an earthly voice because our ears can hear no other. But how, then, does one recognize its divine nature? Upon asking a hallucinating woman who that interlocutor was who spoke to her by mysterious waves, she responded cautiously, "He says that he is God, but *I* don't know him." Moses could have felt the same mistrust about the voice that came out of the burning bush or that rumbled at the top of Mount Sinai.[48] Whether the voice comes from a cloud, a church, or a confessor's mouth, the transcendent must always manifest himself through an immanent presence in the world. His transcendence will always escape us. Even in my heart, this order I hear is ambiguous. There lies the source of Abraham's anguish, which Kierkegaard describes in *Fear and Trembling* [1843].[49] Who knows if it's not a question of a temptation of the devil or my pride? Is it really God who is speaking? Who will distinguish the saint from the heretic? Kafka describes the same uncertainty in *The Castle* [1926].[50] Man can receive messages and even see the messenger. But isn't this one an impostor? And does *he* know who sends him? Hasn't he forgotten half the message along the way? Is this letter that he hands over to me authentic, and what is its meaning? The Messiah says that he is the Messiah; the false messiah also says it. Who will distinguish one from the other?

One will be able to recognize them only by their works. But how will we decide whether these works are good or bad? We will decide in the name of a human good. All morality that claims to justify itself by divine transcendence proceeds this way. It posits a human good and affirms that it is willed by God because it is the good. Claudel asserts that we must prefer order to disorder because order is, while disorder is the negation of being; because order is in itself superior to disorder we proclaim that it conforms to God's designs. But Claudel is forgetting that, as Spinoza and Bergson have shown,[51] only man's point of view makes order seem like order. Is Claudel's order the same as God's? There is a bourgeois order, a socialist order, a democratic order, a fascist order, and each one is disorder in the eyes of its adversary. Every society always claims to have God with it. It recreates him in its image; the society speaks, not God. But if I turn toward myself to question myself, I hear only the voice of my own heart. The Catholic Church and the Protestant individualist can rightly reproach each other for taking the echo of their personal convictions as a divine inspiration. I will not meet God himself outside of myself anymore than within myself. I will never notice any celestial sign written on the earth. If it is written down, it is earthly. Man cannot enlighten himself through God; through man one tries to shed light upon God. God's call [*appel*] is always made to be heard through men, and through human undertakings man will respond to this call [*appel*]. God, if he existed, would therefore be powerless to guide human transcendence. Man is never in situation except before men, and this presence or this absence way up in heaven does not concern him.

Humanity

We must therefore turn toward men. Can't we find in humanity itself that absolute end that we were first looking for in heaven? If we see it as closed upon itself, as needing to attain a state of unchanging equilibrium someday or to annihilate itself in death, we can undoubtedly transcend it toward nothingness and anxiously ask ourselves: and after that? If, with Laforgue,[52] we imagine the terrestrial globe rolling frozen through a silent ether, what good does it do to preoccupy ourselves with the transient fauna that lives on it? But those are the visions of poets, wise men, or priests. Nothing allows us to affirm that humanity will ever die out. We know that each man is mortal but not that humanity must die. And if it does not die, it will never stop in any stage; it will not cease to be a perpetual surpassing of itself. However, if we envision only the indefinite nature of this race where one generation follows another only to disappear in turn, then it seems to us rather useless [*vain*] to take part in it. Our transcendence would be dissipated in time's elusive flight. But humanity is more than this endless dispersion; it is made of flesh-and-blood men. It has a singular history, a definite shape. In order for us to be able to transcend ourselves safely toward humanity, it must present itself to us in these two aspects at once: as open and as closed. It must be separated from its being so that it has to realize its being through us, and yet it must be. This is how humanity appears to those who propose the cult of Humanity to us. It is never completed; it unceasingly projects itself toward the future. It is a perpetual surpassing of itself; an appeal in need of a response constantly emanates from it; a void in need of fulfillment is constantly being hollowed out in it. Through each man, humanity searches indefinitely to rejoin its being, and its very being consists of that. Our transcendence can never surpass humanity but only accompany it, and yet it will be completely grasped again in each instant because in each instant Humanity is.

But *is* it really? Can one speak of *a* humanity? Undoubtedly it is always possible to use a collective noun for the ensemble of men, but this would be to consider them from the outside, as objects unified by the space that they take up. This collectivity would be only a herd of intelligent animals. We have nothing to do with this given, fixed in the plenitude of its being. In order for us to be able to act *for* humanity, it must demand something from us. It must possess a unity acting as a totality that seeks to realize itself, and it must appeal to us in a single voice.

Humanity takes this form in the myth of solidarity. Often since the famous apologue of the limbs and the stomach, men have been represented as the parts of an organism. By working for one of them, one would be working for them all. There is said to exist a natural economy according to which the place of each one is defined by the place of all the others. But this is defining man in terms of exteriority. In order to occupy a determined [*déterminée*] place in the world,[53] man himself must be determined: a pure passivity. He would not, then, put the goal of his actions into question; he would not act. But he does act; he does question himself. He is free, and his freedom is interiority. How, then, would he *have* a place on earth? He will *take* a place by throwing himself into the world, by making himself exist among other men through his own project. Often the young man agonizes: how to integrate oneself into this plenitude? No drop of water is lacking from the sea. Before his birth, humanity was exactly as full; it will remain as full if he dies. He can neither diminish nor increase it, any more than a point can increase the length of a line. He does not feel at all like a cog in a precise mechanism. On the contrary, it seems to him that no corner of the world was reserved for him: he is everywhere too much [*de trop*]. And indeed, his place was not marked ahead of time as an absence. He came first. Absence does not precede presence; being precedes nothingness, and only through man's freedom do voids and lacks spring up in the heart of being.*[54]

It is true that at every moment men make this void spring up around them. In transcending the given toward a plenitude to come, they define the present as a lack. They constantly wait for something new: new goods, new techniques, social reforms, new men. And the young man encounters even more precise appeals around him; each year a certain number of government workers, doctors, fitters are needed; the world *lacks* manpower. He can slip into one of these voids, but there is never one that is molded exactly for him. He can become one of those new men for whom others were waiting, but the new man they awaited was not *him*. Another would have done just as well. The place that each one occupies is always a foreign place. The bread that one eats is always the bread of another.

And besides, if I wait for men to give me a place, I would not know where to put myself; they do not agree with each other. The country lacks men; it makes that decision for itself. In the eyes of the neighboring country, it is overpopulated. Society needs government workers to persevere in its routines, but the revolution needs militants who undermine society. A man finds

---

*See *L'etre et le néant* [Being and Nothingness], by J-P Sartre, page 38 and following.

his place on earth only by becoming a given object for other men, and every given is destined to be transcended. One transcends it by using it or combating it. I am an instrument for some only by becoming an obstacle for others. It is impossible to serve them all.

Wars, unemployment, crises plainly show that there doesn't exist any preestablished harmony between men. Initially, men do not depend on one another because initially they *are* not: they have to be. Freedoms are neither unified nor opposed but separated. In projecting himself into the world, a man situates himself by situating other men around him. So solidarities are created, but a man cannot enter into solidarity with all the others, because they do not all choose the same goals since their choices are free. If I serve the proletariat, I combat capitalism; the soldier only defends his country by killing its adversaries. Class and country define themselves as a unity through the unity of their opposition to the other. There is a proletariat only as long as there is a struggle against capitalism. A country exists only through its borders. If one does away with opposition, the totality comes apart; we are no longer dealing with anything but a plurality of separate individuals. In transcending oneself toward the proletariat, one cannot at the same time transcend oneself toward all of humanity because the only way to transcend oneself toward the proletariat is to transcend oneself with it against the rest of humanity. One might say that with the proletariat, one transcends oneself toward a future humanity where the separation of the classes will be abolished, but one must first expropriate one or several generations of capitalists and sacrifice the proletarians of today. One will always work for certain men against others.

Nevertheless, can't one count on a higher reconciliation beyond these oppositions?[55] Don't singular sacrifices find a necessary place in world history? The myth of evolution wants to delude us with this hope. It promises us the accomplishment of human unity across temporal dispersion. Here transcendence takes the shape of progress. In each man, in each of his actions, the entire human past is written and immediately surpassed entirely toward the future. Reflecting upon old technologies, the inventor invents a new technology, and pushing off from this springboard, the following generation invents a better technology. The innovator salutes the success of his own project in this future humanity who only surpasses it by pushing off from it. "Those who are born after us will, because of us, belong to a history higher than any other one ever was until us," writes Nietzsche in *The Gay Science*.[56] In this way human transcendence would be entirely grasped again within each moment because within each moment the preceding one would be conserved. And yet it would not become fixed in any of them, since progress always continues.

But the idea of evolution assumes a human continuity. In order for an action to persist in time like waves in ether, humanity must be a docile, passive medium. But how is it, then, that man acts?

If my son is a determined [*déterminé*] being who submits to my actions without resistance,[57] then I am also determined; I do not act. And if I am free, my son is also free. But then my action cannot be transmitted across successive generations as if it were gliding along calm water. Other men act on this action in turn. Humanity is a discontinuous succession of free men who are irretrievably isolated by their subjectivity.

So an action thrown into the world is not propagated infinitely like the wave in classical physics. Rather, the image proposed by the new wave mechanics would be appropriate here: an experiment can define a wave in terms of probability and give an equation for its propagation, but it does not allow us to predict a later experiment that will throw new givens into the world from which the wave must be reconstructed anew. The action does not stop the instant that we accomplish it. It escapes us toward the future, where it is immediately grasped again by foreign consciousnesses. It is never a blind constraint for the other but a given to be surpassed, and the other surpasses it, not I. From this fixed act, the other throws himself into a future that I have not mapped out for him. My action is for the other only what he himself makes of it. How then would I know in advance what I do? And if I don't know, how can I intend to act for humanity? I build a house for the men of tomorrow; perhaps they will shelter themselves there, but it could also get in the way of their future constructions. Maybe they will put up with it; maybe they will demolish it; maybe they will live in it, and it will collapse upon them. If I bring a child into the world, tomorrow he might be a criminal, a tyrant. He is the one to decide, and each of his children's children will decide for himself. Do I then procreate for humanity? How many times has man exclaimed, "I didn't want that to happen!" when contemplating the unexpected result of his action. Nobel thought he was working for science; he was working for war. Epicurus did not anticipate what would later be called Epicureanism, nor Nietzsche Nietzscheanism, nor Christ the Inquisition. Everything that comes from the hands of man is immediately taken away by the ebb and flow of history, remolded by each new minute, and gives rise around it to a thousand unexpected eddies.

There are nevertheless some goals upon which human freedoms agree. If I intend to enlighten humanity, to increase its power over nature, to improve its hygiene, isn't the destiny of my action certain? The scholar is content if he brings a tiny rock to the edifice of science; it will remain eternally in its necessary place, and eternity will infinitely increase its dimensions.

It is true that men agree about science, since a thought is scientific only when it is such that all men can agree upon it. But in working for science, is it really for humanity that one works? Each one of its inventions defines a new situation for men. To decide that it is useful, the situation that it creates must be better than the former situation. Generally, the idea of progress requires such comparisons. But can one compare the diversity of human situations? Whether there are fifty million men on earth or twenty, humanity is exactly as full, and in its heart, it still has that "constant emptiness of the future" that prevents it from ever becoming a paradise. If it can be seen as a goal impossible to surpass, it is because humanity itself is not limited to any goal. By its own élan it sets goals that constantly draw back before it. But this is when what seems to us to be the promise of salvation turns against our hopes: neither science, nor technology, nor any sort of action will ever bring humanity close to this moving goal. Whatever situation is created, it is, in its turn, a given to be surpassed. A successful man is said to have "arrived." Where has he arrived? One never arrives anywhere. There are only points of departure. With each man humanity makes a fresh start. And that's why the young man who seeks his place in the world does not initially find it and feels forsaken, useless, without justification. Whether he studies science, writes poetry, or builds motors, he transcends himself; he transcends the given situation, but he does not transcend himself for humanity. Humanity transcends itself through him. This transcendence isn't *for* anything; it is. Each man's life and all of humanity thus appear absolutely gratuitous at every instant, as neither required nor called [*appelées*] by anything. Their movement creates requirements and appeals to which only the creation of new requirements will respond. No accomplishment is merely imaginable.

But can this endless becoming itself be considered an accomplishment? Humanity does not move closer to a goal that has been fixed from the start, but if in each one of its successive stages the preceding one is conserved and takes on a higher form, couldn't we speak of progress? We see a contradiction in it, Hegel tells us, only because we stop at some of its avatars. But if we envision the totality of its history, we see the apparent separation of events and men vanish; all moments are reconciled. The obstacle is part of the struggle that breaks through it; cubism combats impressionism,[58] but the former exists only through the latter, and the painting of tomorrow will be defined by going beyond them both. Robespierre is brought down by the revolution of Thermidor, but Robespierre and Thermidor together are found in Bona-parte.[59] By realizing his historic and singular destiny, each man can thus find his place at the heart of the universal. My accomplished act becomes something other than what I had first wanted it to be, but it does not undergo a foreign perversion because of this. It completes its being, and thus it truly accomplishes itself.

In order to subscribe to Hegelian optimism, it must be established that the synthesis effectively conserves the thesis and the antithesis that it surpasses; each man must be able to recognize himself in the universal that envelops him. He must recognize himself there, says Hegel, since the concrete universal is singular, and it is through singular individualities that it finds its shape. It would not be what it is if each of its moments had not been what it was.[60] Let us therefore admit that the presence of each man is written in the world for eternity. Would a defeated man be consoled by showing him that the triumph of his victor would have been less brilliant without his resistance? Would that be sufficient to make that victory his own? To tell the truth, it is *his* defeat that belongs to him. We have seen that man is present in the world in two ways: he is an object, a given that foreign transcendences surpass, and he is himself a transcendence who throws himself toward the future. What is his is what he founds by his free project, and not what is founded by others based on him. But what is conserved of a man in the Hegelian dialectic is precisely his facticity.[61] The truth of a choice is the living subjectivity that makes it a choice of that end, and not the fixed fact of having chosen. Hegel retains only this dead aspect. As long as he falls into the world as a thing passed by and surpassed, man cannot find himself there. On the contrary, he is alienated there. One cannot save a man by showing him that that dimension of his being by which he is a stranger to himself and an object for others is conserved. Undoubtedly man is present to the entire universe as a given. At each instant, I have the entire past of humanity behind me, before me its entire future; I am situated in one spot on the earth, in the solar system, among the nebulae. Each of the objects that I handle refers me to all the objects that constitute the world, and my existence refers me to that of all men, but this is not sufficient for the universe to be mine. What is mine is what I have founded; it is the accomplishment of my own project.

And also, Hegel would say, man will indeed find the accomplishment of his project in universal becoming, if only he knew how to extend that project far enough. The only disappointment will be for the foolish stubbornness that will persist within a finite purpose. But if man adopts the universal's point of view, he will recognize his victory even in the appearance of defeat. Demosthenes was shortsighted when he was in despair over the ruin of Athens;[62] what really mattered to him was civilization, and it was civilization that Philip and Alexander realized in the world.[63] All is well if only I am capable of wanting it all.

But is such a desire possible?

Sheltered in the unique and impassive heaven, the wise man would see revolutions pass by like shadows on the eternally changing face of the earth. He would not lift a finger to secure the triumph of a certain shape of the world, which will be erased tomorrow. He would prefer nothing since all would be his. In this way the optimistic economist of the nineteenth century admires overpopulation for bringing an excess of labor and a correlative decrease in salaries, which leads to the mortality and sterility of the working class, thus leading back to depopulation, and so forth.

And indeed, if we are floating in Hegelian ether, neither the life nor the death of these particular men seems important to us. But why does the economic equilibrium still remain important? The universal spirit does not rejoice here over this machinery; the bourgeois economist does. The universal spirit is voiceless, and every man who claims to speak in its name only lends it his own voice. How could he adopt the universal's point of view since he *is* not the universal? One cannot have a point of view other than his own. "Where is hell?" Marlowe's Faust asks Mephistopheles, and the demon replies, "It is where we are."[64] Thus man can say, "The earth is where I am." There is no way for him to escape to Sirius. To claim that a man renounces the singular nature of his project is to kill the project. What Demosthenes really wanted was *one* civilization resting upon that of Athens, blossoming out of it.

Undoubtedly, it can happen that the project aimed for an end through means that have been shown to be inadequate. In this case, a man can congratulate himself on the success of another means that he had not initially chosen. A man desires the prosperity of his town; he votes for a leader. His rival is elected, but he shows himself to be a good leader; the town is prosperous in his hands. The voter can be satisfied with his election because the end for which he had aimed is accomplished in spite of everything. And it was a definite, singular end.

If one claims that every end can be seen as a means toward an end that is farther off, one denies that anything is really an end. The project is emptied of all its contents, and the world crumbles by losing all form. Man finds himself plunged into the heart of an expanse of equal indifference where things are what they are, without him ever choosing to make them be. Since there will always be a civilization, it may be useless to defend Athens. But then one must give up ever regretting anything or rejoicing for anything. To act for a goal is always to choose, to define. If the singular form of his effort appears to man as indifferent, his transcendence vanishes by losing all shape. He can no longer want anything since the universal is without lack, without expectation, and without appeal.

In this way, every effort by man to establish a relationship with infinity is futile [*vain*]. He can enter into a relationship with God only through humanity, and in humanity, he never reaches but a few men and can found only limited situations. If he dreams of expanding himself to infinity, he immediately loses himself. He loses himself in a dream because, in fact, he doesn't stop being there [*être là*],[65] attesting to his finite presence by his finite projects.

Situation

Therefore, Candide's garden can be neither reduced to an atom nor merged with the universe. Man is only by choosing himself; if he refuses to choose, he annihilates himself. The paradox of the human condition is that every end can be surpassed, and yet, the project defines the end as an end. In order to surpass an end, it must first have been projected as something that is not to be surpassed. Man has no other way of existing. It is Pyrrhus, and not Cineas, who is right. Pyrrhus leaves in order to conquer; let him conquer, then. "After that?" After that, he'll see.

Man's finiteness is therefore not endured [*subie*]; it is desired. Here, death does not have that importance with which it has often been endowed. It is not because man dies that he is finite. Our transcendence is always concretely defined on this side of death, or beyond it. Pyrrhus does not wait to have traveled around the world to return home; the revolutionary worries little about no longer being there the day that the revolution triumphs. The limit of our undertaking is at its very heart, not outside of it. A man takes a trip; he hurries to arrive in Lyon that evening because he wants to be in Valence tomorrow in order to be in Montelimar the day after tomorrow, in Avignon the day after that, in Arles the following day. One may laugh at him; whatever he does, he must return home without having seen Nîmes, Marseilles; he won't have seen Bône or Constantinople. But that matters little to him; he will have taken the projected trip: his trip. The writer is impatient to have finished a book in order to write another one. Then I can die happy, he says, *my* work will be completed. He does not wait for death in order to stop, but if his project engages him right into future centuries, death will not stop him either. The octogenarian builds and plants; Moses knows that he will not enter into the Promised Land; Stendhal writes to be read a hundred years later.[66] My death stops my life only once I am dead, and in the eyes of others. But for the living me, my death is not; my project crosses it without meeting obstacles. There exists no barrier against which my transcendence collides at full élan. It dies of itself, like the sea that runs into a smooth beach and comes to a stop and goes no farther.

Therefore, one must not say, with Heidegger, that man's authentic project is being for death [*être pour mourir*],[67] that death is our essential end, that there is no other choice for man than the flight from or the assumption of this ultimate possibility. According to Heidegger himself, there is no interiority for men; his subjectivity is revealed only through an engagement in the objective world. There is choice only through an action that bites onto things. What man chooses is what he makes; what he projects is what he founds, but he does not make his death; he does not found it. He *is* mortal. And Heidegger has no right to say that this being is precisely *for* death. The fact of being is gratuitous; one is *for nothing*, or rather, the word *for* makes no sense here. Being is project because it posits an end, says Heidegger. But as being, being posits no end; it is. The project alone is what defines its being as being *for*. Heidegger agrees that, compared to other ends, this supreme end is not defined as an end by any act. The resolute decision that throws man toward his death does not lead him to kill himself, but only to live in the *presence of* death. But what is presence? It is nowhere else than in the act that presences [*présentifier*]; it is realized only in the creation of concrete links. Thus the Heideggerian conversion is shown to be as ineffective as the Stoic conversion.[68] After, as before, life continues, identical. It is only a matter of an interior change. The same behaviors that are inauthentic when they appear as flights become authentic if they take place in the face of death. But this phrase *in the face of* is only a phrase. In any case, while I am living, death is not *here,* and in whose eyes is my behavior a flight if for me it is a free choice of an end? Heidegger's hesitations concerning the degree of reality of inauthentic existence have their source in this sophism. In truth, only the subject defines the meaning of his action. There is no flight except through a project of flight. When I love, when I desire, I flee nothing: I love; I desire. The nothingness that anguish reveals to me is not the nothingness of my death. It is the negativity at the heart of my life that allows me to constantly transcend all transcendence. And the consciousness of this power is translated not by the assumption of my death, but rather by this "irony" of which Kierkegaard or Nietzsche speaks: even though I would be immortal, even though I would try to identify myself with immortal humanity, every end would remain a departure, every surpassing an object to surpass, and that in this game of relationships there is no other absolute than the totality of these very relationships, emerging in the void, without support.

Thus one is not *for* death [*pour mourir*]; one is, without reason, without end. But as J.-P. Sartre has shown in *L'être et le néant* [Being and Nothingness] [1943] man's being is not the fixed being of things.[69] Man has to be his being. Every moment he is seeking to make himself be, and that is the project. The human being exists in the form of projects that are not projects toward death [*projets vers la mort*] but projects toward singular ends. He hunts, he fishes, he fashions instruments, he writes books: these are not diversions or flights but a movement toward being; man makes so as to be [*faire pour être*].[70] He must transcend himself since he *is* not, but his transcendence must also grasp itself anew as a plenitude since he wants to be. Within the finite object that he founds, man will find a fixed reflection of his transcendence. Why will he found this object rather than that one? One cannot respond to this question because, precisely, the project is free. An existential analysis would allow us to extract the global meaning from a man's different choices, and to understand its development and its unity. But it would have to come to a halt before the uncompromising fact of that singular option by which each man freely throws *himself* into the world.[71] We do not want to examine the contents of the project here, but, its original and free character being posited, we are only trying to define the general and formal conditions of its existence.

We have arrived at the conclusion that the project is singular and therefore finite. The temporal dimension of transcendence is not desired for itself; it depends on the nature of the founded object. A man may want to construct an edifice that will last through the centuries; he may also endeavor to succeed in a dangerous leap. He does not aim here at time for itself; time is only one particular quality of the object. In any case, whether it passes in an instant or endures across centuries, the object always has a duration [*durée*].[72] The plenitude of being is eternity. The object that will collapse one day is not, truly. "And after that?" Man seeks to grasp his being again, but he can always transcend anew the object in which his transcendence is engaged. Even were it indestructible, the object would appear only as contingent, finite, a simple given that must still be surpassed. The object is sufficient as long as it is sufficient to me, but reflection is one of the forms that transcendence spontaneously takes on, and, in the eyes of reflection, the object is there, without reason. A man alone in the world would be paralyzed by the manifest vision of the vanity of all his goals. He would undoubtedly not be able to stand living.

But man is not alone in the world.

Part 2

Others

"How lucky she is!" said a psychasthenic watching a woman who was crying. "She is crying *for real*." The psychasthenic also cried rather often, but they weren't real tears; *her* tears were a comedy, a parody. The normal man does not think he is made of glass or wood. He does not think he is a puppet or a ghost, yet neither can he ever fully believe in his tears or his laughter. Nothing that happens to him is completely true. However long I look at myself in a mirror and tell myself my own history, I never grasp myself as a solid object. I feel within me that void which is myself; I feel that I *am* not. And that is why any cult of the self is truly impossible; I cannot destine myself to myself. Often in my youth I was in despair over not having any personality while certain classmates dazzled me with the brightness of their originality. The other easily takes on that marvelous and inaccessible character because he alone experiences for himself the void in his heart. For me, he is an object in the world, a plenitude. I who am nothing, I believe in his being, and yet he is also something other than an object. He has the infinity of his transcendence that can constantly push back the horizon toward which it rushes. I don't know if God exists, and no experience can make him present for me. Humanity never realizes itself. But the other is there, before me, closed upon himself, open onto infinity. If I destined my actions to him, wouldn't they also take on an infinite dimension?

As soon as a child has finished a drawing or a page of writing, he runs to show them to his parents. He needs their approval as much as candy or toys; the drawing requires an eye that looks at it. These disorganized lines must become a boat or a horse for someone. So the miracle is accomplished, and the child proudly contemplates the multicolored paper. From then on there is a real boat, a real horse there. By himself, he would not have dared to put confidence in those hesitant lines. Undoubtedly, we do not try to thus change all the instants of our lives into hard diamonds. We often seek to accomplish our being without help; I walk in the country, I break off a stem, I kick a pebble, I climb a hill; all that without witnesses. But no one is satisfied with such solitude for his entire life. As soon as my walk is completed, I feel the need to tell a friend about it. King Candaule wanted his wife's beauty to shine for everyone's eyes.[73] Thoreau lived for years in the woods, alone, but upon returning he wrote *Walden* [1854].[74] And Alain Gerbault wrote *Seul à travers l'Atlantique* [The Flight of the "Firecrest"].[75] Even Saint Teresa wrote *The Interior Castle*,[76] and Saint John of the Cross his canticles.[77]

What, then, do we expect from others?

I would be wrong to hope that others could take me far away across an endless becoming. No human act is propagated to infinity; what others create based on me is no longer mine. The sick person whom I cure may be hit by a bus his first time out; I do not say that my care killed him. I bring a child into the world; if he becomes a criminal, I am not an evildoer. If I claimed to assume for infinity the consequences of my actions, I could no longer want anything. I am finite; I must desire my finitude. But what I desire is to choose an end that could not be surpassed, that would truly be an end. And if the object, fixed upon itself, is not sufficient to stop me, wouldn't others have this power?

Devotion

Let's suppose the other needed me and that his existence had an absolute value. Then my being is justified since I am for a being whose existence is justified. I am released from both the risk and the anguish. By positing an absolute end before me, I have abdicated my freedom; questions are no longer posed; I no longer want to be anything but a response to that appeal which requires me. The master is hungry and thirsty; the devoted slave desires only to be the dish that he prepares and the glass of water that he brings to appease the hunger and thirst; he makes himself into a docile instrument. If his master requires it, he will kill himself, and will even kill his master because there exists nothing beyond the master's will, not even what might seem to be his own good. To attain his being, the slave wants to be a thing before the one who possesses being. Many men, and even more women, wish for such a rest: let us devote ourselves.

But first, to whom shall I devote myself? The value of the life to which my own is destined must appear as absolute to me. If a woman asked herself what her old, incompetent husband was good for, she would also ask herself: what's the use of devoting myself to him? She avoids asking herself questions, but then her security is rather precarious because the question may be asked at any moment. I will tranquilly devote myself only if I will the existence of the other in an unconditioned way. Such a will may spring up out of love, admiration, or respect for the human person. Is it then legitimate to dedicate myself, body and soul, to this child, master, or invalid? Will my being be able to accomplish itself in this way?

The devoted man often complains of meeting with only ingratitude around him; his kindnesses go unnoticed or even seem irritating. The justification that he was expecting is refused him by the very person who alone could grant it to him. He bitterly invokes man's perversity. But aren't there more specific reasons for this ingratitude? Does devotion ever conform to what it claims to be? And does it ever attain the results that it intends?

"I did not ask to be born," says the ungrateful child. These words sting his father to the quick because devotion appears first of all as a total resignation [*démission*] in favor of the other. "I lived only for you; I sacrificed everything for you," says the father. But he must clearly recognize that he couldn't resign in favor of what did not yet exist. To bring a child into the world is not to devote oneself to anyone. It is indeed to throw oneself into the world by way of an anonymous child, without submitting to any foreign will. "So be it," says the father, "but ever since the child was born, he has asked for and demanded things, and I gave him what he wanted." "If he gave me everything, it's because he wanted to," says the ungrateful child, and indeed, the father gave in freely to his demands. A man can never abdicate his freedom; his claims to renounce it are only a masquerade that he freely performs. The slave who obeys chooses to obey, and his choice must be renewed at every moment. One is devoted because one wants to be; one wants to be because one hopes to regain his being in this way. . . . "I gave you my life, my youth, my time," says the scorned woman. But what would she have done with her youth and her time if she had not given them away? In love and friendship, the word "gift" has a rather ambiguous meaning. The adulated tyrant thinks that he is doing his slave a great favor by accepting his services. He would be right if the slave were content with his slavery. The mother who contemplates her grown son like the volunteer nurse who contemplates her cured patient says with regret, "You no longer need me!" This regret often takes on the form of a reproach. The need that I saw in the other was therefore really a gift that he was giving me. It is hard to say who are the winners and losers. The object of devotion very often feels irritation; he asked for nothing. His mother, his wife, or his friend ask that their devotion be accepted. They rejoice in the other's misfortunes because they hope to console him and they feel betrayed and blame him when happiness renders them useless. Far from being a resignation, devotion very often takes on an aggressive and tyrannical shape. We want the other's good without him and against him.

But is it indeed the other's good that one wants? It is evident that one can speak of devotion only on this condition. If I set a goal for myself that another did not set for himself, it is *my* goal, and I am not being devoted; I am doing. In looking at his son who did not ask to be born and who is presently a handsome and robust little boy, the father may proudly think: "See what I have made," and not "See what I have devoted myself to." There is devotion only if I take an end defined by the other as my end. But then it is contradictory to suppose that *I* could define that end for him. The despotic father who prevents his son from marrying whom he wishes would still like to think that he is devoted to him, but it is in the name of his own good that he chooses one situation rather than another for his son. He avoids taking responsibility for his own will by declaring that he acts for *the* good and posits the objectivity of accepted values such as health, fortune, and glory. In Bernanos's *Journal d'un curé de campagne* [Diary of a Country Priest],[78] the defrocked priest who bores his unfortunate companion stiff with his lessons believes he is acting for her own good. Isn't knowledge a good thing? Likewise the inquisitor has the heretic burned at the stake in the name of what is good; no one would claim that he is devoted to him. To devote oneself is to act *for* another, giving to the word "for" the meaning of the German expression *warum willen* [*sic*];[79] it is to respond to the appeal that emanates from his will. His only good is what he wants as his good. When a man posits an end for itself unconditionally, then no one can deny it this character; and if he does not attain it, no foreign success could compensate for this failure. And, as Hegel has so clearly shown, we must ensure that the end includes the means by which we intend to reach it. Suppose a child tries to climb up a tree; a well-meaning and presumptuous adult lifts him off the ground and hoists him up to a branch. The child is disappointed; he wanted not only to be in the tree but to climb there himself. We see right away that there are certain goods that others cannot attain through us. We can do nothing *for* him unless he expects something from us, and by giving him precisely what he expects.

Many so-called devotions thus contradict what they claim from the beginning. They are in truth tyrannies. But can there be devotions that are not tyrannical? Suppose I want to devote myself, knowing that in so doing I remain free, and that nothing will deliver me from the risk and anguish of my freedom. But if I freely choose to accept as my own end the end posited by the other's will, am I not really seeking his good?

But first I would have to know what the other's will is, and that is not so easy. Every project extends across time; it envelops a plurality of elementary projects. We must know how to distinguish those that accord with the essential project, those that contradict it, and those that relate to it only in a contingent manner. The other's will must be distinguished from his whims. Suppose the convalescent wants to go out despite the doctor's orders, and I give in to his wishes, causing him to become sick again. My excuse that "I am not responsible; I did what he wanted," would not be acceptable. "You shouldn't have listened to me," the patient himself will angrily say. After becoming a man, the spoiled child will address similar reproaches to his parents. They may seem harsh, but they are not unfair. Because I know the other's desires, I transcend them; they are only givens for me, and it's up to me to decide if they express his true will. For a man is something else besides what he is at this moment. No word, not even any gesture could define a good that surpasses each instant. It would be rather foolish to trust words: Orestes was careless in believing that Hermione wanted Pyrrhus's death because she demanded it at the top of her voice.[80] Neither are singular behaviors sufficient to convince us; it is the totality of a life that we must be able to examine. Thwarting the ruses of bad faith, the psychiatrist discovers ends in his patient that are his own ends and yet which are completely different from those that the patient admits. We give credit to the lucidity of people whom we admire, whom we respect, but that again is a decision. The good of the other is what he wants, but when it is a matter of discerning his true will, we can only resort to our judgment alone.

Isn't that becoming a tyrant again? It would be easy for the despotic father to think that he judges what's good for his son better than his son does himself. "Deep down," he says, "my son wants the same thing as I do. He persists out of ignorance, carelessness. He will recognize his error later on." He appeals to his future son against his present son. But he will never be sure, in the future any more than in the present. Will the future submission be more real than today's revolt? If the latter does not worry the father, why would the docility on which he is counting satisfy him? It may even happen that some parents despair because they have been obeyed too well. They no longer recognize the voice of the little boy whom they have mastered in the mouth of the young man who accepts what they think is best for him. They did not want what's good for this young man, but what was good for the little boy as he would still exist in the young man. They were dupes, here, of an illusion. The successive moments of a life cannot be preserved in their surpassing; they are separated. For the individual as for humanity, time is not progress but division. Just as one can never act for humanity as a whole, one never acts for one entire man. A man's will does not remain the same during an entire life. Future blame or approval will not be an objective observation but a new project that enjoys no privilege over the project that it confirms or contradicts. There is no instant in a life where all instants are reconciled. Not only can one not know beyond doubt the other's good, but there is not *one* good that is definitively this good. One often has to choose between these different goods posited by a man's different projects. The child must be betrayed for the man, or the man for the child.

One therefore devotes oneself amid risk and doubt. We must take a stand

and choose without anything dictating our choice for us. But posing such choices belongs precisely to our freedom. I choose to prefer the man to the child if it is the man whom the child will become, and not the child, who is of interest to me. Or I prefer the child because the child exists, and I love him, and I am indifferent to that future man whom I do not know. One cannot condemn devotion simply because it requires that our actions be limited to this or to that. We never act except by creating limits for ourselves.

Let's admit, then, that, conscious of the freedom of my actions, the risks that they involve, the limits of their success, I still decide to answer that appeal which wells up toward me. The child asks me for a toy; I give it to him; he is happy. Can't I be satisfied with his joy? The obliging mother looks at the child who is smiling at the toy and smiles, but her smile stiffens. Now the child wants a drum, a set of tools; the old toy no longer amuses him. "After that?" he says impatiently. However hard his mother tries to satisfy him, there will always be an "after that." Devotion claims to fulfill the other, but one cannot fulfill a man. A man never arrives anywhere; one will wear oneself out by following him, without ever arriving either. Let us recall that man is transcendence; what he demands, he only demands in order to surpass. The sick man requires care; I give it to him; he recovers. But the health that he recovers through me is not a good if I stop him at that. It becomes a good thing only if he makes something of it. If I prevent him from using it, he will ask me angrily: "Why have you saved my life? Why have you given it back to me?" This is why tales in which the hero, saved from mortal peril, is forced by his savior to one preset day give up his own life for him seem so cruel to us. The saved man will give back something quite different from what he received, and the demanding benefactor looks like an unjust tyrant. I never create anything for the other except points of departure. The health, the instruction, and the fortune that a father has provided for his son must appear not as givens to him, but as possibilities that only the son can use. I am not the one who founds the other; I am only the instrument upon which the other founds himself. He alone makes himself be by transcending my gifts.

The father and the benefactor often fail to recognize this truth. "I am the one who made him what he is. I pulled him up from nothing," they say about their obligee. They would like the other to recognize the foundation of his being in them, outside of himself. Such a gratitude is sometimes found. "What would I have become without you?" says the distraught man snatched from a disaster. He refuses to project himself beyond that disaster; by saving his situation, one has saved *him*. But a proud man rebelliously refuses to be thus merged with a given thing, to deny his freedom. No matter what someone has done for him, he does not feel affected in his being. When it comes to his being, he is the only one who makes it. Therein lies the essential source of those misunderstandings that often separate the child from his parents: "You owe your life to me," says the father when demanding obedience from his son. But to give a life confers no right over a freedom. The father thinks that he has given his child the greatest of gifts since he brought him into the world, but the child knows that there is no world for him except through his presence in that world. He is himself only through his own project. His birth, his education are only the facticity that is for him to surpass. What one has done for him forms part of the situation that his freedom transcends. Though, of course, he had to be in one situation or another, he does not coincide with his situation since he is always elsewhere.

The fundamental error of devotion is that it considers the other as an object carrying an emptiness in its heart that would be possible to fill. Even when it aims at the future, it still assumes such a lack. A son wishes to marry; the marriage will impose heavy burdens upon him and risks leading him to misery. His father opposes it, saying: "I am acting for his own good." But how would he act for that man who does not yet exist and does not project before him any good? The father imagines his son as he would have been without him: an impoverished man, overwhelmed with worries. Then he imagines him as he will be thanks to him: rich and free; and he claims to see in the latter an impoverished man saved from misery by him. But the impoverished man does not exist anywhere; no appeal rose up from his lips; there was no emptiness there to fill. Likewise, a child who is happy to live is not a child who asked to be born and who was born. When I was little, I often thought with a sort of vertigo about all the children who would never be born, as if they had existed somewhere as a potentiality, as if they had been appeals not heard, voids not filled. But that was a childish imagination. Life is a plenitude preceded by no painful absence.

A Celtic legend recounts that someone predicted to a young woman that her child would be a "worthy druid" if she brought him into the world that very night, and that he would be a great king if she didn't give birth until the next day. She heroically remained seated on a rock all night long, and the child wasn't born until the morning. He had a flattened head, but he was a great king.*[81] Obviously the heroic mother did not devote herself to her son. Insofar as he already existed, he was asking only to be born. And if one questions the future, one thinks that if he had been a wise druid, he would have

---

*Cited by Dumézil in *Les Horaces et les Curiaces* [*sic*].

been happy to be one. In choosing the existence of a king, one has rejected that of a druid. In either one, the child would have fully realized his destiny. In a way, a man is always all that he has to be, since, as Heidegger shows, it is his existence that defines his essence.[82] However, one must not believe that the young mother acted for *herself*. The error of an ethics of self-interest is the same as that of devotion. One assumes that an emptiness was there first, in me or in another, and that I would not have been able to act if the place for my action had not already been carved out. But our actions are not waiting to be called forth [*appelées*]; they are rushing toward a future that is not prefigured anywhere. Our actions always create a future, and the future explodes into the full world like a new and gratuitous plenitude. One does not desire for others or for oneself; one desires *for nothing*, and that is what freedom is. It is for nothing that the young mother in the legend wanted a son who would be a king; for nothing that a flesh-and-blood mother wants her son to become a strong, rich, educated man. And that is exactly what makes for the touching character of maternal love, properly understood. We must know that we never create anything for the other except points of departure, and yet we must want them for ourselves as ends.

The generous man knows well that his action reaches only the outside of the other. All that he can ask is that this free action not be confused with a pure facticity without foundation, that it be recognized as free by the one who benefits from it. The ingrate often refuses such a gratitude. He does not like to admit to himself that he was viewed as an object by a foreign freedom; he only wants to believe in his freedom alone. So he tries his best to not think of his benefactor, or he claims to see only a mechanical force in him. He explains: the benefactor acted out of vanity, out of a sense of importance. If his decision appears to be subject to a psychological determinism, it is no longer offensive; it is no longer anything but a simple fact among others. In enlightened, consenting gratitude, one must be capable of maintaining face to face these two freedoms that seem to exclude each other: the other's freedom and mine. I must simultaneously grasp myself as object and as freedom and recognize my situation as founded by the other, while asserting my being beyond the situation.

It is not a matter of paying off a debt here. There exists no currency that allows for paying the other in return. Between what he has done for me and what I will do for him, there can be no measure. In order to get rid of all worries about gratitude, it happens that a man tries to reimburse a kindness with gifts. These gifts are not touching; they wound. They appear to be the price of a favor whose value one is therefore claiming to measure like that of a thing.

A tip given in thanks for a generous act is insulting. It is a way of denying the act its freedom by supposing that it was not done freely, for nothing, but out of self-interest. Generosity wants and knows itself to be free and asks for nothing but to be recognized as such.

A lucid generosity is what should guide our actions. We will assume our own choices and posit as our ends the situations that will be new points of departure for others. But we must not delude ourselves with the hope that we can do anything *for* others. That is what we learn in the end from this analysis of devotion: its pretensions cannot be justified; the goal that it proposes to itself is impossible. Not only are we unable to abdicate our freedom in favor of the other, or ever act entirely for one man, but we cannot even do anything for any man. Since there exists for him no immobile happiness with which we can gratify him, no paradise into which we can make him enter, his veritable good is that freedom which belongs only to him and which brings him beyond every given. It is out of our reach. Even God would have no hold on it.

And if I can do nothing for a man, I can do nothing against him either. The disappointment of the mother who does not succeed in completely fulfilling her child corresponds to the exasperation of the executioner who is challenged by a proud soul. However hard he tries, if his victim wants to be free, she will remain free even during torture, and struggling and suffering will only elevate her. One can kill her only because she was carrying her death in her. From what point of view can we say that it is an evil that this death occurred today rather than tomorrow? How can one harm a man? Did it harm Socrates to make him drink the hemlock?[83] Did it harm Dostoevsky to send him to the penal colony?[84]

Of course, violence exists. A man is freedom and facticity at the same time. He is free, but not with that abstract freedom posited by the Stoics; he is free in situation. We must distinguish here, as Descartes suggests, his freedom from his power.[85] His power is finite, and one can increase it or restrict it from the outside. One can throw a man in prison, get him out, cut off his arm, lend him wings, but his freedom remains infinite in all cases. The automobile and the airplane change nothing about our freedom, and the slave's chains change nothing about it either. He freely lets himself die or gathers his strength to live; he freely resigns himself or he revolts; he always surpasses himself. Violence can act only upon the facticity of man, upon his exterior. Even when it stops him in his élan toward his goal, violence does not reach him in his heart because he was still free in the face of the goal that he proposed to himself. He wanted to succeed without merging with his success. He can transcend his failure as he would have transcended his success. And that is also why a proud man refuses pity as he refused gratitude; he is never fulfilled, but he is never without resources. He does not want others to pity him. He is beyond his misfortune as he is his happiness.

We are therefore never anything but an instrument for the other, even when we are an obstacle, like the air that supports Kant's dove while resisting it.[86] A man would be nothing if nothing happened to him, and it is always through others that something happens to him, starting with his birth. One cannot treat the other as an instrument if he refuses to be one. On the contrary, I am the instrument of his destiny. And this is why our actions toward the other seem to us so heavy and at the same time weightless. No doubt, the life of the other would have been completely different if I hadn't crossed his path, pronounced those words, if I hadn't been there. But that would have been *his* life; through him our words and our gestures received a meaning. He freely decided their meaning. Everything around him would have been as full if I had not existed.

Must we, then, conclude that our conduct toward the other does not matter?

Far from it. It is indifferent *for him,* because it is a part of those things that the Stoics would call "ouk ephiemenon,"[87] things that we ourselves have not wanted. But it concerns me, it is *my* conduct, and I am responsible for it. The most striking illustration of this paradox is found in the Christian religion. The Christian is *for others* only an instrument in the hands of God, and yet he is accountable to God for all *his* actions. What good is it to care for the sick and relieve the suffering when sickness and misery are tests willed by God and good for the soul? In order to justify himself, a Christian father whose tyrannical conduct provoked or hastened the death of his daughter said, "After all, I was only an instrument in the hands of God." The Christian knows that through him it is always God who acts. Even if he leads his neighbor into temptation, it is because the neighbor was supposed to be tempted. And yet Christ said, "Woe to those who cause others to sin."[88] The sincere and scrupulous Christian rejects this weak defense, "I am but an instrument," because if he is only an excuse for others, an occasion for salvation or ruin, he is free before God. Death is not an evil for the man whom I kill; through my crime, God's will calls him home. And yet in killing him, I, myself, have sinned. A given for others, my act is a free act for me. And in this way, from the Christian point of view, it is never for others that one can want anything; it is for God. One must accomplish one's own salvation. One cannot bring about the other's salvation, and that is the only good that exists for him. This truth can be expressed in another language: as freedom, the other is radically separated from me; no connection can be created from me to this pure interiority upon which even God would have no hold, as Descartes has clearly shown. What concerns me is the other's situation, as something founded by me. One must not believe that I could elude the responsibility for that situation on the pretext that the other is free. That is his business, not mine. *I* am responsible for what I can do, for what I am doing. There is a convenient and false way of thinking that authorizes all abstentions, all tyrannies. Peaceful and satiated, the egoist declares, "The unemployed, the prisoners, the sick are as free as I am; why reject wars or misery if a man remains just as free in the worst circumstances?" But only the impoverished man can declare himself free in the midst of his misery. In abstaining from helping him, I am the very face of that misery. The freedom that rejects or accepts it absolutely does not exist for me. It exists only for the one in whom it is realized. It is not in his name; it is in the name of *my* freedom that *I* can accept or reject it.

And I must accept or reject. I say that I can do nothing for the other or against him, but that does not release me from caring about my relationship with him because whatever I do, I exist before him. I am there, and for him, I am confused with the outrageous [*scandaleuse*] existence of all that is not him. I am the facticity of his situation. The other is free based on that, totally free based only on that, but free facing this and not that, facing me. The fate that weighs on the other is always us. Fate is the fixed face that the freedom of all the others turns toward each of us. It is in this sense that Dostoevsky said that "each person is guilty for everything, before everyone."[89] Immobile or in action, we always weigh upon the earth. Every refusal is a choice, every silence has a voice. Our very passivity is willed; in order to not choose, we still must choose not to choose. It is impossible to escape.

Communication

An initial analysis of my relationships with others has thus led me to this result: the other asks me for nothing and he is not a void that I would have to fill; I can discover no ready-made [*toute faite*] justification of myself in him.[90] And yet each of my actions by falling into the world creates a new situation for him. I must assume these actions. I want certain situations and I reject others. But why is it, then, that they do not appear to me as indifferent, that I can choose between them? In what way do they concern me? What is my true relationship with the other?

We must first turn away from the errors of false objectivity.[91] The serious mind considers health, fortune, education, and comfort as indisputable goods whose worth is written in heaven. But he is duped by an illusion; ready-made values whose hierarchy is imposed upon my decisions do not exist without me. What's good for a man is what he wants as his own good. However, this will is not sufficient to define ours. Is it good that this man attains *his* own good? As we have seen, man himself is divided between his present and his future; we must often choose. And man is not alone in the world. What is good for different men differs. Working for some often means working against the others. One cannot stop at this tranquil solution: wanting *the* good of *all* men. We must define *our* own good. The error of Kantian ethics is to have claimed to make an abstraction of our own presence in the world. Therefore, it leads only to abstract formulas. The respect of the human person in general cannot suffice to guide us because we are dealing with separate and opposed individuals. The human person is complete both in the victim and the executioner; should we let the victim perish or kill the executioner?

We have already seen that, if I efface myself from the world, if I have the contradictory pretension of judging human situations without adopting any human point of view on them, they appear to me as incomparable among themselves, and I can want nothing. An attitude of contemplation never allows any preference. It delivers what is with indifference. There is preference only when the subject transcends the object. One prefers for an end, from a definite point of view. One prefers one fruit over another in order to eat it or paint it, but if one had nothing to do with it, the word "preference" loses all meaning. "Do you prefer the ocean or the mountains?" It should be understood as: "Do you prefer to live by the ocean or in the mountains?" If one doesn't care about sewing or riding a bicycle, one cannot choose between a bicycle and a sewing machine. A past moment can appear as better or worse to me to the extent that I transcend it with my own project. If I want the blossoming of culture, I prefer the Renaissance to the Middle Ages, and I consider it as a progression toward *my* end, but I can speak of progress only in relation to a goal that I have fixed. If I am transported outside of all situations, any given seems equally indifferent to me. So it is impossible for me to choose between the diverse moments of history; they appear as givens to me, identical in that they all represent the fixed élan of a transcendence, and radically heterogeneous in the singular facticity of their existence. One can establish a hierarchy neither in the heart of identity nor in absolute separation. Spinoza rightly said that one cannot compare the perfection of horses with that of dogs.[92] How does one decide what is worth the most *in itself:* the life of a cathedral builder or that of a pilot? And if we consider the human essence that is common to them, it is complete in each one of them.

In *Histoire véritable* [True Story], Montesquieu tells that one day a genie offered a poor man his choice of becoming a king, a rich landowner, or an opulent merchant whose happiness he had so often envied.[93] The poor man hesitated and in the end could not reconcile himself to any exchange; he remained himself. Each man is apt to envy the fate of another, Montesquieu concludes, but no one would accept to be the other. And in fact, I envy the situation of the other if it appears to me as a point of departure that I myself would surpass, but the other's being, closed upon itself, fixed and separated from me, can be made the object of no desire. It is from the core of my life that I desire, prefer, and reject.

Answering the question "How to choose?" is possible because each one of us is truly at the core of his life. "I want the biggest piece," says the child looking greedily at the cake that his mother has just cut up. "Why would it be yours rather than another's?" "Because it's me." The clever businessman knows how to cultivate this taste for privilege in his clients: "I'll let you have it for twenty francs, but only because it's you," he says to the flattered housewife. She readily believes him. How could *I* be just anyone? Other men exist only as objects; we alone grasp ourselves in our intimacy and our freedom as a subject. What is puerile in the child and the housewife is believing that their privilege exists in the eyes of others, because each person is only a subject for himself. But it is true that I am just anyone only in the eyes of the others, and ethics cannot demand from me that I realize this foreign point of view. That would be to cease being me; it would be to cease being. I am; I am in situation before the other and before the situations in which he finds himself. And that is exactly why I can prefer and desire.

So we must now try to define what *my* situation is before others. Only then can we attempt to find a foundation for our actions.

We have seen that it is only through the presence of man that what J.-P. Sartre calls *négatités,* i.e., voids, lacks, absences, seep into the world.[94] Some men refuse to make use of this power. Everything around them is full; they see no place for anything else. Every novelty frightens them and reforms must be forcibly imposed upon them. "One did fine in the past without these inventions," they say. Others, on the contrary, are in a state of waiting; they hope and demand. But they never demand *me,* and yet I wish to be necessitated by them in the very singularity of my being. The book that I write does not fill a void shaped in advance exactly like it. The book is first, and once it is, it is up to the reader to grasp its presence as the reverse of an absence: his freedom alone decides. "How could one do without railroads or airplanes? How can one imagine French literature without Racine or philosophy without Kant?"[95] Beyond his present satisfaction, man retrospectively projects a need behind him. And indeed, now that it exists, the airplane responds to a need, but it is a need that it created by existing, or more exactly, that men freely created based on its existence. Human freedom must then carve out a place for this new plenitude that we cause to spring forth in the world. This place was not, and neither are we the ones who made it; we have only made the object that fills it up. Only the other can create a need for what we give him; every appeal and every demand comes from his freedom. In order for the object that I founded to appear as a good, the other must make it into his own good, and then I would be justified for having created it. The other's freedom alone is capable of necessitating my being. My essential need is therefore to be faced with free men. My project loses all meaning not if my death is announced, but if the end of the world is announced to me. The time of scorn is also that of despair.

Thus it is not *for* others that each person transcends himself; one writes books and invents machines that were demanded nowhere. It is not *for* oneself [*soi*] either, because "self" [*soi*] exists only through the very project that throws it into the world. The fact of transcendence precedes all ends and all justification, but as soon as we are thrown into the world, we immediately wish to escape from the contingence and the gratuitousness of pure presence. We need others in order for our existence to become founded and necessary.

It is not a matter of making recognized in us the pure abstract form of the self [*moi*], as Hegel believes. I intend to save my being in the world, such as it is realized in my actions, my works, my life. Only through these objects that I make exist in the world can I communicate with others. If I make nothing exist, there is neither communication nor justification. But many men fool themselves here. We have seen that, out of irresponsibility or laziness, man often claims to find his being where he has not engaged it and declares objects that he has not founded as his. He demands the other's approval for these foreign things, and he tries his best to believe that it's really *he* who benefits from it. In such a case a man is accused of stupid vanity, when, for example, he boasts about his ancestors, his fortune, or his good looks. In an even more puerile way, the jay adorns himself in peacock feathers and the handsome Christian borrows Cyrano's voice under Roxanne's balcony.[96] But in the end, it is Cyrano whom Roxanne loves. If we really cared about ourselves, we would refuse to let ourselves be loved or admired for "the wrong reasons," that is to say, through goods that are not our own. Thus some women want to be loved just as they are [*sans fard*], and some men, incognito. The conceited man seems to imagine that others possess being, and that one can capture this precious wealth by surprise, but others can only clothe with a necessary dimension what I do in order to make myself be; I must do something first. In this sense one is right to say that whoever seeks himself will lose himself, and that it is in losing himself that he finds himself. If I seek myself in the eyes of others before I have fashioned myself, I am nothing. I take on a shape and an existence only if I first throw myself into the world by loving, by doing.

And my being enters into communication with others only through those objects in which it is engaged. I must resign myself to never being entirely saved. There are endeavors that extend over an entire life; others are limited to an instant, but none expresses the totality of my being since this totality *is not.* We are often fooled by a mirage. If, for example, I have written two verses that are admired, I readily believe that I am necessitated, even in my way of eating and sleeping, because my self is dispersed and unified at the same time. It is like the mana of the primitive man—entirely whole in each point. And as the primitive man thinks that if one possesses a single hair of his, one possesses his entire mana, we imagine that the praise given to one of our actions justifies our entire being. This is why we worry about being named. The name is my total presence magically assembled into the object. But in truth, our actions are separate, and we exist for others only insofar as we are present in our actions, and therefore in our separation.

If first I must know *what* I communicate, it is no less important for me to know with whom I can and want to communicate. Looking for just any approval is another one of the weaknesses of vanity, as when Mr. de Montherlant demands praise from critics whom he claims to scorn and asks for the admiration of a public that he judges to be imbecilic.[97] Truly, in order for the other to possess this power of making the object that I founded necessary, I must not be able to transcend him in turn. As soon as the other appears to me as limited or finite, the place that he creates for me on earth is as contingent and useless [*vaine*] as himself. "He needs me, but what need is there for him? How could this unjustifiable existence justify me?" The coquette looks at her suitor with disgust; if her beauty is useless in the depths of her mirror, isn't it also useless in the depths of his eyes? Many women give up their lovers on the advice of their concierges because the lover is only a man; the concierge is the voice of the public, that mysterious *they* that exists and yet extends to infinity.[98] A writer looks up with satisfaction when someone tells him, "*They* admire you," but as soon as he knows the name of his admirers, he is disappointed. Usually, the blame or the esteem of those close to us hardly touches us. We know their motives too well; they are facts that we can predict and transcend. Parents may be irritated to see their son give their lost prestige to a friend; the friend is a stranger whom the child does not transcend, while his parents have become fixed as objects in his eyes. In this way the man who suffers from an inferiority complex will not let himself be reassured by any approval. The one who approves of him is only a single individual; he transcends him toward that innumerable, mysterious stranger in whose eyes he feels inadequate. Inversely, a man can always believe himself to be an unappreciated genius. Those who condemn him are only finite individuals whose judgment he challenges in order to appeal to an enlightened, impartial, and free posterity.

For I must have a freedom facing me. Freedom is the only reality that I cannot transcend. How can one surpass what is constantly surpassing itself? If a being appears to me as pure freedom, if he is capable of founding himself entirely by himself, he can also justify what I have founded by taking it on as his own. Such a being would be God. The magic of love, fear, admiration, and respect can change a man into God. The humble adorer is nothing but an object, and his idol is not an object before anyone; toward whom could one transcend this pure and sovereign freedom? There is nothing beyond it.

But if suddenly other freedoms are revealed to me, the fascination dissipates. I remember the shock [*scandale*] I felt as a thirteen-year-old when a friend whom I admired violently contradicted an opinion of my father's. She judged my father; my father judged her in return. I could therefore appeal to my father against my friend, to my friend against my father. In this going back and forth, the absolute slipped away. I could no longer rely on anyone. My dismay lasted a long time. Whom should I care about pleasing?

I am dealing not with one freedom but with *several* freedoms. And precisely because they are free, they do not agree among themselves. Kantian ethics enjoins me to seek the support of all of humanity, but we have seen that there exists no heaven where the reconciliation of human judgments is accomplished. If certain works are hardly discussed anymore, it's because they have ceased to move us; they have become museum objects or relics. But one must not believe that they are justified simply because they are written down in history. Certainly without Sophocles or Malherbe,[99] literature would not have been what it is, but that confers no necessity upon their works because literature need not be what it is. It is; that's all. Here, one finds the point of view of the universal that allows neither praise nor blame since no void within it could even be supposed. Success appears only through a definite project that posits an end and carves out a retrospective appeal behind it. The dilettante who claims to love everything loves nothing. In order to be pleased about the existence of Rimbaud or Cézanne,[100] one must prefer a certain poetry and a certain way of painting above all others. An object is grasped as having needed to

131

be what it has been only if a singular choice flows back from the future toward it. This very reality that we throw into the world will be saved only if others found a future that envelops it by surpassing it, and only if new objects choose it in the past for the future. We cannot, therefore, be satisfied with a simple verbal approval; only the conceited man is content with that because he is only looking for the hollow appearance of being. But a more demanding man knows that words cannot suffice to necessitate the object that he has founded. He asks that a real place be reserved for him on earth. It is not enough that others listen to my tale; the listener must wait hungrily for my words. A woman quickly tires of an indifferent admiration; she wants to be loved because love alone will create an essential need of her. The writer does not only want to be read; he wants to have influence, he wants to be imitated and pondered. The inventor asks that the tool he invented be used. But human projects are separate and may even fight against each other. To me, my being appears condemned to remain forever divided. A loyal ally is also a traitor, and a venerable wise man a corrupter. No man is a hero to his valet. I can laugh at the hero with the valet, but the hero and his friends will laugh at me. If I laugh at the valet, he will laugh at me at the same time as at the hero. However, if I laugh at everyone, I end up alone in the world and everyone will laugh at me.

The most convenient solution would be to challenge the judgments that bother me by considering the men who pass them as simple objects, denying them their freedom. "They are barbarians, slaves," thought the decadent Romans in seeing themselves cursed by the men working and suffering for them. "He's a Negro," thought the planter of Virginia. And by rigid taboos, these parasitic societies try their best to defend the masters against the consciousnesses of the creatures whom they are exploiting. They must not be recognized as men. It is told that some white women used to get undressed in front of Indo-Chinese servant boys with indifference; those yellow people were not men.

But then the parasite ignores the human character of the objects that he uses. He lives in the midst of a foreign nature, among inert things, crushed by the enormous weight of things and subjected to a mysterious fate. In the tools, the machines, the houses, and the bread he eats, he does not recognize the mark of any freedom. Only the matter remains, and to the extent that he depends on matter, he also is only matter and passivity. In suppressing man's empire over things, he makes himself a thing among things. And he gains nothing in this metamorphosis. If we assume that, for security reasons, one administered to the servants a magic potion that transforms them into beasts, no reconciliation would be thus realized between men. Faced with this new animal species, the masters would still constitute a divided humanity. The parasite becomes human again only in turning toward his peers, and he then finds himself in danger before their freedoms.

And besides, man is not free to treat other men as things, as he likes. In spite of taboos, prejudices, and his willful blindness, the master knows that he must speak to the slave. One speaks only to men. Language is an appeal to the other's freedom since the sign is only a sign through a consciousness that grasps it again. He feels the look of the slave. As soon as he is looked at, he is the one who is object.*[101] He is a tyrant who is cruel or timid, resolute or hesitant; if he tries to transcend that transcendence, thinking, "Those are the thoughts of a slave," he knows that the slave also transcends that thought, and in the struggle that unfolds here, the slave's freedom is recognized by the very defense that the master puts up. All men are free, and as soon as we deal with them, we experience their freedom. If we want to disregard these dangerous freedoms, we must turn away from men. But then our being draws back and loses itself. Our being realizes itself only by choosing to be in danger in the world, in danger before the foreign and divided freedoms that take hold of it.

However, we have a recourse against these freedoms: not stupid blindness but struggle, because we can in turn transcend the action by which they transcend us. "Who will be my witness?" wonders the pilot in Saint-Exupéry's *Pilote de guerre* [Flight to Arras],[102] who is sent on a dangerous mission at the moment of defeat. He challenges all testimonies; he himself witnesses others' cowardice and abandonment. I don't wish to be recognized by just anyone, because in communication with others, we look for the completion of the project in which our freedom is engaged, and therefore others must project me toward a future that I recognize as mine. For me it would be a bitter failure if my action were perpetuated by becoming useful to my adversaries. The project by which others confer necessity upon me must also be my project. There are blames and hatreds that I joyfully accept. The revolutionary who combats the conservative's project wishes to appear as a hostile force to him. In her memoirs, Gertrude Stein tells that Fernande Picasso was happy with a hat only if she heard bricklayers and workmen exclaim at length when they saw her, because for her, elegance was defined as a challenge to plain good sense.[103] If we struggle against a project, we choose to appear as an obstacle before it. There are projects that simply do not concern us; we consider the judgments where they are expressed with indifference. If, for example, it is a question of appreciating a poem, a banker is not competent,

*See *L'etre et le néant* [Being and Nothingness], by J-P Sartre, page 330.

133

and the banker would smile at the poet's advice. It may be that my disdain envelops not one particular competence but an entire man. It is the global project of his being that we reject and combat. So disdain becomes contempt. I am indifferent to any opinion of those whom I despise. "I didn't ask you for your opinion," one says in contempt, and even, "I am not speaking to you." For any speech, any expression is an appeal; true contempt is silence. It takes away even the taste for contradiction and for outrage. In the case of outrage, we ask that the other prove that his project is separate from ours. We want to become a ridiculous or hateful object for him. Thus there will no longer be complicity between us. But this is leaving him the initiative and consenting out of defiance to make ourselves into a thing. It is up to us to assert calmly that we are separating ourselves from him, that we are transcending him and that he is but an object before us.

It would be convenient to be able to use contempt as a weapon. One often tries hard to do this. A child or a young man, for example, who is esteemed by those around him chooses not to confront a foreign judgment face to face. He confines himself to his sphere and, in order to run no risk, disarms the rest of the world's opinion in advance. He goes through life with a sure step; whoever condemns him condemns themselves. But in doing this, he denies his freedom. To be free is to throw oneself into the world without weighing the consequences or stakes; it is to define any stake or any step oneself. The overly prudent man, on the contrary, must take care to not found any project other than that which enhances the prestige of the people who enhance his prestige. This timid vanity is the opposite of true pride. It also happens that a man who at first meets only with failure and disdain around him defends himself with repudiation. He wanted to be an athlete; he fails, so he begins to scorn athletes and sports. He esteems only bankers or soldiers now. But in thus renouncing his project, he betrays himself. And besides, one cannot at will cause contempt or esteem to be born within oneself. It is through the same project that, by defining the objects I found, I define myself and the public to whom my appeal is addressed. To love books, admire writers, and want to write: these were one and the same project for me in my childhood. Once the global choice has been posed, we can partially contradict it only through blindness and bad faith,[104] and bad faith carries doubt and uneasiness along with it. That is why so many conceited men are so unhappy with themselves. A fool always finds a greater fool who admires him, but he cannot at will hide from himself the fact that that fool is a fool, nor can he take foolishness for a virtue whenever it suits him. Freedom commands and does not obey. In vain does one try to deny or force it. If sports are truly my project, I still prefer being an unsuccessful athlete rather than being an honored obese man. This is why one cannot so easily triumph, even interiorly, over a hated rival. If I want to be courageous, skillful, and intelligent, I cannot scorn the courage, skill, or intelligence in the other.

The attitude of those who love only those who love them and indiscriminately scorn all those who scorn them is rightly seen as a weakness. One is rather suspicious that their love and their scorn are only a hollow appearance. Only by my free movement toward my being can I confirm in their being those from whom I expect a necessary foundation of my being. In order for men to be able to give me a place in the world, I must first make a world spring up around me where men have their place; I must love, want, and do. My action itself must define the public to which I propose it. The architect loves to build; he builds an edifice that will remain standing for centuries; he appeals to a long posterity. An actor, a dancer appeal only to their contemporaries. If I perfect an airplane motor, my invention is of interest to millions of men. If it is a matter of getting approval for my daily actions or passing words, I address myself only to those who are close to me. I can concretely appeal only to the men who exist for me, and they exist for me only if I have created ties with them or if I have made them into my neighbors. They exist as allies or as enemies according to whether my project agrees with theirs or contradicts it. But how would I not assume this very contradiction since I am the one who makes it exist by making myself such as I make myself?

Action

So here is my situation facing others: men are free, and I am thrown into the world among these foreign freedoms. I need them because once I have surpassed my own goals, my actions will fall back upon themselves, inert and useless, if they have not been carried off toward a new future by new projects. A man who survives alone on earth after a worldwide cataclysm must strive, like Ezekiel,[105] to resuscitate humanity, or he will have nothing left to do but die. The movement of my transcendence appears futile [*vain*] to me as soon as I have transcended it, but if, through other men, my transcendence is always prolonged further than the project I am now forming, I could never surpass it.

In order for my transcendence to be absolutely impossible to transcend, all of humanity must extend my project toward ends that were mine. Who, then, would transcend it? Outside of it, there would be no one, and it would be entirely my accomplice; no one would judge me. But I must renounce this hope; men are separate, opposed. I must reconcile myself to the struggle.

But for *whom* shall I struggle? My goal is to achieve being. Let's repeat again that it is not a question of egoism here. The idea of self-interest is based on the idea of a ready-made self toward which the subject that I am would transcend itself, taking it for a supreme end, instead of throwing myself through the project toward different ends of a self that doesn't exist anywhere as a given. To seek to be is to seek *being*, because *there is no* being except through the presence of a subjectivity that discloses it, and it is necessarily from the heart of my subjectivity that I rush toward it. I therefore struggle in order to be. I struggle in order to possess a toy or a jewel, in order to take a trip, eat a fruit, or build a house. But that is not all. I adorn myself, I travel, and I build among men. I cannot live shut away in an ivory tower. Some theories such as those about art for art's sake are wrong to imagine that a poem or a painting is an inhuman and self-sufficient thing. It is an object made by man, for man. Of course, it is made neither to entertain nor to edify. It does not respond to a preexisting need that it must fulfill. It is a surpassing of the past, a gratuitous and free invention, but in its newness, it demands to be understood and justified. Men must love it, want it, and prolong it. The artist cannot lose interest in the situation of the men around him. His own flesh is engaged in others. I will therefore struggle so that free men will give my actions and my works their necessary place.

But how does one resort to struggle here since these men must freely grant me their approval? Of course, wanting to obtain a spontaneous love or admiration by violence is absurd. One laughs at Nero,[106] who wanted to seduce by force. I want the other to recognize my actions as valid and to make them into his good by taking them up in his name toward the future. But I cannot count on such gratitude if I first contradict the other's project. He will see me only as an obstacle. I make an error in judgment if I force the other to live, even though he would like to die, on the pretext that I need a companion likely to justify my existence. He will curse me throughout his life. Respect for the other's freedom is not an abstract rule. It is the first condition of my successful effort. I can only appeal to the other's freedom, not constrain it. I can invent the most urgent appeals, try my best to charm it, but it will remain free to respond to those appeals or not, no matter what I do.

But in order for this rapport with the other to be established, two conditions must be met. First, I must be allowed to appeal. I will therefore struggle against those who want to stifle my voice, prevent me from expressing myself, and prevent me from being. To make myself exist before free men, I will often be compelled to treat some men as objects. A prisoner will kill his jailer to join up with his comrades. It's a shame that the jailer cannot also be a comrade, but it would be even more of a shame for the prisoner never to have any comrades again.

Next, I must have before me men who are free *for me,* who can respond to my appeal.

In any situation, the other's freedom is total because the situation is only to be surpassed, and freedom is equal in every surpassing. An ignorant man who strives to educate himself is as free as the scholar who invents a new hypothesis. We respect equally in all beings the free effort to transcend oneself toward being. What one scorns are the resignations of freedom. One cannot establish a moral hierarchy among human situations. But, as far as I am concerned, there are some of these transcendences that I can transcend, and that become fixed for me as objects. There are others that I can only accompany or that surpass me. Tess d'Uberville [*sic*] loves Clare.[107] The three farmer's daughters who also love Clare do not transcend Tess's love. With Tess, they transcend themselves toward Clare. But if we discover Clare's weaknesses, if we do not love him, all the while recognizing Tess's freedom, we see only an object that is foreign to us in her love. The other's freedom exists as separate from me only when it reaches for a goal that is foreign or has already been surpassed. The ignorant man who uses his freedom to surpass his state of ignorance can do nothing for the physicist who has just invented a complicated theory. The sick man who wears himself out by struggling against sickness or the slave against slavery care for neither poetry, nor astronomy, nor the improvement of aviation. They first need health, leisure, security, and the freedom to do with themselves what they want. The other's freedom can do something for me only if my own goals can, in turn, serve as its point of departure. In using the tool that I have fabricated, the other prolongs its existence. The scholar can speak only to men who have arrived at a degree of knowledge equal to his own, so he proposes his theory to them as the basis for new work. The other can accompany my transcendence only if he is at the same spot on the path as I.

In order for our appeals not to be lost in the void, there must be men ready to hear me close by, and these men must be my peers. I, myself, cannot go backward, because the movement of my transcendence is carrying me ceaselessly forward, and I cannot walk toward the future alone. I would lose myself in a desert where none of my steps would matter. I must therefore strive to create for men situations such that they can accompany and surpass my transcendence. I need their freedom to be available to use and conserve me in surpassing me. I ask for health, knowledge, well-being, and leisure for men so that their freedom is not consumed in fighting sickness, ignorance, and misery.

Thus, man must be engaged in two convergent directions. He founds ob-

137

jects where he finds the fixed reflection of his transcendence. He transcends himself by a forward movement that is his freedom itself, and at each step, he strives to pull men to himself. He resembles the leader of an expedition who marks out a new route for his march and who constantly goes back to gather up the stragglers, running forward again to lead his escort further on. But, all men do not consent to follow. Some stay put or engage themselves on divergent roads. Some even try their best to stop his march and that of his followers. Wherever persuasion fails, only violence remains to defend oneself.

In one sense, violence is not an evil, since one can do nothing either for or against a man. To bring a child into the world is not to found him; to kill a man is not to destroy him. We never reach anything but the facticity of others. But precisely in choosing to act on that facticity, we give up taking the other for a freedom, and we restrict, accordingly, the possibilities of expanding our being. The man to whom I do violence is not my peer, and I need men to be my peers. The resort to violence arouses correspondingly less regret in cases where it seemed less possible to appeal to the freedom of the man to whom violence has been done. One unscrupulously uses force against a child or a sick person. But if I did violence to all men, I would be alone in the world, and lost. If I make a group of men into a herd of cattle, I reduce the human reign accordingly. And even if I oppress only one man, all of humanity appears in him as a pure thing to me. If a man is an ant that can be unscrupulously crushed, all men taken together are but an anthill.[108] One cannot, therefore, lightheartedly accept resorting to force. It is the mark of a failure that nothing can offset. If the universal ethics of Kant and Hegel end in optimism, it is because in denying individuality, they also deny failure. But the individual is; failure is. If a scrupulous heart hesitates so long before making a political decision, it is not that political problems are difficult, but that they are unsolvable. And yet abstention is also impossible; one always acts. We are condemned to failure because we are condemned to violence. We are condemned to violence because man is divided and in conflict with himself, because men are separate and in conflict among themselves. Through violence the child will be made into a man and the horde into a society. Renouncing the struggle would be renouncing transcendence, renouncing being. However, no success will ever erase the absolute outrage of each singular failure.

We should not believe either that success consists of calmly attaining a goal. Our goals are never anything but new points of departure. Everything begins when we have led the other to this goal. From there, where will he go? I do not content myself with the idea that he will always go somewhere. Without me, he would have also been somewhere. I want it to be *my* project that he prolongs. It is up to each person to decide how far his project extends without being destroyed. Would Kant have found himself in Hegel? Would he have seen the Hegelian system as his negation? In order to respond, one must know what, in his eyes, the essential truth of his philosophy was. But in any case, his project did not extend to infinity. If Kant had wanted only philosophy, he would not have needed to write. In any event, philosophy existed. He wanted *a* philosophy created by a philosophical development that was his own. We want to be necessitated in our singularity, and we can be so only through singular projects. We depend on the other's freedom; he can forget, ignore, or use us for ends that are not our own. One of the meanings of the *Trial* [1925] described by Kafka is that no verdict can ever come to a conclusion. We live in a state of indefinite procrastination. This is also the meaning of what M. Blanchot says in *Aminadab:* the most important thing is to not lose, but one never wins.[109] We must assume our actions in uncertainty and risk, and that is precisely the essence of freedom. Freedom is not decided with a view to a salvation that would be granted in advance. It signs no pact with the future. If it could be defined by the final point [*terme*] for which it aims, it would no longer be freedom. But an end is never a final point; it remains open to infinity. It is only an end because freedom stops there, thus defining my singular being at the heart of formless infinity. What concerns me is only to reach my end; the rest no longer depends on me. What the other will found based on me will belong to him and does not belong to me. I act only by assuming the risks of that future. They are the reverse of my finitude, and I am free in assuming my finitude.

Thus man can act; he must act. He is only in transcending himself. He acts in risk, in failure. He must assume the risk. By throwing himself toward the uncertain future, he founds his present with certainty. But failure cannot be assumed.

Conclusion

"And after that?" says Cineas.

I ask that freedoms turn back toward me in order to necessitate my actions. But can't reflection surpass this very action that claims to justify me? Men approve my work; their approval is in turn fixed as an object. It is as futile [*vaine*] as my work itself. Shouldn't one conclude that all is vanity?[110]

What reflection reveals to me is that every project leaves room for a new question. Within myself I have a negative power with respect to my project and myself through which I appear as emerging in nothingness. It releases me from the illusion of false objectivity. I learn from it that there is no other end in the world besides my ends, and no other place besides the one that I carve out for myself. And other men do not have in their possession the values that I wish to attain either. If I transcend them, they can do nothing for me. In order to be recognized by them, I must first recognize them. Our freedoms support each other like the stones in an arch, but in an arch that no pillars support. Humanity is entirely suspended in a void that it creates itself by its reflection on its plenitude.

But since this void is only a reverse side, since reflection is possible only after spontaneous movement, why grant it a predominance and condemn human projects by comparing them with the tranquillity of nothingness? Reflection makes nothingness spring up around me, but reflection is not carried in its heart; it is not authorized to speak in its name and judge the human condition from its point of view. Wherever there is a point of view, there is not nothingness. And to tell the truth, I can take no other point of view but my own.

One and the same finite project throws me into this world and toward these men. If I love a man with an absolute love, his approval is sufficient for me. If I act for a city, a country, I appeal to my fellow citizens, to my fellow countrymen. If I create real ties between me and future centuries, my voice crosses the centuries. Of course, in any event, there is a point where my transcendence runs aground, but reflection cannot surpass it. I exist today, and today throws me into a future defined by my present project. Wherever the project stops, my future also stops, and if I claim to contemplate myself from the depths of this time where I am not, that is but a pretense and I am only uttering empty words. For eternity a minute is equal to a century, for infinity the atom is equal to the nebula. But I am floating neither in infinity nor in eternity; I am situated in a world that my presence defines. One only transcends oneself toward an end, and if I have precisely posited my end before me, toward what could I surpass it? Toward what could I transcend an exclusive love during the time that I love? When other men have begun to exist for me, then I could transcend that love. But I cannot transcend toward nothing the totality of men whom my project causes to exist for me.

One can surpass one project only by realizing another project. To transcend a transcendence is not to effectuate a progress, because these different projects are separate. The transcendent transcendence can in turn be transcended. No instant joins up with the eternal. Ecstasy and anguish still take their place in time; they are projects themselves. Every thought, every feeling is project. Thus the life of man does not appear as a progress but as a cycle. "What good does it do?" he says, and he continues his task. I now see that moment of doubt or of ecstasy where all projects seem useless [*vain*] to me as a fit of ill humor or puerile exaltation. Between these two moments, who will judge? They exist together only by a third moment that must in turn be judged. That is no doubt why so much importance is attached to the last wish of a dying man. It is not only one wish among others, but it is the one in which the dying man has grasped his whole life again. Whoever wants to continue to affirm a dear friend's life against death prolongs his last instant by maintaining its privilege. It is only when I separate myself from the dead person in order to look at him from the outside that the last instant becomes an instant among others. Then the dead person is really dead; I transcend all his wishes equally.

We are free to transcend all transcendence. We can always escape toward an "elsewhere," but this elsewhere is still somewhere, in the heart of our human condition. We never escape from that human condition, and we have no way to envision it from the outside in order to judge it. It alone makes language [*la parole*] possible. It is with our human condition that good and evil are defined. The words "utility," "progress," and "fear" have meaning only in a world where the project has made points of view and ends appear. They presuppose this project and cannot be applied to it. Man knows nothing other than himself and cannot even dream of anything that is not human. To what can he therefore be compared? What man could judge man? In whose name would he speak?

NOTES

1. Pyrrhus (319–272 B.C.E.) was the militaristic king of Hellenistic Epirus, on the Ionian Sea. In 281, Cineas, his chief adviser, attempted without success to dissuade Pyrrhus from invading Italy. After a victory against the Romans in 279, his heavy casualties caused Pyrrhus to declare, "One more such victory and I am lost," thus the origin of the term "Pyrrhic victory."

2. Benjamin Constant (1767–1830) was a Franco-Swiss political writer and forerunner of the modern psychological novelist. The quote is from Constant's novella *Adolf: A Narrative Found among the Papers of an Unknown Person,* trans. Paul Hookum (New York: Knopf, 1925): "I came to the conclusion that there was no object of desire worth the trouble of effort" (28).

3. Élan refers to *élan vital,* the vital impetus, or creative surge of life, from Henri Bergson (1859–1941), *Creative Evolution,* trans. A. Mitchell (1907; New York: Modern Library, 1911), 58. "Spontaneity" comes from Bergson's distinction between mind (characterized by spontaneity, unforeseeability, and freedom) and matter (characterized by inertia and necessity), in *Time and Free Will: An Essay on the Immediate Date of Consciousness,* trans. F. L. Pogson (1889; New York: Macmillan, 1913), 220.

4. Don Juan was a legendary libertine whose story is dramatized in Molière's *Le festin de Pierre* (1665) and Mozart's opera *Don Giovanni* (1787), among others. Hegel's reference to Don Juan and Faust (*Phenomenology of Mind,* trans. J. B. Baillie [New York: Harper, 1967],

section 5.B.a., "Pleasure and Necessity") provides an argument against Faust that equally works for Don Juan. Here, hedonism appears as the beginning of the movement toward the good life. But even Don Juan will eventually be led out of hedonism toward a more ethical life. This is the section to which commentators refer in speaking of Don Juan, but Hegel mentions only Faust, though many use Don Juan interchangeably. However, Kierkegaard's book *Either/Or,* volume 1, is riddled with references to Don Juan and the similarities and differences from Faust.

5. *Candide* (1759), a satiric novel by the French Enlightenment writer Voltaire (1694–1778), deals with the cruel truths of this "best of all possible worlds," a place where unguarded optimism is foolish and relentless pessimism leads nowhere. The novel's conclusion is that we should tend our own garden rather than speculate on unanswerable philosophical questions.

6. "What happens . . .": the French expression is "après nous, le déluge." Charlemagne (742–814) was king of the Franks (768–814), king of the Lombards (774–814), and emperor of Western Europe (800–814).

7. The question of the measure of man is a play on the claim of the Greek philosopher Protagorus (ca. 490–ca. 420 B.C.E.) that "of all things the measure is Man."

8. Albert Camus (1913–60) was a French existentialist writer and 1957 Nobel laureate; *L'étranger* (1942) was translated as *The Stranger* in the United States and *The Outsider* in the U.K.

9. The word "inert" is from Bergson's distinction between spontaneity and inertia; see note 3, above.

10. The Nazi occupation of France began in June 1940.

11. "Being made" (*se faisant*), or becoming, is contrasted with "the ready-made" (*tout fait*), or inert, in Bergson's *Creative Evolution:* "Our consciousness . . . must detach itself from the already-made and attach itself to the being made" (259).

12. Vincent Van Gogh (1853–90) was a Dutch postimpressionist painter. Paul Gauguin (1848–1903) was a French painter, printmaker, and sculptor.

13. "Lazy": see Bergson's *Time and Free Will:* "We often resign our freedom . . . by inertia or indolence" (169); and *Creative Evolution,* on man's "tendency . . . toward the vegetative life," where "torpor and unconsciousness are always lying in wait" (125).

14. Indra is a Vedic god of India.

15. Aristippus (435–366 B.C.E.), a Greek philosopher, was a disciple of Socrates and founder of the Cyrenaic school of hedonism, the ethic of pleasure. Horace (65–8 B.C.E.) was a Latin lyric poet and satirist under the emperor Augustus. The familiar phrase "seize the day" (*carpe diem*) occurs in his *Odes* (I, xi). André Gide (1869–1951), a French writer, humanist, and moralist, received the Nobel Prize for literature in 1947. His novel *Nourritures terrestres* (The Fruits of the Earth) was begun in 1893 but not completed until 1896–97.

16. The duke of Mantua is incorrectly cited as a character in William Shakespeare's play *Twelfth Night.* The Shakespearean character is Orsino, the duke of Illyria. Mantua is a city in northern Italy; Illyria is an ancient country in the northwestern part of the Balkan peninsula. We find the first reference to *Twelfth Night* in the journal of John Manningham in 1602. It is convincingly argued, however, that a more likely date for its first appearance is 1600–1601.

17. See Bergson, in *Time and Free Will:* "A sensation, by the mere fact of being prolonged, is altered to the point of becoming unbearable" (153).

18. For "presence" and "absence," see Bergson's description, in *Creative Evolution,* of the thread of experience as "the existence of the present" (319–20), and the starting point of every human action as a dissatisfaction and "a feeling of absence" (323).

19. A Stoic is a follower of Stoicism, the Greek school of philosophy founded by Zeno, who taught that men should be free from passion and submit to unavoidable necessity. G. W. F. Hegel's *Phenomenology of Mind* (pub. 1807) describes stoicism as a withdrawal and abstraction from the world into interiority that results in an empty and subjective concept of freedom.

20. See Gide's *The Fruits of the Earth,* trans. Dorothy Bussy (New York: Knopf, 1949): "But now I understand that God, permanently present in all that passes, dwells not in the object but in love; and now I know how to enjoy the quiet eternity in the fleeting moment" (199).

21. The citation is not from *Incidences* but from Gide's *Journals, Volume 1: 1893–1913,* trans. Justin O'Brien (Urbana: University of Illinois Press, 2000): "At San Sebastian, on the square, we ordered Spanish chocolate, thick and strongly flavored with cinnamon; it is served in little cups, much too small to my way of thinking. Jeanne claims she cannot endure Spanish chocolate, so she asks for a French chocolate. Almost at once she is brought some of this chocolate; yes, the same. But the cup is much bigger and Jeanne declares it to be excellent. Em. is willing to try the Spanish chocolate, but shudders at the thought of the cakes made of eggs. And since I am irritated to see them both so resigned (or decided) to enjoy this country only through their eyes or, at most, to taste it with the tip of their tongues, I thought as I sank my teeth into that oily, curdled, saffron-flavored paste that I was biting right into Spain itself; it was terrible" (126).

22. Psychasthenia is a disorder characterized by anxiety, obsessions, and fixed ideas. Pierre Janet (1859–1947), a prominent French neurologist and psychiatrist, first described psychasthenia in *Les obsessions et la psychasthénie* (Obsessions and Psychasthenia) (1903).

23. Epicureans were followers of the Greek philosopher Epicurus (342–270 B.C.E.), who maintained that the highest good is pleasure, interpreted as the freedom from disturbance or pain. "Ataraxia" is a freedom from disturbances of mind or person; a stoical indifference.

24. Beauvoir appropriates Hegel's reading of Stoicism in *The Phenomenology of Mind,* where Hegel claims that Stoicism results only in an empty concept of freedom. See 4.B., on Stoicism, Scepticism, and the Unhappy Consciousness.

25. "Upspringing" (*jaillissement*) comes from Bergson's *Creative Evolution,* 181.

26. Blaise Pascal (1623–62) was a French scientist and religious philosopher whose religious writings were posthumously published as *Pensées de M. Pascal sur la religion et sur quelques autres sujets* (1670). The citation is from Pensée 136; see *Pascal's Pensées,* trans. A. J. Krailsheimer (1966; London: Penguin, 1995), 37.

27. Paul Valéry (1871–1945) was a French poet, essayist, and critic.

28. Georg Wilhelm Friedrich Hegel (1770–1831) was a German idealist philosopher. Beauvoir read his *Phenomenology of Mind* at the start of the Nazi occupation in July 1940; see her *Journal de guerre* (Paris: Gallimard, 1990), 339.

29. See Hegel's *The Logic of Hegel,* trans. W. Wallace, 2nd ed. (Oxford: Oxford University Press, 1892): "Exterior is the same content as Interior. . . . The appearance shows nothing that is not in the essence, and in the essence there is nothing but what is manifested" (252, ¶139); "Essence accordingly is not something beyond or behind appearance, but just because it is the essence which exists—the existence is Appearance (Forth-shinings)" (239, ¶131).

30. Martin Heidegger (1889–1976) was an influential German philosopher, student of Edmund Husserl, and important influence on French existential phenomenologists, including Beauvoir, who first read Heidegger in July 1939. See Beauvoir's *Lettres à Sartre,* ed. Sylvie Le Bon de Beauvoir, 2 vols. (Paris: Gallimard, 1990), 1:77; and Sartre's *Lettres à Castor,* ed. Simone de Beauvoir, 2 vols. (Paris: Gallimard, 1983), 1:235–36. For "a being of faraway places," see Heidegger's claim that "Dasein, in accordance with its spatiality, is proximally never here

but yonder," in *Being and Time*, trans. John Macquarrie and Edward Robinson (1927; New York: Harper and Row, 1962), bk. 1, ch. 3, ¶21–24.

31. "To what he is in the instant": see Heidegger's discussion of temporality and his claim in *Being and Time* that "[a]ny entity whose Essence is made up of existence, is essentially opposed to the possibility of our getting it in our grasp as an entity which is a whole" (bk. 2, ¶45).

32. The phrase *creux toujours futur* is from Paul Valéry's poem *Le cimetière marin* [The Graveyard by the Sea], ed. and trans. G. D. Martin (Edinburgh: Edinburgh University Press, 1971); first published in *La Nouvelle Revue Francaise,* June 1, 1920. The Centaur Press (Philadelphia) published the English translation in 1932.

33. Marcel Arland (1899–1986) was a French novelist, critic, and essayist. Jacques Chardonne (1884–1968), a French novelist and essayist, is best known for the novel *L'épithalame,* published by Gasset in 1921 and reissued in 1929. The English noun "epithalamium" refers to a wedding hymn in praise of the bride and bridegroom, often a metaphor for Christ and the church.

34. *Terres étrangères* (Foreign Lands) is a novel written in 1923 by Marcel Arland.

35. From Pensée 136: "That is why gaming and feminine society, war and high office are so popular. It is not that they really bring true happiness, nor that anyone imagines that true bliss comes from possessing money to be won at gaming or the hare that is hunted: no one would take it as a gift. What people want is not the easy peaceful life that allows us to think of our unhappy condition, nor the dangers of war, nor the burdens of office, but the agitation that takes our mind off it and diverts us. That is why we prefer the hunt to the capture" (*Pascal's Pensées,* 139).

36. Benedict de Spinoza (1632–77), a Dutch-Jewish philosopher, was the foremost exponent of seventeenth-century rationalism.

37. Ambiguity is a central concept in Beauvoir's ethics; see *Pour une morale de l'ambiguïté* [The Ethics of Ambiguity] (Paris: Gallimard, 1947).

38. Although the French term *scandale* can convey the same meaning as its English cognate, it can also mean "a troubling, contradictory religious fact." In this text, *scandaliser* has been translated as "to outrage" and *scandale* as "outrage," unless otherwise noted.

39. Zeno of Elea (ca. 495–ca. 430 B.C.E.), a Greek philosopher and mathematician, formulated paradoxes to defend Parmenides's theory of Being and demonstrate that motion and multiplicity are impossible. One of them used Achilles and the tortoise to show that if the tortoise has a head start in the race, then Achilles will not be able to beat him because he must first cross one-half the distance to the tortoise and then half of the remainder as the tortoise moves on into infinity. See Bergson's discussion of Zeno's attempt to reduce movement to immobile states, in *Creative Evolution*, 335–38.

40. On the "individual" and the "universal," see Hegel, *The Phenomenology of Mind,* 89–90 and 130; see also William Wallace, trans., *The Logic of Hegel,* 2nd ed. (Oxford: Oxford University Press, 1892), 291–97.

41. The works of Gustave Flaubert (1821–80), along with those of Stendhal and Balzac, presaged the realist French novel.

42. The abbey of Thélème was a fictional abbey given to a monk by Gargantua, in Francis Rabelais (1494–1553), *Gargantua and Pantagruel,* book 1, chap. 1.57.

43. Amalricians were a sect of followers of Amalric of Bena (d. 1207?), a heretical French professor of philosophy. Banned by the pope, their heresy resulted in the temporary ban on Aristotle and the Arabic philosophers at the University of Paris.

44. Paul Claudel (1868–1955) was a French dramatist, poet, and diplomat whose mystical Catholicism was an important early influence on Beauvoir.

45. Saint Francis of Assisi (1182?–1226) was the founder of the Franciscans and a leader of the movement of evangelical poverty in the early thirteenth century.

46. See Claudel's *The Satin Slipper,* trans. Reverend Fr. John O'Connor (New York: Sheed and Ward, 1931): "You had nothing but praise for everything, but it vexes me to see that you make use of none" (95).

47. Angelus Silesius (Johannes Scheffler, 1624–77) was a Lutheran-turned-Catholic poet/hymnist. His most famous work is *Cherubinischer Wandersmann* (The Cherubinic Wanderer) (1674–75), an anthology of theological couplets and aphorisms. The theme of divine reciprocity runs through many of the aphorisms, but Beauvoir is probably referring here to number 18, "I Do as God Does" ("God loves me above all; if I love Him the same, I give Him just as much as I receive from Him"), or perhaps number 100, "One Sustains the Other" ("God shelters me as much as I do shelter Him; His being I sustain, sustained I am therein"). Couplets 272 and 278 refer to man as "God's Other Self."

48. Moses (thirteenth century B.C.E.), a Hebrew prophet, teacher, and leader, delivered his people from Egyptian slavery. According to the Book of Exodus, God spoke to Moses from a burning bush and from on top of Mount Sinai.

49. Abraham (early second millennium B.C.E.), the first of the Hebrew patriarchs, was considered the "father of faith" and was revered in Judaism, Christianity, and Islam. According to the Book of Genesis, Abraham heard God tell him to kill his beloved son, Isaac, as a demonstration of his faith. Søren Kierkegaard (1813–55) was a Danish religious philosopher, existentialist, and critic of rationalism. Abraham is the privileged figure in Kierkegaard's *Fear and Trembling,* trans. Walter Lowrie (1843; Princeton: Princeton University Press, 1968); see, for instance, pages 22–37.

50. Franz Kafka (1883–1924) was a Czech-born German-language writer of visionary fiction.

51. Henri Bergson, the leading French philosopher in the early twentieth century, won the Nobel Prize for literature in 1927. He was an important early philosophical influence on Beauvoir, whose 1926 diary quotes at length from his *Time and Free Will* (1889).

52. Jules Laforgue (1860–87) was a French symbolist poet.

53. "A determined [*déterminée*] place in the world": *déterminée* here seems to imply both "definite" and "subject to determinism."

54. Beauvoir is referring here to the chapter on "the origin of negation," in Jean-Paul Sartre, *Being and Nothingness,* trans. Hazel Barnes (New York: Philosophical Library, 1953), 3–45.

55. "Reconciliation" refers to Hegelian *Aufhebung,* which is the raising and preserving of a contradiction through synthesis. Beauvoir criticizes reconciliation because, as she will explain further in *Pour une morale de l'ambiguïté* (The Ethics of Ambiguity), it evades the paradoxical condition of ambiguity.

56. Friedrich Nietzsche (1844–1900), a German existentialist philosopher, challenged the foundations of traditional morality and Christianity. *The Gay Science* was first published in 1882.

57. "My son is a determined being": "determined [*determiné*]" here implies "subject to determinism" rather than "resolute."

58. Cubism was a reaction to impressionism, a late nineteenth-century French movement in painting.

59. Maximilien Robespierre (1758–94) was a radical Jacobin leader of the French Revolution and the chief instigator of the Reign of Terror. Thermidor was the eleventh month (July

19–August 18) of the French Republican calendar. During the French Revolution, the revolution of Thermidor was the revolt initiated on 9 Thermidor, year II (July 27, 1794), resulting in the fall of Robespierre and the end of revolutionary fervor and the Reign of Terror. The ascent to power of Napoleon Bonaparte (1769–1821), French general, first consul (1799–1804), and emperor of France (1804–15), officially ended the French Revolution.

60. A "moment" in Hegelian dialectics is a temporal stage in the dialectic or one essential part of reality.

61. "Facticity" (*Faktizität*), from Heidegger's *Being and Time*, means self-understanding as inextricably bound up with the Being of those entities encountered in the world (bk. 1, ch. 2, ¶12).

62. Demosthenes (384–322 B.C.E.), an Athenian statesman and orator, roused Athens to oppose Philip of Macedon and, later, his son, Alexander the Great.

63. Philip (382–336 B.C.E.) was the eighteenth king of Macedonia (359–336 B.C.E.). By 339 B.C.E. he had gained domination over all Greece by military and diplomatic means, thus preparing the way for its expansion under his son, Alexander III (356–323 B.C.E.), also known as Alexander the Great. Alexander succeeded his father as king of Macedonia (336–323 B.C.E.), overthrew the Persian empire, and laid the foundation for the Hellenistic world of territorial kingdoms.

64. Christopher Marlowe (1564–93), the great English writer and playwright who perfected dramatic blank verse, wrote several versions of the play *Dr. Faustus*. Faust, a legendary hero in Western folklore, is a German necromancer or astrologer who sells his soul to the devil in exchange for knowledge and power. Mephistopheles, a name probably invented by the anonymous author of the first *Faustbuch* (1587), is the familiar spirit of the Devil in late settings of the legend of Faustus.

65. *Être là* is the standard French translation of Heidegger's *Dasein* or *Da-sein*, generally left untranslated in English or rendered as "being-there." The term was mistranslated as *réalité humaine* in the first translations of Heidegger into French, which resulted in serious misunderstandings of Heidegger.

66. Stendhal (1783–1842) was the pseudonym of Marie-Henri Beyle, a French writer who played a major role in the development of the modern novel; see Beauvoir's chapter on Stendhal in *The Second Sex*.

67. *Être pour mourir* is the French equivalent of the Heidegger term conventionally translated as "being toward death." We translate *pour* as "for" to preserve the continuity of the translation of *pour* in the passage below.

68. "Conversion" is Beauvoir's interpretation of the relationship between inauthenticity and authenticity in Heidegger's *Being and Time*. In *The Ethics of Ambiguity*, Beauvoir will use "conversion" to mark Husserl's phenomenological reduction.

69. Jean-Paul Sartre (1905–80), the French novelist, playwright, and leading existential philosopher, was an intimate friend and lifelong associate of Simone de Beauvoir.

70. "Man makes so as to be" (*l'homme fait pour être*) also means "man makes for being."

71. "Throwness" (*Geworfenheit*), from Heidegger's *Being and Time*, describes the sense in which Dasein finds itself delivered over to a very specific, situated existence; it is intimately connected to "facticity" (see note 61 above), which is disclosed to Dasein in throwness; see bk. 1, ch. 5, ¶38: "Falling and Throwness."

72. "Duration," or persistence through the flow of time, was, for Bergson, an aspect of freedom: "To act freely is to recover possession of oneself, and to get back into pure duration" (*Time and Free Will*, 231–32).

73. King Candaule is a character in a tale from Herodotus 1.7–14 and a play (1901) by André Gide. King Candaule was so proud of his wife's beauty that he had her dance naked in front of a friend, Gyges, who later killed the king and wed the queen.

74. Henry David Thoreau (1817–62) was an American author and naturalist.

75. Alain Gerbault (1893–1941), a French navigator, crossed the Atlantic Ocean alone in 1923 in a small sailboat, the *Firecrest.*

76. Saint Teresa of Avila (1515–82), a Spanish nun and the author of spiritual classics, was one of the great mystics and religious women of the Roman Catholic Church.

77. Saint John of the Cross (1542–91) was one of the greatest Christian mystics and Spanish poets. He was the subject of a 1924 doctoral thesis by Jean Baruzi, Beauvoir's mentor in philosophy at the Sorbonne in 1927.

78. Georges Bernanos (1888–1948) was a French novelist and essayist. *Diary of a Country Priest* was first published in 1936 and was translated into English in 1937.

79. The phrase *worum willen,* from Heidegger's *Being and Time* (84), is hyphenated in the later German editions and translated as "for-the-sake-of-which" (see Heidegger, *Being and Time,* bk. 1, ch. 3, ¶18, p. 116, n. 2, and p. 119, n. 1).

80. In Homer's *Odyssey,* Orestes, the son of Agamemnon and Clytemnestra, avenges his father's death by killing his mother; Hermione is the daughter of Helen and Menelaus.

81. See *Horace et les Curiaces* (Paris: Gallimard, 1942).

82. "Existence . . . essence": see Heidegger's *Being and Time:* "The 'essence' of Dasein lies in its existence" (bk. 1, ch. 1, ¶9).

83. Socrates (470–399 B.C.E.) was the first of the trio of great ancient Greeks—Socrates, Plato, and Aristotle—who laid the foundations of Western philosophy. Tried for "impiety against the gods of the city" and "corrupting the young," he was condemned to death and forced to drink a poison, hemlock.

84. Fyodor Dostoevsky (1821–81), a Russian novelist and short-story writer, was sentenced to four years at hard labor in a Siberian penal colony in the 1840s for his involvement with a group of radical utopians.

85. René Descartes (1596–1650), a French mathematician, scientist, and philosopher, is considered the father of modern philosophy. In Meditation Four of *Meditations on First Philosophy* (1641), Descartes distinguishes between the freedom of willing and the power or faculty of willing in order to explain the possibility of erroneous judgments.

86. Immanuel Kant (1724–1804) was a German philosopher and founder of critical transcendental philosophy. See Kant's *Critique of Pure Reason,* trans. N. Kemp Smith, 2nd ed. (New York: St. Martin's, 1965): "The light dove, cleaving the air in her free flight, and feeling its resistance, might imagine that its flight would be still easier in empty space" (47).

87. *Ouk ephiemenon* means "something not aimed at or desired," what the Stoics termed "an indifferent"; there is an apparent typo in the French edition, "Ouch ephiemon."

88. Beauvoir paraphrases the standard French translation of Matthew 18:6–8 and Luke 17:1–2.

89. "Each person is guilty . . ." (Chacun est responsible de tout devant tous) is from Dostoevsky's *The Brothers Karamazov,* trans. R. Pevear and L. Volokhonsky (New York: Vintage Books, 1991), 164. It also appears as the epigraph for Beauvoir's novel *Le sang des autres* [The Blood of Others] (Paris: Gallimard, 1945), written during the Nazi occupation.

90. See note 11, above, on Bergson's distinction between the "ready-made" (*tout fait*) and the "being made" (*se faisant*).

91. "False objectivity" is a consciousness of the world that mistakenly takes values as always already given.

92. Beauvoir often cited other authors from memory, occasionally confusing one work with another, or capturing the gist of a passage without quoting the words precisely. This appears to be an example of the latter. Spinoza was fond of using dogs and horses to illustrate points, but the passage to which Beauvoir is referring probably comes from the end of the preface of the *Ethics*, book 4: "say that something passes from a lesser to a greater perfection, and opposite, I do not understand that he is changed from one essential form to another. For example, a horse is destroyed as much if it changes into a man as if it is changed into an insect. Rather, we conceive that the power of acting, insofar as it is understood through his nature, is increased or diminished."

93. Charles-Louis de Secondat, baron de La Brède et de Montesquieu (1689–1755), was a French political philosopher and satirist. His *L'Histoire veritable d'Arsace et Ismenie* was composed around 1730 but was not published until after his death.

94. *Négatités:* see Sartre's *Being and Nothingness,* "The Phenomenological Concept of Nothingness" (21).

95. Jean Racine (1639–99), a French dramatic poet and historiographer, was renowned for his mastery of French classical tragedy.

96. Christian, Cyrano, and Roxanne are characters in the play *Cyrano de Bergerac,* written by the French playwright Edmond Rostand (1868–1918).

97. Henry de Montherlant (1896–1972) was a French novelist and dramatist whose works reflect his own egocentric and autocratic personality; see Beauvoir's discussion of Montherlant in *The Second Sex.*

98. "The they" (*das Man*) is Heidegger's term for the anonymous and inauthentic everyday being with others in the public sphere that is a flight from death.

99. Sophocles (ca. 496–406 B.C.E.), with Aeschylus and Euripides, was one of the great tragic playwrights of classical Athens. François de Malherbe (1555–1628) was a French poet who prepared the way for French classicism.

100. Arthur Rimbaud (1854–91), a French poet and adventurer, won renown within the symbolist movement and markedly influenced modern poetry. The French painter Paul Cézanne (1839–1906) was one of the greatest postimpressionists; his work was one inspiration for cubism.

101. See *Being and Nothingness,* 283. See Beauvoir's *L'invitée* (She Came to Stay), on the look of the other.

102. Antoine de Saint-Exupéry (1900–1944) was a French aviator and writer.

103. Gertrude Stein (1874–1946) was an American avant-garde writer whose Paris home was a salon for leading artists and writers of the period between World Wars I and II. Fernande Olivier Picasso (1881–1965), born Amelie Lang, was Pablo Picasso's live-in model and lover during his formative years as an artist.

104. Bad faith, or self-deception, is the subject of Beauvoir's early (1935–37) philosophical short-story cycle, *Quand prime le spirituel* (When Things of the Spirit Come First) (1979); see Sartre's chapter on bad faith, in *Being and Nothingness,* 47–70.

105. Ezekiel (sixth century B.C.E.), a prophet-priest of ancient Israel, was the subject and author of the Old Testament book that bears his name.

106. Nero (37–68), the fifth Roman emperor (54–68), was infamous for his personal debaucheries and extravagances.

107. Tess d'Urberville and Clare are characters from *Tess of the D'Urbervilles* (1891), a novel by Thomas Hardy (1840–1928).

108. Beauvoir also utilizes the "anthill" metaphor in an entry dated January 9, 1941, in her *Journal de guerre:* "Se faire fourmi parmi les fourmis, ou conscience libre devant des consciences. Solidarité *métaphysique* qui m'est une découverte neuve, pour moi qui étais solipsiste. Je ne peux être conscience, esprit, parmi des fourmis" (To make yourself an ant among ants or a free consciousness faced by other consciousnesses. Metaphysical solidarity is for me, who used to be a solipsist, a new discovery. I cannot be mind and consciousness among ants) (362).

109. Maurice Blanchot (1907–2003) was a French novelist, philosopher, and critic. *Aminadab* was first published in 1942.

110. "All is vanity" recalls *Ecclesiastes* 1:2, "Vanity of vanities. All is vanity!" (Revised Standard Version).

4

A Review of
The Phenomenology of Perception
by Maurice Merleau-Ponty

INTRODUCTION
by Sara Heinämaa

In 1945, Merleau-Ponty published an extensive study in the philosophy of experience, titled *La phénoménologie de la perception*.[1] The book is a phenomenological inquiry into the living body; it studies the perceptions, emotions, and movements of the body as well as the world surrounding the body and appearing to it. In addition to traditional philosophical topics, Merleau-Ponty addresses the problem of sexuality. He argues that sexuality cannot be explained as a specific function of the body but must be understood as an expression of existence.

Merleau-Ponty's first publication, *La structure du comportement* (finished 1938, published 1942),[2] had dealt with similar subjects but was different in its methodology. Merleau-Ponty had acquainted himself with Edmund Husserl's phenomenology through secondary sources already in the late 1920s and early 1930s, but it was not until 1939 that he started to work systematically with Husserl's publications and manuscripts.[3] This research period led Merleau-Ponty to adopt Husserl's descriptive transcendental approach and the methods of reduction that made possible a philosophical study of experience.[4] The new work testified to a comprehensive phenomenological turn in Merleau-Ponty's thinking.

Especially important to Merleau-Ponty were Husserl's detailed descriptions of the body and his late reflections on the crisis of science.[5] But Merleau-Ponty was also influenced by several interpreters and critics of Husserl, above all Eugen Fink, Martin Heidegger, and Aron Gurwitsch. He did not uncritically accept Husserl's descriptions and analyses but reworked several of his basic distinctions.

Merleau-Ponty's phenomenology had a crucial importance to Simone de Beauvoir's thinking. We can see his influence in the reference that she makes to his *Phénoménologie* in the introduction to *Le deuxième sexe* (The Second Sex) (1949). The three central ideas that she leans on are Merleau-Ponty's description of the living body, his notion of sexuality, and his understanding of the temporal nature of experience.

But *Le deuxième sexe* is not the first document of Beauvoir's philosophical encounter with Merleau-Ponty. Beauvoir wrote a review for *Les temps modernes* on Merleau-Ponty's *Phénoménologie* right after its appearance in 1945.[6] The text is short—in its original printing only five pages long—but it has a great importance to our understanding of Beauvoir's thought. It illuminates the phenomenological background of Beauvoir's own inquiries, most importantly *Le deuxième sexe*, which for a long time has been considered as lacking any philosophical content.

When Beauvoir read Merleau-Ponty's phenomenology, she was already familiar with the principles of Husserl's new philosophy. She tells in her autobiography that in 1934 and 1935 she studied Husserl's works in German as well as Fink's explications of them.[7] She also knew Heidegger's critical response to Husserl, *Sein und Zeit* (Being and Time) (1927), as well as Emmanuel Lévinas's early study *Théorie de l'intuition dans la phénoménologie de Husserl* (1930), and discussed all these sources eagerly with Sartre (*FA*, 157, 404, 497; *PL*, 135–36, 355, 433).[8]

So Beauvoir read Merleau-Ponty's book with a good background in phenomenological philosophy. This made it possible for her to find easily the core of Merleau-Ponty's argumentation and to identify the original aspects of his work. She gives a clear view of the merits of the book and takes on a comparison between Merleau-Ponty's approach and that of Sartre, presented in *L'être et le néant* (Being and Nothingness) two years earlier (1943).

Beauvoir emphasizes that Merleau-Ponty's descriptions of the body, its expressivity and sexuality, are faithful to experience as it is lived. Merleau-Ponty does not build a theoretical system, as Hegel and Sartre did. His philosophical goal is not constructive but critical: he aims at revealing the flow of experiences as the hidden basis of all theoretical and conceptual constructions.

There are two remarks in Beauvoir's review that are especially important from the point of view of understanding her own philosophical work. The first discussion concerns ethics, and the second is about the notion of subjectivity.

Ethics

Beauvoir starts her review by reminding her reader of the achievements of phenomenological philosophy. She points out that this philosophy abolishes the opposition between subject and object. In the phenomenological framework, the object is always given to a subject, and the subject is always directed toward an object. The two are interdependent but can be separated by analysis (see FA, 157, 404, 497; PL, 135–36, 355, 433).

Here Beauvoir refers to Husserl's well-known thesis about the intentionality of experience. Husserl argued that every experience is intentional; that is, every experience is an experience of something, directed toward some kind of an object or another.[9] The subjective side of the experience includes such states or acts as perceiving, imagining, knowing, valuing, and desiring. The objective side includes different kinds of objects, for example, perceivable things, imaginable things, facts, states of affairs, and values. The two sides correlate in systematic ways, and the correlation can be studied by the phenomenological methods of reduction.[10]

In the review, Beauvoir states that the phenomenological notion of intentionality has far-reaching philosophical implications that are especially important to our understanding of ethics. She does not, however, specify what these ethical implications are. To find an account, one has to turn to her essay *Pour une morale de l'ambiguïté* (The Ethics of Ambiguity) (1947).[11] In this text, Beauvoir argues that values are not provided by nature or by God. The source of values is not in some natural or supernatural being but in our own actions, interactions, and practices. For Beauvoir, an existentialist attitude in ethics means that we recognize our role in the constitution of values and take responsibility for it (MA, 20–21; EA, 13–15).

Le deuxième sexe is an application of this notion of ethics to the problem of women's subordination. Beauvoir argues that every explanation offered thus far for women's subjection rests on a naïve notion of values. Thus, a radical philosophical inquiry into the subjection of women must problematize the validity and origin of human and natural values.[12]

Subjectivity

The other important aspect of Beauvoir's review concerns the notion of subjectivity. The traditional understanding has been that Beauvoir was Sartre's faithful pupil and that she merely applied Sartre's philosophy to concrete problems—in *Le deuxième sexe,* to the problem of the sexual hierarchy.

It is only recently that scholars have approached Beauvoir's texts without assuming that they are applications of Sartre's ontological doctrines. This work has shown that Beauvoir's philosophy has several sources and that her analysis of sexual relation is based on her original understanding of existentialist ethics.[13]

The review, even if short, testifies to the complexity of Beauvoir's thinking. Beauvoir distances herself from Sartre's ontology and describes Merleau-Ponty's philosophy as a fruitful alternative. Its strength is in its nondualist notion of subjectivity, based on a phenomenological inquiry into the experience of temporality. This includes an implicit criticism of Sartre's account of consciousness and subjectivity.

In 1936–37, Sartre had published an article, "La transcendance de l'ego: esquisse d'une description phénoménologique" (The Transcendence of the Ego), which criticized Husserl's notion of the subject. Sartre argued that Husserl's claims about the subject or the ego are unwarranted and defy Husserl's phenomenological method.

In *Ideen* (Ideas), Husserl had claimed that the phenomenological reduction that discloses the pure consciousness does not nullify the ego as a principle that unifies the passing experiences. The ego necessarily belongs to every possible experience. Sartre stated against Husserl that the ego is nothing but an object of consciousness. Consciousness has no ipseity; it is nothing but a series of nonmotivated nihilating acts. As such it is empty of all content and form, "absolutely empty," as Beauvoir explains in *La force de l'âge* (FA, 240; PL, 208).

In the review, Beauvoir points out that Merleau-Ponty's work offers an alternative to the doctrine of the empty consciousness. In Merleau-Ponty's description, consciousness is not opposed to being but forms "a hollow, a fold" in it.

As noted, commentators have traditionally assumed that Beauvoir follows Sartre in the controversy about subjectivity. The review gives evidence that the question of interpretation is more complex.

Beauvoir's discussions of subjectivity have many more starting points than just Sartre's works. They are inspired by Kierkegaard's critique of Hegel, Nietzsche's attack on Christian morality, and the different interpretations of phenomenology that she studied. To these she adds a radical question about the sexual hierarchy, stemming from the works of Virginia Woolf and other woman writers.

If we let go of the assumption that Beauvoir's philosophical position adheres to the commitments of her private life, then it becomes possible to pose scholarly questions of interpretation. We can ask if Beauvoir's discussion of subjectivity really is similar to that of Sartre, or perhaps nearer to that of Merleau-Ponty or Heidegger. These questions are still largely unanswered, but the discussion of Beauvoir's philosophy has already begun.

NOTES

1. See Merleau-Ponty, *Phenomenology of Perception,* trans. Colin Smith (New York: Routledge and Kegan Paul, 1962).

2. See Merleau-Ponty, *The Structure of Behavior,* trans. Alden L. Fisher (Boston: Beacon, 1963).

3. On Merleau-Ponty's reading of Husserl's texts, see Ted Toadvine, "Merleau-Ponty's Reading of Husserl: A Chronological Overview," in *Merleau-Ponty's Reading of Husserl,* ed. Ted Toadvine and Lester Embree (Dordrecht: Kluwer, 2002), 221–86.

4. On Merleau-Ponty's interpretation of Husserl's phenomenology, see Sara Heinämaa, "From Decisions to Passions: Merleau-Ponty's Interpretation of Husserl's Reduction," in Toadvine and Embree, *Merleau-Ponty's Reading of Husserl,* 127–46.

5. Husserl gives a detailed description and analysis of the experience of the living body in the second book of his *Ideen*. This work was not published until 1952, long after Husserl's death, but Merleau-Ponty studied it as a manuscript in the Husserl archive in Louvain. He was also well acquainted with the late work *Die Krisis der europäischen Wissenschaften und die transzendentale Phänomenologie,* which involved an extensive critique and analysis of the crisis of science. For Husserl's description of the body and its influence on the so-called existentialist philosophies, see Sara Heinämaa, *Toward a Phenomenology of Sexual Difference: Husserl, Merleau-Ponty, Beauvoir* (Lanham, Md.: Rowman and Littlefield, 2003).

6. Simone de Beauvoir, "*La phénoménologie de la perception* de Maurice Merleau-Ponty," *Les temps modernes* 1, no. 2 (1945): 363–67. See also Beauvoir's later essay, "Merleau-Ponty et le pseudo-sartrisme," in *Privilèges* (Paris: Gallimard, 1955), reprinted from *Les temps modernes* 10, nos. 114–15 (1955): 2072–2122; it appears in English as "Merleau-Ponty and Pseudo-Sartreanism," trans. Veronique Zaytzeff, in Jon Stewart, ed.: *The Debate between Sartre and Merleau-Ponty* (Evanston, Ill.: Northwestern University Press, 1998), reprinted from *International Studies in Philosophy* 21 (1989): 3–48.

7. See Simone de Beauvoir, *La force de l'âge* (Paris: Gallimard, 1960), 231, 254 (hereafter referred to as *FA*), trans. Peter Green as *The Prime of Life* (Harmondsworth, Middlesex, Eng.: Penquin Books, 1962), 201, 221 (hereafter referred to as *PL*).

8. See Martin Heidegger, *Being and Time,* trans. John Macquarrie and Edward Robinson (New York: Harper and Row, 1962); Emmanuel Lévinas, *The Theory of Intuition in Husserl's Phenomenology,* trans. André Orianne (Evanston, Ill.: Northwestern University Press, 1973).

9. A good nontechnical introduction to Husserl's notion of intentionality is given by Robert Sokolowski, *Introduction to Phenomenology* (Cambridge: Cambridge University Press, 2000), 8–21.

10. Husserl's notion of intentionality has its roots in Brentano's philosophy, and from there we can trace the notion back to medieval discussions of the different modes of existence. But Husserl gave Brentano's idea of intentionality a whole new interpretation and developed methodological and conceptual tools that made possible a detailed description and analysis of the different modes, aspects, and levels of intentionality.

11. Simone de Beauvoir, *Pour une morale de l'ambiguïté* (Paris: Gallimard, 1947), trans. Bernard Frechtman as *The Ethics of Ambiguity* (New York: Carol Publishing Group, 1994) (hereafter referred to as *MA* and *EA,* respectively).

12. A more detailed account of this argument is given in Heinämaa, *Toward a Phenomenology of Sexual Difference;* see also Heinämaa, "Simone de Beauvoir's Phenomenology of Sexual Difference," *Hypatia* 14, no. 4 (1999): 114–32, and idem, "The Body as an Instrument and the Body as an Expression," in *The Cambridge Companion to Simone de Beauvoir,* ed. Claudia Card (Cambridge: Cambridge University Press, 2003), 66–86.

13. See Michèle Le Dœuff, "De l'existentialisme au *Deuxième sexe,*" *Le Magazine Littéraire* 145 (1979), in English, "Simone de Beauvoir and Existentialism," *Feminist Studies* 6, no. 2 (1980): 277–89; Margaret A. Simons, "Beauvoir and Sartre: The Question of Influence," and "The Silencing of Simone de Beauvoir: Guess What's Missing from *The Second Sex,*" both in *Beauvoir and "The Second Sex": Feminism, Race, and the Origins of Existentialism* (Lanham, Md.: Rowman and Littlefield, 1999); Margaret A. Simons, "Beauvoir and Sartre: The Philosophical Relationship," in "Simone de Beauvoir: Witness to the Century," ed. Hélène Vivienne Wenzel, *Yale French Studies* 72 (1986): 165–79; Judith Butler, "Sex and Gender in Simone de Beauvoir's *Second Sex,*" ibid., 35–49; Michèle Le Dœuff, *L'étude et le rouet* (Paris: Seuil, 1989), trans. Trista Selous as *Hipparchia's Choice: An Essay Concerning Women, Philosophy, etc.* (Oxford: Blackwell, 1991); Sonia Kruks, *Situation and Human Existence: Freedom, Subjectivity, and Society* (New York: Routledge, 1990); Eva Lundgren-Gothlin, *Kön och existens: Studier i Simone de Beauvoirs "Le Deuxième Sexe"* (1992), trans. Linda Schenck as *Sex and Existence: Simone de Beauvoir's "The Second Sex"* (London: Athlone, 1996); Sara Heinämaa, "What Is a Woman? Butler and Beauvoir on the Foundations of the Sexual Difference," *Hypatia* 12, no. 1 (1996): 20–39; Debra B. Bergoffen, *The Philosophy of Simone de Beauvoir: Gendered Phenomenologies, Erotic Generosities* (Albany: State University of New York Press, 1997); Kate Fullbrook and Edward Fullbrook, *Simone de Beauvoir: A Critical Introduction* (Cambridge: Polity, 1998); Heinämaa, "Simone de Beauvoir's Phenomenology of Sexual Difference"; Jo-Ann Pilardi, *Simone de Beauvoir Writing the Self: Philosophy Becomes Autobigraphy* (Westport, Conn.: Greenwood, 1999); Eleanore Holveck, *Simone de Beauvoir's Philosophy of Lived Experience: Literature and Metaphysics* (Lanham, Md.: Rowman and Littlefield, 2002); and Heinämaa, *Toward a Phenomenology of Sexual Difference.*

TRANSLATION BY MARYBETH TIMMERMANN
NOTES BY STACY KELTNER

A Review of
The Phenomenology of Perception
by Maurice Merleau-Ponty

One of the essential goals proposed by children's education is to make the child lose the sense of his presence in the world. Ethics teaches him to renounce his subjectivity, to give up the privilege of affirming himself as "I" when faced with others. He must consider himself as a human person among others, subjected, like the others, to universal laws written in an anonymous heaven. Science enjoins him to escape out of his own consciousness, to turn away from the living and meaningful world that this consciousness disclosed to him, and for which science tries to substitute a universe of frozen objects, independent of all gaze and all thought. However, in spite of ethics, every man knows a mysterious intimacy with a unique existence that is precisely his own, and, in spite of science, every man sees with his eyes. From this is born the divorce that one so often notices between theory and practice, between open opinions and hidden convictions, between learned precepts and the spontaneous movement of life. The world having been torn from the sub-

This essay first appeared as "*La phénoménologie de la perception* de Maurice Merleau-Ponty," *Les temps modernes* 1, no. 2 (1945): 363–67. Its subject is Maurice Merleau-Ponty, *La phénoménologie de la perception* (Paris: Gallimard, 1945) (hereafter referred to as *PDP*), trans. Colin Smith as *The Phenomenology of Perception* (London: Routledge and Kegan Paul, 1962) (hereafter referred to as *POP*).

ject, and the subject pushed outside the world, it becomes impossible to possess the world and oneself at the same time. Some throw themselves resolutely toward the foreign things and strive to forget that they are losing themselves; others choose a turning inward toward oneself, but it then seems to them that the rest of the universe escapes them. One of the great merits of phenomenology is to have given back to man the right to an authentic existence, by eliminating the opposition of the subject and the object. It is impossible to define an object in cutting it off from the subject through which and for which it is object; and the subject reveals itself only through the objects in which it is engaged. Such an affirmation only makes the contents of naïve experience explicit, but it is rich in consequences. Only in taking it as a basis will one succeed in building an ethics to which man can totally and sincerely adhere. It is therefore of extreme importance to establish it solidly and to give back to man this childish audacity that years of verbal submission has taken away: the audacity to say: "I am here." This is why *The Phenomenology of Perception* by Maurice Merleau-Ponty is not only a remarkable specialist work but a book that is of interest to the whole of man and to every man; the human condition is at stake in this book. Empiricism, like intellectualism, separates the world from consciousness; in order to succeed thereafter in reuniting them, one asked consciousness to abdicate before the opacity of the real; the other dissolved the real in the light of consciousness, and in the end, both failed to give an account of that unique experience: the consciousness of the real. Merleau-Ponty shows us that the phenomenological attitude allows man to access the world, and to find himself there: it is in giving myself to the world that I realize myself, and it is in assuming myself that I have a hold on the world.

There is one existence in particular that science claims to annex to the universe of objects, from which phenomenology returns it to man's possession: it is the existence of his own body. In pages that are perhaps the most definitive of the entire book, Merleau-Ponty demonstrates, by the analysis of normal processes and of pathological cases, that it is impossible to consider our body as an object, even as a privileged object. For example, none of the explanations that have been proposed for the famous "amputee's illusion," based on the notion of the body as an object, are valid, or even plausible. On the contrary, the phenomenon of the phantom limb becomes intelligible if one defines the body as our manner of being in the world, our "anchorage" in this world, or even the collection of "holds" we have upon things. One then understands that the world, which had been constituted by my body as handleable, remains that way at the moment, even if I have lost the power to handle it. The handleable object refers me to a hand that I no longer have, but whose presence is posited by the environment [*milieu*] that surrounds me. Merleau-Ponty also analyzes a curious psychosis: a patient suffering from a disorder of the cerebellum is incapable of pointing out any part of his body or of making any abstract movement such as bending a finger or a leg on command, but he can grab his nose or his ankle, take his handkerchief from his pocket, react to any concrete situation. That is to say he has his phenomenal body at his disposal. His body has stayed intact as a vehicle of his being in the world. Where the patient fails is when he must see his body as an object among others that occupies its place between the wall and the table, in objective space. He can live his body, not represent it to himself, which clearly demonstrates that the represented body is a secondary construction that is added on to the reality of the lived body, and which can, in certain cases, become disunited from it. Our body is not first posited in the world the way a tree or a rock is. It lives in the world; it is our general way of having a world. It expresses our existence, which signifies not that it is an exterior accompaniment of our existence, but that our existence realizes itself in it.

Thus, in restoring our body to us, phenomenology also restores things to us. Through the body we can "frequent" the world, understand it; we can "have a world." The space in which we situate objects is not an abstract form imposing itself upon us from outside; our perception of space expresses the manner in which we stretch out toward the future through our body and through things. It expresses the entire life of the subject. The experience of spatiality is the experience of our situation in the world. It allows us to understand that an original spatiality exists for primitives, schizophrenics, hallucinators, sleepers, painters; it also allows us to elucidate the classic problems of "inverted vision,"[1] of the perception of depth. It is known that a subject who is made to wear glasses that correct the retinal images eventually regains normal vision.[2] The same goes for a subject who is made to perceive his bedroom in a mirror tilted at a 45-degree angle; he ends up orienting himself in such a way that he sees the oblique lines of his room as vertical lines. This can be understood only if one envisions the body as constituting by its action a perceptual ground, a basis of life, a general setting [*milieu*] for my coexistence with the world.[3] It carries out the necessary transpositions in order to be able to live in a new perceptual field and to anchor itself there. As for depth and size, they come to things with no comparison to any reference object. They are rooted in our situation; they are defined with respect to a certain range of our gestures, a certain hold on our surroundings [*entourage*]. Only this conception of space also accounts for the phenomena of movement. If we are engaged in an environment [*milieu*], movement appears to us as an absolute, and its relativity is reduced to the power we have to change domains within the interior of the larger world.

The role of the body is not limited to projecting into the space that it constitutes qualities whose heaviness and opacity would be foreign to it. Sensation is neither a quality nor the consciousness of a quality; it is a vital communication with the world, an intentional network [*tissu intentionnel*]. Every supposed quality is inserted into a certain behavior and possesses a vital signification. Laboratory experiments, for example, show that the gesture of raising one's arm is modified by a red, yellow, blue, or green field of vision. To look at a blue beach is to give my body that particular way to fill up the space that is blue. The sensible is "a certain way of being in the world that is proposed to us from a point in space, and that our body takes back and assumes."[4] And in order for the sensible to be sensed, it must be subtended by my gaze or by the movement of my hand.[5] To perceive the blue sky is not a matter of positing myself in front of it. I must abandon myself to it, so that it "thinks itself within me." At the moment that I perceive it, "I am the very sky that pulls itself together, collects itself and begins to exist for itself."[6] The "thing," then, first defines itself not as a resistance but, on the contrary, as the correlative to my existence: it is a "structure" accessible to inspection by the body, and it is why reality seems to us to be full of human significations. It is why we can conceive of a thing only if it is perceived or perceptible. Thus, perception is not a relationship between a subject and an object foreign to one another; it ties us to the world as to our homeland, it is communication and communion, "the taking back into ourselves of a foreign intention," or inversely, "the exterior accomplishment of our perceptual powers." Things *speak* to us, and one must not give these words a figurative or symbolic meaning. Nature is truly language, a language that would teach itself, where signification would be secreted by the very structure of signs. With this, one understands that we could never be out of place [*dépaysés*] in the world. The most savage desert, the most hidden cave still secrete a human meaning. The universe is our domain.

However, at the same time as they offer this familiar aspect, things offer another side: they also are silence and mystery, an Other who escapes us. They are never completely given but, on the contrary, always open. The world in the full sense of the word is not an object; it transcends all the perspective views that I take of it. Although real, the world is always incomplete, and this contradiction corresponds to the one that opposes the ubiquity of consciousness to its engagement in a field of presence. In order to perceive, I must be situated, and the same movement by which I accede to the world by rooting myself, here and now, pushes away the world to the always inaccessible horizon of my experience. Indeed, I am not an impersonal and timeless consciousness. If I exist as subject, it's because I am capable of tying together a past, a present, and a future; it's because I make time. Perceiving space, perceiving the object, is unfolding time around me, but the perceptual synthesis always remains incomplete because the temporal synthesis is never completed.

It is therefore by temporality that the opacity of the world is explained, and it is also in temporality that the opacity of the subject has its root. While Sartre, in *Being and Nothingness,* first emphasizes the opposition of the "for-itself" and the "in-itself" and the nihilating power of the mind in the face of being, and the absolute freedom of the mind, Merleau-Ponty, on the contrary, concentrates on describing the concrete character of the subject that is never, according to him, a pure for-itself. Actually, he thinks that our existence never grasps itself in its nakedness but as it is expressed by our body. And this body is not enclosed in the instant but implies an entire history, and even a prehistory. For example, it can situate itself in space only by defining its current milieu in relation to a previously given spatial milieu that itself refers to a prior level without ever being able to stop at a first level that would not be anchored anywhere. Therefore, the perception of space, like all perception in general, presupposes an indefinite past lying behind oneself, a "communication with the world that is older than thought," which is made concrete by the fact of my birth. My history is incarnated in a body that possesses a certain generality, a relationship with the world prior to myself, and that is why this body is opaque to reflection. That is why my consciousness finds itself "engorged by the sensible." It is not a pure for-itself, or to use Hegel's phrase, later used by Sartre, a hole in being, but rather "a hollow, a fold that has been made and can be unmade."[7]

From these definitions of the world and of man, Merleau-Ponty considers most of the main problems that are of interest to the human condition, and he offers some very rich suggestions, particularly about the question of sexuality and that of language. But what seems to me to be the most important in his book, both by the method used and the results gained, is the phenomenological elucidation of a lived experience, the experience of perception. Hegel rightly says that one can understand a truth only by reattaching it to the movement of thought that engendered it. The ideas that I have just summarized too briefly can keep all of their value only if one reattaches them to the concrete analyses that support them. Merleau-Ponty does not invent a system; he starts from established facts and he demonstrates that it is impossible to account for them on an experimental plane. Instead they imply an entire relationship between man and the world, and it is this relationship that he patiently brings out. One of the main merits of this book is that it's convincing. Another one of its merits is that it does not ask us to force ourselves. On the contrary, it suggests that we embrace the very movement of life that is belief in the things of the world and in our own presence.

NOTES

1. See *POP* (244–47) and *PDP* (282–85).

2. Paraphrased from *POP* (244) and *PDP* (282).

3. Paraphrased from *POP* (248–50) and *PDP* (287–90); see *POP:* "The constitution of a spatial level is simply one means of constituting an integrated world: my body is geared to the world when my perception presents me with a spectacle as varied and as clearly articulated as possible, and when my motor intentions, as they unfold, receive the responses they expect from the world. This maximum sharpness of perception and action points clearly to a perceptual *ground*, a basis of my life, a general setting in which my body can co-exist with the world" (250); and *PDP:* "Ce maximum de netteté dans la perception et dans l'action définit un *sol* perceptif, un fond de ma vie, un milieu général pour la coexistence de mon corps et du monde" (290).

4. Quoted from *PDP* (245–46), which Smith translates as "a certain way of being in the world suggested to us from some point in space, and seized and acted upon by our body" (*POP*, 212).

5. Here, and with "the blue sky" example that follows, Beauvoir alludes to Merleau-Ponty's discussion on *PDP* (248) and *POP* (214).

6. Quoted from *PDP* (248), which Smith translates as "I am the sky itself as it is drawn together and unified, and as it begins to exist for itself" (*POP* 214).

7. Quoted from *PDP* (249) and *POP* (215).

Moral Idealism and
Political Realism

INTRODUCTION
by Sonia Kruks

Simone de Beauvoir was concerned with the question of the vexed relationship between ethics and politics throughout her active life. She addresses this topic in many of her novels, her autobiography, and her travel writings, as well as in the group of early works sometimes referred to as her "ethical writings." "Moral Idealism and Political Realism," first published in 1945, belongs to this latter group. Published between her two book-length works on ethics, *Pyrrhus et Cinéas* (1944) and *The Ethics of Ambiguity* (1947), it shares many of their preoccupations. Indeed, Beauvoir later repeated certain formulations from it in *The Ethics of Ambiguity.*

"Moral Idealism and Political Realism" was first published in November 1945. It appeared in the second issue of *Les temps modernes,* the radical monthly journal of politics, philosophy, and culture founded by Beauvoir, Sartre, Merleau-Ponty, and others. The piece was republished in 1948 in the collection of her essays Beauvoir entitled *L'existentialisme et la sagesse des nations.*[1] Its critique of "intransigent moralists," those who insist on following absolute principles and keeping their consciences pure irrespective of the costs to others or themselves, takes up a theme to which Merleau-Ponty had already introduced the journal's readers in the very first issue. In October 1945, in "The

War Has Taken Place," Merleau-Ponty discusses the moral and political lessons taught to their generation by the war and the experiences of daily life in German-occupied Paris. He asserts the impossibility of remaining a moral purist. "No one's hands are clean. . . . We have unlearned 'pure morality.' . . . We are in the world, mingled with it, compromised with it," he writes.[2] Beauvoir's essay begins where Merleau-Ponty's left off the previous month: if pure morality is impossible, are we then condemned to an irresponsible realism? she asks. Or is moral action still possible in the midst of the ambiguous and violent world of politics?

In addressing such questions Beauvoir builds on her own earlier meditations on ethics and politics. These notably include her discussion of violence and responsibility for others in the novel *The Blood of Others* (set in the Resistance and written between 1941 and 1943) and her discussions of the vulnerability of individuals to injury through each others' actions in *Pyrrhus et Cinéas* (1944). Although much of "Moral Idealism and Political Realism" is written at a fairly abstracted level, it is also very much a text for its times. Beauvoir's inquiry is driven by her passionate concern about concrete political events and actions: the loss of life that had resulted from the French Resistance; the claims of Nazi collaborators (then on trial) to have acted for "principled" ends, such as saving France from further bloodshed; and the question of means and ends as it was unfolding above all in the trajectory of the Russian Revolution.

Beauvoir begins the essay by considering the drama of Antigone as the quintessential expression of two conflicting positions: moral idealism and political realism. Antigone, in her insistence on following the prescribed rites and burying her brother, is the moral idealist, the dangerous purist. She is concerned only with the rightness of her own actions and not with their mundane consequences. By contrast, Creon "incarnates the political realist," concerned only with state interest or with what works in attaining immediate goals. In Beauvoir's view, what these otherwise conflicting positions share is that both offer us (false) grounds to evade one's own freedom. The moralist claims to be bound to an inner, subjective necessity, to a preordained principle or duty; the realist claims to be bound to the objective necessity decreed by the circumstances. In either case necessity, and not one's own free will, is said to determine what we shall do; and in each case we have found a means to evade our own freedom with its attendant anxiety and responsibility.

Much of Beauvoir's essay is devoted to an exposition and critique of the two positions, while in the final portion she sketches out her own alternative view of morality in politics. She begins with a fairly brief consideration of the position of the moral idealist, for this position is in her view patently indefensible. The idealist's neo-Kantian commitment to the "great idols" of abstract principles is untenable in politics. First, it predisposes one to inaction, since in the world of politics one cannot avoid violating "pure" principles. In clinging to atemporal verities, an ethical idealism "severs its earthly roots." Consequently, it can inadvertently contribute to the very ends to which it is opposed. For example, she notes, in the face of the growing Nazi threat in the 1920s and 1930s, French pacifism "served the cause of peace poorly." Second, Beauvoir points out, abstract principles still do not tell us what to decide in a specific case; we must always make our own decisions, develop our own interpretations, even if we claim we are bound by universal rules. Both collaborators and members of the Resistance claimed to be acting to "serve France," but they had divergent concepts of what, in practice, that meant; and their actions created new and very different values for which particular individuals were accountable.

Beauvoir next turns to "political realism." She wrestles with this position at far more length than idealism, for it at least has the merit of starting with its feet on the ground and enabling one to engage with the surrounding world. But when it claims to be driven by the exigencies of that world alone, it too falls into a dangerous denial of one's own freedom in the name of the objective, or preordained, goal. In relation to such a goal, Beauvoir observes, "the political man becomes simply a technician. . . . [T]he only problems posed to him are of a tactical nature."

Whether or not "the end justifies the means" has been a matter of debate among political actors and thinkers alike ever since Machiavelli, and indeed earlier. Beauvoir distinguishes two kinds of political realism in the world around her: a "conservative" type and a "revolutionary" one. Although their political goals are very different, what they share is their inattention to the meaning of means. In the name of pregiven goals, they erase the freedom that is always affirmed in the struggle to reach them.

Thus, the conservative realist will oppose working-class demands as foolish and dangerous and will argue that poverty can better be relieved through charity than through radical politics. "After all, bread is bread," he argues. It does not matter how the poor obtain what they need, as long as they are provided for. But this point of view denies the *meaning* of the struggle, Beauvoir points out. The significance of a strike, for example, is not to increase wages, not to put bread on the table. Rather, a strike is in itself important as a value-affirming and transcendent action. In the demand for bread, "each demands for all the others, and the goal pursued infinitely surpasses the immediate satisfaction of an animal appetite." What is at issue is not the "objective" end—that is, more bread, higher wages—but obtaining it through one's own free actions. The demand the worker makes is "the objective form that a transcendence takes on."

Beauvoir later chided herself for the idealism of this analysis. In 1963, looking back to the 1940s in her autobiography, she questions why she had gone through the "detour" of values, rather than simply recognizing the demands of need itself: "Why," she asks, "did I write *concrete freedom* instead of *bread* and subordinate the will to live to the meaning of life? I never confined myself to saying: these people must eat because they are hungry. However, that was what I thought."[3]

Was Beauvoir guilty of the kind of purist, ethical idealism of which she here accuses herself? Certainly, in "Moral Idealism and Political Realism" (as in *The Ethics of Ambiguity*, which she began the following year) she not only affirms the value of freedom as what uniquely defines our humanity but tends also to claim that free, transcendent, action is possible and should be chosen in any and all circumstances. It is perhaps against this tendency that she later reacted: for those who are actually starving, bread may be more important than freedom; and for another to assert otherwise is to make of freedom an absolute end.

Yet, both as a general political analysis and in its specific context, Beauvoir's critique of realism is important. Conservative "realism" does generally set out to foreclose possibilities and to discourage transformative social action, thereby denying the value of freedom. In postwar France, conservative realism represented an attempt to set the clock back to the prewar status quo and to destroy the sense of new beginnings ushered in with the Liberation. Beauvoir was an astute political analyst, and her critique constitutes a significant political intervention. To offer militant workers charity while opposing their self-mobilization surely was, as she argued, a "bad faith" defense of elite interests and a refusal to acknowledge the values that do inhere in solidaristic social movements. In the guise of common sense, conservative realism was proposing to foreclose the new, more egalitarian and democratic possibilities of the postwar era.

Although Beauvoir examines conservative realism at considerable length, it is "Left" or "revolutionary" realism (especially in its Communist version) that concerns her more profoundly. In postwar France, Communism largely defined Left politics. The Communist Party, popular because of its participation in the Resistance and the Soviet role in defeating the Nazis, entered electoral politics and even participated in a coalition government for a while.

Many still saw in the Soviet Union the promise or vision of a new world to come. Beauvoir, and others involved with *Les temps modernes,* shared this desire for a new world. But the group offered only what they called "critical support" to Russia and the French Communist Party. While they believed in the possibilities of a democratic and humanist socialism, they were skeptical about a revolution that claims its ends are "objectively" assured because the motor of history guarantees them. Left realists claim that history has a knowable and necessary trajectory and that one acts only to bring it to fruition. For many Communists these claims may unproblematically vindicate revolutionary violence: it is an objective necessity, not a matter of human decision and responsibility.

Beauvoir's own position, however, is not to reject revolutionary violence out of hand (as Albert Camus did a few years later in *The Rebel*).[4] Rather, Beauvoir criticizes the facile and dishonest good conscience that too often accompanies this violence. The political actor who wishes to change the world in accordance with his or her values does have to act—and it is not unlikely that one's actions may injure others.

In the face of this dilemma one must not, however, claim the ethical idealist's high ground, keep one's hands clean, and refuse to act. Nor may one, like the realist, deny one's own accountability for injuries to others that result from one's actions. Rather, a "lucid political action" must accept the agonizing contradictions of a human condition that may require us to do violence to others in order to be effective, even as we acknowledge that we ourselves are guilty of the harm done. Alas, "it is not possible to act for man without treating certain men, at certain times, as means." But it is bad faith to claim that one therefore is merely history's "technician." For it is through one's own decisions and actions that one both affirms values and may cause injury to others in their name. The central dilemma that Beauvoir thus poses and addresses in the essay is whether there can be a reconciliation of morality and politics. Can the pitfalls of both idealism and realism be avoided in moral political action? She wrestles with this dilemma in fertile, but ultimately inconclusive, ways.

Beauvoir sets out toward the end of the essay to "reconcile" morality and politics by arguing that our ends demand means that are consonant with them, and that the means we choose themselves affirm new values or ends. "The means can be understood only in light of the desired end," she writes, "but inversely, the end is inseparable from the means by which it is carried out." Here, her conception of temporality becomes pivotal: what we choose as a future is part of our present, and our present actions affirm futures. Thus, we should not compromise the present for the future since "the value of the future is that it is the future of my present. . . . [P]resent and future are joined in the unity of the project." For example, to sacrifice the lives of some people now for future world peace, or for the future of the revolution, is to make a choice of *present* values for which we are responsible. We cannot ever claim that history makes such a choice on our behalf, since the future is always open and unknowable.

Yet to say we are responsible does not help us to decide what decision we should make in particular circumstances. For example, we can decide to sacrifice the life of one man to save many, or we can decide not to do so—but either way the decision is ours. For, "it is not reality that imposes a choice on me, it is only after the choice that reality takes on a value." But how then, we must ask, do I make my choice? What enters into my decision whether or not to save the one man? It is here that Beauvoir fails to offer us a sufficiently full analysis of the problem she addresses. For while she is surely correct that universal principles cannot tell us what we should do in a particular instance, still our choices rarely are arbitrary: the judgments that we make do not come out of thin air, or from pure freedom.

What Beauvoir's analysis lacks is what we might call a phenomenology of judgment. Once we accept responsibility for our own decisions, how do we go about making them? Why do we not just arbitrarily toss a coin? How do our prior choices shape (though not determine) our future ones? How does the social milieu we live in, with its normative and cultural practices, inform (though not determine) our choices and the meanings we create? How, in short, does our situation color our freedom? Later, in her autobiography, Beauvoir harshly criticized her ethical essays. She accused herself of excessive individualism, of lacking a philosophy of history, and of mistakenly trying to define morality independently of any social context.[5] Although the tone of this later critique was overly dismissive, her diagnosis had some merit. Between the claims of idealists and realists alike, that values are imposed on us (be it either by principles or by the objective givens of the world), and Beauvoir's counter-affirmation that we *alone* and freely create our own values, a more nuanced position, one attentive to the social dimensions of the self, is needed. For were nothing to constrain or shape our choices they would indeed be wholly free—but, lacking any inherence in the world, also arbitrary. Thus we need also to examine the social and historical nature of individual selves, to explore the ambiguities of human situatedness and freedom.

Beauvoir was to develop such an account of freedom a few years later, in *The Second Sex.*[6] There she recognizes that women (and men) are, paradoxically, at once free subjectivities and subject to "destinies" that are socially produced. Thus, in spite of its inadequacies, "Moral Idealism and Political

Realism" should be read as a key work in Beauvoir's philosophical development. For in it we see Beauvoir working out the "freedom" side of the account of freedom-in-situation and its ambiguities that she subsequently elaborated in *The Second Sex*. Moreover, the significance of the essay also endures today in its profound critique of any contemporary politics (be it of Right or Left) that continues to evade responsibility for its consequences.

NOTES

1. *L'existentialisme et la sagesse des nations* (Paris: Nagel, 1948).

2. Maurice Merleau-Ponty, "The War Has Taken Place," in *Sense and Non-Sense,* trans. Hubert L. Dreyfus and Patricia Allen Dreyfus (Evanston, Ill.: Northwestern University Press, 1964), 147.

3. Simone de Beauvoir, *La force des choses,* vol. 1 (Paris: Gallimard, 1963), 100.

4. See Albert Camus, *The Rebel: An Essay on Man in Revolt,* trans. Anthony Bower (1951; New York: Knopf, 1956).

5. See Beauvoir, *La force des choses,* 99–100.

6. Beauvoir began work on *The Second Sex* in 1946. Parts of it were published as essays in *Les temps modernes* in 1948, and the book was published the following year; see *Le deuxième sexe,* 2 vols. (Paris: Gallimard, 1949).

TRANSLATION BY ANNE DEING CORDERO
NOTES BY REBECCA JEYES

Moral Idealism and Political Realism

The drama of Antigone,[1] who upholds against Creon's human laws the divine laws engraved in her heart, appears as the ancient symbol of a conflict that continues to this day. Antigone is the prototype of those intransigent moralists who, while being contemptuous of earthly goods, proclaim the necessity of certain eternal principles and insist at any cost on keeping their conscience pure—even though they may forfeit their own lives or the lives of others. Creon incarnates the political realist concerned only with the interests of the state and determined to defend them by every possible means. All through history this conflict has persisted, neither side being able to convince the other of the validity of its values—each side is imprisoned in its own value system in the name of which it rejects the values of its adversary. The realist boasts in vain about his effective methods and the useful results achieved; the moralist, enamored with eternal principles only, will always look at the realist's actions as being futile, of little consequence. Whatever the success he may pride himself on, the political man is unable to reach what

"Idéalisme moral et réalisme politique," *Les temps modernes* 1, no. 2 (1945): 248–68; reprinted in *L'existentialisme et la sagesse des nations* (Paris: Nagel, 1948), 49–88, © Sylvie Le Bon de Beauvoir (hereafter referred to as *ESN*).

is truly good. The rise and collapse of empires, the discovery of the world, the invention of machines, the increase in the human species, and the proliferation of cities and factories will not make the soul that is dedicated to the cult of virtue waver in its haughty disdain. But the moralist upbraids the man of action in vain for the faults that sully him and the futility of his objectives, for the man of action considers these ends unconditionally desirable. He knows that despite the edifying fables intended for children, in this world, which is his, virtue is poorly rewarded; only force reigns supreme. Speeches on morality are nothing but useless [*vain*] chatter, and scruples, nothing but a tactical weakness.

For a long time, this duality was based on man's belief that he belonged at once to two worlds. At the time of Antigone, the Greek considered himself the son of the state but also a descendant of ancestral human larvae. As an inhabitant of the earth he was at the same time a future guest of hell; he owed obedience both to terrestrial governments and underworld powers.[2] This obligated him at times to choose between two irreconcilable orders of values. Between Antigone, faithful to the cult of the dead, and Creon, concerned with the future of Thebes, no understanding was possible. In the Middle Ages, the Christian belonged to the kingdom of God and the secular world. As a rule there were conflicts between spiritual and worldly interests. If he really wanted to save his soul, the most prudent path to take was to renounce this world. If he committed himself to earthly endeavors, he brazenly accepted to sin even as this meant redeeming his faults by doing penance. The importance given to the idea of penance proves that politics and religion were routinely separated. When pursuing worldly ends, man was practically sure of losing his soul; to obtain a pardon, he deliberately had to enter another domain, that of prayer, almsgiving, pilgrimage, and gratuitous and symbolic expressions.

Today, when a great number of men believe neither in heaven nor hell, the conflict that opposes moralists and realists takes on an entirely different meaning. In the past, man was torn between two worlds, but in this world his situation was simple. He was enclosed within the confines of a town, a province, a nation, or a civilization. Furthermore, except in rare circumstances, managing public affairs was within the purview of a few specialists. At present, almost all men live a political existence, and so almost all are faced with the problem of action. And never before has this problem been so complex because each individual no longer belongs to one country alone; he is also a member of a self-conscious class, a civilization that reaches beyond national borders, and a world whose parts are tightly interconnected. He knows that his actions affect the future as much as the present, that they exist as much through the effects they set off as through themselves; his projects are more far-reaching than in the past; they are manifold and often contradictory. Must class be sacrificed to nation or nation to class? Today's generation to tomorrow's generation? Must the future be sacrificed to a temporary peace? What should we want? And to reach what we want, what should we do? Men hesitate to answer. The idea of solving these problems without help fills them with anguish. They are still not used to being their own masters on earth; their freedom frightens them. There are many, therefore, who seek refuge in one of two conflicting attitudes, either of which can free man from himself: an intransigent moralism or a cynical realism. If they decide on moralism, they choose to obey an interior necessity, and enclose themselves in pure subjectivity; if on the other hand they choose realism, they decide to submit to the necessity of things, and lose themselves in objectivity. Both, moralists and realists, agree on rebuking those who attempt to reconcile ethics and politics. As a result, there develops a gulf between the two disciplines that widens with each passing day. Will ethics then have no hold on the real world and will the real world be stripped of any moral significance? Or, on the contrary, can the two planes of human activity meet and merge? To be able to decide this question, ethics and politics must attain a clearer consciousness of themselves, their essence, and their objectives.

We must admit that, despite all the verbal assertions through which it is perpetuated, ethics, as conceived by most moralists, is in the process of being discredited. The traditional, classical ethics by which society claims to live nowadays is a more or less adulterated legacy of Kantian ethics. It enjoins men to submit their behavior to universal, timeless imperatives, to model their actions on great idols inscribed in an intelligible heaven—Justice, Law, and Truth—and, positing its principles as absolutes, it considers itself as being in itself its own end.[3] Any individual who acts in pursuit of earthly ends thus situates himself forthwith outside of ethics.[4] He can either avoid transgressing the supreme laws or else actively oppose them. If he opts for the former, his action will not be called good; it will remain neutral in value; while in the latter case it will be condemned as reprehensible. Having thus no possibility of attaining the good, a man engaged in political ventures risks, on the contrary, doing harm. It is, therefore, in the interest of the virtuous soul to abstain from action as he is concerned with keeping himself pure; at the very most will he affirm by symbolic gestures his loyalty to great principles. He will be a witness, a martyr. This is precisely the meaning of Antigone's stubbornness; but she will not get involved in struggles whose stakes she deems to be without value.[5] Such an ethics can be of no real help to the political man. Since it scorns the ends that he is pursuing, it offers him nothing but a set of negative precepts; moreover it is negative also because it is situated at the level of generality and abstraction. It is impossible—Kant has often been criticized for this—to derive from the universal form of the maxim any definite application.[6] The map of the future world is not laid out in the idea of Justice, the idea of Law. Just as the general laws of gravity cannot suggest to an inventor the design for a flying machine but can only show him its conditions of possibility, so the general and abstract precepts of ethics can only set limits to the political man's range of action without helping him to find the solution to the singular problems he is facing. In his eyes, this sterile ethics, which does nothing but deny him certain means of action, is only an obstacle; and since the role of the political man is to change the face of the earth and surpass the given, it is natural for him to try to break through this barrier. In fact, he sees no reason to respect it; the moralist's claims do not seem justified to him. Engaged in the present and busy building the future, the political man experiences the historical and contingent character of human things and denies to ethics any absolute and timeless character. Ethics attempts to remove itself from time but, in doing so, simply relegates itself to the past and appears as a useless legacy of bygone ages. Wishing to be absolute, it severs its earthly roots, and the man of action who is rooted on earth no longer recognizes foundations there. Ethics claims to define the Good objectively. But, against this good that he does not recognize as his, the political man opposes the obvious fact of his own will and ends. Ethics, ultimately, speaks this haughty language in the name of man, but is the political man not himself a man? Why would he favor outdated traditions, an uncertain public opinion? It is noteworthy, besides, that public opinion is only mildly indignant about the man of action's rebellion against accepted ethics. The public knows that an ethics that does not bite into the world is nothing but an ensemble of dead structures. Public opinion itself is not convinced of the ethics that it has adopted; it admits that there is much truth in the maxim "The end justifies the means," and that the means cannot be judged independently of the end for which it aims. The means and the end form part of a unique process, and the means find their signification only in the light of the completed operation. Finally, the public hesitantly wonders whether true ethics does not lie in efficacy.

As a result, ethics, being in practice rejected by the very persons who still pay lip service to it, seems hardly more than a gratuitous and ceremonious pastime reserved for a few specialists. Many political men deliberately turn away from it. While scorning the subjective concerns of virtuous souls, they seek the solution to their problems in objectivity and hope to find assurance there. They openly declare themselves to be realists. The realist scorns both the utopian, who underestimates the forces of opposition in the world, and the idealist, who, with his useless [*vain*] scruples, adds superfluous resistance to this world. As for himself, the realist claims to have a precise knowledge of things and to respond to their appeal without wavering on the choice of means. There are various kinds of realists, but they are all alike in their intention to subordinate their activities to the one reality and in their refusal to integrate into this reality human freedom, whose anguishing presence is precisely what they want to conceal from themselves. To what extent is such an attitude valid?

We will not discuss here politicians, i.e., men for whom politics represents only a personal career and whose activity is not defined by principles or objectives, but the true political man who intends to map out the world to come. Such a man is not focused on himself but on things, and because of this, it is in the midst of things that he finds his objectives; he believes that the ends that he is pursuing are imposed on him from the outside, without his consent, that they assert themselves as ends in the same way a stone asserts itself as a stone. When Louis XI or Richelieu set out to unify or preserve the kingdom of France,[7] or when the Emperor Charles V attempted to revive the Holy Roman Empire[8]—with such passion that he did not hesitate to enter into alliances with the Lutherans in order to ensure victory for the Church—they did not question the necessity of those grand designs: it was France, it was the Empire dictating their actions. If, however, they had reflected on their endeavors, even for a moment, they would have discovered that neither the kingdom of France nor the Holy Empire that they sought to establish could lay claim to existence, precisely because they did not as yet exist. It is obvious, then, that no end can be inscribed in reality. By definition an end is not; it has to be; it requires the spontaneity of a consciousness that, surpassing the given, throws itself toward the future. No historical tradition, no geographical structure, no economic fact can impose a course of action. They merely constitute situations that make it possible for man to pursue the most diverse projects. And whether he takes it upon himself to recapture the ideal of his ancestors, of a faction,[9] or of a party, whether he loses himself in the violence of a passion or is fascinated by a myth, it is always man who fashions the great idols to which he devotes his life. As a result, we may state without paradox that any coherent and valid politics is first of all idealist inasmuch as it is subordinate to an idea that it intends to carry out. Whether one fights for his country's independence, his integrity, prestige, or prosperity, whether he fights for the happiness of man, for peace, justice, comfort, or freedom, the goal to be reached is an unreality [*un irréel*].

The realist must recognize the fact that the end does not precede action, but he believes that at least its conditions of possibility are inscribed in reality. Contrary to the utopian, who aims at unreachable ends or deceives himself about the means that could serve his purpose, the realist claims to define clearly the feasibility of his action and to know how to choose effective means to carry it out. He criticizes Wilson, for example, for having been a utopian; Wilson indeed sought an impossible end, at least in 1918, namely, world peace.[10] And the means he advocated to guarantee it implied a misconception of human nature. The realist admires, on the other hand, the fact that the three great powers,[11] concerned not to make the same mistake twice, adopted a resolutely realistic politics. They refused to place their trust in men or nations; what they were seeking was to establish a stable balance of power among the existing forces.

Obviously, the utopian is by definition destined to fail, and for a politics to be valid it must first and foremost be successful. However, upon closer examination, the lines separating utopianism from realism are less distinct than they may have appeared at first. In fact, we can prove that squaring the circle and perpetual motion are impossible, but man is not what he is in the way a circle is, whose radii remain invariably equal. He is what he makes himself be, what he chooses to be. Whatever the given situation, it never necessarily implies one future or another since man's reaction to his situation is free. How can he decide in advance that peace, war, revolution, justice, happiness, defeat, or victory are impossible? When Lenin was preparing in Switzerland for the coming of a new order, he could have been taken for a great dreamer;[12] and if no one had been so bold as to want the Russian Revolution, if Lenin and all the revolutionaries had thought of themselves as insane, they would indeed have been so, for the revolution would not have happened.

That is why, when a reform is suggested, the first reaction of the political conservative is always to declare it impossible, because he knows that by declaring it impossible, he contributes to making it so. It was, no doubt, not enough, as French pacifists imagined it was, simply to declare "There will be no war" for it not to happen. However, it is also true that the impulse through which we accept the advent of a certain future contributes to its formation. We therefore do not accept the collaborators' excuse of having been victims of a simple intellectual error. They argue that they believed Germany's defeat to be impossible. That means that they consented to her victory. In reality, they opted for the German supremacy that they claimed merely to have recognized. Furthermore, the word "recognition" is in itself ambiguous, because when we recognize a government, we make it exist as such. Gaining an awareness is never a purely contemplative process; it is engagement, support or rejection. In 1940 some Frenchmen accepted collaboration with Germany in the name of realism. But they are striking proof of the weakness of an attitude that mutilates and distorts the very reality on which it claims to base itself, since it refuses to make the fact of human freedom an integral part of this reality. If all nations had resigned themselves to accept Hitler's triumph, Hitler would indeed have triumphed; but they could refuse and they did. It is this refusal that the collaborator was unable to foresee. Anxious to give up his own freedom, he wished to be carried along on the great current of history, forgetting that history is made by men. To be sure, the occupation of France by Germany was a reality. But it was equally real that the French remained free to give to the event the meaning they chose. If everyone had collaborated, Germany would have become an ally. If they resisted, she would remain an adversary. A defeat is not final until the vanquished has admitted it as such. The first mistake of the political realist is to underestimate the existence and weight of his own reality. This reality is not given. It is what it decides to be. The lucid political man who truly has a hold of things is also conscious of the power of freedom in him and in others.

The ends of action, therefore, are neither given nor even prefigured in reality; they have to be willed. Despite his desire to lose himself in pure objectivity, the realist cannot avoid the question of what to will. But he will try to regain on the level of values the objectivity that eludes him on the level of being.

As politics attains consciousness of itself, it indeed becomes clear that the essential problem posed is to reach valid ends; reaching the goal does not suffice in itself, the goal has to be justified as such. Throughout history we see wars follow upon wars, revolutions upon revolutions that seem to us to be nothing but sterile agitations because their goals were vain. If the outcomes do not serve man, if they are nothing to him, then they are absolutely nothing. To annex a territory without knowing how to administer it is doing nothing. To increase production without thereby changing men's standard of living is doing nothing. Gradually men have become conscious of the following truth: that they themselves are their own end. Marx expressed this idea when he said, "Man represents the highest goal for man."[13] The political man who claims to be a realist can hope to find in this statement the objective justification for his endeavors; he knows what he must want; he must want to serve man. Therefore, since there is no other value besides this one, all means employed are indifferent by themselves: there exists no taboo. The end being posited as an absolute, and the means as relative to the end, the realist evades any moral indecision. The goal is fixed and the means are determined by the goal. As a result, the political man becomes simply a technician; he need not concern himself with ethics any more than does the mason building a house; the only problems posed to him are of a tactical nature.

The preceding describes the most modern and conscious form of political realism. But it becomes obvious right away that equally realist politics can differ greatly depending on the conception of man that they adopt. At present, we can roughly distinguish between two kinds of realism: a conservative realism employed defensively by a certain bourgeoisie, and a revolutionary realism employed by its proponents in the opposite attempt to capture and utilize precisely those forces capable of building the future.

The conservative associates the interests of the bourgeois class with the preservation of spiritual values whose guardian it claims to be. At the same time he strives to demonstrate the primitive and purely material character of the interests of the working class. An idealist and a spiritualist in the positive aspect of his doctrine, yet the conservative becomes a stubborn realist when it comes to defending his interests against the demands of the proletariat. He likes to think—thereby subscribing to the old naturalist and utilitarian tradition—that any action taken by the working class is solely motivated by the pursuit of what is useful and that the useful is defined by the elementary needs of human nature. And he uses these assumptions on the one hand as a pretext to criticize the members of the proletariat for their "sordid materialism," and on the other to accuse them of frivolity if they appear to have other concerns besides the necessities of food and clothing. In the name of his spiritual superiority, the bourgeois declares himself to be in a better position to define the conditions suitable for the working class than the working class itself. This entitles the conservative to approve with a clear conscience an authoritarian regime that, while providing the worker with what he needs, namely the satisfaction of his material instincts, would reserve the exercise of freedom and the advantages that accompany it for the privileged class. The conservative will thus prove triumphantly that it is childish to get annoyed at the excessive fortunes of big capitalists, because if their wealth were distributed to all the workers, each would receive only a pittance. He will also explain that it is folly to attempt by means of strikes or bloody revolutions to gain advantages that would not be worth the sacrifice of a single human life and that could be patiently won by peaceful means. Charity and aid are in his opinion valid remedies to relieve poverty. After all, bread is bread, whether given out of pity, earned through work, or obtained by violent means. When the behavior of the proletariat refutes this rudimentary philosophy, we look to a mechanistic psychology for an explanation. Thus, if we observe that for the most part the working class does not fight to keep itself alive, but rather to defend and obtain a certain standard of living, we will declare that the worker suffers from an inferiority complex. In this way the workers' demands are stripped of any moral signification; we refuse to recognize in them the élan of human transcendence.

However, the very fact that the workers' demands assume a political form precludes mistaking them for a simple instinctual movement. Just as in knowledge, empiricism is false because science begins only when the individual fact is surpassed toward a general theory, so any naturalistic interpretation of a political attitude is erroneous, because politics begins only when men surpass themselves toward general human values. In politics, the individual must tear himself away from his individual situation, transcend himself toward others, and transcend the present toward the future. A man who tries only to keep himself alive has no political existence and the horror of his situation stems precisely from the fact that, wholly taken up with not dying, he cannot give value to his existence by surpassing it toward something other than itself. But men who together make demands, even if only for a piece of bread, could not be accused of "sordid materialism" because each demands for all the others, and the goal pursued infinitely surpasses the immediate satisfaction of an animal appetite. A piece of bread is also life, the right to life for oneself and for others, in the present as in the future. There is no space between matter and the idea incarnated in it, between the thing and its signification. The standard of living that the worker demands is not required by his immediate needs, nor is it called forth by dreams of compensation. It is the actualization, the expression of the idea that the worker has of himself, in the same sense that our body is the expression of our existence. It is the objective form that a transcendence takes on. For this reason it is not absurd that a man is willing to risk his life in a strike, or in war, in order to maintain or gain a certain standard of living. The aim of the striker is not so much an increase in salary, as a crude amount of money, but an increase as something that he has gained; it affirms his power to improve his condition on his own. That is precisely what the conservative's limited good sense refuses to understand. Like Pascal, he likes to think that the hunter is not interested in the hare but in the hunt.[14] In reality he is interested in the hare that *he* is hunting. They constitute an indivisible totality. In August 1944,[15] there were prudent people who, invoking the well-known realist wisdom, were asking, "What good would there be in liberating Paris ourselves? In any case, Paris will soon be liberated."[16] But the goal was not a liberated Paris, it was the liberation itself; for the combatants having Paris liberated was not enough, they wanted to liberate it themselves. For the same reason, the idea of revolution falls apart if we value only its end results, or, rather, if we believe that we could ever separate the result from the movement that engendered it. Our well-meaning historians are eager to prove that the king and his ministers could have brought about, without bloodshed, the reforms that were achieved by the Revolution of 1789.[17] They forget that, if this had been so, the reforms would have had a totally different meaning, that our political system and our institutions have been deeply marked by the event that gave them birth: the specific form democracy took in France, the system of political parties and how they interact can be explained only by their origin. For this very reason, the revolutionary's action is aimed not only at the time following the revolution; he wants the revolution for its own sake, since it serves as a means of confirming his freedom and his transcendence. The good for man cannot be given to him from the outside; it is a good only because man engages himself in it. Here again, we find in realism the glaring contradiction that, out of respect for reality, it denies the very reality that gives all others their value and meaning, namely, human reality. Given the context, there is nothing surprising here. Such defensive realism is nothing but bad faith; it aims precisely at nothing but the negation of an entire class of men. Fascism, paternalism, all forms of authoritarianism are based on a lie.

Realists on the left have often exposed this bad faith, this lie. They say that they are not fighting for material goods but to enable man to realize himself as transcendence and freedom. We could blame them for refusing to become aware of all the implications of such an attitude and this leads them to serious inconsistency. If man's good is constituted by the élan of human transcendence, and if the result forms a single process with the movement leading to it, then it becomes impossible to disassociate the end from the means. The means can be understood only in light of the desired end, but inversely, the end is inseparable from the means by which it is carried out, and it is a fallacy to believe that the end can be achieved by just any means. The relation of means to end is difficult for the realist to imagine, since he views the end as something static, closed in on itself and separate from the means that is also defined as a thing, a simple instrument; between them there could exist only a mechanical link, that of a cause and the effect it produces. But just as our body is a mechanical force capable of producing definite effects in the material world yet is, at the same time, the expression of our existence, so too our actions belong to the category of material phenomena, but they are also realities that signify. The desired end is always a human situation, that is to say, a signifying fact. The actions, therefore, that aim to bring about an end must both create a thing and give it meaning. If this thing is not animated by meaning, then the failure is just as complete as if the meaning were never incarnated at all.

Michelet in *Histoire de la Révolution française* [History of the French Revolution][18] writes that a town in the east, besieged by the Austrians and its resources depleted, considered for a moment chasing women, children, and the elderly outside its walls, but the Commissioner of the Republic opposed this measure, declaring, "We want freedom for all."[19] The goal was not only to save the town from the Austrians; the town was valuable because it embodied the new principles of freedom and equality; a victory won by renouncing the ideal that was being defended would have been the worst of defeats. During the German occupation, people often thought it unfortunate that certain groups of resistance fighters were inept in defending themselves against stool pigeons, against traitors; and doubtless some of them were inept, because a secret society is not easy to organize.[20] But also, many resistance fighters found it repugnant to adopt among themselves the police tactics of informing and distrust. They were fighting for the respect of man, for fraternity and human friendship, and in everything they did they affirmed this respect and friendship, even if they were to pay for this trust with their own lives. The realist laughs at these scruples. He cynically agrees to lie and slander. But if one is ready to inform and lie to ensure man's triumph then it turns out that the man who was made to triumph will be a being unworthy of respect, a man it is legitimate to dupe, slander, and betray. He will be banned from friendship and trust, and he will have been saved only by being mutilated. It is not out of vain idealistic scruples that the antifascist is reluctant to become a fascist in order to fight fascism, the pacifist to become a warrior in order to fight warriors. For what is the point of fighting if by doing so one destroys all reasons for which one chose to fight? No doubt, French pacifists in the 1920s and 1930s served the cause of peace poorly. It is absurd to ensure the defeat of those values that one wants to triumph, out of respect for them. But it is no less absurd to renounce an idea under pretext of ensuring its effectiveness. Politics often chooses the latter path. This also lends politics its incoherent and disappointing character. Charles V, wanting to bring back to life the Holy Roman Empire in the name of a Catholic and mystical idea, agreed to enter into Lutheran alliances against the pope while burning at the stake all heretics in Flanders and Spain. But his clumsy opportunism only undermined, throughout all Christendom, the spiritual convictions necessary to accomplish his work. The men of the Vichy regime,[21] who claimed to be saving France by collaborating with Germany, refused to understand that through their submission they were killing everything that lent meaning and value to the French reality; what remained to them was nothing worthwhile; there was nothing left to save. Men often hide their willingness to accept defeat under the name of opportunism. Through opportunism liberals have been known to support tyranny, socialists to espouse fascism, nationalists to take sides with a foreign country, and revolutionaries to defend the established order. This resulted in the destruction of freedom, of justice, of the nation, and of the revolution. In this interplay of means and ends, if the end recedes further and further into the distance, then the means themselves appear as an end, but an end stripped of all meaning and importance. Under the pretext of going forward with firm resolve, the realist in the end goes nowhere.

The realist is not unaware of this danger. He hopes to avoid it by reducing the antinomy between ends and means to that of present and future, of the part and the whole. All political action is transcendence of the individual toward the human totality, transcendence of the present toward the future. The realist considers this totality as one and complete; he considers the future as a given. Just as the ancients imagined the sky as a ceiling that a sufficiently high tower could reach,[22] so at the end of time instants and centuries are fused. The future appears as a large, fixed, immobile canvas, immobile: a terrestrial eternity. In its most accentuated form, this illusion gives rise to great myths: the golden age, the promised land, paradise found. It then seems natural to sacrifice a few individuals to the ensemble of humanity, to sacrifice the transitory instant to a success destined to perpetuate itself endlessly, to sacrifice what is temporary to the eternal and what is contingent to the absolute.

It is a fact that the individual exists only as surpassing of himself toward others, and the present exists only as a movement toward the future. If human existence were closed in on itself, it would be no more than a vegetative state. This is why we readily accept the sacrifice of individuals to the community, or of a living generation to men who are not yet born. I can lie to some men today so that all men may some day know the truth; I can have some men killed (a million is insignificant for the price of the infinite), if it will bring lasting peace to the world. This is how the realist justifies himself. However, this reasoning, which he thinks will put him at ease, is not so sure. The collectivity is not cut from a different cloth than the individuals who compose it; neither is the future of a different cloth than the present that it prolongs. The collectivity is an ensemble of individuals, none of whom is more real than the next. The future is nothing but a series of moments that, one after another, each become present, and so are transitory. If the realist placidly prefers the whole over the part, it is because he has adopted a material and quantitative point of view: a thousand men are more than one man, if one looks at man as something countable. But quantity is not value; one thousand francs are more than one franc, if you want to buy objects that are themselves valuable. In a desert, one thousand francs and one centime are equivalent; for a thirsty man, a waterfall is worth no more than a modest brook; it is a purely mathematical mirage that makes us attach an absolute meaning to the words "more" and "less."[23] If man is finally nothing but himself, then *for whom* are a thousand men worth *more* than a single one? The only possible answer is: for himself. However, this numerical superiority is not inscribed in reality; it is not a given fact; it still is subject to a human decision. If, therefore, man declares that in certain cases the sacrifice of one man is in his eyes more important than the victory of ten thousand others, he can refuse such a sacrifice. He must choose and decide. The brute fact imposes nothing on him.

Likewise we must ask ourselves from whence comes the value we attribute to the future. It is easy to scorn the present, if, by cutting it off from the future, we reduce it to itself; but then we also cut each future moment off from the others and, reduced to themselves, they also lose all their value. In truth, what constitutes [*fait*] the value of the future is that it is the future of my present, the accomplishment of my project. Present and future are joined in the unity of the project, which is nothing but empty if it is not accomplished. But before it can be accomplished, it must be, it must spring up within me and this upspringing defines my present. Therefore, it is not due to its temporal situation that the result seems desirable; it is because it is the result, because in it my entire élan toward it comes together and becomes concrete. Here again, it is not reality that imposes a choice on me; it is only after the choice that reality takes on a value. Human totality and the future appear to dictate my action only to the extent that my action posits them there. But these are not things separate from myself. I prefer them only inasmuch as I find in them the movement of my transcendence, it is therefore impossible for me to subordinate this movement to them. This means that the political man cannot avoid making decisions or choices; things will not give him any ready-made answers, neither on the level of being nor on the level of values. In each new situation he must question himself anew about his ends, and he must choose and justify them without assistance. But it is precisely in this free engagement that morality resides. If morality is discredited today, it is because it hesitates in affirming itself in its truth. The sterile attitude of the moralist enclosed in his own subjectivity is rightfully scorned. The political man, who has the audacity to choose his ends and to reach them without allowing taboos to get in his way, affirms the preeminence of the future over the past. He affirms the subject's independence against the objectivity that ready-made values claim to have. He affirms himself as transcendence and freedom; he is more genuinely ethical than the theorist who claims to enslave man to abstract principles. But if ethics became aware of its essential significance, we would realize that, on the contrary, there is no domain that should not be subject to it.

Ethics is not an ensemble of constituted values and principles; it is the constituting movement through which values and principles are posited; it is the movement that an authentically moral man must reproduce for himself. The great moralists were not virtuous souls, docilely subject to a preestablished code of good and evil. They created a new universe of values through words that were actions, through actions that bit into the world; and they changed the face of the earth more profoundly than kings and conquerors. Ethics is not negative; it does not require that man remain faithful to a static image of himself: to be moral means to seek to found one's own being and to transform one's contingent existence into a necessity. But man's being is "a being in the world"; he is indissolubly linked to the world in which he lives and without which he can neither exist nor even define himself. He is linked to this world through his actions, and it is his actions that he must justify. Since each act transcends a concrete and singular situation, each time one must invent anew a mode of action that carries within it its own justification. When in 1940 the French had to decide what their attitude toward the occupier should be, no preexisting system could dictate their behavior. They had to choose freely, and through their practical choice of a course of action they defined the values that made this choice necessary. If, during the course of the trials where they presented their defense, the collaborators managed to create an uneasy atmosphere in the courtroom, this is because they skillfully exploited the ambiguous nature of what society nowadays calls ethics.[24] It was easy for them to show that they had not violated any of the great eternal maxims. With respect to the particular situation in which France found itself in 1940, these neither commanded nor forbade anything. Ethics requires that one serve one's country; but it does not say which concept of country one should choose; it does not say what will serve the country. All the collaborators pleaded that they wanted the good of France, except that this France whose good they wanted was defined by their action in such a way that it was no longer ours. They also pleaded that they wanted to serve peace, justice, and order; but the real question is to know which peace, which justice, which order are valid. We can only condemn the collaborators in the name of new values that were created and imposed during those years; or rather, their condemnation is one of the processes by which these values are affirmed. However, the judges themselves did not dare to sweep away traditional prejudice and affirm that ethics was solely the expression of human will. The deficiency of classical ethics is evident to all; and yet, few men resolutely dare to free themselves from it. From thence the profound malaise that men's conscience suffers today. We no longer believe in the kind of ethics whose principles we flaunt; we dare not explicitly formulate nor draw out the final consequences of the ethics that we practice and so believe. The result is much confusion, hypocrisy, bad faith, doubt, and reluctance. Even so, it is time for man to become aware of what is his human domain and to assume fully his condition. Then ethics would find its true expression; it is nothing but concrete action itself, insofar as this action attempts to justify itself. In other words authentic ethics is realist; through it man realizes himself by realizing the ends that he chooses. It can even be said that the authentically ethical man is more realist than any other, for there is no reality more complete than that which carries within itself its own reasons. And since the political man cannot avoid questioning himself about the justification for his actions, and since a politics is not valid unless its ends are freely chosen, ethics and politics seem one and the same to us. Man is one, the world he inhabits is one, and with the actions he performs in the world, he engages himself in his totality.

Reconciling ethics and politics is thus reconciling man with himself; it means affirming that at every instant he can assume himself totally. However, this requires that he give up the security that he hoped to gain by enclosing himself within the pure subjectivity of traditional ethics or the objectivity of realist politics.

"I have my conscience, I have justice, I have all," says Electra in the play by Giraudoux, heedless of the cataclysm that she sets off in Argos.[25] This is the arrogant certainty sought by the idealist. He wants to keep his hands clean, his conscience clear, and intends to escape all earthly defilement. This dream of purity is not possible within a realist ethics. If man is the supreme end of every action, then reciprocally, man should always be considered as an end, as Kantian ethics requires.[26] But the part-whole, present-future antinomy demands sacrifices because, if we must not destroy the goal while reaching for it, neither should we give up the idea of reaching it for fear of destroying it. It is not possible to act for man without treating certain men, at certain times, as means. The drama of lucid political action is that in its attempt to achieve human freedom as an end, it can proceed only on the basis of givens, of corporeal presences. By definition, interiority, the subjectivity of man, and the freedom by which he affirms himself as an absolute value escape anyone's hold over them. We can act on men only as long as they are givens, as long as they are objects coexisting in the same world. Among these objects are some that serve as instruments for my purposes, others that are obstacles; but none of the singular men through whom the political man transcends himself toward "man" is ever an end himself. However, treating man as a means is committing violence against him; it means contradicting the idea of his absolute value that alone allows the action to be fully founded. If I were to kill only one man in order to save millions, an absolute outrage [*scandale*] would break out in the world because of me, an outrage that could not be compensated for by any success and that could neither be overcome or remedied, nor integrated into the totality of action. The moralist who wants both to act and to approve of himself would want to use only means that are in themselves ethical, that is to say, only those whose meaning is in keeping with the end he is aiming for. However, this dream is impossible, and if he insists, he will only vacillate between heaven and earth without being able truly to engage himself in this world. To come down to earth means accepting defilement, failure, horror; it means admitting that it is impossible to save everything; and what is lost is lost forever.

Does this mean that we must finally return to justifying any means for the sake of the end? No, we need to understand that end and means form an indivisible totality. The end is defined by the means, which receive their meaning from it. An action is a signifying ensemble that unfolds across the world, across time, and whose unity cannot be broken. It is this singular totality that we must construct and choose at every instant. It is for us to decide whether one man must be killed in order to save ten, or to let ten die so as not to betray one. The decision is inscribed neither in heaven nor on earth. Whatever I may choose to do, I will be unfaithful to my profound desire to respect human life; and yet, I am forced to choose; no reality exterior to myself can direct me in my choice.

Let man therefore lose any hope of escaping into his inner purity or of losing himself in some foreign object; temporal dispersion and the separation of consciousnesses will not allow him to dream of a definitive reconciliation with himself. The lot of being torn apart [*déchirement*] is the ransom for his presence in the world, for his transcendence and for his freedom. If he tries to flee, he will be lost for good, because then he does nothing, or, what he does is nothing. He must give up any idea of finding rest; he must assume his freedom.[27] Only at this price will he become able truly to surpass the given, which is the veritable ethics; truly to found the object in which he transcends himself, which is the only valid politics. At this price his action is concretely inscribed in the world, and the world where he acts is a world endowed with meaning, a human world.

NOTES

1. The tragedy *Antigone* (442 B.C.E.), by Sophocles (496–406 B.C.E.), was used by Hegel in the *Phenomenology of Mind* to illustrate several critical oppositions in man's ethical/political structures: divine law in opposition to earthly law; the family in opposition to the community; the individual in opposition to the whole; the female in opposition to the male. Antigone's central drama—the conflict that occurs when reverence to divine obligations stands in unyielding opposition to obedience to the laws of man—weaves its way through the ethical portions of the *Phenomenology*.

2. The Greeks were dualists who believed that the mortal body is a sort of tomb in which the soul is held captive. This belief is connected with the Orphic myth of Dionysus, the child of Zeus and Persephone who is captured and eaten by the Titans. On discovery of this crime, Zeus punishes the Titans with lightning; from their ashes emerges humanity, at once as divine as Dionysus and as corrupt as the Titans. After the death of the body, the soul may be purified of its physical taint, but only after it descends to the underworld and endures grueling punishment.

3. "Positing its principles as absolutes, it considers itself as being in itself its own end": in the phrase "comme absolus, elle se considère comme étant à elle-même sa propre fin," in *ESN*, 54, the words "absolus, elle se considère comme" are omitted.

4. The ethics of Immanuel Kant (1724–1804), as outlined in *Fundamental Principles of the Metaphysic of Morals* (1785), posits a self-existing Good that is found in—is, in fact, synonymous with—the Good Will; that is, in the will that acts only upon what it *ought* or *should* do, without consideration of personal satisfaction or gain. Thus the pure will to do good and the good itself are encompassed within the same universal principle and are governed by the (natural) law—the *categorical imperative*—of Duty. One does good because it is one's duty to do good; one does one's duty because to do one's duty is good. Kant allowed no other acceptable moral position.

5. After Antigone's brother is killed in the commission of a treasonous war, the wronged king, Creon, forbids the burial of the traitor's body, a pointed act of desecration and blasphemy against the man, his family, and their gods. Unwilling to disobey divine law, Antigone defies Creon and buries her brother. Antigone's treason, while "good" according to her custom and belief, directly opposes Creon's understanding of good for the state. Her tenacious loyalty to the gods' requirements escalates into a conflict that results in death and destruction for her supporters and enemies alike.

6. From section 2 of Immanuel Kant's *Foundations of the Metaphysics of Morals,* trans. Lewis White Beck (Indianapolis: Bobbs-Merrill, 1959): "There is, therefore, only one categorical imperative. It is: Act only according to that maxim by which you can at the same time will that it should become a universal law" (39).

7. Louis XI (1423–83), son of Charles VII, was an early nationalist whose efforts following the Hundred Years' War focused upon a unified France. The duke of Richelieu (Armand-Jean du Plessis, 1585–1642) was chief minister to Louis XIII; he was called the "iron cardinal."

8. The Holy Roman Empire (800–1806) began with the rule of Charlemagne in 800 C.E.,

when efforts were made, with varying degrees of success, scope, and duration, to restore to Europe the traditions, boundaries, and glories of Rome. Charles V (1500–1558) was one of the seven rulers of the Holy Roman Empire.

9. The word "faction" is given as "action" in *ESN*, 60.

10. Woodrow Wilson (1856–1924) was a devout Presbyterian and scholar who constructed his most significant political decisions around his belief in absolute universal truths. When escalating tensions with the Central Powers (particularly Germany) forced Wilson to lead the United States into World War I, Wilson rationalized American involvement by saying that its success would "make the world safe for democracy." Meanwhile, Wilson researched the world's problems, soliciting the help of experts in law, science, mathematics, and the humanities. At the 1918 peace conference in France, Wilson is said to have commented to such a committee of experts, "Tell me what is right, and I'll fight for it." Wilson's dream of a worldwide governing body committed to maintaining peace (the League of Nations) was disappointed, however, when the United States refused to join, in spite of Wilson's architecture.

11. Beauvoir is probably referring to the prevailing alliance of the First World War: France, Great Britain, and Russia.

12. Lenin's position of anti-involvement in the war forced him into exile in Switzerland until 1917. It was during this time that Lenin found the sympathetic "party within a party" and began laying out the structure for the revolution that decisively ended the monarchy.

13. See Marx's essay "Contribution to the Critique of Hegel's *Philosophy of Right*": "The criticism of religion ends in the teaching *that man is the highest being for man*, hence in the categorical imperative to overthrow all those conditions in which man is a debased, enslaved, abandoned, contemptible being—conditions that cannot be better described than the exclamation of a Frenchman on hearing of a proposed tax on dogs: Poor dogs! They want to treat you like men" (*The Portable Marx*, trans. Eugene Kamenka [New York: Penguin Books, 1983], 119).

14. The religious writings of Blaise Pascal (1623–62), French scientist and religious philosopher, were posthumously published as *Pensées de M. Pascal sur la religion et sur quelques autres sujets* (1670). Here, Beauvoir is referring to his Pensée 136; see *Pascal's Pensées*, trans. A. J. Krailsheimer (1966; London: Penguin, 1995): "That is why gaming and feminine society, war and high office are so popular. It is not that they really bring true happiness, nor that anyone imagines that true bliss comes from possessing money to be won at gaming or the hare that is hunted: no one would take it as a gift. What people want is not the easy peaceful life that allows us to think of our unhappy condition, nor the dangers of war, nor the burdens of office, but the agitation that takes our mind off it and diverts us. That is why we prefer the hunt to the capture" (139).

15. "August 1944" is "l'année dernière" in *Les temps modernes*, 259.

16. France was liberated from the Nazi occupation on August 25, 1944.

17. The Revolution of 1789 began in Paris, on July 14, with the liberation of the Bastille. It culminated with the ousting of Louis XVI's *ancien régime*.

18. Jules Michelet (1788–1874) was one of the first historians to apply "interdisciplinary" methods to his research and narrative.

19. See Beauvoir's play *Les bouches inutiles* (1945), based on this story of the besieged town.

20. Beauvoir had some firsthand knowledge of these difficulties. In 1941 Sartre attempted to form a resistance organization, which he called "Socialism and Liberty" (see Beauvoir's

The Prime of Life, trans. Peter Green [New York: Lancer, 1973], 581). But the group was not effective: "Politically, we found ourselves reduced to a condition of total impotence. . . . Already the various movements that had sprung up right at the beginning were disbanded or in the process of breaking up. Like ours, they had come into being through individual initiative and consisted mainly of middle-class intellectuals without any experience of underground action—or indeed of action in any form" (ibid., 601).

21. The Vichy regime was the collaborationist government of Nazi-occupied France, headed by Marshal Philippe Pétain. The regime's slogan was "Work, Family, and Fatherland."

22. The Judaic myth of the Tower of Babel is found in Genesis 11:1–9.

23. Hegel wrote in the *Phenomenology of Mind,* trans. J. B. Baillie (New York: Macmillan, 1955): "It is quantity, a form of difference that does not touch the essential nature, which alone mathematics deals with. It abstracts from the fact that it is the notion which separates space into its dimensions, and determines the connexions between them and in them. . . . The principle of quantity, of difference, which is not determined by the notion, and the principle of equality, of abstract lifeless unity, are incapable of dealing with that shear restlessness of life and its absolute and inherent process of differentiation" (103–5).

24. Beauvoir also discusses the post–World War II trials of Nazi war criminals in the essay "An Eye for an Eye." See part 8 in the present volume.

25. Jean Giraudoux (1882–1944) adapted his *Electra* from the version by Euripedes (Sophocles having written one as well) of the Trojan tale of revenge. Of his play Giraudoux said, "The thesis of my play is this: that humanity, by its ability to forget and by a fear of complication, absorbs great crimes against it. But in every epoch surge forth these true beings who don't want the crime to be absorbed, and who prevent that absorption and call a halt to these means which only provoke more crimes and new disasters. Electra is one of those beings. She attains her goal, but at the price of horrible catastrophes." From an interview by Warnod Andre, "Le buste d'Electre, nous dit M. Jean Giraudoux," *Le Figaro,* May 11, 1937.

26. Kant wrote in the second section of the *Fundamental Principles,* "So act as to treat humanity, whether in thine own person or in that of any other, in every case as an end withal, never as means only."

27. "He must give up any idea of finding rest; he must assume his freedom": in the sentence "il doit renoncer à connaître le repos, il doit assumer sa liberté," in *ESN,* 87, the words "doit renoncer à connaître le repos, il" are omitted.

Existentialism and
Popular Wisdom

INTRODUCTION

by Eleanore Holveck

In the second volume of her autobiography, *Force of Circumstance,* Simone de Beauvoir describes the literary, political, and personal situations in Paris that gave rise to her essay "Existentialism and Popular Wisdom," which was first published in the third issue of *Les temps modernes,* 1945. In 1948, it became the title essay in a collection of previously published short pieces. The year 1945 was the occasion of an "existentialist offensive."[1] Beauvoir's novel *The Blood of Others* and Sartre's *The Age of Reason* and *The Reprieve* were published; *Les temps modernes* was launched; Sartre lectured on existentialism as a humanism, while Beauvoir spoke on the novel and metaphysics; and Beauvoir's play *Les bouches inutiles* (The Useless Mouths) was produced. Beauvoir, like Sartre, first rejected the name existentialism, coined by Gabriel Marcel, but accepted it in the end.

At first the public, disillusioned with ideologies based on neo-Kantian universal values, reason, and progress, viewed existentialism's emphasis on free individual choice as compatible with bourgeois values; amidst the ruin of all other absolute values, at least freedom remained. Soon, however, right-wing critics attacked Sartre and, by association, "la grande Sartreuse" (*FC,* 46), as a "poet of the sewers, philosopher of nothingness" (*FC,* 45). Communists found *Being and Nothingness* a barrier to a philosophy of history (*FC*, 43) and classified it as a minor aspect of bourgeois ideology. *Les temps modernes* allowed Beauvoir to respond. "I would read an article that made me angry and say to myself immediately: 'I must answer that!' That's how all the essays I wrote . . . came into being" (*FC*, 48).

To give a brief summary, then, "Existentialism and Popular Wisdom" is a defense of existentialism against its right- and left-wing critics in post–World War II France. Beauvoir argues that popular wisdom is characterized by two contradictory and ultimately unacceptable views of man: ideal versus real; a rational Kantian idealism versus an egoistic, utilitarian pessimism. Existentialism's view of singular, existing freedom undermines both contradictions and presents a view of human beings as having the free choice to act authentically in the world, thereby taking responsibility for all past and future values. Despite the ephemeral character of this essay, its major themes reveal serious philosophical issues echoed in works that Beauvoir wrote at the same time and illuminate Beauvoir's philosophical development up to *The Ethics of Ambiguity.* The essay also sheds light on Beauvoir's philosophical method in *The Second Sex.*

Beauvoir begins her essay with the accusation that existentialism emphasizes man's wretched condition; it denies friendship and love and abandons man in pure subjectivity, bereft of an objective world and any objective values. Beauvoir answers that popular wisdom cannot face and accept the finite character of human existence; therefore, it attempts to deal with human problems by means of two contradictory strategies. On the one hand, human beings turn to the arts to give them heroic portraits of noble human beings; popular songs, films, novels, public ceremonies, and epitaphs in cemeteries conspire to present an ideal man: patient, modest, selfless, courageous. At the same time, however, popular wisdom mocks a degraded image. From the fathers of the church to literary and philosophical moralists like Pascal and La Rochefoucauld, human nature is characterized by a psychology of cynical self-interest. Under his heroic armor, man is a Hobbesian wolf to other men.

To exemplify this stark dichotomy between the ideal and the real, Beauvoir turns to marriage, love, and friendship. Love is loftily affirmed in speeches at weddings and funerals and in light novels, operas, and films. Lip service to the noble institution of marriage, however, gives way to the shrewish wives and lecherous husbands of comedy routines in farce and vaudeville. As early as her 1935–37 collection of short stories, *When Things of the Spirit Come First,* Beauvoir underlined the contradiction between spiritual ideals and brutal reality. Jacques Maritain's "greatest freedom of spirit,"[2] reason following faith, turns into Madam Vignon's attempt to force her daughter, Anne, to give up her true love in order to marry the richer, older man chosen by her parents.[3] In *Les bouches inutiles,* the important men of Vaucelles are building a monument to human freedom, a stone belfry, at the same time that they are planning to abandon the elderly, infants, and women to enemies outside the city gates, in order to preserve enough food for themselves until they are rescued by an approaching army.

Beauvoir's use of popular wisdom in common sayings, newspapers, and best sellers obviously owes something to Martin Heidegger's discussion of the they-self in *Being and Time.* For Heidegger, Dasein loses his authentic self in the world of everydayness, characterized by *das man.* An analysis of this phenomenon precedes Heidegger's discussion of authentic existence, just as Beauvoir's analysis of the many things that "they say" precedes her discussion of authenticity. Perhaps more important, Beauvoir reveals her interpretation of Hegel in her discussion of the contradiction between the "image of the generous and heroic man erected in public places and the image of the bestial and selfish man forged by the bitterness of daily life." What is at stake is the status of the individual in reference to the universal.

In his *Présentation* of the first issue of *Les temps modernes,* Sartre describes two methods of dealing with the individual/universal distinction in Hegel. The bourgeoisie use the myth of the universal to approach individual men by means of the analytic method. From this viewpoint, the individual is a simple element, "the vehicle of human nature . . . like a pea in a can of peas. . . . All men are *brothers:* fraternity is a passive bond among distinct molecules."[4] Individuals are social or psychological atoms viewed from a universal point of view. *Les temps modernes,* on the other hand, uses a method Sartre calls "synthetic anthropology" (Sartre, 261), viewing men as having in common "not a nature but a metaphysical condition . . . the necessity of being born and dying, that of being *finite* and of existing in the world among other men" (Sartre, 260). Viewed synthetically, men make themselves. A man, for example, makes himself a worker. "Though he is completely conditioned by his class . . . conditioned even in his feelings and his thoughts, it is nevertheless up to him to decide on the meaning of his condition and that of his comrades" (Sartre, 265).

Beauvoir's analysis might seem to agree with Sartre's; however, I would submit that there is a major difference in emphasis. Beauvoir argues in "Existentialism and Popular Wisdom" that contradictions in popular wisdom permit men "to jump from one plane of truth to another." The self of the ethics of self-interest is "an object of the world." Likewise, "[i]n edifying stories, young people smile as they die for their country. . . . [W]e are demigods as we eat and sleep." For Beauvoir, one must reject both the universal and the individual, which lead to bad faith, and her solution anticipates her position in *The Ethics of Ambiguity*. "I exist as an authentic subject, in a constantly renewed upspringing that is opposed to the fixed reality of things. I throw myself without help and without guidance into a world. . . . I am free, and my projects are not defined by preexisting interests." Instead of floundering between an ideal of perfect love between soul mates united in a permanent sacred union, or giving in to a brute desire to possess, which day by day forges a chain that weighs down two people who ultimately loath their cellmates, two people can freely choose to meet, to act together, to love each other today, knowing that their free choice must be constantly renewed.

In *The Ethics of Ambiguity* Beauvoir describes existential conversion, which brackets all beliefs in absolutes, whether that absolute be a universal value or a factual individual, as analogous to Husserl's phenomenological *epoché*. Existential conversion reveals not my stance as an individual in the light of the universal, but my free existence as a singular, gushing, spurting spontaneity.[5] At the same time, the existential freedom of others is revealed. In this essay about popular wisdom, Beauvoir seems not to have quite formulated existential conversion. She emphasizes, rather, that existing freedoms are separate and that action in the world overcomes the separation. "The separation of consciousnesses is thus a metaphysical fact, yet man can surmount it. He can, through the world, unite himself to other men. Existentialists are so far from denying love, friendship, and fraternity that in their eyes the only way for each individual to find the foundation and accomplishment of his being is in these human relationships." Hence, by acting freely in the world, by recognizing the freedom of others in my action, I create myself and others as free and accept responsibility for my choice.

The emphasis on action, without prior description of existential conversion, is characteristic of *Pyrrhus and Cineas* and *The Blood of Others*. In the latter novel, Beauvoir describes the creation of a new sense of family through actions centering around the heroine, Hélène Bertrand. In occupied France, a young girl, a stranger, rescues Hélène by giving her food and finding transportation for her by claiming that she is her sister. Hélène is not Yvonne's biological sister nor is Paul her brother, but she creates them as free sister and brother with her free action of driving a truck to help them escape Nazi prisons.

Beauvoir's emphasis on freedom of action is more radical, more existential, more grounded in the world, than Sartre's. A woman is not completely conditioned by class or biological facts, or even in her feelings and thoughts, as

Sartre would have it. Beauvoir's method in *The Second Sex* is both analytic and synthetic. She studies the universals, and then she studies how the universals are used to create the individuals, how women are not born but rather become, that is, develop into, grow up to be, similar peas in the same can. But in the midst of all the descriptions on the level of things—universal things, individual things—there is the hope that what man has made might be unmade and remade by women. Beauvoir's political actions for and with other women after writing *The Second Sex* suggest that her position in 1945 remained with her. She chose to act in the world with other women. Her autobiography is not filled with heroic clichés, nor is it the saga of a woman determined by her sex, her psychological makeup, or her class. Rather, her autobiography presents an example of a singular freedom struggling to act in the world, creating a world where she is free and others are free with her, and taking responsibility for her actions as a real woman.

NOTES

1. Simone de Beauvoir, *Force of Circumstance,* trans. Richard Howard (New York: Putnam, 1965), 38 (hereafter referred to as *FC*).

2. Jacques Maritain, *The Things That Are Not Caesar's,* trans. J. F. Scanlon (London: Sheed and Ward, 1930), 25.

3. Simone de Beauvoir, *When Things of the Spirit Come First,* trans. Patrick O'Brian (1935–37; New York: Pantheon, 1982), 119–20.

4. Jean-Paul Sartre, "Introducing *Les temps modernes,*" in *"What Is Literature?" and Other Essays,* trans. Bernard Frechtman (1948; Cambridge, Mass.: Harvard University Press, 1988), 256 (hereafter referred to as "Sartre," followed by page number).

5. Simone de Beauvoir, *The Ethics of Ambiguity,* trans. Bernard Frechtman (1948; New York: Citadel, 1976), 25.

TRANSLATION BY MARYBETH TIMMERMANN

NOTES BY SABINE CRESPO AND TRICIA WALL

Existentialism and Popular Wisdom

Few people understand this philosophy baptized somewhat randomly as existentialism, and many attack it. Among other things, it is criticized for offering man an image of himself and his condition such as to make him despair. Existentialism (justified or not, we will keep this name for simplicity's sake) supposedly does not acknowledge man's greatness and chooses to paint only his misery. It is even accused of "miserablism," according to a recent neologism. It is, they say, a doctrine that denies friendship, fraternity, and all forms of love, enclosing the individual in an egoistic solitude. It cuts him off from the real world and condemns him to remain entrenched in his pure subjectivity for it refuses any objective justification to human undertakings, the values posited by man, and the ends that he pursues. Does existentialism really conform to this image? The critics do not expand upon this question, and their readers meekly accept their interpretation. This should not sur-

"L'existentialisme et la sagesse des nations," *Les temps modernes* 1, no. 3 (1945): 385–404; reprinted in *L'existentialisme et la sagesse des nations* (1948; Paris: Nagel, 1963), 13–48, © Sylvie Le Bon de Beauvoir. It is followed here by Simone de Beauvoir's "Preface" to *L'existentialisme et la sagesse des nations* (9–11), a volume reprinting four articles from *Les temps modernes:* "L'existentialisme et la sagesse des nations," "Idéalisme moral et réalisme politique," "Littérature et métaphysique," and "Œil pour œil."

prise us. It is more surprising that this image, true or false, should raise so much outrage. There have always existed schools and authors that were not tender toward man. They were often received favorably. From where do these very particular resistances that we now encounter come?

One might believe that men are always reluctant to consider their weaknesses, and that they ask the arts to present them with a retouched and embellished portrait of themselves. And it is true that they like sentimental songs, heroic films, generous novels, and edifying speeches that give their feelings, acts, and life that moving plenitude that is also affirmed by epitaphs and funeral busts in cemeteries. Particularly when they feel menaced in their privileges, faced with hordes of dissenters like anarchists, revolutionaries, criminals, and delinquents, respectable people experience the need to give themselves a hand to hoist themselves up onto a pedestal. In order to obtain by trickery the respect of those newcomers who are wide-eyed children, the fraternity of adults also strives, through chosen texts and anecdotes, to raise before them the intimidating figure of man such as he dreams himself to be: patient and modest like Pasteur, passionate and selfless like Bernard Palissy, heroic like Bara the little drummer boy.[1] Commemorative ceremonies, front-page articles in newspapers, and books by certain specialized writers are specifically destined to maintain this secular faith. And just as the megalomaniac in the grip of his ravings is enraged if someone declares to his face, "You are not Napoleon," the man who has situated himself on the plane of official truths is indignant at the least hint of cowardice, egoism, or weakness. A lawyer who pointed out to a presiding judge that the wife of a prisoner, alone and poor, was exposed to many temptations, heard the judge answer [s'entendit répondre] with righteous anger: "You are insulting all the women of France!" However, the psychiatrist knows that if he casually asks the self-proclaimed Napoleon, "What do you do for a living?" the response will simply be, "I am a hair stylist," just as in the intimacy of his living room, the presiding judge would laugh heartily if someone were naïve enough to insinuate that all prisoners' wives were Lucreces.[2] As soon as they no longer feel obligated to give a public account of themselves and they give in to their private convictions, people willingly admit their weaknesses. If it is presented to them in a tone of good-natured complicity, they calmly accept the most degrading image of themselves. After exalting in reading Cyrano de Bergerac or the songs of Déroulède, they savor what they call the human truth in Le voyage de M. Perrichon [Monsieur Perrichon Goes Abroad] or Maupassant's stories.[3] From their conversations, proverbs, favorite books, and jokes emanates such a dark picture of man that one wonders what miserablism could still frighten them.

The theme of man's misery is not new. The Church fathers, Pascal, Bossuet, Massillon, preachers, priests, the entire Christian tradition has for centuries tried its best to fill man with the feeling of his abjection.[4] It is true that for the believer, the original sin that corrupts human nature can be redeemed with the help of grace, but among the people who repeat along with the believer that man's heart is full of garbage, there are many who do not believe in the supernatural or who hardly give it a second thought. In either case, they deny that any innocence or virtue exists on the natural plane. Man appears to them as a bestial being whose vulgar appetites would lead to the worst excesses if the fear of hell and society didn't put the brakes on them. It is known, for example, that in the eyes of most priests and staunch believers, an honest friendship between a man and a woman is absolutely impossible. The purity of a young girl and the chastity of a woman seem too fragile to them to resist one hour alone with a male who is obviously lustful. I knew a very pious general's widow who had such a terrifying idea of masculine lust that she approved of the existence of organized prostitution. "Without that, a respectable woman wouldn't be able to walk down the street," she would say. The many precautions that parents and Christian teachers take regarding children are enough to show that they imagine a propensity for all perversions within these young souls.

Sensuality, lust: Christian pessimism especially emphasizes the misery of the flesh. Secular moralists have more readily attacked social behaviors. La Rochefoucauld, La Fontaine, Saint-Simon, Chamfort, and Maupassant have vied with each other in denouncing baseness, futility, and hypocrisy.[5] According to them, man's heart is a vulgar mechanism whose only profound motivation is self-interest. Far from being indignant at such a mean interpretation, men enthusiastically adopted it. No platitude is more solidly anchored in people's minds than this one: "Man always seeks his own interest." An ethics was even founded upon this superficial psychology. Utilitarianism, which allows the concern for public well-being to be reconciled with a disenchanted conception of human nature, was invented. There is no blame and scarcely a nuance of irony in the proverb: "Charity begins at home."[6] Such a thought even has a reassuring character. It allows a common measure to be assigned to all human acts and provides a clear and easy explication for them. Only when an action is presented as disinterested do people get worried. They suspiciously seek hidden reasons. "No one does something for nothing," they say. They are bothered and suspect some treacherous machination of which they risk being the dupes. Outraged, they say "I don't understand." On the contrary, as soon as they clearly see what tangible profit an individual has gained, be it from betrayal or villainy, they are all ready to excuse him. They are not indignant about cynical egoism, and they accept the struggle for life. The only faults that revolt them are those that seem unjustified and gratuitous. They are indignant about Weidmann and Hitler because, first of all, these men's crimes were useless.[7] They didn't bring anything to those who committed them (a triumphant Hitler would have surely incited much less outrage than a defeated Hitler). But it is especially because these enterprises were extravagant. They displayed a sort of generosity of evil and a lust for cruelty that upset and shocked the conscience of the average man. Again, he does not understand. This is his criticism of great criminals as well as unrecognized heroes. About both of them he says, "They are madmen." The vampire who disembowels a woman is a madman, but Bernard Palissy would be considered a madman if they had discovered him burning his furniture before they had officially erected a statue of him. Public opinion understands all behaviors that have self-interest as their motive. When faced with greed, envy, calumny, perfidy, or lies, people need only to grasp what all this baseness is for in order to say indulgently, "That's human!" With an excuse like that, they clearly show that they are renouncing any expectations of generosity or greatness from man. Indeed, their response to someone naïve enough to count on a less sordid future is, "Human nature will never change." It is particularly edifying to glance through the columns and short letters in women's newspapers where idealistic yet well-informed ladies and gentlemen dispense the treasures of their experiences to their young readers. They warn them that all men are pitiful beings, that their husband will be no exception, and that they must indulge his weaknesses, use cunning to get around his vanity, make concessions to his puerile tyranny, humor his pride, conceal, and prevaricate. They advise counting on his faults and not trying to correct them. "To know how to get a man," which is the ultimate feminine wisdom, is to treat him like a mechanism whose cogs are well known and to accept him in his irremediable misery while feigning to respect an illusory freedom in him. People accept seeing themselves described as lustful, egoistic, cowardly, hypocritical, and conceited in humorous newspapers, "vicious" songs, funny stories, caricatures, comedies, and novels about which they say in admiration, "That's so true! That's human nature!" And maybe they are quick to laugh at such a portrait for fear of being compelled to cry about them. The fact is that they laugh. Isn't such a resignation really a shameful form of despair?

As for love, friendship, and human fraternity, one can easily see that a psychology of self-interest cannot allow a very large place for them. Just like man's greatness, love is affirmed in wedding speeches and on funeral steles, in serialized novels, operas, and films, but on the plane of everyday truths, people hardly pay any attention to it except as a touching illusion of youth or a guilty folly. When it slips into social settings, it is smiled upon indulgently, or in the opposite case, people deny it any reality and try to dissipate its mirage by a lucid analysis. They readily imagine, for example, that in a couple of lovers, one of the two has manipulated the other for money or vanity, and the other one has let himself be seduced, swept away, trapped, bewitched, or hood-winked by the partner who is good at exploiting his weaknesses or vices. In a case where no manipulation is conceivable, they talk of sensual follies. In no circumstance do they recognize in love the engagement of a freedom. They see only the result of a play of mechanical forces. What's more, the same mechanical fate condemns it to be nothing but a straw fire destined to go out. Time dulls sensuality: "Possession kills love," and it dissipates illusions: "Novelty always appears handsome." The feeling withstands neither daily life nor absence: "Out of sight, out of mind." Fleeting and capricious, passion does not, therefore, have a veritable existence. Yet there are cases where a man and a woman are stubborn enough to love each other faithfully for a long time, and people still find a mechanical explication to take this obstinacy into account: they are victims of routine and lazy habits. This is what is expressed by referring to their liaison by these awful words: pasted together [un collage]. No doubt the legitimate affections guaranteed by the bonds of marriage are spoken of with more consideration, but what they respect is marriage as an institution, and marriage insofar as it represents, precisely, a sort of insurance against love. On the contrary, marriage is ridiculed as soon as someone envisions it as an individual relationship. Ever since the Middle Ages, husbands and wives are the classically ridiculous characters of farces, operettas, vaudevilles, tales, and comedies that amuse the public. It is admitted that there is no good marriage, that the most ardent feelings cannot withstand the test of conjugal life, that all wives are either unfaithful or bad tempered, and all husbands cheat or are cheated on.

One might scoff at love out of preference for other types of human relationships. But actually, public opinion doesn't really believe in friendship either. It is seen only as an illusion of youth that life soon takes care of dissipating. If a man gets married or engages himself in a career, insurmountable distances come up between him and his former friends. Inequality of conditions separates as surely as divergence of interests. Such themes have been exploited time and time again: a successful man feeling embarrassed when he happens upon a childhood friend who has sunk into misery, or a band of enthusiastic and intransigent young people feeling nothing but an egoistic indifference toward each other once they have reached a comfortable maturity.

If some friendships live on, it is because they have found a way to base themselves on a play of mutual self-interest, but they would quickly dissolve if this self-interest disappeared on either side. *Si tempora erint nubila, solus eris,* says the Latin poet who has been translated in so many different ways.[8] La Fontaine places true friendship in Monomotapa,[9] where Princess Mathilde says, "How many friends would still come see me if I lived in an attic?" What is called solid friendship is merely a habit based on a firm core of indifference. It excludes neither jealously nor malevolence, particularly among women whose affections are capricious and perfidious. At least these are the widely accepted platitudes on the subject.

So friendship will not shatter the solitude in which man is enclosed. It is never possible for an individual to share the joys and sorrows of another, nor even understand them: "Beings are impenetrable, and consciousnesses are incommunicable." In love, friendship, and all affections, each person remains a mysterious stranger for the other. In his home, among his friends, and at his work, man can never experience anything but a "solitude in common." The betrayals of language, politeness, decency, and routine prevent any true communication. And men certainly don't make much effort to establish a real contact between themselves. They are enclosed in their own preoccupations and worries, and they are not interested in what happens in spheres that are not their own. "When a viscount meets another viscount, they recount viscount stories," sang Chevalier.[10] Everyone loves to tell their own stories but gets bored with listening to others' stories. The worst misfortune is easily accepted if it has fallen upon a neighbor and not oneself. Oftentimes, it is even welcomed with malicious pleasure—*suave mari magno*[11]—while the joy of others irritates easily. Men are hard on each other, either out of cynical egoism because their interests are divided—*Homo homini lupus*[12]—or out of a lack of imagination, a harshness and emptiness [*vide*] of the heart. This is why wisdom consists of counting only on oneself: "If you want to be well served, serve yourself." In life, we must arrange things so that we need no one and never ask for anything, which allows us to have nothing to give either. A bit of kindness is fine; after all, we are not brutes, but too much kindness becomes weakness and foolishness. A man who is too good sets a bad example; he is blamed; he is almost a criminal. For example, Van Gogh, who was responsible for distributing official aid to the Borinage,[13] was blamed by his superiors and relieved of his position because he was living with the aid recipients as an equal and sharing his resources with them. What you need to do is to interfere in other people's business as little as possible, avoid getting in trouble, and use discretion in order to be spared useless responsibilities. Don't give too much advice; you

could be criticized for it. Don't do too many favors; you will receive no gratitude for it, and people will possibly even be irritated by it. Such is the usual
way people look upon their relationships with their fellow man.

One cannot have a very exalted idea of life with such a conception of man
and human relationships. Men didn't wait for the "Mythe de Sisyphe" [The
Myth of Sisyphus] [1942] to think that life was, as Shakespeare said, "a tale
told by an idiot";[14] in other words an absurd adventure. And indeed, if the
psychology of self-interest is true, all existence is a radical failure, for man's
only goal is to assure his own happiness, and happiness is impossible. "Love
is but a lie, happiness but a dream," is an old tune sung a thousand different
ways with almost identical words. Happiness is like a butterfly whose brilliant
colors are tarnished as soon as they are touched. One must never enter into
promised lands; the only paradises that exist are lost paradises.[15] Reality is always beneath the dream;[16] nothing is more disappointing than to obtain what
has been desired. Everything passes, everything breaks, and everything grows
wearisome. Or, in more definitive terms, "Happiness is not of this world." It
is also expressed by slightly more severe expressions: "We are not on earth to
enjoy ourselves," and "Life is not a storybook." We must therefore ask the
least possible from life in order to not be disappointed. We must know that
in this world we never do what we want, and that we are the plaything of circumstances that, most of the time, are against us. Wisdom is giving misfortune the least hold possible, which leads to an ethics of mediocrity. "The quiet
life is the happy life." Let's not be noticed, and not try to embrace too much:
"He who grasps at too much loses all." Let's content ourselves with a respectable mediocrity: not too much, not too little. Let's tranquilly cultivate
our garden. All ambition is dangerous, even moral ambition. Let's not try to
be a hero or a saint but only what is called a respectable man. Virtue is finding the appropriate mean; he who tries to be an angel ends up making a fool
of himself. Besides, it is pointless [vain] to hope for an exceptional destiny; it
is only a mirage that makes certain lives appear more enviable than others. In
the end, they are all equivalent. Even the scholar, the artist, or the poet about
whom they speak so reverently in award speeches and on diplomas are but
pitiful men, slaves to human weaknesses: their wives have cheated on them;
they have had sicknesses and money problems. "No man is a hero to his valet."
The Persian poet Ferdousi was wise when, after trying for twenty years to capture the history of humanity in a long poem, he summed it up in one single
verse: "Men have been born, they have suffered, and they have died."[17] Re-
buses that express the same philosophy can be deciphered on the bottom of
old faience plates: "You enter, you cry out, and you're alive; you cry out, you

leave, and you're dead."[18] Since all men die, and since everything ends up coming to an end, nothing that happens has much importance. We would be just as wrong to hope as to despair.

And indeed, it is not existentialism that has revealed to men that they must die someday. They have always known it, and even the most lighthearted hardly forget it. Whether they believe in an afterlife or not, death's shadow hangs over their earthly existence anyway. Since we must die, why are we born? What are we doing on earth? What is the point of living and suffering? Tired old people and overworked housewives expand upon these bitter or anguished questions at length. They take on a pathetic tone in the songs of Damia or Yvonne Georges.[19] Yet many also find a sort of peace in this insignificance that death confers upon life. Seeing that we die, nothing is so important, and resignation becomes legitimate; all our undertakings take on a temporary and relative character, and it is foolish to persist with so much passion. One must look on the bright side of things. "Take it easy." If absolute stakes existed, this opportunism would be impossible. One could not find a positive side of a failure or accept a defeat with good humor. But death, while making life taste like cinders and dust, also makes it light and easy to bear because it removes all objective value from it. Death appears as a convenient alibi that allows men to entrench themselves in their subjectivity, exempts them from wanting anything passionately, and authorizes all resignations. Man willingly sees himself enclosed in the narrow circle of his own interests, enclosed in a life that death limits and empties of all meaning. Can one imagine a darker pessimism? What doctrine opens fewer doors to hope? How can people who have such an idea of their condition reproach existentialism for its lack of optimism?

"All sound reasoning is offensive," says Stendhal profoundly.[20] People get scared when faced with an uncompromising opinion or a definitive truth. They will complacently list off someone's faults, saying that so-and-so is conceited, egoistic, mean, and greedy, but if you conclude that "he is a bad man," your interlocutor protests, "I didn't say that." And he might add, "In spite of everything, the core is good." In this way, man accepts being painted by cruel little brushstrokes, but if you force him to take a step back to contemplate his full-length portrait, he looks away; he does not want to summarize or conclude. No doubt this is partly because he senses that reality goes beyond any description that can be attempted of it.[21] It is therefore unwarranted to draw a line, figure the total, and close the account. But he is especially reluctant to take a stand. God only knows what consequences might result from an overly rigorous logic. Man likes to hear himself talk and feel himself think, and by so doing, to affirm man's superiority over beasts, but on the condition that his thoughts do not engage him and remain in a favorable half-light. Men do not believe wholeheartedly in what they say, which is what allows them to jump from one plane of truth to another without embarrassment. In fact, they are never really situated on any of them. The image of the generous and heroic man erected in public places and the image of the bestial and selfish man forged by the bitterness of daily life are absolutely irreconcilable. This is why one never tries to form a synthesis of them. Depending on the occasion, they evoke one or the other, but they believe in neither the truth of funeral orations and prop-aganda movies nor that of sententiously spouted proverbs and disillusioned platitudes. People's ordinary behavior clearly shows that it is not natural for them to devote themselves unreservedly nor to restrain themselves without any generosity. La Rochefoucauld cultivated friendship, Swift cherished Stella,[22] and the disillusioned skeptic has children against his interests, against his ego-istic wisdom, and against death. If they were criticized for these contradictions, they would respond that the exception proves the rule and each one sees him-self as an exception. But people are especially shocked if perfect coherence is required of them. They know perfectly well that their thoughts are neither gra-tuitous nor completely sincere. Their thoughts do not seek the universal but are circumstantial thoughts commanded by practical ends. If one claims to take them literally, they get irritated. In order to prevent her son from persist-ing in a stupid marriage, a mother tells him that love is a delusion, yet she is convinced of having married her husband out of love. It is to defend his own interests that an old man joyously sends young people off to be killed, declar-ing that there is no more beautiful fate than to die for one's country, but as for him, he wants to save his skin. Idealism and skepticism are but weapons that men use according to their needs. But the reaction they have today before a singular situation does not fetter their future. One of the circumstances that allows them to put up with the very somber pessimism that we have described is that they do not adhere to it completely. And the first reproach they address to existentialism is that of being a coherent and organized system, a philo-sophical attitude that demands being fully adopted. By assuming a vision of the world that is defined too precisely, they fear burdening themselves with re-sponsibilities that are too heavy.

For men fear responsibilities above all. They do not like taking risks, and they are so afraid of engaging their freedom that they prefer to renounce it. And that is the most profound reason for their reluctance in regard to a doc-trine that places this freedom in the forefront. If one considers the criticisms directed against existentialism, one cannot help being struck by an obvious contradiction: the people who accuse it of subjectivism are the very same who take delight in Montaigne, La Rochefoucauld, and Maupassant.[23] They are decided supporters of a pure psychology of immanence in which the projects and feelings of the individual all appear to turn back toward himself. On the contrary, existentialists affirm that man is transcendence; his life is engagement in the world, movement toward the Other, surpassing of the present toward a future that even death does not limit. How dare they accuse the existentialists of according too much importance to subjectivity? Actually, the subject never appears in the ethics of self-interest. The self that they talk about is an object of the world. One can love one's self and take it as a pole for one's behavior because it exists in the manner of a thing. One supposes that within it there are instincts to subjugate and voids to fill. By its very existence my self imposes objective ends upon me that swallow up my freedom. I must satisfy its needs, provide it with what pleasure it wishes, and defend it against suffering. Since my energies are thus channeled, their use is determined even before they appear. It is not a question of asking me how to direct them. In existentialism, on the contrary, the self is not. I exist as an authentic subject, in a constantly renewed upspringing that is opposed to the fixed reality of things. I throw myself without help and without guidance into a world where I am not installed ahead of time waiting for myself. I am free, and my projects are not defined by preexisting interests; they posit their own ends. In the philosophy of immanence, the outcome [*le point d'aboutissement*] of my actions is given. If I go back from there to their starting point, it appears itself as defined. It is a sort of projection of the object self onto the plane of interiority. In the philosophy of transcendence, the subject exists uniquely as a starting point. I cannot mask its presence, and I cannot conceal from myself the fact that all my acts have their source in my subjectivity. When people resent existentialism for its subjectivity, they are really reproaching it for assimilating subjectivity and freedom.

To define man as freedom has always appeared as the distinctive feature of optimistic philosophers. And so it is false to consider existentialism as a doctrine of despair—far from it. It does not condemn man to an irremediable misery. Man may not be naturally good, but he is not naturally bad either; he is nothing at first. It is up to him to make himself good or bad depending on whether he assumes his freedom or renounces it. Good and evil appear only beyond nature and beyond all givens. This is why one can describe reality in complete impartiality. There is never reason to be distressed about it; it is neither sad nor happy; facts are facts, nothing more. What is important is the way man surpasses his situation. The separation of consciousnesses is thus a metaphysical fact, yet man can surmount it. He can, through the world, unite himself to other men. Existentialists are so far from denying love, friendship, and fraternity that in their eyes the only way for each individual to find the foundation and accomplishment of his being is in these human relationships. But they do not consider these feelings as given at first; one must conquer them. Death is another fact for which there is no reason to either grieve or rejoice. It inflicts no denial upon human undertakings, for they take their value from the freedom that is engaged in them. Freedom posits the ends that it posits absolutely, and no foreign force, even death, could destroy what it has founded. Man is the unique and sovereign master of his destiny if only he wants to be. This is what existentialism affirms, and certainly this is an optimism. And in reality, this optimism is what worries people. If one gets indignant about certain impartial descriptions of the world and man, it is not, as one claims, because they are "depressing"; Maupassant's books are much more so. It is because the evil that they reveal comes out of man's freedom. The "bastards" of *La nausée* [Nausea] chose to be that way;[24] it is completely up to them to be lucid and honest, and to repudiate the lie behind which they shelter themselves. The idea of such responsibility terrifies the reader. To this demanding ethics, he prefers a pessimism that leaves no hope for man but also asks nothing of him.

The ethics of self-interest and naturalistic sadness are welcomed with such favor because the despair they express has a soft and comfortable character. It supposes a determinism that relieves man of the burden of his freedom. Man is a mechanism for whom self-interest and lust are the essential motivations. His feelings are reduced to a more or less subtle play of forces. Popular wisdom affirms this unique postulate under diverse forms. If man cannot modify his essence, and if he does not have a hold on his destiny, all he has left is to accept himself indulgently, which saves him the weariness of the struggle. Existentialism, which puts his fate back into his hands, comes and disturbs this repose.

People like to think that virtue is easy. In edifying stories, young people smile as they die for their country, fathers and mothers smile as they break their backs to nourish their children, and children smile as they sacrifice themselves to their old parents. They also resign themselves, without much trouble, to believing that virtue is impossible. But they are reluctant to envision that it could be possible and difficult. If we proclaim that life is a magnificent adventure, then we are delivered of all worries; we are demigods as we eat and sleep. Each beat of our heart allows us to participate effortlessly in the great human escapade. Or, if we admit that it is but a farcical comedy, nothing that we do has any importance any longer, and so we can eat and sleep in peace.

But if our hand is neither lost nor won in advance, we must struggle and risk every minute, and this disturbs our idleness. If need be, people consent to wage one or two battles, but they must at least be able to rest definitively in their victory or their defeat. If an engineer constructs a dam, or a woman brings children into the world, they want the dam or the children to justify definitively that they exist. They want the ends that they pursue to be affirmed as absolutely useful. If, on the contrary, a man has failed in his undertakings, he likes to repeat with Ecclesiastes that "All is vanity."[25] But to declare that it is I who, in choosing my goals, found their value is to refuse myself all alibis. No success saves me. In order for it to continue to appear as a success to me, I must continue to want [*vouloir*] it, and this volition is necessarily manifested by new acts. And no failure exempts me from pursuing the struggle. There exists no point of view exterior to myself from which I could scorn my own volitions. Likewise, a man raised by circumstances to the dignity of a hero would like to think that he is marked on the forehead with a star, that he drinks, eats, and sleeps as a hero, and that from now on, in danger or in torture, he is assured of behaving in a way that conforms to his essence as a hero. This is an idea that saves him the anxiety of true heroism. As for the coward, he is not altogether dissatisfied with being a coward. He is one and can do nothing about it, so he settles himself in his cowardice with the tranquility of the valets in comedic plays who congratulate each other for not having any honor to defend. It is much less reassuring to admit that courage can always be conquered without ever being able to count on possessing it.

One sees that existentialism is worrisome not because it despairs of man, but because it demands a constant tension from him. But one may wonder: why such exigency? why persist in ousting people from positions where they find their security? And that is indeed a question that critics have often posed: what does one gain by being an existentialist?

The question will seem strange to any philosopher. Neither Kant nor Hegel ever asked himself what one would gain by being Kantian or Hegelian.[26] They said what they thought was the truth, nothing more. They had no other goal but the truth itself. But perhaps it is the philosopher who is wrong here; perhaps he is a victim of a distortion endemic to his profession [*une déformation professionnelle*]. Is it good to speak the truth? If it is useless or harmful, shouldn't it be masked? Such prudence makes sense only if the truth is seen as exterior to reality. If it is a light that a foreign heaven pours out onto the world, one may wonder whether or not it is opportune to let it dissipate our darkness. But this conception is radically false. The truth is nothing other than reality. One can refuse to apprehend it through words and sentences, that is to say, express it systematically, but one cannot elude it. The very effort one makes to escape it is one of the ways of manifesting it. This is what clearly emerges from the discoveries of psychoanalysis, for example. It may seem useless and even nefarious to reveal to an adolescent that he hates his father, but not admitting this hate with words does not mean he affirms it any less in his feelings, behaviors, dreams, and anxieties. The psychoanalyst is not choosing to brutally and gratuitously uncover an unknown truth; he is trying to help his patient modify the behaviors by which he reacts to this reality. Instead of using his strength to hide from his hate, the subject must liberate himself of it, not by denying it but by assuming it and surpassing it, which requires that he first recognize it explicitly and understand it. Existentialism does not intend to disclose to man the hidden suffering of his condition either, but only wants to help him assume this condition that is impossible for him to ignore. Instead of looking the truth in the face, man wears himself out by fighting against it. We have seen that he is situated alternately on two planes that he cannot manage to reconcile. He also cannot manage to maintain himself on either of them. As early as adolescence, he begins to laugh at ethics teachers' idealized images and lofty speeches. He becomes disillusioned [*désabusé*], which means that he believes himself to have been illusioned [*abusé*] at first. He thus throws himself willingly into cynicism. He is passionately pessimistic, which does not, however, prevent him from undertaking, loving, and living. Between what he does and what he says, what he affirms in acts and what he believes in words, there is always an abyss. And this is a source of uncertainty and unease. Most men spend their life crushed by the weight of clichés that smother them. If they resolved to acquire a clear awareness of their situation in the world, then only would they find themselves in harmony with themselves and reality.

There are certain domains in which men of our day are making a decisive effort toward sincerity. No one will deny that through this, they have realized some important gains. Thanks to psychoanalysis, sexual hypocrisy has been in part dissipated. Taking the existence of certain instincts as a fact, psychoanalysis rejects as meaningless the expressions human nature is perverse, and human nature is innocent and good. Man can confidently look within himself; nothing that he might encounter is monstrous since sexual morality is constructed beyond the tendencies and complexes that make up his particular temperament. There is no state of equilibrium or health that is moral in and of itself, and there is no singularity that is immoral. With this in mind, one starts to admit that morality is the privilege of no man and that everyone can conquer it.

Since the war of 1914–18, a conception of courage that is very different than that of past centuries has appeared. No doubt Turenne's statement "You tremble, carcass" has always been respectfully quoted, but in the past you had to be Turenne to be allowed to say it.[27] To be afraid seemed the deed of a coward; every soldier was a professional hero, and a hero laughed at bullets and shells. This cliché was extremely widespread in 1914. But afterward, in France, England, and America, the generations who harbored a profound hatred toward war dared to treat warrior virtues without consideration. The combatants of 1940 were more lucid than enthusiastic;[28] in becoming soldiers, they remained men. Courage had value in their eyes as a human, not military, virtue. And this is what makes the accounts of so many English, French, and American soldiers so moving. These young parachutists, pilots, and infantrymen do not aspire to what used to be called heroism; they tell us that their hearts beat faster, their throats tightened, and they were afraid. And in spite of this fear, they simply did what they had to do. They knew each time that the outcome was not certain, that tomorrow they would again be afraid, and that they risked succumbing to their bodies and having something to despise themselves for, but they also knew that it was up to them alone to overcome their anguish.

The value of such examples is that they don't allow anyone to declare himself an irremediable coward and they prevent man from the disillusion and "deflating" that are the ordinary price of all too easy lies. Yet they touch us especially because we see in them the human condition fully assumed. And it appears to us that in being assumed,[29] this condition is justified. Existentialism in general aims for precisely this goal: it wants to prevent man from the morose disappointments and sulking that the cult of false idols brings about. It wants to convince him to be authentically a man and it affirms the value of this accomplishment. Such a philosophy can boldly refuse the consolations of lies and resignation; it has confidence in men.

Preface

"In France, you pose problems without resolving them," an American told me one day. "*We* don't pose them, we resolve them."

In this aggressive quip, he summarized the reproaches that have always been addressed to speculative thought: it does not help one to live and even diverts one from living, yet one must live.

Today, when existentialism is attacked, it is not usually out of preference for another definite doctrine, but rather out of a refusal to give any credit to philosophy in general.

Such an attitude is innate in its roots; it rests upon biases that are neither a priori axioms nor experimental laws, and that themselves fall under philosophy.[30]

For example, it is not true that the mass of those who denigrate existentialism see the world with ingenuous eyes. They grasp it through the platitudes constituted by Popular Wisdom. Incoherent and contradictory, this wisdom is nevertheless a vision of the world that should be questioned. And if one puts it to a serious examination, one understands that it cannot satisfy an honest mind. It's only out of laziness that so many people rally to it.

Likewise, one cannot find fault with the existentialist aesthetic in the name of absolute principles; they do not exist, for literature is what man makes it be. In fact, another aesthetic is often put forth in contrast, generally a vague naturalism that does not possess an unconditioned guarantee. One of the domains into which the intrusion of philosophy is challenged most intensely is the political domain; political realism, they say, should not be encumbered by abstract considerations. But if one looks a little closer, one quickly sees that political and moral problems are indissolubly linked. In any case it is a matter of making human history and making man, and since man is to be made, there is the question of his making—a question at the source of both action and its truth.

Behind the most narrow-minded and stubborn politics, there is always an ethics hidden away. This is clearly discovered as soon as the concrete case is considered.

The problem of punishment that troubled so many consciences after the liberation could be resolved neither on the purely political plane nor according to the norms of an abstract ethics. By choosing charity rather than justice, or severity rather than clemency, each person defined a global attitude toward other men that is precisely the metaphysical attitude: each one brings himself entirely into question facing the entire world. Man cannot escape philosophy because he cannot escape his freedom, which implies questioning and refusal of the given. That is what these essays strive to show. They do not seek to define existentialism once again, but to defend it against the reproach of frivolity and gratuity that has so often been frivolously and gratuitously addressed to all organized thought since Socrates. In truth, there is no divorce between philosophy and life.

Every living step is a philosophical choice and the ambition of a philosophy worthy of the name is to be a way of life that brings its justification with itself.

NOTES

Sabine Crespo and Tricia Wall would like to thank William Hamrick, Matthew Schmitz, and Carl Springer for their helpful advice on annotations.

1. Louis Pasteur (1822–95), the French chemist and microbiologist, was the first to formulate vaccines for rabies, anthrax, and chicken cholera and was the originator of the pasteurization process (named for him), which removes dangerous pathogenes by heat. Bernard Palissy (1510–89) was a French potter and Huguenot who was persecuted and imprisoned as a Protestant. He was also known to have burned his furniture in order to fire his kilns in a vain effort to imitate white-glazed pottery. Joseph Bara (1780–93), a drummer boy in the French Revolution, was fatally shot by the royalists for having cried out, "Vive la République" (long live the Republic), instead of "Vive le roi" (long live the king).

2. Lucrece, or Lucretia, in Roman legend, was a Roman matron illustrious for her virtue. See Shakespeare's *Rape of Lucrece*.

3. The play *Cyrano de Bergerac* (1897) was written by the French dramatist Edmond Rostand. Intelligent and witty, Cyrano, the hero, feels that his enormous nose will impede his chance at obtaining the love of Roxanne. Paul Déroulède (1846–1914) was a French politician and the author of patriotic poems. *Le voyage de M. Perrichon* (1868) was written by the famous French playwright Eugène Labiche (1815–88). Guy de Maupassant (1850–93), French novelist and short-story writer, portrays his characters as driven by greed and desire.

4. "Church Fathers" is the collective name for the Christian writers of early times whose work is considered generally orthodox; the traditional Four Doctors of the Latin Church are Saint Ambrose, Saint Jerome, Saint Augustine, and Saint Gregory the Great. Blaise Pascal (1623–62) was a French scientist and religious philosopher. In the *Pensées* (1670), Pascal states his belief in the inadequacy of reason. Jacques-Bénigne Bossuet (1627–1704), French prelate, orator, and moralist, attacked Fénelon and the quietists, the Jesuits, and the Protestants. Jean Baptiste Massillon (1663–1742), French clergyman and bishop of Clermont from 1717, was celebrated for his preaching, especially at the courts of Louis XIV and Louis XV.

5. Duke de François VI La Rochefoucauld (1613–80) was a French writer who believed that selfishness is the source of all human behavior, a philosophy evident in his collection of moral maxims, *Réflexions ou sentences et maximes morales* (first published in 1665). Jean de La Fontaine (1621–95) was a French poet and celebrated author of fables in which beasts behave like men and serve as a comment on human behavior. Duke de Louis de Rouvroy Saint-Simon (1675–1755) was a French courtier whose memoirs of the court of Louis XIV are an apology of a grand seigneur who was prevented, by his proud temperament and his limited intelligence, from accepting the rise of the bourgeoisie. Sébastien-Roch Nicolas Chamfort (1740–94) was a French writer whose maxims and epigrams were popular at court, despite his republican beliefs.

6. The saying in French reads as follows: "Charité bien ordonnée commence par soi-même."

7. Eugene Weidmann (d. 1939), convicted of six murders, was the last person to be guillotined in public in France. Adolf Hitler (1889–1945) was the German leader of the National Socialist (Nazi) Party (from 1920/21) and the chancellor and führer of Germany (1933–45). He initiated World War II and sought to exterminate Europe's Jewish population.

8. The Latin phrase reads in English "if times become cloudy (troubled), you will be alone"; it is from Ovid's *Trista* (1.9). The preceding line reads "[a]s long as you are lucky you will have many friends."

9. Monomotapa was an area of southeastern Africa, in present-day Zimbabwe, that served as an exotic location in the *Fables* of La Fontaine and the works of his contemporaries.

10. Maurice Chevalier (1888–1972) was a French singer and film actor.

11. The phrase in English reads "[i]t is sweet when on the great sea." This line comes from the first line of the second book of *De rerum natura,* by Lucretius. The full sentence and the following one read as follows: "It is sweet when on the great sea the winds are stirring up the surface of the waters to watch the great struggling of someone else from the shore."

12. "Homo homini lupus" (a man is a wolf to a man) is borrowed from the Roman playwright Plautus (*Asinaria,* line 495). The full line reads "[a] man is a wolf to a man instead of a man, when he does not know what he's like." Hobbes uses the expression in the dedicatory epistle to *De Cive.*

13. Borinage is a coal-mining region in southern Belgium.

14. Albert Camus wrote an essay entitled "Mythe de Sisyphe" about the mythical Sisyphus, who was condemned by the gods to endlessly push a huge rock up a mountain only to have it fall down again. The phrase "a tale told by an idiot" comes from Shakespeare's *Macbeth,* act 5, scene 5: "life . . . is a tale told by an idiot, full of sound and fury, signifying nothing."

15. "Paradises" (*paradis*) is capitalized, as *Paradis,* in *Les temps modernes* (393).

16. "Beneath" (*au-dessous*) is given as *en-dessous* in *Les temps modernes* (393).

17. Shahnameh Ferdousi (935–1020) was a Persian poet and author of *The Epic of Kings,* the most important work of Persian literature.

18. A rebus is a representation of words or syllables by pictures of objects or by symbols whose names resemble the intended words or syllables in sound; it also can refer to a riddle made up of such pictures or symbols.

19. Damia was the stage name of Marie-Louise Damien (1889–1978), a French actress and singer known for her "realistic songs." Yvonne George, a French cabaret singer, was the first woman to sing a male repertory, during a short career (1924–30).

20. The French writer Stendhal, pseud. of Marie-Henri Beyle (1783–1842), was recognized as one of the great French novelists; see Beauvoir's discussion of Stendhal in *The Second Sex.*

21. "Attempted of it" (*qu'on en peut tenter*) (*Les temps modernes,* 396) is "qu'on peut tenter" in *L'existentialisme et la sagesse des nations* (32).

22. In 1689, Jonathan Swift (1667–1745), the English satirist, met and formed his lifelong attachment to Esther Johnson, the Stella of his famous journal.

23. Michel Eyquem, seigneur de Montaigne (1533–92), was a French essayist.

24. *La nausée* (Paris: Gallimard, 1938) is a novel by Jean-Paul Sartre.

25. The verse "vanity of vanities. All is vanity!" is from Ecclesiastes 1:2 (Revised Standard Version).

26. Immanuel Kant (1724–1804) was a German philosopher and the founder of critical transcendental philosophy. Georg Wilhelm Friedrich Hegel (1770–1831), the German idealist philosopher, is the author of *Phenomenology of the Mind* (1807), which Beauvoir read at

the start of the Nazi occupation in July 1940; see her *Journal de guerre* (Paris: Gallimard, 1990), 339.

27. Henri de la Tour d'Auvergne, vicomte de Turenne (1611–75), one of the greatest of French military commanders, was made marshal of France in 1643; he was reburied in the Invalides in Paris by order of Napoleon. See Paul Robert, *Dictionnaire alphabétique et analogique de la langue française* (Paris, 1951), under *carcasse:* "Quelquefois, pendant une bataille, il (Turenne) ne pouvait s'empêcher de trembler; . . . alors, il parlait à son corps comme on parle à un serviteur. Il lui disait: 'Tu trembles, carcasse; mais si tu savais où je vais te mener tout à l'heure, tu tremblerais bien advantage.' Lavisse, *Histoire de France (Cours moyen, 1re et 2e années)*, Ch. XIV, p. 107." (Sometimes during a battle he could not help trembling. Then he talked to his body as one talks to a servant. He said to it: "You tremble, carcass; but if you knew where I am taking you right now, you would tremble a lot more.") The quote appears as an epigraph to book 5 of Friedrich Nietzsche's *The Gay Science* (1887), trans. W. Kaufmann (New York: Random House, 1974), 277.

28. "Combatants of 1940" refers to individuals who fought against Germany and the German invasion of France.

29. "In being assumed" (*en s'assumant*) is "en assumant" in *L'existentialisme et la sagesse des nations* (46).

30. In translating the passage "elle repose sur des partis pris qui ne sont ni des axiomes à priori, ni des lois expérimentales et qui relèvent donc elle-même de la philosophie," the translator assumed that "elle-même" must be a typo for "eux-mêmes," which would refer to "les partis pris."

Jean-Paul Sartre

INTRODUCTION
by Karen Vintges

In January 1946 Simone de Beauvoir published a commissioned article, entitled "Jean-Paul Sartre, Strictly Personal," in the fashion magazine *Harper's Bazaar.*[1] A study of the recently discovered original French typescript of the article, which is published here in translation, indicates that the published title and organization of the article were dictated by the editors, who also deleted fifty-five lines from the original article, resulting in an important shift in the focus of the article, which will be discussed below.

Sartre had just come back to New York for the second time when Beauvoir's influential piece came out. It was extensively quoted in *Time* magazine, in an article thus announcing the arrival of Sartre: "The literary lion of Paris bounced into Manhattan last week."[2] In no time Sartre's star was rising in the United States and existentialism became "the talk of the town." Articles on existentialism started to appear in magazines such as *Life,* the *New York Times Magazine,* and *Newsweek* and in fashion magazines such as *Vogue.* However, none of these articles dealt with existentialism on a philosophical level. Existentialism was fashion rather than thought in the States and it would take years before serious books and articles came out on the subject.[3]

It has been suggested that "the existentialists," mainly Sartre, Camus, and

Beauvoir, launched themselves in the United States as "personalities," as a strategy to gain influence in the intellectual field.[4] It is said that Sartre and Beauvoir carefully organized the publicity offensive that made Sartre into a star. In this context Beauvoir's profile of Sartre in *Harper's Bazaar* is interpreted as purposely focusing on Sartre's personal life instead of his work.[5] However, this is a severe misunderstanding of the text, and one unfortunately encouraged by the editor, whose cuts eliminated much of Beauvoir's discussion of Sartre's philosophy and his philosophical way of life (*mode d'existence*) from the original text.

For the existentialist philosophers Sartre and Beauvoir, philosophy was no abstract, timeless reasoning but a *way of life*—and in this they were in good company. Ancient philosophy also was a *way of being* that engages the whole of existence, as Hadot has argued.[6] Remainders of this concept of philosophy as a way of life can be seen in works of Descartes, Spinoza, Nietzsche, Schopenhauer, Marx, and even Husserl, among others, and last but not least in "the movement of thought inaugurated by Heidegger and carried on by existentialism [that] seeks—in theory and in principle—to engage man's freedom and action in the philosophical process."[7]

Not only did the existentialists see philosophy as a way of life, they furthermore wanted to invent alternative ways of life—alternative to the dominant culture, that is. They wanted to invent new forms of imagination, writing, thinking, working, and living. In her profile of Sartre, Beauvoir took Sartre's life and work together and dealt with his existentialist thought as a *way of being*. Clearly she wanted to present Sartre's mode of being as one that offered an alternative to prevalent ones.

Sartre's thinking in *L'être et le néant* (Being and Nothingness) (1943), the work to which Beauvoir refers in her article, was all about human freedom. Sartre distinguished two kinds of being: being-in-itself (*être en-soi*) and being-for-itself (*être pour-soi*); the first refers to the existence of material things, the second to that of consciousness. Sartre's primary goal was to articulate consciousness as opposed to the being of material things; consciousness was characterized by non-being: in itself, it is no-thing, or rather nothing(ness) (*néant*). In order to exist, consciousness is doomed to surpass itself and reach out for a thing (*en-soi*) or it will cease to be consciousness and will coincide with the being of things. The fact that human consciousness is no thing means a human being is not a permanent essence but continually creates itself through intentional activity. The existence of a human being thus precedes every essence. As a consequence, Sartre argued, the human being is fundamentally free. Freedom and non-being are the characteristics of human existence.

In her article Beauvoir shows how this philosophy was "lived" by Sartre, and how, as he himself always indicated, he felt at ease only in freedom—escaping objects and escaping himself.[8] She first of all describes him as a man who opposes the *en-soi,* or the world of "inert," "stupid and stubborn" things. Sartre hates nature: the country, the swarming life of insects, the pullulation of plants. He detests raw vegetables, oysters, and natural—instead of preserved—fruit. She then states that he not only detests things, but thing-like persons as well: he hates people who rely complacently on the mere fact of their presence in the world. Man as consciousness, according to Sartre, has to tear himself loose from the "sticky" mass of the given. Man should not try to live as a tree or a stone but should make use of his freedom, surpassing the given by projecting himself in the future. He should choose his own ends and pursue them with passion, not forgetting that he himself is the one who has defined those ends. Like the Stoics, Sartre wants us to affirm our freedom, escaping everything that does not depend on ourselves. This is the mode of existence that Sartre strives to attain for himself, Beauvoir then states, again underlining the unity of life and letters for Sartre.

Apart from drinking and eating copiously and smoking heavily, Sartre almost escapes his body. He can ignore it when ill, and he can easily undergo privations. His definition of man as projecting himself in future actions also makes him indifferent toward his own past life. "Already, he no longer sees himself in that man about whom he speaks." Even one's former self is something from which one has to tear oneself loose at all times. Sartre is always focused on the things he intends to do in the future. He refuses to be chained down by circumstances. "He expects nothing except of himself."

In short, Beauvoir describes Sartre as someone who wants to tear loose from nature, thing-like fellow men, his body, and his own past life. Thus he absolutely refuses to live as an *en-soi.* She continues to describe Sartre as being interested only in his freedom as a human being and trying to live this freedom to the full. He passionately wants to be consciousness all of the time. He cannot sit still; he always has to be active. He finds great joy in the consciousness of his own freedom and he in no way is the pessimistic or troubled man that people reading his novels and plays expect him to be. Beauvoir concludes that Sartre, on the contrary, is at present a person in perfect harmony with himself, a happy man.

In Beauvoir's description of Sartre, his relationship to other people comes forward as a rather external one. He is profiled as a person who is self-sufficient, who in other words does not need other people to be happy. Compared to Sartre's philosophical *way of being,* Beauvoir's is completely different. To characterize the differences, I shall briefly indicate her own philosophy—especially her existentialist ethics—which she also "lived," in the same way as Sartre "lived" his.

Like Sartre, Beauvoir was strongly opposed to moral theory as such. Existential philosophy states that every human being is free and has to invent his or her own behavior and there are no positive maxims or general rules that we can apply. But unlike the existentialist Sartre, Beauvoir kept a lifelong interest in ethics. In her philosophical essays, among them *The Ethics of Ambiguity* (1947), she tried to work out a type of ethics that does not consist of general moral rules, but that consists of an attitude. In *The Ethics of Ambiguity* she states that we have to adopt a "moral attitude," one of "willing ourselves free," which amounts to a striving for not only our own freedom but also that of all other human beings.

Willing ourselves free is wanting to *practice* our freedom. This means that we must accept the fact that we have to surpass ourselves and reach out for the world. To realize our freedom, we have to act as a body in the world. The attitude of willing oneself free thus implies that we, by way of a so-called "moral conversion," accept our bodily and emotional dimension and transform our pure freedom into a concrete commitment to the freedom of our fellow men; in other words, get involved.[9] Beauvoir argues for living in narrow bonds with others, but she wants these to be chosen bonds. In this sense, she wants everybody to have the social freedom to create their own trajectory in life and to shape themselves into a specific and responsible (relational) self. With this aim in mind, we must constantly and carefully style our daily behavior.

Beauvoir's own life, as recorded and constructed in her autobiographical work, should be seen within the framework of her ethical theory, which reconciles the two ambiguous sides of the human condition: the one of consciousness and freedom on the one hand, and the one of our bodily and situated dimension on the other. She loved nature, the country, and the bodily dimension of life, and above all she was emotionally involved with other people. But she also wanted to develop a *self*. She was convinced that every person has to live his or her own life and should not try to live "through" others, because only in that way can we avoid tyrannizing other people and using them for our own ends. In *The Second Sex* (1949) she put forward that men used women for their own ends by denying them the status of *pour-soi*, reducing them to nature, the body, and so on. She argued that women have to fight their oppression as well as their own tendency to adapt themselves to the role society and men have imposed on them. In other words, they should refuse to be thing-like persons and instead develop an *ethical self.* One could say that Beauvoir's own project was this winning of an ethical self.

She saw her own inclination to cling to Sartre as something she had to combat. She wanted to create an identity of her own. Famous are the passages in her autobiography about her arrival in Marseilles, where she started to work and live on her own, thereby training herself to thrust forward on her own again. She took long walks on her own, to test her capacity to be alone. Later, she created her own professional practice by introducing a serious working pattern, according to fixed rituals. She also traveled extensively on her own, to force herself to be someone by herself and to keep faithful to her philosophical project of the constant winning of an ethical self.

To the tradition of "philosophy as a way of life," Beauvoir has added precisely the dimension of coping with the immediate feelings that drive us to others. She thereby emphasizes the importance of emotional life and our feelings of symbiosis with other persons, something Sartre never really addressed. Striving to become the type of ethical self she had put forward, she consciously created in her own life and work an identity: where Sartre focused on living past a self, Beauvoir's project was rather the striving to win an *ethical* self.

The last lines of the original French typescript read, in translation: "If Sartre's attitude may seem paradoxical, it is because the human condition is ambiguous, and Jean-Paul Sartre is a man who has fully assumed his condition as man." Beauvoir thus concludes her article by putting forward her own ethics of ambiguity.

NOTES

1. See "Jean Paul Sartre, Strictly Personal," trans. Malcolm Cowley, *Harper's Bazaar,* January 1946, 113, 158, 160; see also Annie Cohen Solal, *Sartre: A Life* (New York: Pantheon, 1987), 271.

2. *Time,* January 28, 1946, 28–29.

3. See George Cotkin, "French Existentialism and American Popular Culture, 1945–1948," *The Historian* 61, no. 2 (Winter 1999): 327–40.

4. See Anna Boschetti, *The Intellectual Enterprise: Sartre and "Les Temps Modernes"* (Evanston, Ill.: Northwestern University Press, 1988).

5. See Cotkin, "French Existentialism."

6. See Pierre Hadot, *Philosophy as a Way of Life: Spiritual Exercises from Socrates to Foucault,* ed. and intro. Arnold I. Davidson (Oxford: Blackwell, 1995). Hadot put forward that ancient philosophy should be conceived of mainly as spiritual exercises that were practical, required effort and training, and were lived. He calls these "spiritual" because the twofold goal of ancient philosophy's exercises is the transformation of our vision of the world and the

metamorphosis of our being. These exercises therefore have not merely a moral but also an existential value.

7. Ibid., 272.

8. Solal's *Sartre* opens with the following quotation from Sartre's *War Diaries:* "I am ill at ease except in freedom, escaping objects, escaping myself. . . . I am a true nothing, drunk with pride, translucid. Therefore it is the world that I wish to possess" (v).

9. Through the "moral conversion" Beauvoir "reconciles" freedom and the bodily dimension, this being the reason why she calls her ethics "an ethics of ambiguity." She argues that we are both empty consciousness and incarnated beings; the human condition is ambiguous. The ethical attitude of "willing ourselves free"—an attitude that demands constant exercise—implies that we, through a moral conversion, accept our bodily and emotional dimension and transform our pure freedom into a concrete commitment. We have to rise up, so to speak, from the empty consciousness to the level of the senses, emotion, and connectedness to others. See Karen Vintges, *Philosophy as Passion: The Thinking of Simone de Beauvoir* (Bloomington: Indiana University Press, 1996 [Dutch original, 1992]).

Jean-Paul Sartre

One of the dominant ideas of Jean-Paul Sartre's great philosophical book *L'être et le néant* [Being and Nothingness] [1943] is that there are two ways of existing: in the world, one comes across inert things that remain indefinitely equal to what they are; and on the other hand, men who are consciousnesses and freedoms live in this world.[1] Many men envy the slumber of trees and rocks and strive to resemble them. They put their consciousness to sleep, and they make no use of their freedom. On the contrary, Sartre can be defined as a man who passionately refuses to exist in the way things do, and who chooses to affirm himself as pure consciousness and pure freedom.[2]

The "thing," the stupid and stubborn presence of what is posited there without reason, has always filled Sartre with horror. As we know, he has described this horror in *La nausée* [Nausea] [1938], and one supposes that the disgust that overtakes Antoine Roquentin before a pebble, a mauve pair of suspenders, or a tramway bench isn't a simple literary theme.[3] When Sartre was a student at the École Normale, his friends dreaded what they called his

Untitled and undated typescript in the collection of Sylvie Le Bon de Beauvoir, apparently the original French text of "Jean Paul Sartre: Strictly Personal," trans. Malcolm Cowley, *Harper's Bazaar*, January 1946, 113, 158, 160 (hereafter referred to as *HB*).

morning bad moods. Scowling and unblinking, his face swollen with a smoldering anger, Sartre would sit at his desk and puff on his pipe while staring into the void, and it was better to avoid talking to him at such times. Still groggy from sleeping, he felt stuck in the soft, formless, nauseating paste of the contingent world where all existence is "too much" [*de trop*]. Roquentin's crisis reaches its paroxysm in a public park, and nowhere does the presence of things show itself with more indiscretion than in the heart of nature.[4] Sartre detests the country, with its proliferation of plants and swarms of insects. At most, he tolerates the level sea, the smooth desert sands, or the mineral coldness of mountain peaks, but he is really happy only in cities, at the heart of a universe constructed and populated with fabricated objects. He likes neither raw milk, nor raw fruits and vegetables, nor shellfish, but only processed food, and he always prefers canned fruits and fish over the natural product. More than the pure air of the mountain peaks or the open sea, he enjoys an atmosphere full of tobacco smoke and warmed by human breath.[5]

However, all human presence is not indistinctly a source of joy for Sartre; far from it.[6] In *La nausée*, Sartre scoffs at humanists who preach love for the "human race" or for man as a given. For when man lets himself go to be nothing but a thing, he is the most heinous of all things. Sartre has often cruelly described the faces and bodies of those whose existence seemed to him more naked and more unjustified than that of a pebble. He particularly detests gestures, facial expressions, and voice inflections that betray a tranquil abandon or a blind gluttony; he detests when a man complacently relaxes in the brute fact of his presence in the world. But there is still another way in which men petrify themselves; they enclose themselves in their human dignity and armor themselves with duties and rights, making their past into a protective coating and forming their own rigid personalities. Sartre has always felt the most violent antipathy for people inflated by their importance, embalmed by seriousness and dignity. He doesn't like doctors, engineers, or government officials, and he generally prefers the company of young people and women to that of mature men because he thinks that one finds more spontaneity and truth in them.

Sartre began by opposing the imaginary world of works of art to the disappointing and often repulsive universe of things and man-things. As a small child, he was thrilled by illustrated magazines that carried him away with Nick Cartre [*sic*] into a dreamlike Chicago, or with Buffalo Bill into a legendary Arizona.[7] And he delighted in inventing complicated and mysterious adventures on his own, whether he was acting out his own plays in a little puppet theater in Luxembourg Gardens or covering pages of paper with his writing.

He was particularly happy when he didn't completely understand what he was writing, because then it seemed to him that his work therefore had the depth and richness of grown-ups' books. All throughout his youth, Sartre never stopped writing—poems, essays, dialogues, narratives—and seeing no other means of salvation, he indiscriminately exhorted all of his friends to write. This is also the solution that is proposed to Antoine Roquentin at the end of La nausée, and so it seemed to Sartre that only by existing in an imaginary plane, as creator of imaginary works in the consciousness of a reader, could he escape from getting stuck in the paste of contingent life.

Of course, Sartre was already fiercely determined to be a free man, and he refused anything that could have weighted down his existence or rooted him in the earth. He did not marry and has never possessed anything—not a piece of furniture, bibelot, painting, nor book. He lives in hotel rooms where even a copy of his own works would not be found and whose bareness often surprises his visitors. He has always spent his money as soon as he earned it, sometimes even a bit before. But then this freedom had only a negative character, that of Orestes' tutor in Les mouches [The Flies] [1943] and of Mathieu in L'âge de raison [The Age of Reason] [1945].[8] Considering only his work to be important, Sartre was engaged as little as possible in life; he paid little attention to politics and abstained from voting. An evolution that began a little before the war and that was precipitated in the prison camp where he spent nine months led him to a very different attitude.[9] It appeared to him that one must seek refuge against the horror and insufficiency of things in the very heart of man rather than in an imaginary world. As a consciousness, man tears himself away from the sticky mass of the given, and as a freedom, he surpasses it in order to throw himself toward the future. If a man chooses his ends and pursues them passionately without forgetting that they are only ends by his own choice, then he posits himself as an absolute existence that carries its justification within itself. Literary creation keeps its value in Sartre's eyes, but as one of the possible manifestations of his freedom, as one means among others of communicating with other men and teaching them, precisely, to affirm themselves as consciousnesses and freedoms.

Indeed, it seems to Sartre, as to the Stoics of old whose ethics he loves,[10] that by this affirmation and by it alone, man can escape the menaces of all those unyielding and hostile things, which do not depend upon us.[11] And as far as he is concerned, this is the mode of existence that he strives to attain.[12] Being in excellent health, he is lucky to be rarely troubled by his body; and insofar as this body is manifest, Sartre refuses any solidarity with it. He is a stranger to letting-go [laisser-aller] and abandon but must always be active, making use of his body yet not resting in it. He likes to eat, drink, and smoke but easily tolerates privations; if he happens by chance to be sick, he goes so far as to deny the pain he feels, making it very difficult for doctors to diagnose him. He does not think he has any more solidarity with his past, and he evokes memories only rarely. He recognizes his mistakes with a disconcerting good faith and can describe and criticize himself with the most severe impartiality. Already, he no longer sees himself in that man about whom he speaks, but always sees his true face in the future. He is therefore never full of vanity concerning the things he has done, and while he is extremely proud when he envisions the things he will do, it is the impersonal and metaphysical pride of a freedom who wills itself as absolute and doesn't feel enslaved by any givens. This audacity has often allowed Sartre to push back the limits of what at first seemed possible. He has also sometimes been cruelly thwarted by events, but Sartre is indifferent to his failures and undertakes without hoping in the sense that he does not believe he has any right over the world and expects nothing from it. He expects nothing except of himself; he feels no desire and no regret; he does not suffer from any of the limitations that life imposes on every individual. For him, it is enough to be what he is. One of the qualities that strikes all of Sartre's friends is his immense generosity; he gives of himself and everything that he possesses without counting and is always ready to show an interest in others and share his time and thoughts with them. Yet he doesn't want to receive anything from them and needs no one. He detests conversations about ideas because no idea ever comes to him from the outside. He reads little, and if by chance he feels like reading, any book can delight him—he asks only that the printed pages act as a support for his imagination and his thoughts, a bit like fortunetellers who look in coffee grounds for a support for their visions. Even the prospect of death doesn't bother Sartre; he rarely thinks about it and is very calm when he does think about it. It seems to him that his death is yet another part of his life and this supreme limitation is necessary in order to finish defining him. Active yet never tense, enterprising yet never worried, passionate yet without experiencing the anguish nor the bitterness of disappointments, Sartre is presently a man in perfect harmony with himself: a happy man. And he is happy without qualms because he is convinced that any man can, more or less readily, discover a joy as solid as his own at the heart of himself and in the consciousness of his freedom.[13]

When those who have read *La nausée, Le mur* [The Wall] [1938], *Les mouches,* or *Huis clos* [No Exit] [1947] meet Sartre,[14] they are oftentimes surprised by a gaiety, a youth, an almost childish freshness, whose reasons and meaning I have just provided. One must not believe, however, that Sartre denies this vision of the world that has so often been qualified as "morbid," "black," or "depressing," and that he showed in his first works.[15] The apparent paradox of Sartre is that although he is profoundly optimistic in his ethics and his temperament, he revels in the darkest imaginations and feels more than anyone all that is horrible and troubling in this world. But that is precisely what gives him, in his work as in his life, his exceptional value. Ordinarily, the horrible and the disreputable frightens or fascinates; either one avoids looking directly at them, or one revels and gets lost in them. Sartre looks and does not get lost. He never wanted to lose himself—the drugs and concerted perversions that were rather fashionable in his youth never attracted him—but neither did he want to cheat, and he went rather far in his relationship with the horrible. During an entire season, when he was writing *La nausée* and studying in himself the nature of the image,[16] he fell into a depression, letting himself go to the point of quasi-hallucinations, and was haunted by the idea that he had chronic hallucinatory psychosis. It must be understood that for Sartre, the "nausea" before a contingent and insipid given and the joy of overcoming this given by existing as a freedom are two moments of the same experience.[17] The more disreputable the things surrounding him are, and the more mediocre the people are, the more necessary it becomes for a man to seek aid within himself, and the more moving his effort appears. Sartre did not write so many cruel pages out of his love for naturalism, but rather [his love of] heroism. On the other hand, he is passionately interested in limit-situations like insanity, torture, vice, and agony not out of his love for the morbid and strange, but because it is in these privileged cases that man discloses and manifests his essence in a way that is more pure and necessary than in daily life.

If Sartre's attitude may seem paradoxical, it is because the human condition is ambiguous, and Jean-Paul Sartre is a man who has fully assumed his condition as man.

NOTES

1. Beauvoir begins her text with the following: "Une des idées dominantes du grand livre philosophique de Jean-Paul Sartre, *L'être et le néant,* c'est qu'il y a deux manières d'exister: on rencontre dans le monde des choses inertes qui demeurent indéfiniment égales à ce qu'elles sont; et d'autre part ce monde est habité par des hommes qui sont des consciences et des libertés." In *HB,* Cowley adds the sentence "Jean-Paul Sartre is a new sort of figure in life and letters" before his translation of this sentence, which includes another addition: "One of the leading ideas expressed in his big philosophical work, *L'être et le néant*—and

also exemplified in his novels, his stories, and the two plays that all Paris has gone to see—is the idea that there are two modes of existing. On the one hand, there is the mode proper to things that always remain exactly what they are, in the 'given' world of contingencies and circumstances; on the other hand, there is the mode proper to persons who represent consciousness and liberty." Notice that "and also exemplified . . . all Paris has gone to see" does not appear in the original French.

2. This first paragraph appears as the second paragraph in *HB*.

3. Antoine Roquetin is the protagonist in Sartre's *La nausée* who becomes physically ill at the obscene overabundance of the world around him.

4. The whole first part of the paragraph up to this point is omitted in *HB*.

5. This description of Sartre's likes and dislikes is the opening paragraph in *HB*, although the last sentence is omitted.

6. This sentence is omitted in *HB*.

7. Nick Carter was a popular nineteenth-century dime novel character in Street and Smith's *New York Weekly* created by John R. Coryell (1848–1924). Buffalo Bill was the name by which William Frederick Cody (1846–1917) was known. He was a hunter, U.S. Army scout, and Indian fighter whose real-life exploits became fictionalized in popular dime novels in the United States and abroad. After 1883 Buffalo Bill's Wild West Show toured for many years in the United States and in Europe.

8. Orestes was a Greek mythological figure and the main character in Sartre's *Les mouches*. The reference to specific works, i.e., "that of Orestes' tutor . . . *L'âge de raison*," is omitted in *HB*.

9. In *HB*, this appears as follows: "An evolution in another direction began shortly before the war and continued more rapidly in the German prison camp where he spent nine months. It led him to play an active part in the resistance movement, but this was only the outward sign of a changed attitude." But the original here makes no reference to the French resistance: "Une évolution commencée un peu avant la guerre et qui s'est précipitée dans le camp de prisonniers où il a passé neuf mois l'a conduit à une attitude fort différente."

10. The Stoics comprised an ancient school of philosophy founded by Zeno (c. 300 B.C.E.), so called because they met in the Stoa Poecile (painted porch) at Athens. The Roman Stoic Epictetus (C.E. c. 50–c. 138) defines the highest good in life as virtue, which is achieved only by putting aside passion, unjust thoughts, and indulgence and by bringing one's conduct into agreement with the laws of nature.

11. The last sentence of the preceding paragraph and the first sentence of this paragraph, i.e., "Literary creation . . . depend upon us," are omitted in *HB*.

12. Beauvoir writes, "Et pour son compte c'est ce mode d'existence qu'il s'efforce d'atteindre," which is rendered in *HB* as follows: "This absolute life of the person is what Sartre tries to lead," followed by "Short and square (some of his American friends call him '*Monsieur Cinq-par-Cinq*')," which does not appear in the original.

13. The last part of this paragraph ("Even the prospect of death . . . a joy as solid as his own") is moved to the end of the *HB* article, with the rest of this sentence ("at the heart of himself and in the consciousness of his freedom") omitted.

14. Beauvoir writes, "Lorsqu'un lecteur . . . rencontre Sartre," which is translated in *HB* as "[s]ometimes a reader . . . has the good fortune to be introduced to Sartre."

15. Beauvoir writes, "[I]l est souvent surpris par cette gaieté, cette jeunesse, cette fraîcheur presque enfantine dont je viens de donner les raisons et le sens; il ne faudrait pas croire

cependant que Sartre renie cette vision du monde qu'on a si souvent qualifiée de 'morbide,' 'noire,' 'déprimante,' et qu'il a exposée dans ses premières oeuvres." This is translated in *HB* as follows: "Still shaken by literary creations that have often been described as morbid, dark, depressing, strangers are amazed to find that the author himself is full of youthfulness, optimism, and almost childish high spirits. These qualities, like the pessimism of the novels and plays, are an essential part of Sartre's temperament and philosophy."

16. "Studying in himself the nature of the image" is "étudiait sur lui-même la nature de l'image," in French.

17. This sentence directly follows the first two sentences of this paragraph and the resulting passage appears as the beginning of the last paragraph in *HB*. The remainder of this paragraph and the final paragraph, i.e., "The apparent paradox of Sartre . . . hallucinatory psychosis" and "The more disreputable . . . assumed his condition as man," are omitted.

8

An Eye for an Eye

INTRODUCTION

by Kristana Arp

This essay was first published in *Les temps modernes* in February 1946 and then later in a collection of Beauvoir's essays published by Les Éditions Nagel in 1948. The immediate inspiration for it was the trial and subsequent execution of Robert Brasillach by the French government after World War II. A graduate of the elite École normale supérieure, Brasillach was a well-known author and critic who served as the editor of the fascist newspaper *Je suis partout* from 1935 to 1943. A lifelong anti-Semite, he published a column during the German occupation that revealed the pseudonyms and whereabouts of French Jews, who then could be stripped of their citizenship and jobs and eventually deported under the new anti-Jewish legislation. Beauvoir attended his trial on January 19, 1945, where he was convicted of treason. A petition urging a pardon was circulated among French intellectuals. Forty-nine people signed, among them Gabriel Marcel and Albert Camus. (Camus signed only because of his opposition to the death penalty, he said.) Sartre, who was in New York during this period, did not respond to a telegram requesting his signature. Beauvoir was asked to sign and explicitly refused. In any case, General de Gaulle refused to grant the pardon and Brasillach was executed by firing squad on February 6, 1945.[1]

In this piece Beauvoir explained why she refused to sign the pardon petition. She also referred to this incident in her third volume of memoirs, *Force of Circumstance* (1963). There she condemns Brasillach specifically for urging and facilitating the persecution of Jews, listing the names of a number of Jews whom she knew personally who were killed or deported during the occupation. This last touch is significant given Beauvoir's insistence in "An Eye for an Eye" that punishment of this sort should redress wrongs committed against actual persons, not just satisfy an abstract notion of justice. In "An Eye for an Eye" Beauvoir also focuses on the suffering caused by the French collaborators, not their betrayal of their country. By contrast, Brasillach's treatment of Jews was hardly mentioned at his trial.[2] The focus of this essay can be explained partially by events that occurred during the year that passed between Brasillach's execution and its publication. For one, during this time the concentration camps were liberated, freeing the few survivors to return home. Second, in November 1945 the Nuremberg trials began, where high-ranking Nazi officials were tried for crimes against humanity.[3] "An Eye for an Eye" can be seen on one level to be an attempt to give a philosophical explanation of what it means to commit a crime against humanity.

In her memoirs Beauvoir responded to the objection that Brasillach did not deserve to die because he had not actually committed any of these atrocities himself by saying: "There are words as murderous as gas chambers."[4] Sartre touched on this theme of the responsibility of the writer in his introductory essay for the first issue of *Les temps modernes*. For the writer, he said, "every word he utters has reverberations."[5] *Les temps modernes* was intended to serve as a forum for those who accepted this responsibility—those who wrote *littérature engagé*. Journalism was included in this category.[6] "An Eye for an Eye," which appeared in the fifth issue, was certainly journalism of this sort.

But "An Eye for an Eye" is not merely a *pièce d'occasion*. It is also a philosophical essay, one in a series of philosophical essays that Beauvoir wrote during the 1940s. In it she introduces a philosophical concept that becomes central to her later work on existentialist ethics, *The Ethics of Ambiguity* (1947). Even though she alludes to this concept of ambiguity at only two places in the text, it serves as the foundation of her argument that those implicated in Nazi atrocities should be executed. The "tragic ambiguity" of the human condition, she says in "An Eye for an Eye," is that every person is "at the same time a freedom and a thing, both unified and scattered, isolated by his subjectivity and nevertheless coexisting at the heart of the world with other men." In *The Ethics of Ambiguity* she puts it this way: a human being is "still a part of the world of which he is a consciousness."[7] Existentialism, she claims there, is the only philosophy that does justice to this fundamental feature of human existence.

It is the first aspect of this ambiguity—that a human being exists both as a consciousness and as a material entity—that is central to her argument in "An Eye for an Eye." This aspect of ambiguity is experienced differently in relation to myself and in relation to others. I am directly aware only of my own consciousness. Since I am not directly aware of the other's consciousness, the other's existence as a material being is more apparent than my own. But to the other the same thing is true of me. Given that everyone is rooted in his own subjectivity, the other is not simply equivalent to oneself. Instead there is a reciprocity between subjects (a reciprocity almost in a mathematical sense—the way the fraction $2/3$ is reciprocal to the fraction $3/2$). This reciprocity has a profound moral significance for Beauvoir. The necessity of affirming it is "the metaphysical basis of the idea of justice." I have a moral obligation to treat others not merely as objects in the world, but as conscious beings aware of what is being done to them.

If one refuses to acknowledge the subjectivity of someone else, if instead someone "deliberately tries to degrade man by reducing him to a thing," then one commits an absolute evil, Beauvoir argues. This crime is different from ordinary crimes like theft, or even murder. (Beauvoir does not mention rape here, to which, interestingly enough, this description does seem to apply.) And the perpetrators are different from common criminals. Only in such cases is violent revenge justified. Indeed in such cases vengeance is a "metaphysical requirement" because it reestablishes the reciprocity between humans that this crime negated. The one committing such a deed ignores the ambiguous nature of human existence. He recognizes only one aspect of his existence, his subjectivity, and only one aspect of his victim's existence, his material reality. When the victim seeks vengeance, however, the tables are turned. When he is subjected to violence himself, the victimizer is made to realize that he too has a material existence and that his previous victim is a subject, not just an object.[8]

The moral goal of this sort of punishment is thus to restore the reciprocity between victim and victimizer grounded in the ambiguous existence that they both share. However, Beauvoir goes on to discuss the many reasons why this goal can only rarely, if ever, be achieved. Human freedom, the subject of much of Beauvoir's philosophizing during this period, proves to be the stumbling block. Because the target of vengeance remains free, even when subjected to violence himself, he can always refuse to accept the significance of what he is undergoing. He can persist in seeing his punishment as merely a blow of fate along the lines of a natural disaster. Trying to break his spirit by increasing his suffering does not have the desired result either. If his subjectivity is eclipsed by the intensity of the pain he feels, he becomes incapable of any understanding. Yet the one who commits the evil of treating another human being as a thing must suffer, must be *forced* to feel remorse, or else his freedom to impose his own interpretation on events mocks his victims. If he chooses to repent all on his own, he remains the sovereign subject. The reason it is hard for vengeance to achieve its goal is that "[t]he foreign consciousness must be led from the outside to draw from itself sentiments that one cannot impose on it without its consent."

It is because he is free, on the other hand, that the one committing such evil ultimately deserves to be punished. Beauvoir explores what she calls the point of view of charity at some length in this essay and grants that it raises many valid points. For one, we can judge a person's actions only from the outside. These actions appear differently to the one performing them. Also, the actions we judge occurred in the past, and, in any case, no one action or set of actions defines a person. Beauvoir appeals to an existentialist conception of subjectivity here: "From the inside a man *is* never anything. He escapes all definition by means of a profound inconsistency." However, none of these considerations has weight when someone commits what Beauvoir designates as the absolute evil of treating another person as a thing. In this case no excuse stands up against the fact of human freedom. The Christian god can forgive anything perhaps, but a "human ethics" cannot. It must create the good by rejecting evil, she says.

Although the person committing such evil must be punished, the way that he is punished is bound to be unsatisfactory. Even in what Beauvoir calls the "privileged case" where the victim directly and immediately enacts violent revenge on his tormentor, rarely is human reciprocity restored. In any case, she judges, the state is right to forbid private acts of vengeance. First, how can one determine the motives of someone claiming to be seeking revenge? Some people are eager to claim the status of victim, perhaps because it carries with it the moral privilege to punish others that Beauvoir is talking about here. Second, if the target of vengeance refuses to acknowledge its justice, he is likely to strike back at the avenger in turn, and then vengeance leads to a perpetuation of violence. Private vengeance is problematic, Beauvoir says, because "the freedom of those seeking revenge risks transforming itself into tyranny."

Yet vengeance is even less likely to achieve its metaphysical aim of restoring reciprocity when a third party takes revenge for the victim. In acting for another, a person becomes an agent of an abstract justice, and this is not a legitimate role for a private individual to take on. The state *is* justified in taking on this role, but in doing so it no longer aims at reestablishing the reciprocity between victim and victimizer the way vengeance does. The state cannot really redress wrongs done in the past; it aims only to create a future where the wrongs punished will not occur again. For this reason the trials and executions of people like Brasillach function mainly as social rituals. The unfortunate consequence is that "[p]unishment thus takes on the symbolic role and the condemned is never far from appearing as an expiatory victim."

The ultimate failure of punishment to achieve the moral purpose behind it deeply disturbs Beauvoir. Nonetheless, it is important that she points out that punishment is not simply "the serene recovery of a reasonable and just order." This is one reason why extreme punishments like execution are deeply problematic. In any case, Beauvoir asks, what measures that people take *are* ever certain of reaching their goals? "In the same way as hatred and revenge do, love and action always imply a failure," she writes, "but this failure must not keep us from loving and acting." In her other philosophical essays from this period, especially "Existentialism and Popular Wisdom" (1945), Beauvoir stresses that existentialism is not a pessimistic philosophy. But since Beauvoir's existentialism sees ambiguity and freedom to be the defining features of human existence, there can be no easy, reassuring answers to significant moral questions like those raised by the executions of war criminals. In *The Ethics of Ambiguity,* Beauvoir says, "morality resides in the painfulness of an indefinite questioning."[9] Beauvoir's treatment of this concrete ethical question in this essay is certainly in line with her approach to ethical questions generally there.

NOTES

1. All of this information about Robert Brasillach comes from Alice Kaplan, *The Collaborator: The Trial and Execution of Robert Brasillach* (Chicago: University of Chicago Press, 2000).

2. See Kaplan, *Collaborator,* xi.

3. See Kaplan, *Collaborator,* 217–18.

4. Simone de Beauvoir, *Force of Circumstance,* trans. Richard Howard (New York: Putnam, 1964), 22.

5. Jean-Paul Sartre, "Introducing *Les temps modernes,"* in *"What Is Literature" and Other Essays* (Cambridge, Mass.: Harvard University Press, 1988), 252.

6. "It strikes us, in fact, that journalism is one of the literary genres and that it can become one of the most important of them." Sartre, "Introducing *Les temps modernes,"* 266–67.

7. Simone de Beauvoir, *The Ethics of Ambiguity,* trans. Bernard Frechtman (New York: Carol Publishing Group, 1991), 7.

8. Beauvoir wrote before the day of gender-neutral usage, and she uses the male pronoun to refer to individual humans, a feature of her prose that has been retained in the translation. I, of course, have no such excuse. But in the present case, it would be awkward to use the he/she, her/him construction. To refer to the victim or victimizer as "she," on the other hand, might have misleading implications. So I also have reverted to using the male pronoun.

9. Beauvoir, *The Ethics of Ambiguity*, 133.

An Eye for an Eye

"Our executioners have passed on very bad morals to us," Gracchus Babeuf once wrote with regret.[1] Under the Nazi oppression, faced with traitors who have made us their accomplices, we saw poisonous sentiments bloom within our hearts of which we never before had any presentiment. Before the war we lived without wishing any of our fellow humans any harm. Words like vengeance and expiation had no meaning for us. We scorned our political or ideological opponents rather than detesting them. And as for individuals like assassins and thieves, whom society denounced as dangerous, they did not seem to be our enemies. To our eyes their crimes were only accidents provoked by a regime that did not give everyone an equal chance. These people did not compromise any of the values that we were attached to. We would not have consented to bring a complaint against a thief, because we would not think we had a right to any of our possessions. An assassination could inspire us with horror, but not resentment. We would not have dared to demand respect for our lives from those whose misery, whose very birth, places them outside

"Œil pour œil," *Les temps modernes* 1, no. 5 (1946): 813–30 (hereafter referred to as *TM*); reprinted in *L'existentialisme et la sagesse des nations* (Paris: Nagel, 1948), 109–43, © Sylvie Le Bon de Beauvoir (hereafter referred to as *ESN*). Differences in the two versions are annotated below.

of the human community. Conscious of our privilege, we forbade ourselves to judge them. And we would not have wanted to align ourselves with tribunals that persisted in defending an order we disapproved of.

Since June 1940 we have learned rage and hate. We have wished humiliation and death on our enemies. And today each time a tribunal condemns a war criminal, an informer, a collaborator, we feel responsible for the verdict. Since we have desired this victory, since we have craved these sanctions, it is in our name that they judge, that they punish. Ours is the public opinion that expresses itself through newspapers, posters, meetings, the public opinion that these specialized instruments are designed to satisfy. We were pleased at the death of Mussolini, at the hanging of the Nazi executioners at Kharkov,[2] with the tears of Darnand.[3] In so doing have we participated in their condemnation. Their crimes have struck at our own hearts. It is our values, our reasons to live that are affirmed by their punishment.

It goes without saying that our attitude with regard to those called common criminals has not changed. They retain in our eyes the same excuses, since on this plane the social order has not become more just. But to the extent that it refuses tyranny, that it strives to reestablish the dignity of man, we claim this society as ours. We feel a solidarity with it; we are complicit in its decisions.

It is not a small thing to suddenly find oneself a judge, much more an executioner. During the years of the occupation we claimed this role with enthusiasm. Then, hate was easy. When we read the articles of *Je suis partout*,[4] when we heard on the radio the voice of Ferdonnet or Hérold Paquis,[5] when we thought about the arsonists of Oradour,[6] of the torturers of Buchenwald, of the Nazi leaders and of their accomplices, the German people, we said to ourselves in an outburst of anger, "They will pay." And our anger seemed to promise a joy so heavy that we could scarcely believe ourselves able to bear it. They have paid. They are going to pay. They pay each day. And the joy has not risen up in our hearts.

No doubt our disappointment is due in part to circumstances. The purge has not been straightforward [*franche*]. Many of the worst war criminals met such a brutally disastrous end that it did not have the appearance of an atonement; others remain out of reach. The attitude of the German people stymies our hate. But this is not enough to explain why a revenge so eagerly desired has left this taste of ashes in our mouths. It is the idea of punishment itself that is at issue here. Now that we feel in their true concreteness the sentiments and attitudes designated by the words "vengeance," "justice," "pardon," "charity," they have assumed a new meaning that surprises and worries us. Legal sanctions no longer appear to us to be simple police measures that still retain a reflection of past blind beliefs. All of us have more or less felt it: the need to punish, to avenge ourselves. We would like to better understand what this need represents for someone today. Is it well founded? Can it be satisfied? In order to try to answer these questions, it is necessary to both look around us and return inside ourselves.

First it appears obvious that in the moment of punishment the relationship of the two parties facing each other is not one of struggle. During a struggle the enemy is seized as a pure exteriority. He is only a resistance to overcome, a human material. His extermination is not wanted for itself but as a necessary means to a final success. That which is called "exercising reprisals" is still an act of war. No doubt murder and destruction do not have immediate efficacy in this case. One executes hostages already rendered powerless. One annihilates civilian populations whose death will not advance the outcome of the war. But such measures have an indirect utility: they intimidate the enemy. The treatment inflicted on the victims is not directed at them; it is a form of pressure. In all cases where executions serve as an example or proceed from preestablished orders, one should not speak of punishment. What distinguishes punishment is that it aims expressly at the individual who suffers it. It does not seek to prevent the commission of new crimes; only those who can no longer do harm are able to be punished. Nor is it a matter of making an example. It would be absurd to suppose that they shot Mussolini in order to intimidate future dictators. Thus, vengeance is not justified by realistic considerations. On the contrary, a concern for efficacy often demands that one renounce punishment. It would be an absurd politics that sought to satisfy its grudges against Italy, against Germany even, rather than reinstitute a lasting equilibrium in Europe. Vengeance appears to be a luxury. Nonetheless, it answers a need so deep that it can hold practical interests in check. Had the French government decided after the war to use certain men who could render a service to the country but were heavily compromised by collaboration, it would have caused serious outrage [*scandales*]. For man does not live on bread alone.[7] He also has spiritual appetites that are no less essential than any other appetites and the thirst for revenge is one of these. It answers to one of the metaphysical requirements of man.

But in order to discover this deep significance, one must not examine it in the elaborate forms in which society envelopes it. It is necessary to grasp it in its spontaneity. In the revolutionary period that we have lived through in the aftermath of the liberation, there has been license to exact an individual or collective revenge that is subject to no codes: there have been "barberings,"[8] lynchings of snipers, summary executions of certain of the collaborationist police, and massacres of the S.S. prison guards by their freed captives.[9] In all these cases, the punishment had no goal outside of itself. Through inflicting death and suffering, people wanted to reach those individuals they regarded as personally responsible, together and alone, for certain bad acts. The only justification for the treatment inflicted upon them is the hate that they have aroused, and it seemed sufficient justification. Indeed hate is not a capricious passion. It denounces an abominable [*scandaleux*][10] reality and imperiously demands that this reality be eradicated from the world. One does not hate a hailstorm or a plague, one hates only men, not because they are material causes of material damage, but because they are conscious authors of genuine evil. A soldier who kills in combat is not to be hated, because he is obeying orders and because there is a reciprocity between his situation and the situation of his foes. Neither death nor suffering nor captivity are abominable in themselves. An abomination arises only at the moment that a man treats fellow men like objects, when by torture, humiliation, servitude, assassination, one denies them their existence as men. Hatred grasps at another's freedom insofar as it is used to realize the absolute evil that is the degradation of a man into a thing. And it calls immediately for a revenge that strives to destroy that evil at its source by reaching the freedom of the evildoer.

"He will pay for it." The word is telling. To pay is to supply the equivalent for that which one has received or taken. This desire for equivalence is expressed most exactly in that famous law of retaliation: "An eye for an eye, a tooth for a tooth." No doubt this law retains to the present day a whiff of magic. It strives to satisfy some unknown dark god of symmetry. But, above all, it corresponds to a profound human need. I heard a member of the resistance tell how he applied this law to a collaborationist police agent guilty of torturing a woman. "He understood," he concluded somberly. This word, often employed in this elliptical, violent sense, announces the deep intention of revenge. It is meant not as an intellectual abstraction but as exactly what Heidegger designates by "understanding": the process by means of which our entire being realizes a situation. One understands an instrument in using it. One understands torture by undergoing it. But even if the torturer feels in turn what the victim felt, this cannot remedy the evil that the torturer caused. It is necessary, besides this revived suffering, that the totality of a situation also be revived. The torturer believes himself to be sovereign consciousness and pure freedom in the face of the miserable thing he tortures. When his turn comes to be made into a tortured thing himself, he feels the tragic ambiguity of his condition as man. What he must understand, though, is that the victim, whose abjection he shares, also shares with him the privileges that he believed he could arrogate to himself. And he must not understand this by thought alone, in a speculative manner, but must realize this reversal of situation concretely. He must reestablish concretely and genuinely the reciprocity between human consciousnesses the negation of which constitutes the most fundamental form of injustice. An object for others, each man is a subject for himself, and he insistently demands to be recognized as such. One knows how one kick or shove can start a quarrel in a crowd. The individual who is inadvertently struck is not solely a body and he proves it; he defies the other with his voice, by a look; he hits him. The respect that he demands for himself, each person claims for his loved ones and finally for all men. The affirmation of the reciprocity of interhuman relations is the metaphysical basis of the idea of justice. It is what vengeance strives to reestablish in the face of the tyranny of a freedom that wants to be sovereign.

But this enterprise runs up against an essential difficulty. It aims for nothing less than to "compel" [*contraindre*] a "freedom." These terms are contradictory. However, true vengeance is bought only at this price. If the tyrant decided, without pressure from outside, to repent of his errors, even if, carried away by remorse, he were to apply the law of an eye for an eye to himself, perhaps vengeance would be disarmed, but it would not be satisfied. For he would remain the master of his regrets, of his destiny. He would remain a pure freedom and even in the suffering he might voluntarily inflict upon himself, he would continue to mock his victims in spite of himself. He himself must feel himself a victim, must endure violence. But violence alone is not sufficient either. It can serve only to make the guilty party recognize his real condition. And due to the very nature of freedom, it is by no means sure of succeeding at this. Violence can never present more than a temptation. It can never be an absolute constraint. What one wants is for violence to cast a spell over the enemy's freedom analogous to the spell that a seducer seeks to weave: the foreign consciousness must remain free with regard to the content of its acts, it must freely recognize its past faults, repent, and despair, but it must be an exterior necessity that compels this spontaneous movement. The foreign consciousness must be led from the outside to draw from itself sentiments that one cannot impose on it without its consent. It is because of this contradictory character that the intent of vengeance can never be satisfied. If the suffering inflicted is excessive, the consciousness of the criminal is engulfed in it. Entirely occupied in suffering he is nothing more than panting flesh—torture misses its aim. On the other hand, if he is spared physical pain, consciousness is at his disposal again and regains its autonomy. One can profit from moral punishment. One can even recover a type of happiness in captivity or exile. One can also undergo it with a sense of irony, with resistance, with arrogance, with a resignation lacking remorse. Here again punishment suffers a defeat. This is why we see throughout history that truly vindictive people engage all the resources of their imagination in order to punish their enemies. I do not know which Italian tyrant invented "the Great Fast" [le grand carême],[11] which consisted of forty days of slow torture culminating in the gradual elimination of all food and drink. The alternation of horrible suffering and long respites deprived of hope is one of the most effective methods of subduing a consciousness. But even the Great Fast ends in death and the death of the criminal disappoints those seeking vengeance. In dying he slips out of the world; he shrugs off his punishment. One can rain blows on his corpse, defile him with spit, hang him by the feet, thus proving that this haughty tyrant is also a thing of flesh. But one wishes that this truth were recognized by the tyrant himself. The death of Hitler frustrated us: one wished that he had remained alive to realize his ruin, in order to "understand." The ideal revenge is that which Louis XI exacted on La Balue, [or] which Judex enacted on the evil banker by enclosing him his whole life in a cell.[12] There consciousness was present but prisoner of the situation that was imposed on it, congealed in despair. Still it is always possible for this consciousness ultimately to escape into madness. In any case, one can scarcely find the circumstances favorable to accomplishing such perfect acts of revenge any longer except in paperback novels. Lacking the power to control the hated enemy indefinitely, one must resolve to kill him. For the one seeking vengeance must also reckon with the temporal dispersion that limits his hold on the other's consciousness. The moment when Mussolini cries "No, no" in front of the firing squad satisfies hate far more than the moment when he collapses beneath the bullets. But how can this moment be perpetuated? A living Mussolini would serve to cancel it out. Vengeance can in certain instants come near to its goal, e.g., when Paul Chack,[13] when Darnand say, sobbing, "I did not understand." But vengeance cannot keep a consciousness in subjection its entire life. So it resolves to extinguish it, with the hope that the abjection of those last instants will be eternalized by death. But this is only a last resort, since the concrete restitution of the reciprocity between victimizer and victim would require the living presence of the victimizer turned victim in his turn.

And even in the instant when the guilty party's consciousness yields to the solicitations of physical or moral pain, is this reciprocal relation ever really reestablished?[14] The privileged case is the one where the victim takes revenge on his own account. When at the hour of liberation the concentration camp inmates massacred their S.S. jailers, revenge existed for them in the most concrete and obvious way possible.[15] The victims and their torturers had really exchanged situations. However, when one takes revenge for another, when one takes revenge for those who have died, one of the parties refusing to realize the meaning of the punishment and the other being absent, from where then does this punishment draw its signification? A stranger can intervene only insofar as he participates in the universal essence of man that has been injured in the victim. He situates the punishment on the level of the universal; he makes it into an exercise of a right. But he is not qualified to defend the universal rights of man. To want to do this is to set himself up as a sovereign consciousness. He becomes himself a tyrant. That is why private vengeance always has a disquieting character. Granted, it is all the more pure for being founded on a more concrete hate. I do not think anyone was revolted by the way the concentration camp inmates massacred their torturers. But as soon as the avenger aspires to set himself up as a judge, vengeance becomes suspect. Vengeance is a concrete relation among individuals in the same way that struggle, love, torture, murder, or friendship are. It must assume its true nature and not seek universal justifications. The Ku Klux Klan and vigilantes provoke our indignation as much for the tranquil arrogance with which they decide the crime and the punishment as for their cruelty. But even in those cases where vengeance is most authentic, how can one be sure that the one seeking revenge has not been carried away by that will to power that slumbers in everyone? Hate can be nothing more than a pretext. If so, then in wiping out one abomination, one makes a new abomination appear in the world. One act of revenge calls for another act of revenge, evil engenders evil, and injustices pile up without wiping one another out.

That is why society does not authorize private acts of revenge, only allowing them as exceptions, without ever officially legitimating them. From the day after the liberation of France from the Nazis, an ordinance severely forbade individual violence. It delegated the task of punishment to special agencies. The notion of vengeance is replaced by that of sanction, which is elevated to the level of an institution and cut off from its base in the passions. People declare that one must punish without hate in the name of universal principles. But if vengeance inevitably ends up defeated, will social justice be better satisfied?

Here one no longer seeks to reestablish an impossible reciprocity. Although tolerated as a police method, physical torture has no place among social sanctions. Imprisonment, penal servitude, loss of civil rights, loss of citizenship rights, death—these all have the same character. They aim to eliminate the guilty from society. The judges turn away from the criminal's past. They know it is beyond their reach. In truth, one can no more avenge the dead than one can resurrect them. It is the future that the judges aim at. They want to restore a human community to its own idea of itself, to uphold the values that the crime has negated. They refuse in the present, for the future, in the name of the whole society, this wrong that cannot be effaced. But such a refusal cannot be merely a matter of words. Nothing was more laughable than the impotent protestations the European democracies made before 1939 against crimes that were all too real.[16] The refusal must be proved in action. Society solemnly pushes from its breast the man responsible for wrongs it has repudiated, and if a wrong weighs heavily enough, only one penalty is weighty enough to counterbalance it: death. Here death is not demanded by the law of an eye for an eye. Organized justice does not recognize this law. Furthermore neither Brasillach, nor Pétain, nor Laval directly killed anyone.[17] However, death is the only penalty that can express the violence with which society refuses certain crimes. All the trappings of the trial are designed to endow the sentence with the greatest expressive power possible. And, of course, the execution must follow the verdict. If not, the trial would be nothing more than a comedy of words. But the verdict counts more than the execution; it is the will to kill the criminal that matters, more even than his death, to the extent that in the trial of Pétain it seemed plausible to affirm this will on one level by cutting it off from any concrete consequences and condemning Pétain to death with the avowed intention of sparing his life.

This extreme case shows how far removed the idea of sanctions is from that of vengeance. In vengeance the man and the criminal are confounded in the concrete reality of a unique freedom. By discerning in Pétain the traitor and the old man, condemning the one and pardoning the other, the High Court only followed one of the tendencies of social justice through to its logical extreme. Social justice does not consider the guilty party in the totality of his being. It does not engage in a metaphysical struggle with a free consciousness imprisoned in a body of flesh and blood. It condemns the guilty party insofar as he is the substrate and reflection of certain evil acts. Punishment thus takes on the symbolic role and the condemned is never far from appearing as an expiatory victim. Of course in the end it is a man who is going to experience in his consciousness and in his flesh the penalty aimed at this abstract social reality, the condemned criminal. The dissociation is all the more striking the greater the temporal distance that separates the accused from his crimes. He seems to us to be someone other than the person who committed them. What, during the occupation, made hate so easy and clear was that it was aimed at free beings actually engaged in evil. In the moment of his victory one can punish with joy an unjust conqueror. The attack on Henriot was, from this point of view, as satisfying as possible.[18] The more the perpetrator is engaged in his criminal universe, the more punishment seems legitimate. However, official trials involve such long delays that, even in his physical appearance, the accused is sometimes unrecognizable. We did not expect to see that tired old man's face on Laval. A friend who cannot be suspected of sympathy for the Vichy government nor of empty sentimentality told me that he had felt a pang when during Pétain's trial he heard Laval asking the journalists in a certain voice: "Can one sit down? Can one have a glass of water?" The vanquished foe was no more than a poor, pitiful old man. It became difficult to wish for his death. Time is not the sole factor, moreover, that so blurs the features of the accused. The change in situation makes him appear in a new light. In this respect also, it is radically impossible to satisfy hate. Hate wants to strike the criminal at the heart of his evil activity. If one had struck Henriot down during one of his speeches, without him being aware of it, it would have been a failure, since he would not have been conscious of the punishment. But facing his murderers in his bedroom, as he did, and welcoming them with *sangfroid,* he was already less to be hated. The pomp of big trials, their tragic dimension, their ceremonial rites emphasize this reversal in a troublesome manner. I know how I was struck on entering the large hall where the trial of Brasillach was taking place. The public assembled there out of curiosity, the journalists there for professional reasons, the magistrates exercising their function as magistrates and attempting in vain to raise themselves to the level of true grandeur; all were people occupied like myself in living out an everyday mediocre moment of their lives. There were also the jurors with their unreadable faces who seemed to be pure incarnations of an abstract justice. And in his box, alone, cut off from everyone, there was a man whom circumstances had carried higher than himself. This man was put in the presence of his death and, because of that, in the presence of his entire life that he had to assume before death. Whatever this life had been like, whatever the reasons for his death, the dignity with which he carried himself in this extreme situation demanded our respect in the moment we most desired to despise him. We desired the death of the editor of *Je suis partout,* not that of this man completely occupied in dying well.

When, on the other hand, the accused conducts himself as a coward, as Paul Chack did, if he denies his guilt like Darnand, his tears evoke a disgust that also extinguishes the thirst for revenge. We would have rejoiced, if, at the time of their arrogance, someone had predicted their fall to us. For we believed in this arrogance and it would have pleased us to think it secretly fragile. But now that it has declared its fragility, it seems to us to have been a miserable mask behind which weak souls hid their flaws. The acknowledgment of this weakness takes away the relish of triumphing over them. Here again we confusedly aim to achieve the impossible: a force that recognizes itself as weakness without destroying itself as force. Sometimes it happens that the desired synthesis comes close to being realized, when the horror of the crimes being punished swamps even the event of the trial. It was that way at Kharkov, at Lüneburg:[19] the presence of the victims' families, the ringing testimony of the witnesses, the films of the atrocities made the past so close, so real, that the torturers were not able to evade it. They themselves—by their fits of nerves, their suicide attempts—acknowledged that they recognized themselves in the detestable figures evoked by their victims. But such cases are rare. Ordinarily, whether he merits our esteem or our contempt, the man who is condemned is not the man we hate.

Well enough, it is necessary to punish without hate, we are told. Yet I think this is precisely the error of official justice. Death is a real, concrete event, not the completion [*l'accomplissement*] of a rite. The more the trial takes on the aspect of a ceremony, the more abominable it seems that it might end in a real spilling of blood. This also struck me during Brasillach's trial: the lawyers, the judges, even the public played a role. The questioning, the lawyer's summations unrolled with all the pomp of a comic drama. Only the accused belonged to that world of flesh where bullets can kill. Between these two universes no passage seemed conceivable. In renouncing vengeance, society gives up on concretely linking the crime to the punishment. So punishment appears to be but an arbitrarily imposed penalty. For the guilty party it is nothing but an atrocious accident. True, vengeance almost inevitably degenerates into tyranny. But for all their concern for purity, legal sanctions fail to achieve the concrete goal they have set themselves. They are nothing but an empty form that only the plenitude of content could justify.

Thus it appears that all punishment is a failure. Maybe it is the principle itself that is wrong. Is not the justice that we demand merely a deception? Would it not be better to silence our rancor in order to open the door to charity? Let us listen attentively to this voice.

Vengeance is founded on a hate that addresses itself to a freedom that creates evil. But is man really free in committing evil? The scourges that man unleashes on the earth, are they not of the same order as a hailstorm or a plague? The question would be without importance if one considered only the objective aspects of his acts, as one does during the struggle. It becomes essential here since they are to be grasped in their subjectivity. Yet if we adopt the point of view of interiority,[20] does not their abominable character precisely disappear? There is a mirage of exteriority. Seen from the outside, wicked people seem wicked and good people absolutely good, as in the pictures from Épinal.[21] But in truth, from the inside, man *is* never anything. He escapes all definition by means of a profound inconsistency. There is so much wretchedness at the base of all men; they are so totally gnawed away by nothingness, that often, approaching an adversary who from afar appeared as hard and dense as a rock, we notice that, in truth, there is really "nobody" there before us that we could detest. No one really willed those abominable acts. They were not deliberate; they resulted from a whim, from a heedless blunder, by chance, by mistake. And even if they were willed, they were not willed insofar as they realized an evil. "No one is wicked voluntarily," Socrates says. The person who committed these acts was seeking a certain good, at the very least his own good. Perhaps he was an egoist, narrow-minded, thoughtless. But if we look into our own depths, who among us dares say: I am better than that man. It requires a lot of arrogance and very little imagination to judge another. How can one measure the temptations a man could have faced? How can one appreciate the weight of the circumstances that give an act its real shape? One would have to bring his upbringing, complexes, failures, and entire past—the totality of his engagement in the world—into account. Then, without question, his conduct is explainable. One could explain even Hitler's conduct, if one knew him well enough. But to explain is to understand, and to understand is already to accept. To the extent that they flow from a given situation, from a given temperament, even the crimes themselves lose the arrogance that makes them detestable. The objective aspect that they wore at first in our eyes vanishes. This is not the way that they existed for their author. He is certainly sincere when he refuses to recognize his crime, saying: "That's not what I wanted; I did not understand." At the trial at Lüneburg, some of the executioners from Bergen-Belsen wanted to commit suicide after seeing a reconstruction of their crimes. Doubtless they were overwhelmed by the censure of a public composed of their own compatriots and experienced the horror of an intolerable solitude. But I also conjecture that they discovered an atrocious and unknown aspect of their crimes in the light shed by this censure. They had never seen them except from their own point of view and they had never put themselves in the place of their victims or of society. Now let us not forget that hate and vengeance are aiming at the intention of an act; even legal sanctions repudiate it with violence only to the extent that it was willed by a freedom. Moreover, even if we admit that a man is responsible for a misdeed, it does not express him in his entirety. This traitor was also a good husband, a good father, a faithful friend; he used his influence to save human beings. Can one condemn an entire man on the basis of one moment of his life? This would be all the more cruel because this weakness that one reproaches him for is already in the past. It does not exist anymore as the expression of a freedom, but as something fixed that the guilty party trails behind him in spite of himself. Since he is other than the person who committed the crime, can we still hate him? And what good is served by punishment? Christian charity is more sincere than other forms in such pleadings because Christianity finds in original sin an excuse for all other sins. For the Christian there is the same corruption at the heart of all men. Only grace can permit us to overcome it. But it does not belong to any earthly judge to know what succor God has sent to any of his children. God alone can measure the temptation and the wrong. Besides, there is wrong only toward Him. He alone has the right to punish. As to men, they are all brothers in sin and wretchedness. Crime need not appear to them as an earthly abomination because the whole earth is abominable in the eyes of God, who has chosen, nonetheless, to save it through redemption. Men must pardon each other so that God may pardon them.

That there is much truth in the point of view taken by charity, no one, except in the élan of blind hatred, would care to deny. Very often men act without knowing what they do. One could even say that they never know exactly what they do. One cannot hate those youthful sixteen-year-old followers of Hitler in whom Nazism affirmed itself with such savage violence, but who never had the possibility of criticizing it. One reeducates children, the ignorant, those populations that are ill-informed; one does not punish them. Neither does one punish the ill or those mad people in whom conscience has been annihilated. And everyone knows that even a normal adult always acts out of situations that he has not chosen, that numerous physiological and sociological factors weigh on him. One also does not judge the act without judging the man: one does not have meaning or reality without the other. The act bursts from the heart of a life, of a universe in which alone it can find its true shape. That is why one listens to character witnesses during a trial; that is why one can attenuate the import of an act by seeing it in the light of other acts that are otherwise foreign to it. If a crime appears as a pure aberration in a life that entirely contradicts the principles of the crime, one considers it with indulgence. It seems that it has escaped from the guilty person, rather than being willed by him. Finally, it is true that a freedom, although always bound up with the past, is never held captive by it. The guilty party, by a new act, can regain the esteem of his fellows and be rehabilitated in their eyes. They can freely decide, looking beyond the past errors of a man, to opt for his future. Putting their confidence in him, they hold out a chance for him to redeem himself.

But there are cases where no redemption appears possible, because the evil that one runs up against is an absolute evil. Here is where we reject the point of view of charity. We think that such an evil exists. One can excuse all the offenses, even the crimes by which individuals assert themselves against society. But when a man deliberately tries to degrade man by reducing him to a thing, nothing can compensate for the abomination he causes to erupt on earth. There resides the sole sin against man. When it is accomplished no indulgences are permitted and it belongs to man to punish it. It is allowable for Christians to opt for charity since they believe in the existence of a supreme judge. But charity in this radical form is forbidden to men who affirm a human ethics, human values. Certainly, man is wretched, scattered, mired in the given, but he is also a free being. He can reject the most urgent temptations. It is not true that time divides him from himself, for it belongs to each man to realize his unity in assuming his past in his project for the future. For the life of a man to have a meaning, he must be held responsible for evil as well as for good, and, by definition, evil is that which one refuses in the name of the good, with no compromise possible. It is for these reasons that I did not sign the pardon petition for Robert Brasillach when I was asked to.[22] I believe that I understood during the course of his trial, at least roughly, how his political attitudes were situated in the ensemble of his life. And I know that on leaving the courtroom, I did not desire his death, for during that long sinister ceremony he had deserved esteem rather than hatred. Finally, I could not envision without anguish that an affirmation of the principle "one must punish traitors" should lead one gray morning to the flowing of real blood. Nonetheless, I did not sign. First of all, to "understand" is not to excuse: one never understands anything but the situation in which a freedom decides. But the decision itself could have been other than what it was. To grasp the coherence of a life, its relation to the given world, the logic of its development, all this does not prevent a decision from appearing as a choice. I saw clearly that the accused had forged his own opinions, his tastes, that sensibility in the name of which people claimed to excuse him, and of which his wrongs were a perversion. Afterward, the attitude of Brasillach touched me in that he had courageously assumed his life. But precisely because of that he recognized that he was one with his past. In claiming his freedom, he also owned up to his punishment. It seemed to me everyone should want, as he did, this unity that he realized through the months and the years. To deny the rages and desires of another time, to prefer the emotion of the present moment to them, is to break human existence into worthless fragments. It is to annihilate the past, to bury the dead at the bottom of an abyss of absence, to break all our ties with them. In the end it is the hypocritical pomp of official trials that carves out a gulf between principles and reality. But, in truth, if ideas do not have a concrete existence, if concrete facts do not signify anything, a man's death is also something devoid of meaning and, therefore, of importance. If, on the contrary, the values in which we believe are real and have weight, it is not shocking to affirm them at the cost of a life.

But one question still arises: who should punish? We have seen that contrary to what the sociologists claim, the more justice becomes socialized and renounces its repressive character,[23] the more it loses its signification and its concrete hold on the world. The official tribunals claim to take refuge behind an objectivity that is the worst part of the Kantian heritage. They want to be only an expression of impersonal right and deliver verdicts that would be nothing more than the subsumption of a particular case under a universal law. But the accused exists in his singularity, and his concrete presence does not take on the guise of an abstract symbol so easily. The real event that is death, and punishment in general, is justified only if it is one of the moments of a wholly real conflict. It is necessary that the punishment be attached to the wrong by a concrete bond. And this bond can be established only at the heart of a subjectivity. Only vengeance founded on hatred realizes a real reversal of the situation it rejects. Only it bites into the world. Nevertheless, one cannot admit the principle of a prompt and passionate justice administered by individuals, because the freedom of those seeking revenge risks transforming itself into tyranny. Is it really the guilty party that one punishes? Has he really committed a wrong? It is easy to make a mistake and a mistake can be irreparable. In the fever pitch of the Liberation, more than one innocent was shot. It is necessary to institute a trial of the accused; it is necessary that the sentence this person is handed is not dictated by caprice but expresses a true will. Thus we find ourselves facing a choice that it is practically impossible to escape: popular revenge expresses the passions of the moment instead of manifesting a reflective act of will, and professional judges can do nothing but obey commands. In them there is no concrete will.

Thus in the person of the judges as in that of the accused, every attempt to compensate for this absolute event that is the crime manifests the ambiguity of man's condition, that he is at the same time a freedom and a thing, both unified and scattered, isolated by his subjectivity and nevertheless coexisting at the heart of the world with other men. This is why all punishment is partially a failure. In the same way as hatred and revenge do, love and action always imply a failure, but this failure must not keep us from loving and acting. For we have not only to establish what our situation is, we have to choose it in the very heart of its ambiguity. We know enough at present to know that we must stop seeing vengeance as the serene recovery of a reasonable and just order. Nonetheless, we must still want the punishment of authentic criminals. For to punish is to recognize man as free in evil as well as in good. It is to distinguish evil from good in the use that man makes of his freedom. It is to will the good.[24]

NOTES

1. Gracchus Babeuf (1760–97) was a proto-communist revolutionary active after the French revolution who was executed by the government. See R. B. Rose, *Gracchus Babeuf: The First Revolutionary Communist* (Stanford: Stanford University Press, 1978).

2. A war crimes trials was held in 1943 at Kharkov, a city in the Ukraine, at which three Germans and one Russian were condemned to death for committing atrocities against prisoners. Sheldon Glueck, *War Criminals: Their Prosecution and Punishment* (New York: Knopf, 1944), 60, 80.

3. Joseph Darnand, the head of the Milice, or militia, set up by the Vichy government, gave violent speeches against the Resistance and later sponsored a French contingent of the German army. He was executed after his trial in 1945. Herbert R. Lottman, *The Purge* (New York: Morrow, 1986), 179.

4. *Je suis partout* (I Am Everywhere) was the collaborationist newspaper edited by Robert Brasillach.

5. Paul Ferdonnet broadcast Nazi propaganda in French from Stuttgart. He was tried and executed in August 1945. William L. Shirer, *The Collapse of the Third Republic: An Enquiry into the Fall of France in 1940* (New York: Da Capo, 1994), 203. Jean Hérold Paquis, a leading commentator for Radio-Paris during the occupation, followed the retreating Germans to Berlin to broadcast propaganda. He was sentenced to death and executed in September 1945. Lottman, *The Purge*, 140.

6. Oradour sur Glane is a town in the Limousin region of France. A division of German militia passing through there in June 1944 locked almost the entire population in the church and then burned it to the ground. Six hundred forty-two people were killed. Bertram M. Gordon, *Collaborationism in France during the Second World War* (Ithaca, N.Y.: Cornell University Press, 1980), 305.

7. From Deuteronomy 8:3, Matthew 4:4, and Luke 4:4.

8. After the war, people sought out and shaved the heads of women who were known to have kept close company with the Germans.

9. "S.S." is the abbreviation for the *Schutzstaffel* (security echelon), Hitler's elite Nazi militia under Heinrich Himmler.

10. Although the French term *scandale* can convey the same meaning as its English cognate, it can also mean something much graver, the sin of leading someone away from God, although Beauvoir does not use it in a religious sense. Unless otherwise noted, I have translated *scandale* as "abomination" and *scandaleux* and "abominable" in this text.

11. *Le carême*, the French term for "fast," also means Lent, which is often observed with a forty-day fast.

12. La Balue, a French prelate born in 1421, conspired with the enemy of his king, Louis XI. He was held captive for eleven years, legend has it, in an iron cage. *Grand dictionnaire encyclopédie Larousse*, vol. 2, 1982. Judex was the pseudonym adopted by a mysterious avenger in a French film serial from 1917, remade as a movie in 1933 and 1963. See Frank N. Magill, ed., *Magill's Survey of French Cinema*, vol. 4 (Englewood Cliffs, N.J.: Salem Press, 1985), 1604–7.

13. Paul Chack, a former naval officer and popular writer on history, wrote editorials and appeared at rallies for the Germans. He was sentenced and executed in December 1944. Lottman, *The Purge*, 140.

14. "Reestablished" is "rétabli" in *TM* (820) but "établi" in *ESN* (122).

15. "The most concrete, the most obvious" (la plus concrète, la plus évidente): in *ESN* (123) the words "concrète, la plus" are deleted.

16. "Impotent protestations . . . made before 1939" is a reference to the British and French appeasement of the Nazis, for example, in the Munich Pact of 1938, before finally declaring war in 1939.

17. Brasillach is identified in Kristana Arp's introduction to this essay. Marshal Philippe Pétain was a French war hero of World War I who became chief of state of the Vichy government set up by the Germans after their defeat of the French. After the war he was tried and condemned to death, but his sentence was commuted to life imprisonment due to his advanced age. Lottman, *The Purge,* 139. Pierre Laval, the premier of the Vichy government, was executed by firing squad in 1945. Ibid., 177–79.

18. Philippe Henriot, the Vichy minister of propaganda, was shot dead by a Resistance commando in his bedroom three weeks after the Allies landed at Normandy. Lottman, *The Purge,* 32.

19. Lüneburg, Germany, was the site of the Bergen-Belsen concentration camp, where a war crimes trial was held.

20. "Interiority" (l'intériorité) is "l'antériorité" in *ESN* (132).

21. "Pictures from Épinal" refers to popular stylized color prints produced in Épinal, a city in the Vosges region of France, in the nineteenth century.

22. "The pardon petition" is "la pétition" in *ESN* (139) but "le recours en grâce" in *TM* (828).

23. "Repressive" is "répressif" in *TM* (829) but "expressif" in *ESN* (140).

24. I thank Peter Tanzer and Margaret A. Simons for their suggestions on how to translate certain phrases in this piece.

9

Literature and Metaphysics

INTRODUCTION

by Margaret A. Simons

On December 11, 1945, when Simone de Beauvoir presented a lecture titled "Roman et métaphysique" (The Novel and Metaphysics),[1] which she revised for publication in April 1946 as "Littérature et métaphysique" (Literature and Metaphysics), she was already well known in France as a "writer and existentialist philosopher."[2] *L'invitée* (She Came to Stay),[3] her critically acclaimed metaphysical novel on the problem of solipsism and the confrontation with the other had appeared in 1943, followed in 1944 by an essay in existentialist ethics, *Pyrrhus et Cinéas* (Pyrrhus and Cineas),[4] and, in the fall of 1945, by a novel, *Le sang des autres* (Blood of Others),[5] and a play, *Les bouches inutiles* (Useless Mouths),[6] on the problem of political responsibility and relations with others.

Blood of Others, the first novel set in the French Resistance to appear after the Nazi occupation, was initially both a popular and critical success (*FC*, 59). But *Les bouches inutiles* failed to find a receptive audience and was assailed by critics for sacrificing literature to philosophy. A theater critic, Jean-Jacques Gautier, writing in *Figaro,* describes Beauvoir's play as "much less theater than idea." According to Yvon Navy, in *Cité-Soir,* "What we have here is dramatic art confused with the professoriate."[7] Despite its initial success, *Blood of Others* also faced similar criticism.

Maurice Blanchot, a novelist and critic supportive of the philosophical novel, praises *She Came to Stay*, in an October 1945 article, for describing a discovery (of the existence of the other) the meaning of which remains ambiguous at the novel's conclusion, thus safeguarding the "essential conditions" of literature: the "ambiguity" of its message and "the tendency to give itself as a means of discovery and not as a means of exposing what has already been discovered." But Blanchot condemns *Blood of Others* as a "thesis novel," in which we witness not the discovery of an ambiguous truth but a moral "conversion" to political responsibility and action presented as definitive.[8] In a December 1, 1945, interview with Dominique Aury, Beauvoir faced such criticism directly. Asked about the risk that characters in a philosophical novel would be "incarnated ideas rather than characters," Beauvoir replies, "I know well that this is the pitfall [*l'écueil*] of the metaphysical novel."[9]

In "Literature and Metaphysics," Beauvoir defends the metaphysical novel, arguing that the attempt to reconcile philosophy and literature arises from "a profound demand of the mind." Reflecting her rejection of the voice of "abstract objectivity,"[10] Beauvoir opens her essay with a description of her lived experience, an account of feeling "torn apart" in her youth by her love of both philosophy and literature. Beauvoir's early interest in reconciling philosophy and literature is confirmed in her 1927 diary, written while a philosophy student at the Sorbonne, where she declares her intention to "write 'essays on life' which would not be a novel, but philosophy, linking them together vaguely with a fiction."[11] Beauvoir's student diaries also point to Henri Bergson, the leading philosopher of early twentieth-century France, as an influence on her linking of philosophy and literature. In his *Essai sur les données immédiates de la conscience,* Bergson celebrates the novelist as able to disclose reality in its fundamental temporality, an "absurd" reality of changing impressions that is distorted by the intellectual understanding.[12] In her 1926 diary, Beauvoir quotes at length from Bergson's *Essai,* which Beauvoir describes, in an entry dated August 16, as "a great intellectual intoxication."[13]

In a July 1947 article, Beauvoir points to another important influence on her conception of the philosophical novel: the American "realist" novelists. For writers such as John Steinbeck and Richard Wright, Beauvoir argues, "reality is invested with the concreteness of an experience in which an individual consciousness and an individual liberty have been staked." For Beauvoir the appropriation of American literary techniques and the rejection of the "abstract objectivity" of French literary realism makes possible the reconciliation of literature and philosophy: "Neither philosophy nor psychology has anything to lose here; on the contrary: it is thanks to precisely this technical tool borrowed from America that we could undertake to give to philosophy itself a novelistic form."[14]

In "Literature and Metaphysics," Beauvoir argues that if the novel is to be more than trivial entertainment, it must lead the author as well as the reader on an authentic search with no ready-made answers. It thus cannot be the illustration of a preconstructed philosophical system. Working in both the Bergsonian and phenomenological traditions, Beauvoir describes the goal of philosophy as a "disclosure" of metaphysical reality, which she describes in Heideggerian terms as grasping one's "being-in-the-world," that is, one's experience of embodied freedom and abandonment, of the opacity of things and the resistance of foreign consciousnesses. Beauvoir argues that since the metaphysical meaning of human events and objects in the real world cannot be grasped by the pure understanding, but can only be disclosed within an overall relation of action and emotion, philosophers must reject system building and turn to the novel. An authentic metaphysical novel appeals to the reader's freedom, reconstituting our experience on an imaginary plane and imitating life's opacity, ambiguity, and temporality. An authentic novel can thus succeed, where both other novels and the abstract philosophical essay fail, in disclosing the meaning of objects in the real world.

"Literature and Metaphysics" thus sheds light on Beauvoir's early philosophical methodology, showing influences by Bergson, American literary realism, Husserlian and Heideggerian phenomenology, and, in the rejection of philosophic system building, the nineteenth-century French philosopher of science Claude Bernard, the subject of a 1924 student essay by Beauvoir and a philosophical influence on Bergson.[15] "Literature and Metaphysics" also highlights Beauvoir's early philosophical subjectivism. Beauvoir condemns "false naturalistic objectivity," arguing that the value of a novel comes from the author's unique point of view. Although she argues by analogy with science that an authentic metaphysical novel must be a process of discovery for the author as well as the reader, Beauvoir provides a subjectivist interpretation of science as testing a hypothesis not against the external world, but against other ideas. Beauvoir employs a less subjectivist methodology in her nonfiction, including *America Day by Day* (1947), where she quotes at length from a scientific study of the American system of racist segregation, following a moving phenomenological description of her own "meager" experience.[16]

Given the significance of "Literature and Metaphysics," the question arises of why Beauvoir barely mentions it in her autobiography.[17] Does she, perhaps, later disavow the essay as she does much of the work dating from what she describes as the "moral period" of her literary life? Years later Beauvoir concedes that Blanchot was correct in his criticism of *Blood of Others* as a "thesis novel" since it ends "in a univocal conclusion reducible to maxims and concepts."[18] But Beauvoir's project laid out in "Literature and Metaphysics" continued well into the 1950s, when it finally met with success.

Beauvoir's determination to reconcile literature and philosophy, despite the lack of success of her postwar novels, is evident in her 1948 letter to the American writer Nelson Algren, who had just read the English translation of *Blood of Others:* "I guess you are right when you say there is too much philosophy, but that is my genuine way of feeling; . . . it is all mixed: feelings, events and philosophy, it would be rather unnatural for me if I put it away. . . . In fact, I should be rather at a loss if I had to write a novel now. I see the mistakes in the old ones, yet I don't want to give up my own way of feeling and I don't know how I could do really well what I want. Next year, when the essay on women will be over, I'll have to find an answer to this problem."[19]

Beauvoir found an answer in her 1954 award-winning novel, *The Mandarins,*[20] where she sought successfully to avoid the "pitfall" (*l'écueil*) that had plagued her earlier novels (*FC,* 359). "In my estimation *Mandarins* is not a thesis novel," Beauvoir writes in 1963. "I describe certain manners of living the postwar period without proposing any solution to the problems that worry my protagonists. . . . [The novel's conclusion] does not have the value of a lesson" (*FC,* 367). In this account of writing *Mandarins,* Beauvoir reaffirms the claim from "Literature and Metaphysics" that the novel must "imitate life's opacity, ambiguity, and impartiality," as well as its temporality: "Only a novel could, in my eyes, extract [*dégager*] the multiple and swirling significations of this altered world in which I awoke in August 1944: a changeable world that no longer ceases to stir" (*FC,* 358–59).

Although Beauvoir somewhat paradoxically does not explicitly mention philosophy in her autobiographical accounts of *The Mandarins,* her description of metaphysical experience in "Literature and Metaphysics" is echoed in a 1954 interview following the publication of *Mandarins:* "My two principal protagonists, Henri and Anne, represent two completely different attitudes confronting the human condition: for Henri . . . it is life, thus action, that is man's truth: metaphysical anguish in front of death appears to [him] only an easy alibi. . . . Anne is tempted, on the contrary, to adopt the point of view of death and to contest the claim that life is important, since one dies."[21] This observation, evoking Beauvoir's description of the confrontation of Pyrrhus and Cineas in her 1944 essay, clearly shows that Beauvoir's project of the metaphysical novel, first laid out in "Literature and Metaphysics," continued into the 1950s. It thus raises the questions of whether Beauvoir's novels from the 1960s reflect a continuation of the same project and how our understanding of Beauvoir's philosophy should change in order to take into account her philosophical work in literary form.

NOTES

1. There is some confusion concerning the lecture in biographies of Beauvoir. In *Les écrits de Simone de Beauvoir: La vie, l'écriture; Avec en appendice textes inédits ou retrouvés* (Paris: Gallimard, 1979), Claude Francis and Fernande Gontier locate Beauvoir's lecture at the "Club Maintenant le 11 décembre [1945] à la salle des Centraux, rue Jean-Goujon" (135). However, in their biography of Beauvoir, *Simone de Beauvoir: A Life . . . a Love Story* (trans. Lisa Nesselson [New York: St. Martin's, (1985) 1987]; henceforth referred to as *Life*), Francis and Gontier write that the lecture was "in a small lecture room at the Learned Societies in the rue Danton." Deirdre Bair in *Simone de Beauvoir: A Biography* (New York: Summit, 1990) does not mention Beauvoir's December 1945 lecture and claims that "Literature and Metaphysics" was based on a February 1945 lecture to a group of Gabriel Marcel's students, a lecture that according to Beauvoir (in *La force des choses*, folio ed., vol. 1 [Paris: Gallimard, 1963], 98; hereafter referred to as *FC*) was instead the basis for another essay, *Pour une morale de l'ambiguïté* [Ethics of Ambiguity] (Paris: Gallimard, 1947).

2. Dominique Aury introduces Beauvoir as "écrivain et philosophe existentialiste," in their December 1, 1945, interview, "Qu'est-ce que l'existentialisme? Escarmouches et patrouilles," *Les lettres françaises,* December 1, 1945, 4.

3. See *L'invitée* (Paris: Gallimard, 1943), trans. Y. Moyse and R. Senhouser as *She Came to Stay* (Cleveland: World Publishing Co., 1954).

4. See *Pyrrhus et Cinéas* (Paris: Gallimard, 1944).

5. See *Le sang des autres* (Paris: Gallimard, 1945), trans. R. Senhouser and Y. Moyse as *The Blood of Others* (New York: Knopf, 1948).

6. See *Les bouches inutiles* (Paris: Gallimard, 1945), trans. C. Francis and F. Gontier as *Who Shall Die?* (Florissant, Mo.: River Press, 1983).

7. Quoted by Bair, *Simone de Beauvoir,* 311.

8. Maurice Blanchot, "Les romans de Sartre," *L'arche* 10 (October 1945), reprinted in *La part du feu* (Paris: Gallimard, 1949), 200, 203–4.

9. Aury interview, 4.

10. On Beauvoir's criticism of "abstract objectivity," see "An American Renaissance in France," *New York Times,* June 22, 1947, 20.

11. Simone de Beauvoir, Carnets, [1927], unpublished holograph manuscript, Manuscript Collection, Bibliothèque Nationale, Paris, 54–55; translation by Barbara Klaw, Sylvie Le Bon de Beauvoir, and Margaret A. Simons.

12. Henri Bergson, *Essai sur les données immédiates de la conscience,* 6th ed. (1889; Paris: Félix Alcan, 1908), 101, trans. F. L. Pogson as *Time and Free Will: An Essay on the Immediate Data of Consciousness* (New York: Macmillan, 1913), 133; my revised translation. For a fuller discussion of Bergson's influence, see Margaret A. Simons, "Bergson's Influence on Beau-

voir's Philosophical Methodology," in *The Cambridge Companion to Simone de Beauvoir,* ed. Claudia Card (Cambridge: Cambridge University Press, 2003), 107–28.

13. Beauvoir, [1926] Carnet, Bibliothèque Nationale, Paris.

14. "An American Renaissance in France," 20.

15. See Henri Bergson, "La philosophie de Claude Bernard" [1914], in *Œuvres* (Paris: Presses Universitaires de France, 1959), 1433–40.

16. See Simone de Beauvoir, *America Day by Day,* trans. Carol Cosman (Berkeley: University of California Press, 1999), 203, for Beauvoir's phenomenological description ("something fell onto our shoulders that would not lift all through the South: it was our skin that became heavy and stifling, its color making us burn"), and 236 ("my experience is meager for such a vast subject"); see also my introduction to "Analysis of Claude Bernard's *Introduction to the Study of Experimental Medicine,*" in the present volume.

17. See *FC:* "This was thus an 'existentialiste offensive' that we unintentionally set off in the early autumn [of 1945]. In the weeks that followed the publication of my novel, the two first volumes of [Sartre's] *Chemins de la liberté* [Roads to Freedom] appeared, and the first issues of *Les temps modernes.* Sartre gave a lecture—'Existentialism Is a Humanism'—and I gave one at the Club Maintenant on the novel and metaphysics" (60–61; my translation).

18. Simone de Beauvoir, *La force de l'âge,* folio ed. (Paris: Gallimard, 1960), 625 ("La 'période morale' de ma vie littéraire"), 622 ("Je suis d'accord avec lui [Blanchot]").

19. *A Translatlantic Love Affair: Letters to Nelson Algren,* ed. Sylvie Le Bon de Beauvoir, trans. E. G. Reeves (New York: Norton, 1998), 212–13. Thanks to Evangelia Romoudi at St. Louis University for referring me to this letter.

20. See *Les Mandarins* (Paris: Gallimard, 1954), trans. L. Friedman as *The Mandarins* (Cleveland: World, 1956).

21. "Interview de Simone de Beauvoir par J.-F. Rolland," *L'humanité dimanche,* December 19, 1954, reprinted in *Écrits,* 361.

TRANSLATION BY VERONIQUE ZAYTZEFF
AND FREDERICK M. MORRISON
NOTES BY TRICIA WALL

Literature and Metaphysics

When I was eighteen, I read a great deal; I would read only as one can read at that age, naïvely and passionately. To open a novel was truly to enter a world, a concrete, temporal world, peopled with singular characters and events. A philosophical treatise would carry me beyond the terrestrial appearances into the serenity of a timeless heaven. In either case I can still remember the vertiginous astonishment that would take hold of me the moment I closed the book. After having thought out the universe through the eyes of Spinoza or Kant,[1] I would wonder: "How can anyone be so frivolous as to write novels?" But when I would leave Julien Sorel or Tess d'Urberville,[2] I would think it useless [*vain*] to waste one's time fabricating systems. Where was truth to be found? On earth or in eternity? I felt torn apart [*écartelée*].

I think that any mind [*esprit*] sensitive both to the seductions of fiction and to the rigor of philosophical thought has known more or less this distress. For, after all, there is only one reality; it is in the midst of the world that we think the world through. If some writers have chosen to retain exclusively one of these two aspects of our condition, thereby raising barriers between

"Littérature et métaphysique," *Les temps modernes* 1, no. 7 (1946); reprinted in *L'existentialisme et la sagesse des nations* (1948; Paris: Nagel, 1963), 89–107, © Sylvie Le Bon de Beauvoir.

literature and philosophy, others, on the contrary, have long sought to express this condition in its totality. The effort at reconciliation that we witness today follows in this long tradition and answers to a profound demand of the mind. Why, then, should it arouse so much distrust?

We must recognize that the terms "metaphysical novel" and "theater of ideas" may awaken some unease. Certainly, a work always signifies something; even one that deliberately seeks to refuse all meaning still conveys this refusal. But the adversaries of philosophical literature argue, rightly, that the signification of a novel or a play, or of a poem for that matter, cannot be translated into abstract concepts. Otherwise, why construct a fictional apparatus around ideas that one could express more economically and clearly in more direct language? The novel is justified only if it is a mode of communication irreducible to any other. While the philosopher and the essayist give the reader an intellectual reconstruction of their experience, the novelist claims to reconstitute on an imaginary plane this experience itself as it appears prior to any elucidation. In the real world, the meaning of an object is not a concept graspable by pure understanding. Its meaning is the object as it is disclosed to us in the overall relation we sustain with it, and which is action, emotion, and feeling. We ask novelists to evoke this flesh-and-blood presence whose complexity and singular and infinite richness exceed any subjective interpretation. The theoretician wants to compel us to adhere to the ideas that the thing and the event suggested to him. Many minds find such intellectual docility repugnant. They want to retain their freedom of thought; they like instead a story that imitates life's opacity, ambiguity, and impartiality. Bewitched by the tale that he is told, the reader here reacts as if he were faced with lived events. He is moved, he approves, he becomes indignant, responding with a movement of his entire being before formulating judgments that he draws from himself and that are not presumptuously dictated to him. That is what gives a good novel its value. It allows one to undergo imaginary experiences that are as complete and disturbing as lived experiences. The reader ponders, doubts, and takes sides; and this hesitant development of his thought enriches him in a way that no teaching of doctrine could.

A true novel, therefore, allows itself neither to be reduced to formulas nor even to be retold; one can no more detach its meaning from it than one can detach the smile from a face. Although made of words, it exists as objects in the world do, which exceed anything that can be said about them in words. Doubtless, this object was constructed by a man and this man had a design. But his presence must be well hidden, otherwise this magical operation of bewitchment by the novel could not be accomplished. Just as a dream breaks into pieces if the dreamer has the slightest perception that it is a dream, the belief in the imaginary vanishes as soon as one considers confronting it with reality; one cannot posit the existence of the novelist without denying that of his protagonists.

We will thus be tempted to raise our first objection against what is often called the intrusion of philosophy into the novel: any idea that is too clear, any thesis, any doctrine that one attempts to work out in a work of fiction would immediately destroy the work's effect, for it would betray the author's hand and, by the same token, would make the work appear as fiction. However, this argument is hardly decisive; everything here is a matter of deftness, tact, and art. In any case, in pretending to abolish himself, the author cheats and lies. If he lies well enough, he can conceal his theories and his plans. He will remain invisible, the reader will allow himself to be taken in, and the trick will be successfully carried off.

But, it is precisely here that many readers rightly rebel. While admitting that art implies artifice, hence a certain measure of bad faith and lies, they are repelled by the idea of allowing themselves to be tricked. If reading were merely entertainment of no importance, we could situate the debate on the level of technique. But, if one wishes to be "taken in" by a novel, it is not only a matter of killing time. One hopes, as mentioned above, to surpass on the imaginary level the always too narrow limits of actual lived experience. This expectation demands that the novelist himself participate in the same search he has invited his readers on; if in advance he predicts the conclusions to which his readers must come, if he indiscreetly pressures the reader into adhering to preestablished theses, if he allows him only an illusion of freedom, then the work of fiction is only an incongruous mystification. The novel is endowed with value and dignity only if it constitutes a living discovery for the author as for the reader. It is this requirement that one expresses in a romantic and somewhat irritating manner when one says that the novel must escape its author, that the author must not control his characters, but, on the contrary, that they must impose themselves on him. Actually, despite this misuse of language, everyone knows that characters do not haunt the writer's room in order to dictate their wishes to him. But neither does one want fictional characters to be fashioned, a priori, out of a heavy reliance on theories, formulas, and labels. One does not want the plot to be a pure machination unfolding mechanically. A novel is not a manufactured object. It is even derogatory to say that it is fabricated. Doubtless, in the literal meaning of the word, it is absurd to claim that a novel's protagonist is free, that his reactions are unpredictable and mysterious. But, in truth, this freedom one admires in Dostoevsky's characters,[3] for example, is the freedom that the novelist himself has with regard to his own projects; and the opacity of the events he relates shows the resistance that he encounters during the creative act itself. Just as a scientific truth finds its worth in the totality of the experiments that found it and are summed up by it, so the work of art comprises the singular experiment of which it is the fruit. The scientific experiment is the confrontation of the fact, that is, of the hypothesis considered as verified, with the new idea. In an analogous manner, the author must constantly confront his sketches with their realization, which is outlined by them and immediately reacts upon them. If he wants the reader to believe in the inventions he proposes, the novelist must first believe strongly enough in them himself to discover a meaning in them that will flow back into the original idea, a meaning that will suggest problems, new twists, and unforeseen developments. Thus, as the story unfolds, he sees truths appear that were previously unknown to him, questions whose solutions he does not possess. He questions himself, takes sides, and runs risks; and, at the end of his creation, he will consider the work he has accomplished with astonishment. He himself could not furnish an abstract translation of it because, in one single movement, the work gives itself both meaning and flesh. Thus the novel will appear as an authentic adventure of the mind. This authenticity distinguishes a truly great work from a simply clever work, and the greatest talent, the most consummate skill, is no substitute for it. If the metaphysical novel were reduced to imitating this living process from the outside, if instead of establishing a genuine communication with the reader, it cheated him by leading him on a quest that the author had conducted for himself, then, most certainly, it should be condemned.

Certainly the demands of the novelistic experiment are not satisfied if one limits oneself to disguising a preconstructed ideological framework in a fictional, more or less shimmering garment. One renounces the philosophical novel if one defines philosophy as a fully constituted, self-sufficient system. Indeed, the adventure of the mind is lived out in the course of the building of the system. The novel that proposes to illustrate it will only end up exploiting its frozen riches, without risk and without real invention; it will be impossible to introduce these rigid theories into fiction without harming its free development. How could an imaginary tale serve ideas that have already found their proper mode of expression? On the contrary, it could only diminish and impoverish them, for an idea, in the complexity and multiplicity of its applications, always exceeds each of the singular examples in which one claimed to confine it.

Let us note, first of all, that on these grounds one would be led to reject the psychological novel, whose validity, however, one does not dream of debating today. Theoretical psychology also exists, and if the psychological novel were devoted to illustrating Ribot, Bergson, or Freud,[4] it would be utterly useless. One could claim that the protagonists, enslaved to the character the author chose for them and the psychological laws he is obliged to respect, lose all freedom and opacity. If such objections are not raised, it is because people well know that psychology is not, first of all, a special discipline foreign to life; every human experience has a particular psychological dimension; and while the theoretician draws out and systematizes these significations on an abstract plane, the novelist evokes them in their concrete singularity. As Ribot's disciple, Proust bores us;[5] he teaches us nothing; but, as an authentic novelist, Proust discovers truths for which no theoretician of his time proposed an abstract equivalent.

It is suitable to conceive of the relation of the novel and metaphysics in an analogous manner. Metaphysics is, first of all, not a system; one does not "do" metaphysics as one "does" mathematics or physics. In reality, "to do" metaphysics is "to be" metaphysical; it is to realize in oneself the metaphysical attitude, which consists in positing oneself in one's totality before the totality of the world. Every human event possesses a metaphysical signification beyond its psychological and social elements, since through each event, man is always entirely engaged in the entire world; and surely there is no one to whom this meaning has not been disclosed at some time in his life. In particular, it often happens that children, who are not yet anchored in their little corner of the universe, experience with astonishment their "Being-in-the-world" as they experience their bodies. For instance, the discovery of "ipseity,"[6] described by Lewis Carroll in *Alice in Wonderland* or by Richard Hughes in *A High Wind in Jamaica,* is a metaphysical experience.[7] The child concretely discovers his presence in the world, his abandonment [*délaissement*], his freedom, the opacity of things, and the resistance of foreign consciousnesses. Through his joys, sorrows, resignations, revolts, fears, and hopes, each man realizes a certain metaphysical situation that defines him far more essentially than any of his psychological aptitudes.

There is an original grasping of metaphysical reality, and just as in psychology, there are two divergent fashions of making it explicit. We can strive to elucidate its universal meaning in an abstract language, thus developing theories where metaphysical experience will be described, and more or less systematized in its essential character, thus as timeless and objective. If, moreover, the system so constituted affirms that this aspect alone is real, and, if it posits the subjectivity and historicity of experience as negligible, it obviously excludes any other manifestation of the truth. It would be absurd to imagine an Aristotelian, Spinozan, or even Leibnizian novel,[8] since neither subjectivity nor temporality have a real place in these metaphysics. But if, on the contrary, a philosophy retains the subjective, singular, and dramatic aspect of experience, it contests itself if, like a nontemporal system, it makes no allowance for its temporal truth. Thus, as long as Plato asserts the supreme reality of the Forms,[9] which this world only mirrors in a deceptive, debased way, he has no use for poets; he banishes them from his republic. But, when he describes the dialectical movement that carries man toward the Forms, when he integrates man and the sensible world into reality, then Plato feels the need to make himself a poet. He situates his dialogues that show the path to an intelligible heaven amidst blooming fields, around a table, at a deathbed, that is, on earth. Likewise, when spirit [*l'esprit*] has not accomplished itself but is only in the process of accomplishing itself, Hegel must confer on it a certain carnal thickness in order to recount adequately its adventures. In *La phénoménologie de l'esprit* [The Phenomenology of the Spirit] [1807], Hegel resorts to literary myths such as *Don Juan* and *Faust,* because the drama of the unhappy consciousness finds its truth only in a concrete and historical world.[10]

The more keenly a philosopher underscores the role and value of subjectivity, the more he will be led to describe the metaphysical experience in its singular and temporal form. Kierkegaard not only resorts, like Hegel, to literary myths, but in *Fear and Trembling,* he recreates the story of Abraham's sacrifice in a form that approaches the novelistic one, and in *Diary of a Seducer,* he offers the original experience in its dramatic singularity.[11] There may even be thoughts that cannot, without contradiction, be expressed in a categorical manner. Thus, the novel is the sole form of communication possible for Kafka,[12] since he wishes to portray the drama of man confined in immanence. To speak of the transcendent, if only to say that it is inaccessible, would already be claiming to have some access to it. An imaginary account, on the other hand, allows us to respect this silence that is alone appropriate to our ignorance.

It is not by chance if existentialist thought today attempts to express itself sometimes by theoretical treatises and sometimes by fiction; it is because it is an effort to reconcile the objective and the subjective, the absolute and the relative, the timeless and the historical. Existentialist thought claims to grasp the essence at the heart of existence; and if the description of essence is a matter solely for philosophy properly speaking, then the novel will permit us to evoke the original upspringing [*jaillissement*] of existence in its complete, singular, and temporal truth. For the writer, it is not a matter of exploiting on a literary plane truths established beforehand on the philosophical plane, but, rather, of manifesting an aspect of metaphysical experience that cannot otherwise be manifested: its subjective, singular, and dramatic character, as well as its ambiguity. Since reality is not defined as graspable by the intelligence alone, no intellectual description could give an adequate expression of it. One must attempt to present it in its integrity, as it is disclosed in the living relation that is action and feeling before making itself thought.

But one thus sees that philosophical concerns are far from finding themselves incompatible with the requirements of the novel. The novel will no less retain its character as an adventure of the mind for being written into a metaphysical vision of the world. At any rate, today we are no longer dupes of a false naturalistic objectivity.[13] We know that every novelist has his own vision of the world, and it is precisely on this account that he interests us. The metaphysical point of view is no narrower than any other; on the contrary, psychological and social points of view that so often fail to agree and that, taken separately, are each incomplete can even be reconciled in it. Neither should one claim that a character defined by his metaphysical dimension—anguish, revolt, will to power, fear of death, flight, or thirst for the absolute—will necessarily be more rigid, more fabricated than a miser, a coward, or a jealous person, who embodies psychological traits. Everything depends here on the quality of imagination and the power of invention of the author. In particular, one must not believe that the writer's intellectual lucidity may cause him to miss the thickness, the ambiguous richness of the world. Certainly, if one imagines that through the colorful and living paste of things he sees only desiccated essences, one can fear that the author will hand over to us a dead universe, as foreign to the one we breathe in as an X-ray picture is different from a fleshed body. But this fear is well founded only in regard to philosophers who, separating essence from existence, disdain appearance in favor of the hidden reality; fortunately, they are not tempted to write novels. For some, on the contrary, appearance is reality, and existence is the support of essence; a smile is indistinguishable from a smiling face, and the meaning of an event indistinguishable from the event itself. As for them, their vision can be expressed only through the sensible, carnal evocation of the terrestrial domain. A good many examples demonstrate that none of these arguments are valid a priori. *The Brothers Karamazov* and *Soulier de satin* (The Satin Slipper) unfold within the framework of a Christian metaphysics.[14] It is the Christian drama of good and evil that is built up and resolved in these works. One knows well that this hinders neither the protagonists' reactions nor the unfolding of the plot, and that Dostoevsky's world, like Claudel's, is carnal and concrete. Good and evil are not abstract notions. They are grasped only in the good or bad acts accomplished by men; and Doña Prouhese's love for Rodrigue is no less sensual,[15] no less human, and no less overwhelming, because in it she puts her soul's salvation at stake.

Actually, the reader quite often refuses to participate sincerely in the experiment into which the author tries to lead him; he does not read as he demands that one write; he is afraid to take risks, to venture. Even before opening the book, he presupposes that it has a key, and instead of letting himself be taken in by the story, he tries ceaselessly to translate it. He ought to give life to this imaginary world, but instead he kills it and complains that he has been given a corpse. Thus a Russian critic and contemporary of Dostoevsky's criticized *The Brothers Karamazov* for being not a novel but a philosophical treatise in dialogue form. About Kafka, Mr. Blanchot says, very profoundly,[16] that in reading him one always understands either too much or too little. This remark, I believe, can be applied generally to any metaphysical novel. But the reader must not try to elude this uncertainty and his share of the adventure. He should not forget that his collaboration is necessary, since the novel's distinctive feature is, precisely, to appeal to his freedom.

A metaphysical novel that is honestly read, and honestly written, provides a disclosure of existence in a way unequaled by any other mode of expression. Far from being, as has sometimes been claimed, a dangerous deviation from the novelistic genre, it seems to me, on the contrary, to be an accomplishment of the highest level, since, insofar as it is successful, it strives to grasp man and human events in relation to the totality of the world, and since it alone can succeed where pure literature and pure philosophy fail, i.e., in evoking in its living unity and its fundamental living ambiguity, this destiny that is ours and that is inscribed both in time and in eternity.

NOTES

1. Benedict de Spinoza (1632–77), a Dutch-Jewish philosopher, was the foremost proponent of seventeenth-century rationalism; Immanuel Kant (1724–1804) was a German philosopher and founder of critical transcendental philosophy.

2. Julien Sorel is the protagonist of *Le rouge et le noir* (The Red and the Black) (1831), by Stendhal, pseud. of Marie-Henri Beyle (1783–1842); *Tess of the D'Urbervilles* (1891) is a novel by Thomas Hardy (1840–1928).

3. Fyodor Dostoevsky (1821–81) was a Russian novelist and short-story writer.

4. Théodule-Armand Ribot (1839–1916), a French psychologist, attempted to prove that memory loss was linked to progressive brain disease; Henri-Louis Bergson (1859–1941), the leading French philosopher of the early twentieth century, was an early influence on Beauvoir; Sigmund Freud (1856–1939) was an Austrian neurologist and founder of psychoanalysis.

5. Marcel Proust (1871–1922), a French novelist, was best known for his sixteen-volume novel *A la recherche du temps perdu* (Remembrance of Things Past) (1913–27).

6. "Ipseity" refers to selfness.

7. Lewis Carroll (1832–98) was a English logician, mathematician, and novelist whose most famous work is *Alice's Adventures in Wonderland* (1865); Richard Hughes (1900–1976) was a British writer best known for his novel *A High Wind in Jamaica* (American ed., *Innocent Voyage*, 1929).

8. Aristotle (384–322 B.C.E.) was an ancient Greek philosopher; Gottried Wilhelm Leibniz (1646–1716) was a German philosopher and mathematician.

9. Plato (428/27–348/47 B.C.E.), the ancient Greek philosopher, was a student of Socrates and teacher of Aristotle.

10. Georg Wilhelm Friedrich Hegel (1770–1831), the German idealist philosopher, is the author of *Phenomenology of the Spirit* (1807), section 5.B.a. of which, entitled "Pleasure and Necessity," provides an argument against Faust, who, according to legend, sold his soul to the devil for youth and magical power.

11. Søren Kierkegaard (1813–55) was a Danish philosopher. His writings, whose theme is "truth is subjectivity," include *Fear and Trembling* (1843) and "Diary of a Seducer," in *Either/Or* (1843).

12. Franz Kafka (1883–1924) was a German novelist and short-story writer whose posthumously published writings include *The Trial* (1925).

13. Naturalism, a literary movement originated by Émile Zola (1840–1902), claims to examine reality dispassionately and objectively in terms of natural forces.

14. *The Brothers Karamazov* (1879) is a novel by Dostoevsky; *The Satin Slipper* (1929) is a novel by Paul Claudel (1868–1955), a French dramatist, poet, and diplomat, whose mystical Catholicism was an important early influence on Beauvoir.

15. Doña Prouhese and Rodrigue are characters from Claudel's *The Satin Slipper*.

16. Maurice Blanchot (1907–2003) was a French novelist and literary critic.

10

Introduction to an Ethics of Ambiguity

INTRODUCTION
by Gail Weiss

"Introduction to an Ethics of Ambiguity" first appeared in print in 1946, a year before the publication of Simone de Beauvoir's longer work, *The Ethics of Ambiguity*, in which it was incorporated as part of the first chapter. Although there are only a few lines in her introduction that do not appear in the subsequent volume, what is notable about this short piece is that it throws into relief several important themes that preoccupied Beauvoir throughout her life, including the relationship between transcendence and immanence, the difference between the "desire to disclose being" and the "desire to be," and the need to find intrinsic rather than extrinsic justifications for human existence. The central topic that links these themes is the fundamental ambiguity of human existence. Throughout this brief essay, Beauvoir eloquently argues that ambiguity is not an obstacle to, but the very foundation for, an ethical life.

"From the moment he is born, from the instant he is conceived, a man begins to die; the very movement of life is a steady progression toward the decomposition of the tomb." Beginning the essay with these words, Beauvoir immediately calls our attention to a fundamental ambivalence that encompasses all organic matter, namely, that the movement of life is simultaneously the movement toward death. What distinguishes human beings from other creatures, she maintains, is not this "tragic ambiguity" but rather our respective ways of experiencing it. While other animals and plants merely live it out, human beings alone are able to "know it" (*l'homme la connaît*). In what does this knowledge consist? To answer this question not only informs us about what distinguishes human beings from other organisms, but also offers us a new way of thinking about knowledge itself. This is because "knowledge" concerning the ambivalence of life and death is not the outcome of an abstract, rational process (as knowledge is traditionally understood to be) but rather arises out of our experience of being connected to the world even as we detach ourselves from it in reflection.

Paradoxically, Beauvoir observes, it is our very ability to distance ourselves conceptually from the immediacy of our situation that reveals to us how inescapably tied to our situation we are. What reflection promises, then, is not an escape from our situation but rather a new perspective on it, a perspective that transforms the situation in the process. Beauvoir's emphasis on the existentially transformative effects of reflection offers a subtle critique of the dominant Cartesian model of the detached thinker, serenely contemplating his situation from afar. While she agrees with Descartes and the rationalist tradition that our ability to reflect on our situation distinguishes human beings from other types of beings, she also argues that what reflection reveals is what we *share* with all other organisms, namely, the inescapable tension between life and death. How is this insight transformative? To address this point leads us to the very site where ethics, politics, and metaphysics intersect for Beauvoir, namely, in the phenomenon of ambiguity.

In the very first paragraph of "Introduction to an Ethics of Ambiguity," Beauvoir introduces not one but several ambiguities that are constitutive of human existence. First, as mentioned above, we have the capacity to distance ourselves reflectively from our situation even as we remain mired in that situation. We are capable of experiencing the sovereignty of thought, of experiencing our subjectivity as "pure interiority against which no exterior power could take hold," and yet we must also acknowledge the feeling of being "a thing crushed by the obscure weight of other things." In keeping with the existentialist tradition, Beauvoir uses the term "transcendence" to refer to our experience of conceptual detachment from our situation, and she uses the term "immanence" to refer to our sense of being inextricability bound to our situation insofar as we are part and parcel of it. The complex interrelationship and interdependency between transcendence and immanence lies at the foundation not only of Beauvoir's ethics but of her entire philosophy, and it is fitting that this is the first human ambiguity that she invokes in her introduction.

This ambiguity between our experience of ourselves as transcendent on the one hand and immanent on the other is quickly followed by a second, related form of ambiguity because our understanding of ourselves as simultaneously transcendent and immanent is not restricted to the present moment but is temporally indeterminate. More specifically, human existence does not unfold wholly in the present but is defined by the ambiguity of existing in the present, the past, and the future simultaneously. As Beauvoir observes, no matter how lofty our present reflections may be, if we consider them from the standpoint of the past that is "no longer" and the future that is "not yet," we find that the present moment in which we exist "is nothing."

For Beauvoir, the experience of temporal transcendence does not distance me from the ontic dimensions of existence because transcendence is precisely what reveals our immanence to us. We cannot think of immanence as separable from transcendence because even when I feel most trapped in the facticity of my situation, Beauvoir argues, I am nonetheless able, even if only reflectively, to occupy a perspective on that situation that presupposes my transcendence of it.[1] This leads Beauvoir immediately to a third experience of ambiguity, one that is completely inseparable from the first two. It involves an ongoing tension between my understanding of my experience as being unique to myself alone and, conversely, my understanding of my experience as something that is shared with others. For, just as my awareness of my immanence forces me to acknowledge my transcendence, it is when I am most attuned to my transcendence that I can see my situation as not being unique but as similar to the situation of countless others who have existed before me, who coexist with me, and who will exist after me in an as yet unknown future.

Thus, even when we are most aware of the uniqueness of our personal existence, we are forced to recognize that other human beings share this experience of being unique. As Beauvoir notes, each individual alone possesses this "privilege of being a sovereign and unique subject in the middle of a universe of objects, yet he shares it with all those like him." While this experience of uniqueness is clearly dependent upon the experience of transcendence, as we noted above, the awareness that other, equally unique individuals also experience themselves as transcendent is an insight that is dependent upon the immanent presence of others with whom we share a situation. This shows us not only how intertwined all three experiences of ambiguity are but also how fruitless it would be to seek to move beyond them to achieve a nonambiguous understanding of human existence. And yet, Beauvoir maintains, rather than do justice to these ambiguities and the ethical demands that rise out of them, which is precisely her project in *The Ethics of Ambiguity,* the dominant philosophical response has been to seek to eliminate ambiguity altogether.

Whether one chooses the Cartesian route of affirming human transcendence and the irreducibility of subjectivity over the immanence and inherent intersubjectivity of our situation or whether one goes the opposite route and tries to "reduce mind to matter," ambiguity is itself rejected and is therefore fundamentally misunderstood. It is misunderstood not only because the very effort to reject it involves a rejection of existence itself, but also because, for Beauvoir, ambiguity is something we should embrace rather than seek pointlessly to avoid.

Conventional ethics, Beauvoir tells us, offer us varying means of fleeing the ambiguity of our existence. "It was a matter of eliminating ambiguity by making oneself pure interiority or pure exteriority, by evading the world of the senses or by being engulfed in it, by attaining eternity or by enclosing oneself in the pure instant." None of these strategies are effective, she argues, because in denying ambiguity they deny human existence. Indeed, the impotence of these strategies is revealed even as they are promulgated. For, she says, "Despite so many stubborn lies, everywhere, at every instant, at every opportunity, the truth comes to light: the truth of life and death, of my solitude and my connection with the world, of my freedom and my servitude, of the insignificance and the sovereign importance of each man and of all men." Rather than seek to escape our ambiguity, Beauvoir urges us to confront it head-on. Her ethics as well as her politics originate in the demand to affirm the ambiguities that make us human. As she so eloquently asserts: "We try to flee in vain: cowardice doesn't pay. We must, on the contrary, look this undulating truth in the face. We must not conceal but assume our fundamental ambiguity. We intend to draw the strength to live and reasons for acting from knowing the authentic conditions of our life." How do we "assume our fundamental ambiguity"? This guiding question of *The Ethics of Ambiguity* is first posed here, in the "Introduction." Beauvoir's preliminary answer, one which she will continue to develop and refine throughout her life, is that assuming one's fundamental ambiguity means to preserve rather than deny the tensions that animate one's existence, to acknowledge them actively and to determine the meaning of one's existence in relationship to them. Rather than seek to affirm one's transcendence and deny one's immanence, to affirm subjectivity and deny that one's actions have concrete effects on others, to affirm the present and deny the reality of the past and future, an "ethics of ambiguity" requires that we care about and affirm all aspects of our existence, especially those needs, demands, and desires that are in conflict with one another. This does not mean that we will be able to satisfy them all; indeed, Beauvoir emphasizes throughout her philosophical and her literary work that compromises are inevitable. The point is that we must learn to appreciate our failure to harmonize all aspects of our lives into a coherent whole.

The subject of failure is a predominant theme in this "Introduction," and Beauvoir first invokes it in relation to popular critiques that followed in the wake of the 1943 publication of Sartre's *Being and Nothingness,* critiques that accused Sartrean existentialism of failing to be anything more than a "philosophy of anguish and despair." In her defense of existentialism and, in particular, of Sartre's infamous claim that "man is a useless passion" who forever tries "to make himself god," Beauvoir argues that failure is intrinsic to ethics. For, she reminds us, even "the most optimistic ethics have all started by underlining the element of failure included in man's condition; without failure, no ethics." God does not need ethics; only human beings do because we alone can fail to be ethical. While the different ethics that have been proposed over the centuries offer us varied understandings of how we can fail or succeed to be ethical, Beauvoir eloquently argues for an existentialist interpretation that builds upon but also dramatically extends Sartre's work.

Interestingly, Beauvoir situates the turning point between failure and success in ethics at the level of desire. More specifically, she distinguishes between the "desire to be" and the "desire to reveal being," and the last half of the "Introduction" is dedicated to explicating the difference between the two. Both desires are grounded in the recognition that we ourselves lack being, to the extent that our own being as human beings is perpetually in question, never defined in advance. Lacking a fixed essence, we are, in Sartrean language, a nullity of being, forever finding ourselves in a nihilating relationship with a world replete in-itself, a being-in-itself that we are not. For Beauvoir, both the desire to be and the desire to disclose being arise out of our ongoing, intentional orientation toward the world of our concern; together they form two different responses to this world and to our own place within it.

Beauvoir identifies the desire to be as a temptation to overcome our lack of being by identifying ourselves with being, that is, by the acceptance and adoption of a fixed essence that will define who we are. Later on, in *The Ethics of Ambiguity,* she offers the example of the "serious man" as just such a person who accepts a "foreign absolute" as providing the answer to the mysteries of his existence. This foreign absolute can take the form of God, or the State, or even the Other; whatever form it may take, its chief characteristic is to seek to quell our anxiety about the groundlessness of our existence by providing a ground for us. If we seize this ground, however, we fail, ethically speaking, because it is we who posit the ground as our own foundation and, simultaneously, declare this ground to be the transcendental condition of our own being.

The desire to disclose being, by contrast, reflects "an original type of attachment to being that is not the relationship 'wanting to be,' but rather, 'wanting to disclose being.'" Rather than futilely seeking to coincide with a being that I am not, by fulfilling my desire to disclose being I find intrinsic worth in my transcendent capacity to experience the situation as such, that is, as a situation that discloses not one but multiple meanings and therefore multiple possibilities for action. The ongoing challenge, for Beauvoir, is to preserve the openness that belongs to the very act of disclosure rather than seeking to destroy it by converting that which is disclosed into an object I can possess. The desire to reveal being embraces the transcendence that makes disclosure of the situation and of myself possible; the desire to be involves an attempt to abdicate my transcendence by choosing to let the situation totally define me.

In *The Ethics of Ambiguity*, Beauvoir goes on to describe in more depth how difficult it is to content oneself with the desire to disclose being and not yield to the desire to be, since this latter desire alone seems to provide the comfort and security of a stable foundation for existence. Preserving the openness of the act of disclosure, we just noted, involves an active affirmation of my transcendence, which, paradoxically, is precisely what reveals my inherence in the world of my concern. As Beauvoir observes in this "Introduction," "By uprooting himself from the world, man renders himself present to the world and renders the world present to him." What my transcendence reveals to me is a world not of my own making, a world whose immanence constantly tests my transcendence and makes it meaningful in the first place. This is because without the facticity of the situation, my transcendence could not issue forth in concrete action. Disembodied, or "pure," transcendence would be meaningless, an empty intention devoid of content and purpose.

The individual who pursues the desire to disclose being, Beauvoir suggests, must always be on guard against the transformation of this desire into the desire to be. What the desire to be represents, for Beauvoir, is the desire to coincide with one's facticity, to relinquish the burden of transcendence and the responsibility it requires one to assume for all aspects of one's life. The ethical challenge, she argues, is to resist the temptation to possess being once it is disclosed. This means that there is always a tension animating the desire to disclose, a tension between this desire and the desire to be that is produced by it. To preserve this tension by refusing to give in to the desire to be is, on Beauvoir's account, to "win" ethically. And, to the extent that I become more aware of my own desires through this process, disclosure of the world leads to self-disclosure, to a better understanding of myself as a transcendent embodied being. Revealing being, then, also reveals my ongoing, ambiguous relationship to it: "My contemplation is a rending only because it is also a joy. I cannot appropriate the field of snow where I slide; it remains foreign, forbidden, but I delight in this very effort toward an impossible possession. I experience it as a triumph, not as a defeat. . . . *No doubt one succeeds in disclosing being only by an effort to be that never comes to an end. But the fact is that in this aborted effort, being is disclosed* [my emphasis]."

This passage makes it clear that, for Beauvoir, the attainment of an ethical existence does not involve the vanquishing of the desire to be, but an acceptance of it *and* of its failure to be realized. In her words, "The failure is not surpassed but assumed." She claims that the process of recognizing the failure of the desire to be and embracing the desire to disclose being requires an "existential conversion[, which] does not eliminate my instincts, desires, projects, or passions; it merely prevents all possibility of failure by refusing to posit as absolutes the ends toward which my transcendence throws itself and by considering them in their connection with the freedom that projects them." Beauvoir may seem to be equivocating on the issue of failure insofar as we both assume the failure of the desire to be and, at the same time, "prevent all possibility of failure" by refusing to treat the immanent domain as an end in itself; but her larger point is that there is a real difference between ethical success and ethical failure and this difference hinges on how one contends with the inevitable failure of the desire to be. If one continually seeks to satisfy this desire by setting up one's ends as absolutes, then one does not assume the failure but rather simply fails. If one acknowledges the desire but refuses to be seduced by it, then one "prevents all possibility of failure" by rejecting unconditioned values altogether. To succeed ethically, then, one must recognize that "[h]uman existence makes values spring up in the world, and the undertakings in which it will be engaged can be judged according to these values."

Concluding with an affirmation of human values and a refusal of extrinsic justifications for existence, Beauvoir paves the way for a deeper and more detailed discussion of how freedom creates value, a discussion that she goes on to provide in *The Ethics of Ambiguity*. There she will emphasize the intersubjective dimensions of my existence and she will argue that I cannot will my own freedom without, at the same time, willing the freedom of others. She will also acknowledge that some individuals may be so oppressed that freedom may have no meaning for them and that others must endeavor to liberate them so that they, too, can become capable of experiencing this "existential conversion." The groundwork for these claims is laid here in the "Introduction to an Ethics of Ambiguity" with Beauvoir's emphasis on the irreducible ambiguity of human existence. Above all, this short essay beautifully illustrates that the ambiguity of human existence is not a misfortune or something we should seek to eliminate; rather, it is the very motivation for ethics.

Although some of Beauvoir's critics have found her interpretation of ambiguity in terms of the transcendence/immanence distinction to be limiting, insofar as it seems to commit her to a dualistic ontology that they believe smacks of Cartesianism, it is clear that she does not advocate an "either/or" approach, embracing transcendence and rejecting immanence. Instead, she seeks in this essay to show their interdependence and to demonstrate that ethics requires them both.

NOTE

1. An exception needs to be made for the severely oppressed individual whom Beauvoir discusses in *Pour une morale de l'ambiguïté* and in *Le deuxième sexe* (The Second Sex) (1949). For someone whose existence is radically confined by others, it may not be possible to experience transcendence at all. Here, Beauvoir calls upon others to free the oppressed individual so that she, too, can enjoy a hitherto unknown experience of transcendence, that is, an experience of being able to transform one's situation through one's actions.

TRANSLATION BY MARYBETH TIMMERMANN

NOTES BY REBECCA JEYES

Introduction to an Ethics of Ambiguity

From the moment he is born, from the instant he is conceived, a man begins to die; the very movement of life is a steady progression toward the decomposition of the tomb. This ambivalence is at the heart of every individualized organism, but the animal and the plant do nothing but submit to it; man knows it. For him, this life that makes itself by unmaking itself is not just a natural process; it itself thinks itself [*elle se pense elle-même*]. A new paradox is thereby introduced into man's destiny. As a "rational animal" and a "thinking reed,"[1] he frees himself from his immediate condition yet without destroying it. He is part of the world of which he is consciousness.[2] He affirms himself as pure interiority against which no exterior power could take hold,[3] and he also submits himself as a thing crushed by the obscure weight of other things.[4] At each instant he can grasp the timeless truth of his existence, but between the past that is no longer and the future that is not yet, this instant when he exists is nothing. He alone holds this privilege of being a sovereign

"Introduction à une morale de l'ambiguïté," *Labyrinthe* 20 (June 1, 1946); reprinted in *Les écrits de Simone de Beauvoir*, 337–43, © Sylvie Le Bon de Beauvoir. A slightly modified version appeared in Beauvoir's *Pour une morale de l'ambiguïté* (Paris: Gallimard, 1947), hereafter referred to as *PMA;* trans. Bernard Frechtman as *The Ethics of Ambiguity* (1948; New York: Carol Publishing Group, 1996).

and unique subject in the middle of a universe of objects, yet he shares it with all those like him. In his turn an object for the others, he is nothing more than an individual in the collectivity on which he depends.

As long as there have been men who live, they have all experienced this tragic ambiguity of their condition, but as long as there have been philosophers who think, most of them have tried to mask it. They have striven to reduce mind to matter, or to absorb matter into mind, or merge them together within a unique substance. Those who accepted the dualism established a hierarchy between the body and the soul that allowed the part of oneself that could not be saved to be considered as negligible. They denied death either by integrating it with life or by promising man immortality, or they denied life, considering it as a series of illusions under which hides the truth of Nirvana.[5] And the ethics that they proposed to their disciples always pursued the same goal; it was a matter of eliminating ambiguity by making oneself pure interiority or pure exteriority, by evading the world of the senses or by being engulfed in it, by attaining eternity or by enclosing oneself in the pure instant. Hegel, with more ingenuity, claimed to reject none of the aspects of man's condition and to reconcile them all. According to his system, the instant is conserved in the development of time, Nature is affirmed in the face of the Spirit that denies it by positing it, the individual finds himself in the collectivity within which he loses himself, and every man's death is realized by being canceled out in the Life of Humanity.[6] One can thus repose in a marvelous optimism where even bloody wars simply express the fertile restlessness of the Spirit.[7]

To this day there exist many doctrines that choose to leave certain aspects of an overly complex situation in the shadows. However, in spite of these rational metaphysics and consoling ethics, men of today seem to feel the paradox of their condition more acutely than ever.[8] They recognize themselves as the supreme end to which all actions must be subordinated.[9] But the requirements of action drive them to treat each other as instruments or obstacles: as means. The more their hold on the world increases, the more they find themselves crushed by uncontrollable forces; they are masters of the atomic bomb, yet it is created only to destroy them. Each one of them has the incomparable taste of his own life in his mouth,[10] and yet each one feels more insignificant than an insect in the midst of the immense collectivity whose limits merge with those of the earth. Perhaps in no other age have they manifested their greatness more brilliantly, and in no other age has this greatness been so horribly flouted. Despite so many stubborn lies, everywhere,[11] at every instant, at every opportunity, the truth comes to light: the truth of life and death, of my solitude and my connection with the world, of my freedom and my servitude, of the insignificance and the sovereign importance of each man and of all men. There was Stalingrad and there was Buchenwald, and neither erases the other. We try to flee in vain: cowardice doesn't pay.[12] We must, on the contrary, look this undulating truth in the face. We must not conceal but assume our fundamental ambiguity. We intend to draw the strength to live and reasons for acting from knowing the authentic conditions of our life.[13]

Existentialism defined itself from the beginning as a philosophy of ambiguity; Kierkegaard opposed Hegel by affirming the irreducible character of ambiguity,[14] and it is by ambiguity that, in our own day, Sartre, in *L'être et le néant* [Being and Nothingness] [1943], fundamentally defines man, this being whose being is to not be, this subjectivity that realizes itself only as presence in the world, this engaged freedom, this springing forth of the for-itself that is immediately a given for others.[15] But it is also claimed that existentialism is a philosophy of anguish and despair;[16] it encloses man in a sterile anguish, in an empty subjectivity;[17] it is incapable of furnishing him any principle for making choices;[18] let man act as he pleases,[19] for in any case, the game is lost.[20] Doesn't Sartre declare, in effect, that man is a useless passion,[21] that he tries in vain to realize the synthesis of the for-itself and the in-itself, to make himself god?[22] This is true. But it is also true that the most optimistic ethics have all started by underlining the element of failure included in man's condition; without failure, no ethics. For a being who, from the outset, is an exact coincidence with himself, a perfect plenitude, the notion "ought to be" [*devoir être*] would not make sense. One does not propose an ethics to a god. It is impossible to propose one to man if he is defined as nature, as a given. Ethics that are called psychological or empirical are successfully established only by surreptitiously introducing some flaw into the heart of the man-thing that they have first defined. In the second part of *La phénoménologie de l'esprit* [The Phenomenology of the Spirit] [1807], Hegel clearly shows that the ethical consciousness can subsist only to the extent that there is discord between nature and morality;[23] it would disappear if moral law became the law of nature.[24] So by a paradoxical "displacement," if moral action is the absolute goal, the absolute goal is also that moral action not be present. This means that there can be an "ought to be" [*devoir être*] only for a being who, according to the existentialist definition, questions himself within his being, a being who is distant from himself and who has to be [*a à être*] his being.

So be it, one might say, but it still must be possible for the failure to be surmounted, and existential ontology does not allow this hope: man's passion is useless; there is no way for him to become this being that he is not. This, again, is true.[25] It is also true that in L'être et le néant, Sartre particularly emphasized the aspect of lack [côté manqué] in the human adventure.[26] Only in the last pages does he open up the perspective of ethics. Yet if one reflects upon his descriptions of existence, one perceives that they are far from condemning man without recourse.[27]

The failure described in L'être et le néant is definitive, but it is also ambiguous. Man, Sartre tells us, "is a being who *makes himself* a lack of being *so that there might be* being." This means first that his passion is not inflicted upon him from the outside. He has chosen it;[28] it is his very being and as such it does not imply the idea of unhappiness. If this choice is qualified as useless, it is because there exists no absolute value, before man's passion or outside of it, in relation to which one could distinguish the useless from the useful.[29] The word "useful" has not yet received a meaning on the level of description where L'être et le néant is situated.[30] It can be defined only in the human world established by man's projects and the ends he posits. In the original forlornness [délaissement] from which man springs forth, nothing is useful and nothing is useless. It must therefore be understood that the passion to which man has acquiesced finds no external justification. No appeal coming from the outside,[31] no objective necessity permits it to be considered useful. It *has* no reason to will itself. But that does not mean that it cannot justify itself, *give* itself reasons to be that it does not have.[32] And in fact, Sartre tells us that man makes himself a lack of being *so that* there might be being; the term "so that" clearly indicates an intentionality.[33] Man does not nihilate [néantise] being in vain; thanks to him, being is disclosed and wants to be disclosed.[34] There is therefore an original type of attachment to being that is not the relationship "wanting to be" but rather, "wanting to disclose being." And here there is not failure, but on the contrary, there is success. This end that man proposed to himself by making himself a lack of being is indeed realized by him. By uprooting himself from the world, man renders himself present to the world and renders the world present to him. I would like to be the landscape that I contemplate; I would like the sky and this calm water to think themselves in me, that it might be I whom they express in flesh and blood, and that I remain at a distance. But it is also by this distance that the sky and the water exist before me. My contemplation is a rending only because it is also a joy. I cannot appropriate the field of snow where I slide; it remains foreign, forbidden, but I delight in this very effort toward an impossible possession. I experience it as a triumph, not as a defeat. This ambiguity of failure and victory is almost exactly translated by the word "melancholy" and also by so many clichés that one encounters in the language of passion, such as: delicious torment, cruel happiness, blessed torture, etc. No doubt one succeeds in disclosing being only by an effort to be that never comes to an end. But the fact is that in this aborted effort, being is disclosed.[35] This means that in his vain attempt to be god,[36] man makes himself *exist* as man,[37] and if he is satisfied with this existence, he coincides exactly with himself. He is not allowed to exist without tending toward that being which he will never be. But it is possible for him to want this tension even with its inherent failure. His being is lack of being, but this lack has a way of being that is precisely existence.[38] In Hegelian terms, one could say that there is here a negation of negation by which the positive is reestablished. Man makes himself a lack, but he can deny the lack as a lack and affirm himself as a positive existence.[39] So he assumes the failure. And action, condemned as an effort to be, recovers its validity as a manifestation of existence. Rather than a Hegelian surpassing, however, here it is a matter of conversion. For in Hegel, the surpassed terms are conserved only as abstract moments, whereas we consider that existence still remains negativity in the positive affirmation of itself; and it does not appear, in its turn, as the term of a later synthesis. The failure is not surpassed but assumed. Existence affirms itself as an absolute that must seek its justification within itself and not eliminate itself, even if that be by conserving itself. In order to attain his truth, man must not try to dispel the ambiguity of his being but, on the contrary, accept to realize it. He rejoins himself only insofar as he consents to remain at a distance from himself. This conversion is profoundly distinct from the Stoic conversion in that it does not claim to oppose a formal freedom without contents to a sensible universe. To exist authentically is not to deny the spontaneous movement of my transcendence but only to refuse to lose myself in it. The existential conversion must be likened rather to the Husserlian reduction,[40] that man puts his will to be "in brackets" and is thereby brought back to the consciousness of his true condition. And just as phenomenological reduction, by suspending all affirmation having to do with the mode of reality of the exterior world, prevents the errors of dogmatism without however destroying its presence of flesh and blood,[41] so existential conversion does not eliminate my instincts, desires, projects, or passions; it merely prevents all possibility of failure by refusing to posit as absolutes the ends toward which my transcendence throws itself and by considering them in their connection with the freedom that projects them.

The first implication of such an attitude is that the authentic man will not consent to recognize any foreign absolute. When a man projects into a perfect heaven that impossible synthesis of the for-itself and the in-itself that is named god, it is because he hopes that the look of this one who exists will change his existence into being.[42] But if he accepts to not be in order to authentically exist, he will abandon the dream of an inhuman objectivity.[43] He will understand that for him it is not a matter of being right in the eyes of a god but of being right in his own eyes. By renouncing to seek the guarantee of his existence outside of himself,[44] he also refuses to believe in the unconditioned values that would rear up across his freedom like things.[45] Value is this lacking being [*être manqué*] whose freedom makes itself lack,[46] and because its freedom makes itself lack, value appears. It is the desire that creates the desirable, and the project that posits the end. Human existence makes values spring up in the world, and the undertakings in which it will be engaged can be judged according to these values.[47] But first it is situated beyond all pessimism as well as all optimism since the fact of its original spurting forth is pure contingency. There is no reason to exist before existence; nor is there a reason not to exist. The fact of existence cannot be evaluated because it is the fact from which all principles of evaluating are defined. It can be compared to nothing for there is nothing outside of it to serve as a term of comparison.[48] This refusal of any extrinsic justification also confirms the refusal of an original pessimism that we posited at the beginning: since it is unjustifiable from without, existence is not condemned by being declared unjustified from without. And the truth is that outside of existence, there is no one. Man exists. For him it is not a matter of asking himself whether his presence in the world is useful or whether life is worth living. Those are meaningless questions. It is a matter of knowing whether he wants to live and on what conditions.

NOTES

1. "A rational animal" is from Descartes's *Second Meditation:* "But what is a man? Shall I say 'a rational animal?' No, for then I should have to inquire what an animal is, what rationality is." Pascal mentions the "thinking reed" twice in the *Pensées;* first in #113: "Thinking reed. It is not in space that I must seek my human dignity, but in the ordering of my thought. It will do me no good to own land. Through space the universe grasps me and swallows me up like a speck; through thought I grasp it." The second, however, in #200H3, is probably the one to which Beauvoir is referring: "Man is only a reed, the weakest in nature, but he is a thinking reed. There is no need for the whole universe to take up arms to crush him: a vapour, a drop of water is enough to kill him. But even if the universe were to crush him, man would still be nobler than his slayer, because he knows that he is dying and the advantage the universe has over him. The universe knows none of this." *Pascal's Pensées,* trans. A. J. Krailsheimer (1966; London: Penguin), 1995, 347 (#200H3), 348 (#113).

2. The paragraph up to this point is reworded in *PMA* as follows: "'Le continuel ouvrage de notre vie, c'est bastir la mort,' dit Montaigne. Il cite les poètes latins: Prima, quae vitam dedit,

hora carpsit. Et encore: Nascentes morimur. Cette tragique ambivalence que l'animal et la plante subissent seulement, l'homme la connaît, il la pense. Par là un nouveau paradoxe s'introduit dans son destin. 'Animal raisonnable,' 'Roseau pensant,' il s'évade de sa condition naturelle sans cependant s'en affranchir; ce monde dont il est conscience, il en fait encore partie."

3. "Exterior power" is given in the original French article as "puissance intérieure" (interior power), an apparent misprint. It is "puissance extérieure" in *PMA* (9).

4. "Submits himself" (*se subit*) is "s'éprouve" in *PMA* (9).

5. "A series of illusions" (*une suite d'illusions*) is "un voile d'illusion" in *PMA* (10).

6. Although Hegel's texts are notoriously dense, a rudimentary understanding of his system can be attained by reading the preface of the *Philosophy of Right,* along with the preface and final chapter of the *Phenomenology of Mind* (also known as the *Phenomenology of Spirit*).

7. This echoes Hegel: "Consciousness . . . destroys its own limited satisfaction. It can find no rest. Should that anxious fearfulness wish to remain always . . . its restlessness will disturb that indolence." *Phenomenology of Mind,* trans. J. B. Baillie (New York: Macmillan, 1955), 138.

8. In *PMA* (11), the second sentence of this paragraph appears as follows: "Mais c'est en vain qu'on tente de nous mentir: la lâcheté ne paie pas; ces métaphysiques raisonnables, ces éthiques consolantes dont on prétend nous leurrer ne font qu'accentuer le désarroi dont nous souffrons." "Les hommes d'aujourd'hui" (Men of today) begins the next sentence.

9. "All actions" (*toutes les actions*) is "toute action" in *PMA* (12).

10. The preceding phrase may refer to Sartre: "This perpetual apprehension on the part of my for-itself of an insipid taste which I cannot place, which accompanies me even in my efforts to get away from it and which is my taste . . ." *Being and Nothingness,* trans. Hazel E. Barnes (New York: Gramercy, 1956), 338. Prior to Sartre's book, however, the emerging consciousness of Beauvoir's protagonist (Françoise) in *She Came to Stay* makes itself felt through physical—oral—phenomena, particularly the lump in the throat and, once, as "a peculiar taste in her mouth, the taste of metal shavings." *She Came to Stay* (New York: Norton, 1954), 141.

11. "Everywhere" (*partout*) is omitted in *PMA* (12).

12. In *PMA* (12–13), this sentence and the following one appear as follows: "Puisque nous ne réussissons pas à la fuir, essayons donc de regarder en face la vérité. Essayons d'assumer notre fondamentale ambiguïté."

13. "We intend" (*nous entendons*) is "il nous faut" in *PMA* (13).

14. While the systems of Hegel and Kierkegaard were both influential to Beauvoir, she found Kierkegaard's theories more compatible with her own. Here is a passage from the memoir, *Prime of Life:* "I went on reading Hegel, and was now beginning to understand him better. His amplitude of detail dazzled me and his system as a whole made me feel giddy. It was, indeed, tempting to abolish one's own life in the perspective of Historical Necessity, with a detachment that also carried implications concerning one's attitude to death. How ludicrous did this brief instant of time then appear, viewed against the world's long history, and how small a speck was this individual, myself! . . . But the least flutter of my heart gave such speculations the lie. Hate, anger, expectation, or misery would assert themselves against all my efforts to by-pass them, and this 'flight into the Universal' merely formed one further episode in my private development. I turned back to Kierkegaard, and began to read him with passionate interest. The type of 'truth' that he postulated defied doubt no less triumphantly than Descartes' use of 'evidence.' Neither History nor the Hegelian System could, any more than the Devil in person, upset the living certainty of 'I am, I exist, here and now, I am myself.'" *Prime of Life,* intro. Toril Moi, trans. Peter Green (New York: Paragon, 1992), 272–73.

15. This is a fundamental concept that runs through the work of Beauvoir and Sartre alike. It is outlined briefly and concisely in the introduction ("The Pursuit of Being") to Sartre's *Being and Nothingness*.

16. "Anguish" (*l'angoisse*) is "l'absurde" in *PMA* (13).

17. "It" (*il*) refers to "existentialism" in the *Labyrinthe* article, but the word is "elle" in *PMA* (13), which refers to "une philosophie."

18. In the preceding clause, "it" is "il" in the *Labyrinthe* article but "elle" in *PMA* (13). See comment in previous note.

19. "Man" (*homme*) is "il" in *PMA* (13).

20. In the postwar memoir *Force of Circumstance*, Beauvoir discusses the public's misunderstanding of existentialism and of Sartre. Both she and Sartre were less convinced of their status as "existentialists" than was the public, and Beauvoir tells us that Sartre, much more than she, suffered from the public's disapproval and misinterpretation. Called the "poet of the sewer" and the "philosopher of nothingness and despair," Sartre was accused of "miserablism" and attacked as a social danger. Beauvoir was guilty by association. She writes of Sartre's complaints: "'My philosophy is a philosophy of existence. I don't even know what Existentialism is.' . . . I shared his irritation. I had written my novel [*She Came to Stay*] before I had even encountered the term Existentialist. My inspiration had come from my own experience, not from a system. But our protests were in vain. In the end we took the epithet that everyone used for us and used it for our own purpose." *Force of Circumstance*, trans. Richard Howard (New York: Harper Colophon, 1977), 37–45.

21. "A useless passion" (*une passion inutile*) is in quotation marks in *PMA* (13).

22. The word "god" (*dieu*) is capitalized in *PMA* (14). All the following references to "god" are not capitalized in the *Labyrinthe* article and capitalized in *PMA*.

23. The reference to Hegel is reworded in *PMA* (14) as "La conscience morale ne peut subsister, nous dit Hegel dans la dernière partie de la Phénoménologie de l'Esprit, que . . ."

24. "Moral law" (*la loi morale*) is "la loi de la morale" in *PMA* (14). The phrase "it would disappear . . . law of nature" echoes Hegel's *Phenomenology of Mind*: "For, in this highest good, nature has not a different law from what morality has. Moral action itself, in consequence, drops, for action takes place only under the assumption of a negative element which is to be cancelled by means of the act. But if nature conforms to the moral law, then assuredly the moral law would be violated by acting, by canceling what already exists" (632). And this also: "Let us, to begin with, agree to accept the assumption that there is an actual moral consciousness . . . and let us turn to the harmony of morality and nature . . . the harmony of moral purpose and morality itself" (630).

25. On page 15 of *PMA*, "Et" (And) is added at the beginning of this sentence.

26. *Manqué* means both "missing" or "lacking" and "failed" or "unsuccessful."

27. Sartre touches on ethics very briefly in the conclusion of *Being and Nothingness*. Beauvoir, however, saw ethical potential in Sartre's system: "In February of 1945 I had given a lecture at Gabriel Marcel's to a group of mainly Catholic students; I had taken with me an ex-pupil of Sartre's, Misarhi, an Existentialist and a Zionist. . . . Every time Gabriel Marcel attacked me, he would fling himself forward to defend me, vehemently and pertinently; he had made himself thoroughly disliked. When it was over, I had a chat with him upstairs at the Flore; I told him that in my opinion it was possible to base a morality on *Being and Nothingness*, if one converted the vain desire to be into an assumption of existence. 'You must

write it!' he told me. During that winter, Camus had asked me, though I can't remember for what collection, for an essay on action; the reception of *Pyrrhus and Cineas* was an encouragement to return to philosophy. Besides which, when I read Lefebvre, Naville or Mounin, I always wanted to reply. It was partly against them, therefore, that I undertook to write *The Ethics of Ambiguity*." *Force of Circumstance*, 66–67.

28. "Has chosen it" (*l'a choisie*) is in the present tense, "la choisit" in *PMA* (15).

29. "Distinguish the useless from the useful" (*distinguer l'inutile de l'utile*) is "définir l'inutile et l'utile" in *PMA* (16).

30. Sartre does not discuss utility as an ethical value, per se, but as a phenomenon. Inasmuch as material existence is an aspect of otherness, otherness can be employed as an "instrument" or "tool" of the self. Thus, "the soul utilizes the tool which is the body."

31. "From the outside" (*du dehors*) is "de dehors" in *PMA* (16).

32. In this sentence, *"give"* is italicized but "itself" is not, in the *Labyrinthe* article (*se donner*), whereas both are italicized in *PMA* (*se donner*) (16). The phrase *"give* itself reasons to be" (*se donner des raisons d'être*) is "se donner les raisons d'être" in *PMA* (16). "Have" (*a*) is not italicized in the *Labyrinthe* article, but it is in *PMA* (16).

33. Although "so that" (*afin que*) is a fixed expression, *afin que* includes the word *fin*, meaning "end, purpose, or goal" and hence calls to mind the notion of finality from teleological traditions in philosophy. It also echoes the *fins* or "the ends he posits," mentioned above.

34. "Wants to be disclosed" (*il veut se dévoiler*) is "il veut ce dévoilement" in *PMA* (16).

35. This sentence and the preceding one are omitted in *PMA* (17).

36. "To be god" (*être dieu*) is "*être* Dieu" in *PMA* (17), with "*être*" italicized and "Dieu" capitalized.

37. Compare this passage to one from *Being and Nothingness*: "The fundamental value over this project is exactly the in-itself-for-itself; that is, the ideal of a consciousness which would be the foundation of its own being-in-itself by the pure consciousness which it would have of itself. It is this ideal which can be called God. Thus, the best way to conceive of the fundamental project of human reality is to say that man is the being whose project is to become God" (566).

38. In the phrase "a way of being," the article "a" (*une*) is omitted in the *Labyrinthe* article.

39. From the *Phenomenology of Mind*: "Consciousness knows and comprehends nothing but what falls within its experience; for what is found in experience is merely spiritual substance, and, moreover, object of itself. Mind, however, becomes object, for it consists in the process of becoming an other to itself, i.e. an object for its own self, and in transcending this otherness. And experience is called this very process by which the element that is immediate, unexperienced, i.e. abstract—whether it be in the form of sense of a bare thought—externalizes itself, and then comes back to itself from this state of estrangement, and by so doing is at length set forth in its concrete nature and real truth" (96). Furthermore: "The movement of what is partly consists in becoming another to itself, and thus developing explicitly into its own immanent content; partly, again, it takes this evolved content, this existence it assumes, back into itself, i.e. makes *itself* into a moment, and reduces itself to simple determinateness. In the first state of the process negativity lies in the function of distinguishing and establishing existence; in this latter return into self, negativity consists in the bringing about of determinate simplicity" (111).

40. The "Husserlian reduction," also known as the "eidetic reduction," refers to Edmund

Husserl's (1859–1938) system by which the essence of a phenomenon is considered apart from its concrete existence, a response to the question of what a thing is without the definition of the observer.

41. "And just as phenomenological reduction, by . . . blood" (Et de même que la réduction phénoménologique en suspendant toute affirmation touchant le mode de réalité du monde extérieur prévient les erreurs du dogmatisme sans cependant détruire sa présence de chair et d'os) is "[e]t de même que la réduction phénoménologique prévient les erreurs du dogmatisme en suspendant toute affirmation touchant le mode de réalité du monde extéreur dont elle ne conteste pas cependant la présence de chair et d'os" in *PMA* (19).

42. "This one who exists" (*cet existant*) is "cet être existant" in *PMA* (20).

43. "The dream" (*ce rêve*) is "le rêve" in *PMA* (20).

44. "The guarantee" (*le garant*) is "la garantie" in *PMA* (20).

45. "Believe in" (*croire en*) is "croire à" in *PMA* (20).

46. "Makes itself" (*se fait*) is not italicized in the *Labyrinthe* article but is italicized in *PMA* (20).

47. "The undertakings in which it will be engaged can be judged according to these values" (les valeurs d'après lesquelles on pourra juger des entreprises où elle s'engagera) is "les valeurs d'après lesquelles elle pourra juger les entreprises où elle s'engagera" in *PMA* (20).

48. "Outside of it" (*en dehors de lui*) is "hors de lui" in *PMA* (21).

An Existentialist Looks at Americans

INTRODUCTION
by Shannon M. Mussett

In this article, Simone de Beauvoir's view of America and its citizens is critical, penetrating, and unashamed. Many of her works express concern for the practices of America in its treatment of women, African Americans, and labor in the mid-twentieth century. This article, written during her four-month tour of America in the winter and spring of 1947, highlights both her love for and aversion to the United States. Far from merely casting a supercilious eye on another country, Beauvoir encapsulates in this article the ambiguity of an individual, existentialist perspective on a nation full of both the majesty of human achievement and the isolation of unreflective living.

Written for the May 25 issue of the *New York Times Magazine,* "An Existentialist Looks at Americans" is situated in Beauvoir's observations of her travels in America, narrated in *America Day by Day* (1948), and the beginnings of her nearly twenty-year relationship with the American writer Nelson Algren, as recounted in *A Transatlantic Love Affair* (1998). Like many writers, Beauvoir would take commissions to write articles for popular publications in order to support herself financially as well as to reach a wider, less initiated audience. In this particular article, Beauvoir has an additional agenda: political and sociological criticism of a powerful and influential foreign country.

Not even two weeks into her tour of America, Beauvoir was commissioned by the senior editor at the *New York Times* to write an article about America from an existentialist perspective. She expressed enthusiasm over this opportunity to provide a critical analysis of American society and its tendencies towards progress on the one hand and absolutism on the other. She explained that she was somewhat overwhelmed by the deceptive freedom of American capitalism where "even the appearance of democracy itself is fading from day to day, and from day to day despotism breaks out with increasing impudence."[1] The politics of the American government, coupled with its patronizing attitude towards postwar Europe, enraged Beauvoir and motivated her to take on the task of writing this article.

She was immediately aware of the senior editor's condescending and anti-intellectual attitude regarding her work. Under the impression that the American press has great contempt for its product and its audience, Beauvoir chided that "it's a question of concealing from stupid readers the fundamental foolishness of the pages they're offered."[2] Thus, she was faced with a quandary: how would she remain true to her existentialist position while writing for an editor and an audience that were suspicious of this viewpoint even before exposure to it? As Beauvoir aptly remarked, she was faced with "a serious dilemma—propose a subject for an unpublished article, and they tell you that Americans aren't interested in that; choose a question that concerns them, and they object that it's already hackneyed. The trick is to invent a provocative little novelty amid the commonplace."[3] What Beauvoir actually achieves in this article is far from a "provocative little novelty"; it is instead a controversial and astute analysis of the dominant, emerging, capitalist culture.

Beauvoir's article begins by lauding the spirited and generous natures of many Americans as well as the great accomplishments achieved in such a short history. She is captivated by the "poetry" of the dime stores and the "American dynamism" that transforms things into human instruments. Emphasizing the early existentialist thrust to define human beings not by what they "are" or "have," she extols the American tendency to judge people by what they do. Somewhat captivated by the fast pace and hyperactivity of American society, Beauvoir senses a real potential for genuine creation among its citizens.

However, Beauvoir quickly turns to a critique of the American relationship between subject and object. She begins by highlighting the materialistic cult of objects rampant in American society. The public at large is guilty of worshiping the result of labor without concerning itself with the human existence that was employed in its creation. Existentialism, she counters, understands the intimate separation *and* connection between subject and object. To lose sensitivity for the former is to be utterly consumed by the latter and to mistakenly elevate the objective world over and above the subjective creation of it. The obsession with the merely practical and instrumental results of action leads to the two leading challenges facing American society: its relationships to time and to money.

Beauvoir claims that time and money are "abstract conquests" in America because both are so sharply divorced from living the present moment. Despite their nation's rich, albeit brief history, Americans tend to engage in a constant negation of the past in their desperate search for novelty. Conversely, Beauvoir points out, human freedom is not a simple denial of the past but a preservation of it. As she claims, to transcend is also to preserve. If we cannot maintain a living relationship with the past, then the present is merely an "honorary corpse" of a future present. The absence of a meaningful connection to the past also strips the future of meaning and causes our movement toward it to become an empty and "indefinite flight." Taken together, the constant denial of the past and the future in favor of an incessantly novel present infects the present itself with the flavor of death. This theme is more fully elaborated in her major ethical works, *Pyrrhus and Cineas* (1944) and *The Ethics of Ambiguity* (1947), where an authentic existence requires vigilance to the past and the future in present action. In the latter text, Beauvoir informs us that in order to avoid letting an action become a "stupid and opaque fact," I am obliged to "ceaselessly return to it and justify it in the unity of the project in which I am engaged. Setting up the movement of my transcendence requires that I never let it uselessly fall back upon itself, that I prolong it indefinitely. Thus I cannot genuinely desire an end today without desiring it through my whole existence, insofar as it is the future of this present moment and insofar as it is the surpassed past of days to come."[4] The thrust of American ingenuity, for Beauvoir, is the opposite of such a fidelity to the past and commitment to the future. Rather, the drive is to idolize the latest product by denying its past (that is, its production through labor or earlier models of itself) and negating its future (as this product is destined to be quickly replaced by a newer one). But as Beauvoir points out, a present detached from its past and future is nothing in itself.

After addressing the empty and abstract quality of time in American life, she moves to the abstract quantity of money. In American capitalism, the common denominator of experience is reduced to money. Thus money, rather than concrete achievement, becomes the standard by which humans are valued and judged. As she points out, a writer does not undertake the concrete project of writing a "good book"; rather, he wants to write a "best seller." Beauvoir later elaborates on the danger inherent in the cult of money even more scathingly, in her autobiography, *The Force of Circumstance* (1963). Here she writes that for the most part, Americans "were incapable of thinking, of inventing, of imagining, of choosing, of deciding for themselves; this incapacity was expressed by their conformism; in every domain of life they employed only the abstract measure of money, because they were unable to trust to their own judgment."[5] The problem of the American tendency to lose itself in the abstract ideal of money is complicated by the fact that it results from a fundamental human desire to alienate ourselves into things and to define ourselves according to the material world.[6] In the case of money, that in which we lose ourselves isn't even material but an abstract materialist ideal. In addition, there is the seduction of remaining in a childlike and immature innocence where the world of things and values is given to us and we are not responsible for questioning it. Beauvoir explains in *Pyrrhus and Cineas* that such a spirit of seriousness "claims to separate the end from the project that defines it and to recognize in it an intrinsic value."[7] Thus, the end of making money takes on an inflated importance over and against the project that is employed in its amassing—so much so, that the project itself becomes unimportant in the face of the final cash payment.

With such emphasis placed on the abstract concepts of time and money, America soon shows itself to be not a paradise but an empty and lonely desert. Beauvoir concludes the article by emphasizing the despair and loneliness of America's citizens but also the pregnant possibilities latent in its ingenuity and youth. Change will not come, however, until Americans begin to engage in authentic reflection and self-evaluation. Beauvoir remarks here, as elsewhere, that Americans do not relish significant conversation and self-examination. As a result, they hide from their feelings of anxiety and act in a childish and immature manner. Beauvoir warns that this childish adoption of serious, sedimented values in an adult culture is not mere naïveté but the result of a deliberate blindness. Americans fear splitting from the objects in which they have immersed themselves and the consequent loss of the given world. But as Beauvoir's article reminds us, "from this kind of separation the drama of human existence is born; without the pang of separation the drama is not authentically human, lacking consciousness and freedom." For Beauvoir, to be authentic is to lose oneself and to reclaim that self in its loss. The separation of freedom from the given world is necessary, but the two are never fully divorced. Freedom is defined as freedom *from* the given world of ready-made values and things. It is the task of Americans to enact that separation, to become *self-conscious* and to take responsibility for the past, present, and future world that they create.

At first glance, there might be a temptation to take umbrage at Beauvoir's analysis of American life. As a French intellectual, is she truly in a position to judge another country? Beauvoir responds to this kind of criticism in two ways. First of all, she makes no apologies for what she has done. She states immediately that philosophy is arrogant in its analyses and existentialism is no different. But, as an existentialist, she is also aware of the limits of individual perspective. This idea comes across even more clearly in *America Day by Day* where she admits that four months is not enough to have the final word on American life and that she is sharing *her* American experience, not *the* American experience. At the very least, we can grant Beauvoir a sympathetic ear because she did in fact visit America on numerous occasions—as a lecturer, philosopher, tourist, and lover—and she spoke and eventually wrote fluent English. On a deeper level, Beauvoir maintains sentiments that would later be echoed in *The Second Sex* (1949) that thoughtful outsiders to any given system offer the most profound criticism of that system *because* they are marginalized.[8] Beauvoir's differences—as a foreigner, as a woman, and as an existentialist—give her the distance necessary to draw out some of the most charming characteristics and glaring challenges facing American society.

NOTES

1. Simone de Beauvoir, *America Day by Day*, trans. Carol Cosman (Berkeley: University of California Press, 1999), 42.

2. Ibid., 43.

3. Ibid., 44.

4. Simone de Beauvoir, *The Ethics of Ambiguity*, trans. Bernard Frechtman (New York: Citadel, 1997), 27.

5. Simone de Beauvoir, *The Force of Circumstance*, vol. 1, *After the War: 1944–1952*, trans. Richard Howard (New York: Paragon, 1992), 123–24.

6. See *The Second Sex* and Beauvoir's analysis of psychoanalysis and historical materialism for the tendency of human beings to lose themselves in objects (such as the phallus, totems, and mana). *Le deuxième sexe*, vol. 1 (Paris: Gallimard, 1976), 78–106, trans. H. M. Parshley as *The Second Sex* (New York: Vintage Books, 1989), 38–60.

7. See page 99 of the present volume.

8. Although discussions of the marginalization of women run throughout the entirety of *The Second Sex*, see especially the chapter entitled "Myths: Dreams, Fears, Idols" (*Le deuxième sexe*, 1:237–319; *The Second Sex*, 139–98).

An Existentialist Looks at Americans

A philosophy is always arrogant, and has to be. This is because its *raison d'être* is to lay claim to something excessive: possession of truth. Existentialism is no exception. It is a doctrine which aims—like the philosophies of antiquity—at disclosing the true measure of man and of his values.[1]

As it happens, I am an Existentialist. Naturally, I see this country from an Existentialist standpoint, and bring to bear, in trying to judge it, Existentialist criteria.

Now, according to the philosophy I hold, the history of men is the work of men themselves, and concerns no one but them; they must make it meaningful; no one else can; at the start it is neither justified nor absurd. Men may make of their own history a hopeless inferno, a junk yard of events, an enduring value. In trying to come to some conclusions about American civilization, these questions seemed to me essential: Does it provide men with valid reasons for living? Does it justify their existence?

The European who has just arrived in this country is struck first of all by

Reprinted from the *New York Times Magazine,* May 25, 1947, 13, 51, 52; © Sylvie Le Bon de Beauvoir. The article is preceded by the following introduction: "A leading exponent of the new philosophy finds most of us 'isolated,' but sees hope in youth."

the spiritedness and generosity of American life. The skyscrapers, factories, drug stores, bridges slung way up overhead, the roads across the deserts, all perpetuate the victorious movement of the first pioneers. My astonishment increased as train, car and bus took me across the immense areas of California, Nevada, Arizona, Texas, New Mexico. While space seems monstrously swollen (one is often compelled to wait for hours to note any change in the color or curve of the landscape), time seems strangely contracted.

*   *   *

On the fields of Concord and Valley Forge I stood before the statues of the men who created America. These heroes, as distant and as affecting as Alexander, Caesar or Vercingetorix,[2] are less than two hundred years old; it has taken less than two centuries to endow an immense continent with history and civilization, to integrate within humanity a vast portion of the earth: a humanist cannot but marvel at this magnificent triumph of man.

For reasons somewhat akin to this, I found much poetry in the drug stores and the ten-cent stores; the abundance and variety of the industrial products displayed all pointed to a magnificent and immediate taste for the transformation of mere things into instruments adapted to human purposes.

Now, for an Existentialist, it is in the nature of human existence to assert itself against the inertia of the given by dominating things, by invading them, by incorporating their structures into the world of man. What is called the American dynamism assuredly meets this requirement.[3] There is a certain type of wisdom which has often flourished in France and which we totally reject. I have in mind the attitude Voltaire advocated—but fortunately did not adhere to himself—which he asserted in "Candide" that one should cultivate one's own garden.[4] This is the attitude celebrated in the well-known sonnet on happiness: to have a house, a faithful wife, few children, no passions and no cares, that is the condition of happiness.

It means waiting for death, but leisurely, in one's own house, as the author says. But what is the sense of a life spent in awaiting death? Indeed, we scarcely need to wait for death: if this view of things is correct we are dead already.

The philosophy of the petty bourgeois in slippers, who gets away from life as much as he can, granting events as little scope as possible, choosing to be without ambition, love, enthusiasm—this philosophy strikes us as a radical negation of existence.[5] Man is not a stone or a plant and cannot calmly rest his case on the fact that he is present in the midst of the world; man is man only by his refusal to be passive, by the urge which thrusts him from the present toward things with the aim of dominating and shaping them; for him, to exist is to remake existence, to live is to will to live.

We hold that man is free: but his freedom is real and concrete only to the degree that it is committed to something, only if it pursues some end and strives to effect some changes in the world. This is why we approve, to some extent, the American way of judging a man by what he has done. In the United States one is always concerned to find out what an individual does, and not what he is; one takes it for granted that he is nothing but what he has done or may do; his purely inner reality is regarded with indifference, if, indeed, any note is taken of it. A man to be respected is one who has done things that have value.

* * *

There is much truth in this toughness, and we Existentialists also believe that the reality of a man is not hidden in the agreeable mists of his own fancy, but lies beyond him, in the world, and can only be disclosed there. It is by his will to realization, by his project in the world, that a man fulfills himself. And this is why New York did not seem to me the inhuman city it is sometimes said to be in France, but, on the contrary, a magnificent monument to human greatness.

But if we concede that the presence of an individual is expressed only by his acts, equally essential to our way of thinking is the notion that actions are meaningful only in so far as they express a human presence. Man is free only if he sets himself concrete ends and strives to realize these: but an end can only be called such if it is chosen freely. It is in the world that man comes upon the values that justify his existence; but he must have wanted to find these values there.

To say that bread is edible is to say there are stomachs able to digest it; only when a question has been put can the answer to it satisfy; nothing is good that has not been desired. The truth of the world and of man resides in the bond between subject and object. To worship the object isolated from the subject, to make an idol of the thing itself, is to be caught by what we call— following Hegel and Nietzsche—the spirit of serious-mindedness. There is a tendency in America to be fascinated by the bare result without concern for the human existence that was staked on it. To an Existentialist this is a grave danger: for since man can only find himself by committing himself to the world, the loss of the one is ever accompanied by the loss of the other.

"You raise questions without answering them," an American journalist once remarked to me, "while we answer questions without raising any."

I grant that it is fruitless ever to put the questions where no replies are forthcoming; without a doubt this is one of the chief faults of the Latin as of the Greek mind;[6] but surely it is just as absurd to imagine that the reply can exist as such, before the question has dug a place for it. It is as commonplace in science as in philosophy that not knowing what one has been looking for means not knowing what one has found.

Some students at Yale were aware of this. They said to me: "We want to go to Paris for awhile so as to see things from some perspective; we have not even been able to decide what our problems are. All we know is that we have no solution for them."

But I believe these young people were quite exceptional. Even among the American intellectuals there is a very definite tendency to confuse the opaque fullness of the object with real human riches. The intellectuals, too, seem to interest themselves exclusively in the result, rather than in the movement of the spirit which engendered it. A physics professor told me that one day, in trying to explain a very difficult theory to his advanced students, he first stated the theory, gave its mathematical formula, and only then undertook the demonstration. At this point his students stopped him: "Why bother? We take that for granted," they said.

This incident, which I could match with many others, seems to me most significant. These young physicists were interested only in results, in the practical and technical uses of a theory; they refused to interest themselves in the human mind. In the first place this attitude bodes ill for the future of American science; often it is those works which seem most alienated from the practical which ultimately lead to the greatest discoveries.

But that is not all. The bridges, the radio towers, the buildings and the airplanes were all made to be of use to man; if there is no concern for man at the top of his bent, for man at his best, when he strives to be consistent, to invent, to explain and to justify himself, how can there be any great concern shown to aid him in mastering the world?

It is true that it is in the nature of man to transcend the past toward the future without pause or stop. But to transcend is also to preserve; if uprooted, the movement toward the future becomes an indefinite flight. The aim of going faster becomes an alibi for going nowhere. The continual negation of the past in the end wounds the present and the future, also.

"What! You mean to say you are still interested in Faulkner! He is old hat!" a publisher remarked one day.

The phrase "old hat" struck me. For the past has more than a merely sentimental value. What is involved here goes far beyond the question of sentiment. The truth is that the reality of time is frightfully complex; its different moments extend and contradict one another; life is made up of moments which die one by one. If we regard the present as the annihilation of the past, as the bearer of the latter's death sentence, then we condemn the present also; it is negated as a potentiality; it is already an honorary corpse. What was done ten years ago is already worthless? Then what is done today will be worthless ten years from now.

One really does not have to say this to the American, who knows it only too well. He works in the provisional. He does not hope, like the artisan of other times, to confer an eternal value on the object he fashions; he is not concerned with quality, for such a concern implies not the measurement of time but the confident surrender of it; the American wants only to "get on" with his work so that the result be not out of date before completion.

And this is why one soon discovers a flavor of death in this American existence which had seemed at first so joyous and exuberant: the present is already infected with death. Nobody rests in it. Nothing could be more alien to the spirit of this country than André Gide's notion that each instant is infinitely precious because in each instant all eternity is mirrored.[7] Here a vicious circle is formed. It is because the present is permitted to pass unloved that a new present is incessantly required, and feverishly solicited in change, sensation, etc. But the present will never exist other than as an abstraction and a snare, since the way it has been sought for has emptied it of content.

The fact is that the word "abstraction" constantly comes to mind when I try to define my vision of America. This may seem paradoxical since this country is so completely bent on concrete results. But to cut the result from the human movement which engendered it, to deny it the dimension of time, is also to empty it of every sort of quality: only dry bones remain. With quality lacking, the only measure that remains with which to estimate the work and achievement of man is a quantitative one—money. And money is only an abstract sign for real wealth. The cult of money which one encounters here does not spring from avarice or meanness; it expresses the fact that the individual is unable to commit his freedom in any concrete realm; making money is the only aim one can set one's self in a world in which all aims have been reduced to this common denominator.

In the universities and colleges, as elsewhere, I talked with many young people. One characteristic I found in them is particularly disturbing to a European: this is their lack of any authentic ambition. The sort of ambition one finds in the young Frenchman as incarnated by Stendhal in Julien Sorel:[8] he wants to emerge outside the world, so as to oppose it and impose himself on it, realizing himself by means of this victory.

311

The young American generally lacks a sense of personal accomplishment. He does not want to do great things because he is not aware that there are great things to be done. His ambition is restricted to making money. He does not undertake to write a good book but to produce a best seller. And this is not because of small-mindedness or concern for self, but simply because he does not perceive any other objective criterion of value besides money.

Time and money—these, I repeat, are abstract conquests. For what can one do with the time and the money that had been earned except spend them? But on what can one spend them if the only thing at which one may aim is to earn time and money? Leisure, and money in one's pocket would seem to be concrete values, implying some real freedom; and it is indeed in economic success that the American finds a way of affirming his personal independence; but this independence remains wholly abstract for it does not know on what to bestow itself.

The totalitarian regimes veil the character of freedom when they identify the freedom of man with the recognition of necessity; but the atom of Epicurus which jumps to the right or to the left without aiming to get anywhere—since in the emptiness there is no definite place—is not free either.[9] A man tied to a fertile soil which he obediently cultivates is not free. Nor is the man who is abandoned in a desert and told to go where he likes.

Now America is not at all like a desert; when one comes here from Europe it appears rather more like a paradise. But the difference between a desert and a paradise is not great as is generally assumed: in the gardens of Fra Angelico as in the Sahara,[10] there is nothing for men to do. In this rich America, there are thousands of persons who cannot find any task to perform; the age of the pioneers is really over.

Of course, America is young; but she has been young for some time. She has a past, a heritage. The roads and the factories, the fields and the machines are already there, and the young American does not now confront a future that is virginal, yet rich with many appeals. He is in a world that others have created for him, a completed world. I do not say that there is nothing for him to do, far from that; America is not a paradise, it is a living part of the "earth of men" as Saint-Exupéry said.[11] But to discover what is to be done, a human interrogation has to put this world in question.

Many Americans seem to be crushed by the enormous reality of their country. It is, however, by some free movement of this type that they could realize themselves as concrete individuals and by the same token give a real content to American civilization.

As a result of having failed to achieve a concrete bond with the world, most of them feel a great inner emptiness; they feel the abstractness of a content-less freedom; it makes them giddy; they look for a way out.

Here again is a vicious circle to be broken. The more a man seeks to escape from himself, the more reasons he has for so doing. Most Americans are afraid of themselves. Their optimism is wholly external. They trust the world to a certain extent, and themselves, also, in so far as they are parts of it, in so far as they consider themselves capable of this or that objective accomplishment. But they do not trust their individual judgments, their personal feelings; these they do not wish to put in question, which shows how uncertain they are.

Discussion is not relished in America; one hesitates to introduce a significant idea into a conversation. And I do not think self-examination is very popular. The American has a horror of feeling guilty. He has not, like the Slav, a feeling for sin and for remorse, nor like the Frenchman a feeling for anxiety. He likes to be in his own good graces. This doubtless is the result of his Puritan heritage. It is also a sign of that straightforwardness which is one of the attractive traits of some Americans—they cannot endure the feeling of guilt and so they have to change.

The freedom of mind possessed by the French is often not unrelated to the cynicism or indifference with which they are able to accept their weaknesses. Handling ideas is interesting when they don't lead anywhere. Here ideas bear fruit, which is a good thing, but this is the very reason that ideas are avoided.

It might be said that America is in the stage which Hegel designated as the stage of innocence, in which the object and the subject have not yet been divided by the pang of the unhappy consciousness.[12] This is why Europeans find something childish in this country: childhood, too, is innocent. But, long before Freud, La Fontaine said that innocence does not mean purity.[13] In an adult, innocence cannot but mean some voluntary blindness.

The American is afraid of that cold isolation, of that dereliction into which man falls when he splits off from what is given: from this kind of separation the drama of human existence is born; without the pang of separation the drama is not authentically human, lacking consciousness and freedom. The individual has to find himself and assume the task of being what he is in the jeopardy and glory of his lonely freedom; only thus can the world in which he thrusts himself have a human character and value.

* * *

For me the hope of America lies not in the atomic bomb and not in the TVA.[14] It lies in the uneasy hearts of the ex-GI's, and in the hearts of thousands of young people. The future of America lies in the consciousness of its youth, suddenly become aware of what the Spanish philosopher Unamuno called "the tragic sense of life,"[15] and the responsibilities incumbent on a great country. If the immense reality that is America is addressed to serving man's mind and freedom as well as his body it may well become a civilization comparable to Athens and to Rome. If not, it will remain a fact among other facts, in a world it will not have helped to justify.

NOTES

1. In Beauvoir's philosophy the idea of disclosure does not refer merely to verbal confession but also to the activities that reveal being.

2. Vercingetorix (?–42 B.C.E.) was a Gallic leader who led an uprising against Julius Caesar in 52 B.C.E.

3. As described by Nietzsche and Schopenhauer, dynamism is the communication of pure subjectivity, the language of the "thing-in-itself."

4. François-Marie Arouet de Voltaire (1694–1776) wrote the novel *Candide* (1759), which tells the story of the innocent Candide, who learns that, in this "best of all possible worlds," unguarded optimism is foolish, and relentless pessimism leads nowhere. Beauvoir was fond of the idea of tending one's own garden, as expressed in *Candide*. Her essay *Pyrrhus and Cineas* opens and concludes with a reference to Candide's garden, and the reference appears again in *The Ethics of Ambiguity*.

5. Beauvoir distinguishes between *being* and *existence:* being is the more passive term, while existence suggests motion and propulsion, the expression of life through the object. To negate one's existence is to simply be, like a "stone or a plant."

6. "The Greek mind" refers to the Western philosophical tradition, originating with the Greeks, of contriving complex, logical arguments in response to unanswerable questions, such as Does God exist? or What is the nature of the good?

7. "Andre Gide's notion" refers to an idea expressed in Gide's *Journal:* "This terrifies me: to think that the present, which we are living this very day, will become the mirror in which we shall later recognize ourselves; and that by what we have been we shall know what we are." Gide, *Journal, Volume 1: 1889–1913*, trans. Justin O'Brien (New York: Knopf, 1947), 16.

8. Stendhal was the pseudonym of Marie-Henri Beyle (1783–1842). Julien Sorel, the protagonist of Stendhal's 1831 novel *Le rouge et le noir* (The Red and the Black), is a young man of great ambition for whom the end justifies the means.

9. Epicurus (342–270 B.C.E.) was an atomist who was unwilling to abandon the notion of free will, explaining that atoms often moved randomly, frequently "swerving" in ways that made their ultimate shape, form, or function unpredictable.

10. Fra Angelico (Guido di Pietro, 1400–1455), a Florentine painter and muralist, was a Dominican monk. His frescoes and altarpieces employed ethereal colors and delicate lines.

11. The phrase "earth of men" is from a work by Antoine-Marie-Roget de Saint-Exupéry (1900–1944), a French aviator and writer: "And from that earth of men, that earth docile to the reaping of grain and the harvesting of the grape, bearing its rivers asleep in their fields, its villages clinging to their hillsides, our ship was separated by astronomical distances. All

the treasures of the world were summed up in a grain of dust now blown far out of our path by the very destiny itself of dust and of the orbs of night." Saint-Exupéry, *Wind, Sand, and Stars,* trans. Lewis Galantiere (New York: Harcourt, 1940), 16.

12. Hegel's "stage of innocence" is the moment of pure subjectivity in which the self exists and has consciousness but has not yet become an object to itself; at that moment the self possesses neither ethical nor moral reality: "The world is objectively existent spirit, which is *individual* self, that has consciousness and distinguishes itself as other, as world, from itself. In the way this individual self is thus immediately established at first, it is not yet conscious of being Spirit, it thus does not exist as Spirit; it may be called 'innocent,' but not strictly 'good.' In order that in fact it may be self and Spirit, it has first to become objectively an other to itself, in the same way that the Eternal Being manifests itself as the process of being self-identical in its otherness." G. W. F. Hegel, *Phenomenology of Mind,* trans. J. B. Baillie (New York: Macmillan, 1955), 770.

13. Jean de la Fontaine (1621–95) was best known for his twelve-volume *Fables* (1668–94), in which he drew upon Aesop and Asian story traditions to comment upon society, politics, and human moral concerns.

14. The TVA (Tennessee Valley Authority) is an independent U.S. government corporate agency, created in 1933 and responsible for the integrated development of the Tennessee River basin. This was the first time that a single agency addressed the total resource development of a major region.

15. Miguel de Unamuno (1864–1936) was a Spanish (Basque) philosopher whose chief work is *Del Sentimiento tragico de la vida en los hombres y los pueblos* (The Tragic Sense of Life) (1913).

What Is Existentialism?

INTRODUCTION

by Nancy Bauer

What is existentialism? For Simone de Beauvoir in 1947, this question, pressed upon her repeatedly by both admirers and detractors during her first extended trip to the United States, was decidedly narrow in scope. It had nothing to do with Heidegger or Nietzsche or Kierkegaard. Indeed, the question was rarely put to her in the spirit of serious philosophical inquiry. It meant, simply, "Why all the fuss about what's coming out of Paris these days?"

Ironically, both Beauvoir and Sartre had at first resisted identifying their way of doing philosophy as "existentialist." The term had been coined in the early 1940s by Gabriel Marcel, a Catholic philosopher and playwright. Beauvoir reports in the second volume of her autobiography that in early 1943, when a philosopher who was putting together a volume of essays on "contemporary ideological trends" asked her if *she* was an existentialist, her first reaction was embarrassment. Despite having read Kierkegaard and being familiar with Heidegger's "existential" philosophy, she confesses, "I didn't understand the meaning of the word."[1] As late as the summer of 1945, Beauvoir claims, Marcel was still trying to force the term on a resistant Sartre. "I shared his irritation," she notes.[2] But the label stuck. Just a few months later, in the wake of a spate of publications by the pair—Sartre's *The Age of Reason* and

The Reprieve; Beauvoir's *The Blood of Others;* the first issues of *Les temps modernes*—Sartre, "hurled brutally into the arena of celebrity," would give the most famous lecture of his life, under the title "Existentialism Is a Humanism," and Beauvoir would publish an article entitled "Existentialism and Popular Wisdom" in their new journal.[3]

By early 1946, the spotlight was shining on both Beauvoir and Sartre. But it was not always flattering, and since Sartre was all but oblivious to its glare, Beauvoir found herself compelled to take on their critics. "At the time," she writes in her autobiography, "existentialism was being treated as nihilist philosophy, willfully pessimistic, frivolous, licentious, despairing, and ignoble; some defense had to be made."[4] This defense took form as *The Ethics of Ambiguity,* in which Beauvoir sets out to show that existentialism, far from being morally bankrupt, provides the resources for a thoroughly ethical way of being in the world. In the *Ethics,* Beauvoir writes as though her thinking is continuous with that of Sartre—as though there is only one "existentialism" to defend. And yet, as recent scholarship on Beauvoir clearly demonstrates, it is precisely in her defense of "existentialism" that we see Beauvoir clearly taking issue with Sartre's version.[5]

Perhaps the starkest difference between Beauvoir's views and those of Sartre lay in her growing conviction, evident at least as early as *Pyrrhus and Cineas* (1943), that human freedom is boundless only in principle. In reality, she was coming to see, people's choices are often hopelessly constrained by their unpromising circumstances. In other words, Beauvoir was beginning to develop a robust conception of oppression, one that cannot be squared with the metaphysics of *Being and Nothingness.*[6] For Sartre, all human beings are in theory capable at any moment of asserting their subjectivity in the face of others' attempts to objectify them. The task of living, it follows, is to attempt to master one's circumstances. But for Beauvoir, the temptation to mastery is a dead end. Following Hegel, she began in the mid-1940s to see the task of living as coming to grips with the fundamental ambiguity of being a person—that is, a being at once an object and subject in the world.

In "What Is Existentialism?" Beauvoir names this task as an effort to "surpass" (*dépasser*) the opposition between subjectivity and objectivity—and other such binary oppositions prevalent in the history of philosophy—by means of what she calls a "new synthesis." Exactly what this new synthesis is to look like remains rather mysterious, although Beauvoir does attempt to sketch its features. The individual is the source of all signification, but he "has reality only through his engagement in the world." The human will is free, but it cannot be exercised except "against the obstacles and the oppressions that limit the concrete possibilities of man." Each person must achieve "his own salvation," but the only way he can do this is by "working actively for the concrete triumph of universal freedom." Morality and politics thereby dovetail.[7]

Beauvoir wrote "What Is Existentialism?" in the early summer of 1947 for the weekly newspaper *France-Amérique* (published in New York as a version of the French daily *Le Figaro*) shortly after her first trip to the United States, a four-month tour from which she had just returned.[8] During her tour Beauvoir gave talks at numerous colleges (for example, Tulane University and Smith College) on the subject of existentialism, often under the same title as the *France-Amérique* essay. It seems, however, that Beauvoir may have had more than one way of responding to the title question. In reporting on a lecture given at Tulane on April 1, the *Times-Picayune* in New Orleans claimed—plausibly— that Beauvoir emphasized the extent to which "man cannot exist" without "other men to recognize him and understand his thoughts."[9] This emphasis on *recognition*, though absent in the *France-Amérique* essay, would play a key role in Beauvoir's explicitly Hegelian attempt to work out a synthesis between subjectivity and objectivity in *The Second Sex*, a project she was just beginning to undertake.

"What Is Existentialism?" begins with an expression of Beauvoir's exasperation at having been asked on countless occasions, in France as well as in America, to put existentialism in a nutshell. This task is no easier, Beauvoir claims, than summarizing Hegel or Kant "in three sentences." For existentialism is not primarily a pat formula for living or a social fad or a political movement; it is, she insists, first and foremost a philosophy. And like all other philosophies, one cannot understand it or appreciate its novelty unless one studies its historical roots. The best she will be able to do in her short article is to dispel certain misunderstandings.

And yet, Beauvoir concedes, one must explain why nonphilosophers are so interested in existentialism. The answer, she suggests, is that they rightly grasp that existentialism is not just an abstract theory but a philosophy that demands to be *lived*. Like Christianity and Marxism, the two other popular ideologies of the time, it seeks to explain the individual's place "in a world turned upside down"—and here Beauvoir is gesturing at the condition of France in the wake of the German occupation. While Christianity emphasizes the subjective dimension of the struggle for salvation and Marxism the objective dimension, existentialism tries to hold on to "both ends of the chain." But the world would have to wait for *The Second Sex* for a vision of how "existentialism"—or at least Simone de Beauvoir—might tackle this seemingly impossible task.

NOTES

1. See Simone de Beauvoir, *The Prime of Life*, intro. Toril Moi, trans. Peter Green (New York: Paragon, 1992), 433; Beauvoir, *La force de l'âge* (Paris: Gallimard, 1960), 625–26.

2. Beauvoir, *Force of Circumstance*, vol. 1, *After the War, 1944–1952*, intro. Toril Moi, trans. Richard Howard (New York: Paragon, 1992), 38; *La force des choses*, vol. 1 (Paris: Gallimard, 1963), 60.

3. For the "hurled brutally" quotation, see Beauvoir, *Force of Circumstance*, 38; *La force des choses*, 60–61. The article "Existentialism and Popular Wisdom," published in December 1945, is included in the present volume.

4. Beauvoir, *Force of Circumstance*, 67; *La force des choses*, 98.

5. See, for example, Sonia Kruks, *Situation and Human Existence* (London: Unwin Hyman, 1990); Margaret A. Simons, ed., *Feminist Interpretations of Simone de Beauvoir* (University Park, Pa.: Penn State University Press, 1995); Eva Lundgren-Gothlin, *Sex and Existence: Simone de Beauvoir's "The Second Sex"* (Hanover, N.H.: Wesleyan University Press/University Press of New England, 1996); Karen Vintges, *Philosophy as Passion: The Thinking of Simone de Beauvoir* (Bloomington: Indiana University Press, 1996); Debra Bergoffen, *The Philosophy of Simone de Beauvoir: Gendered Phenomenologies, Erotic Generosities* (Albany: State University of New York Press, 1997); Toril Moi, *What Is a Woman? and Other Essays* (New York: Oxford University Press, 1999); Simons, *Beauvoir and "The Second Sex": Feminism, Race, and the Origins of Existentialism* (Lanham, Md.: Rowman and Littlefield, 1999); Kristana Arp, *The Bonds of Freedom: Simone de Beauvoir's Existentialist Ethics* (Chicago: Open Court, 2001); and Nancy Bauer, *Simone de Beauvoir, Philosophy, and Feminism* (New York: Columbia University Press, 2001). The authors of these books disagree about when exactly Beauvoir began to emerge as a mature philosopher in her own right, but all agree that at least by the time she wrote the *Ethics* her views were in tension with those of Sartre.

6. I provide evidence for this claim in *Simone de Beauvoir, Philosophy, and Feminism*; see especially 159–71.

7. Toward the end of "What Is Existentialism?" Beauvoir suggests that Montaigne sums up the main point: "Life is in itself neither good nor evil; it is the place of good or evil, as you make them." This is also the epigraph to *The Ethics of Ambiguity*. I am suggesting that it doesn't quite capture Beauvoir's developing views on oppression, as expressed in both the essay and the book.

8. Beauvoir chronicles her trip to the United States in *America Day by Day*, trans. Carol Cosman (Berkeley: University of California Press, 1999).

9. *New Orleans Times-Picayune*, April 2, 1947, 9.

TRANSLATION BY MARYBETH TIMMERMANN

NOTES BY TRICIA WALL

What Is Existentialism?

I don't know how many times during my trip to America someone made this request, which was also familiar to me in France: "Can you explain what existentialism is?" And my interlocutor, undoubtedly curious about any novelty yet sparing with his time and effort, would add, "in a few words" or "in five minutes." I disappointed many amiable people and made several journalists unhappy by refusing to comply. Some doubted my intellectual capacities; others were suspicious of a doctrine that could not be summarized in one sentence. However, at the risk of disappointing once again, I must say right away that even an article is not enough to give an account of existentialism. I only intend to dissipate some misunderstandings here.

The first error consists precisely in believing that existentialism can be concentrated in one or two immediately efficient, simple expressions. It is not a martingale that guarantees winning at the game of life, nor a recipe capable of erasing the annoyances of existence. Neither is it the art of interpreting dreams, evoking spirits, or holding séances. One must not expect any of these distractions that are so agreeable in society. It is not a social phenomenon analogous

"Qu'est-ce que l'existentialisme?" *France-Amérique*, June 29, 1947, 1, 5, © Sylvie Le Bon de Beauvoir.

to the zazou phenomenon,[1] nor a political movement, nor a postwar fashion, even though it has social repercussions, it does include political implications, and fashion has both served and disserved it. Even less is it a predilection for scandal; the Parisian public who rushed to the first existentialist conferences in the hopes of seeing surrealist extravagances again were extremely disappointed to have to listen to a serious doctrinal lecture like a class at the Sorbonne.[2] Existentialism is first of all a philosophy, analogous in many aspects to classical philosophies and discussed in places as austere and respectable as the French Society of Philosophy [La société française de philosophie], for example.[3]

No one would dream of demanding that the system of Kant or Hegel be dispensed in three sentences;[4] existentialism does not lend itself to popularization any easier. A philosophical theory, like a physics or mathematical theory, is accessible only to the initiated. Indeed, it is indispensable to be familiar with the long tradition upon which it rests if one wants to grasp both the foundations and the originality of the new doctrine. How could you show the audacity of Einstein or de Broglie to someone who was unaware of Newton's mechanics?[5]

The problem is the same here. Many criticisms addressed to us by uninformed minds are aimed at Descartes or Kant rather than existentialism.[6] It is very often philosophy in general that is being questioned by attacking us. In truth, several years of study are needed to be able to detect existentialism's original contribution to philosophy and to be in a position to discuss the validity of it.

However, the fact that nonspecialists, regardless of their incompetence, are interested in existentialism must have an explanation. Symbolic logic, for example, never incited such passionate disputes. The reason, in fact, is that although existentialism claims to rest upon the most serious theoretical bases, it also claims to be a practical and living attitude toward the problems posed by the world today. It is a philosophy yet does not want to stay enclosed in books and schools; it intends to revive the great tradition of ancient wisdom that also involved difficult physics and logic, yet proposed a concrete human attitude to all men. This is why it is not expressed solely in theoretical and abstract treatises but also strives to reach a larger public through novels and plays. This attempt disconcerts many people and makes them doubt that existentialism is truly a philosophy. But this is misunderstanding the truth of philosophy, which, particularly in France, has never appeared as a singular discipline but as a global vision of the world and of man that must embrace the totality of the human domain. Today, the ideologies that gain the approval of most French intellectuals, namely Christianity, existentialism, and Marxism, all have a common pretension of showing man in entirety.[7] They all respond to the same need: in France and all across Europe the individual is seeking with anguish to find his place in a world turned upside down.

Pascal summarized the ambiguity of the relationship between the Universe and man in a famous and striking expression when he called man a thinking reed.[8] From this definition, Christianity retains essentially the aspect of interiority: in the secret of his heart, by the purity of his intentions, and by the individual accomplishment of the ethics dictated by his conscience, man will attain his salvation in this world. On the contrary, Marxism emphasizes that man is a reed, a thing among things, definable by his relationship with the objective reality of the world.

Existentialism strives to hold both ends of the chain at the same time, surpassing [dépassant] the interior-exterior, subjective-objective opposition. It postulates the value of the individual as the source and reason for being [raison d'être] of all significations and all colors, yet it admits that the individual has reality only through his engagement in the world. It affirms that the will of free being is sufficient for the accomplishment of freedom, yet it also states that this will can posit itself only by struggling against the obstacles and the oppressions that limit the concrete possibilities of man. It resembles individualism in the sense that it seems important to it that each individual gains his own salvation, and that each individual appears as being the only one able to obtain it for himself. Yet it also resembles Marxist realism because only in working actively for the concrete triumph of universal freedom, by proposing ends for himself that surpass him, can the individual hope to save himself. Thereby existentialism also seeks a reconciliation of those two reigns whose divorce is so nefarious to men in our time: the ethical reign and the political reign. Ethics appears to existentialism not as the formal respect of eternal and supraterrestrial laws, but as the search for a valid foundation of human history, such as it unfolds on our earth. Politics is not, for existentialism, the simple adjustment of the efficient means toward an unconditioned end, but the perpetual and incessant creation and construction of the end by the means used to produce it. In other words, the task of man is one: to fashion the world by giving it a meaning. This meaning is not given ahead of time, just as the existence of each man is not justified ahead of time either.

Along with the idea of a God guaranteeing Good and Evil, existentialism rejects the notion of ready-made values whose affirmation precedes human judgment. By freely taking his own freedom as an end within himself and in his acts, man constitutes a kingdom of ends.[9] Cut off from human will, the reality of the world is but an "absurd given." This is a conception that appears to many people as hopeless and makes them accuse existentialism of being pessimistic. But actually there is no hopelessness, since we think that it is possible for man to snatch the world from the darkness of absurdity, clothe it in significations, and project valid goals into it. We very simply rediscover the wisdom of old Montaigne, who said, "Life is in itself neither good nor evil; it is the place of good or evil as you make them!"[10] The fact is that the old labels, idealism-realism, individualism-universalism, pessimism-optimism, cannot be applied to a doctrine that is precisely an effort to surpass these oppositions in a new synthesis, respecting the fundamental ambiguity of the world, of man, and of their relationship.

Such a novelty, I repeat, can hardly be summarized; it reveals itself only by a direct intuition that must be sought in the works where it is presented, and that bears fruit only if one takes the time to let it ripen within oneself.

NOTES

1. "Zazou" is the name given to a group of flashy and elegant young French people in the 1940s who loved American jazz music.

2. Founded in 1257, the Sorbonne is one of Europe's oldest universities and the first endowed college in the University of Paris system.

3. The French Society of Philosophy was founded in 1901, with the goal of bringing together scientists and philosophers in an atmosphere that promoted communication.

4. Immanuel Kant (1724–1804) was a German philosopher and founder of critical transcendental philosophy. Georg Wilhelm Friedrich Hegel (1770–1831), a German idealist philosopher, was the author of *Phenomenology of Mind* (1807), which Beauvoir read at the start of the Nazi occupation of France, in July 1940; see Beauvoir's *Journal de guerre*, ed. Sylvie Le Bon de Beauvoir (Paris: Gallimard, 1990), 339.

5. Albert Einstein (1879–1955), a German physicist, transformed scientific and philosophic investigation and earned the 1921 Nobel Prize in physics. Louis-Victor-Pierre-Raymond de Broglie (1892–1987) was a French physicist known for his work on quantum theory. He won the 1952 Nobel Prize in physics. "Newton's mechanics" refers to concepts originated by Sir Isaac Newton (1642–1727), including his Laws of Motion and Law of Universal Gravitation.

6. René Descartes (1596–1650), a French mathematician, scientist, and philosopher, is considered the father of modern philosophy.

7. Marxism takes its name from the economic and political philosophy of Karl Marx (1818–83). It is also known as "scientific socialism" (as opposed to utopian socialism).

8. Blaise Pascal (1623–62) was a French scientist and religious philosopher. The "thinking reed" is explained in chapter 10, n. 1.

9. "Kingdom of ends" is the English translation of *règne des fins,* the French term for a phrase from Kant's *Groundwork for the Metaphysics of Morals.*

10. See Michel Montaigne, "That to Philosophize Is to Learn How to Die," *The Complete Works of Montaigne: Essays, Travel Journal, Letters,* trans. Donald M. Frame (Stanford: Stanford University Press, 1957), 65, where it is rendered as follows: "Life is neither good nor evil in itself: it is the scene of good and evil according as you give them room."

Contributors

KRISTANA ARP is professor of philosophy at Long Island University, Brooklyn. She is the author of *The Bonds of Freedom: Simone de Beauvoir's Existentialist Ethics,* as well as articles on Edmund Husserl, Simone de Beauvoir, and Jean-Paul Sartre.

NANCY BAUER is an assistant professor of philosophy at Tufts University, where she teaches courses in feminism, the history of philosophy, ethics, and film. She is the author of *Simone de Beauvoir, Philosophy, and Feminism* and is working on a book entitled "How to Do Things with Pornography."

DEBRA BERGOFFEN is professor of philosophy, women's studies, and cultural studies at George Mason University. Working within the context of the continental tradition, she examines issues at the intersections of epistemology, ethics, politics, and feminism. She is the author of *The Philosophy of Simone de Beauvoir: Gendered Phenomenologies, Erotic Generosities.* Her essays appear regularly in scholarly journals and anthologies.

ANNE DEING CORDERO is professor emerita of French at George Mason University. She is the author of numerous publications in twentieth-century French literature and translation. She translates from French and German into English.

EDWARD FULLBROOK, with Kate Fullbrook, is the author of a dozen essays on Beauvoir's philosophy and two books, *Simone de Beauvoir and Jean-Paul Sartre: The Remaking of Twentieth-Century Legend* and *Simone de Beauvoir: A Critical Introduction.* He is also an economist whose most recent book is *The Crisis in Economics.* He is a member of the School of Economics of the University of the West of England.

SYLVIE GAUTHERON attended the École Normale Supérieure de Fontenay St-Cloud in France and obtained her Ph.D. from the University of Durham (U.K.) in 2003. She is currently teaching English at the Université de Versailles—Saint-Quentin-en-Yvelines.

SARA HEINÄMAA is a senior lecturer in the Department of Philosophy at the University of Helsinki. She is also professor of humanist women's studies at the Center for Women's Studies and Gender Research at the University of Oslo. She is the author of *Toward a Phenomenology of Sexual Difference.*

ELEANORE HOLVECK is an associate professor of philosophy at Duquesne University. She is the author of *Simone de Beauvoir's Philosophy of Lived Experience: Literature and Metaphysics.* Her speciality is the philosophical novel and the ethics of Immanuel Kant. Her most recent work is on Nelson Algren and Milan Kundera.

SONIA KRUKS is the Danforth Professor of Politics at Oberlin College. She is the author of numerous works that address the social and political thought of the French existentialists, including the intersections of existentialism and feminist theory. Her most recent book is *Retrieving Experience: Subjectivity and Recognition in Feminist Politics.*

MARY BETH MADER is an assistant professor of philosophy at the University of Memphis. She works in the area of European philosophy and feminist philosophy and is the author of essays on Irigaray, Nietzsche, Foucault, and Heidegger. She is the translator of Irigaray's *The Forgetting of Air in Martin Heidegger.*

328

FREDERICK M. MORRISON is an associate professor of Spanish at Southern Illinois University Edwardsville. His translations done in collaboration with Veronique Zaytzeff include *Musorgsky Remembered,* by Alexandra Orlova; sections of *Shostakovich Reconsidered,* by Allan Ho and Dimitry Feofanov; and "Merleau-Ponty and the Pseudo-Sartreanism" and "Literature and Metaphysics," by Simone de Beauvoir.

SHANNON M. MUSSETT is assistant professor of philosophy at Utah Valley State College. Her main research interests center around feminism, nineteenth-century German philosophy, and French existentialism. She has published articles on Simone de Beauvoir and G. W. F. Hegel and continues to explore the connections between Beauvoir and the history of philosophy.

HÉLÈNE PETERS headed the French department at Macalester College and has written and translated articles and books on contemporary France and existential literature. The French government conferred on her the rank of Officier des Palmes Académiques.

MARGARET A. SIMONS, professor of philosophy at Southern Illinois University Edwardsville, is the author of *Beauvoir and "The Second Sex,"* editor of *Feminist Interpretations of Simone de Beauvoir* and two special issues of *Hypatia* on Beauvoir's philosophy (1985 and 1999), and coeditor (with Azizah al-Hibri) of *Hypatia Reborn.*

MARYBETH TIMMERMANN is a certified translator of the American Translator's Association and the Alliance Française de St. Louis. She has taught French at St. Louis Community College and at Southern Illinois University Edwardsville.

KAREN VINTGES is a senior lecturer in political science and social philosophy at the Department of Philosophy of the University of Amsterdam. She has published *Philosophy as Passion: The Thinking of Simone de Beauvoir; Feminism and the Final Foucault;* and several other books in Dutch.

GAIL WEISS is director of the human sciences graduate program and associate professor of philosophy at George Washington University. She is the author of *Body Images: Embodiment as Intercorporeality* and the coeditor of *Thinking the Limits of the Body* and *Perspectives on Embodiment: The Intersections of Nature and Culture.* She has published articles on Beauvoir in *Si-*

mone de Beauvoir Studies; Man and World; and the *Journal of the British Society for Phenomenology.* She is currently working on a manuscript entitled "Beauvoir's Ambiguities: Philosophy, Literature, Feminism."

VERONIQUE ZAYTZEFF is an associate professor in the Department of Foreign Languages and Literature at Southern Illinois University Edwardsville. She translates from French and Russian. Her translations include "Merleau-Ponty and Pseudo-Sartreanism," *Musorgsky Remembered,* and several articles in *Shostakovich Reconsidered.* Her usual collaborator is Frederick M. Morrison.

Index

Abraham (biblical character), 105, 274

absolute: and Beauvoir's appeal to science in support of political change, 20; Beauvoir's rejection of philosophical, 7; and *The Ethics of Ambiguity*, 285–86; evil, 241, 242, 257; and "Existentialism and Popular Wisdom," 197, 200, 210, 213, 217; and "An Existentialist Looks at Americans," 302; and "An Eye for an Eye," 241, 242, 257, 258; and further research on works of Beauvoir, 10; and "Introduction to an Ethics of Ambiguity," 287, 291, 292, 293–94; and "Literature and Metaphysics," 274; and "Moral Idealism and Political Realism," 177, 178, 181, 186, 189–90; philosophical novel as methodological alternative to, 8; and philosophy as way of life, 217; and *Pyrrhus and Cineas*, 82, 104, 106, 115, 117, 131; and scientific experimenta-

tion, 27; and *The Second Sex*, 20; truth as, 26, 27. *See also* doubt

abstract/abstraction: Beauvoir's views about, 39; and existential methodology, 35; and "An Existentialist Looks at Americans," 311, 312, 313; and "Introduction to an Ethics of Ambiguity," 293; and "Literature and Metaphysics," 264, 270; and "Moral Idealism and Political Realism," 178

absurdity, 102, 326

accomplishment, individual, 311–12, 325

accountability, 171. *See also* responsibility

action: in *All Men Are Mortal*, 86; and be and being, 135–38; and Beauvoir's *Harper's Bazaar* article about Sartre, 225; and *The Blood of Others*, 200, 264; and communication, 126, 128, 130, 135; and devotion, 121, 123, 125, 126; and *The Ethics of Ambiguity*, 303;

be and being: and action, 135–38; and
Beauvoir's *Harper's Bazaar* article
about Sartre, 224; and Beauvoir's review of *The Phenomenology of Perception* by Merleau-Ponty, 162, 163; and
communication, 129, 130, 132; as distinctive thesis of Beauvoir, 39; and
The Ethics of Ambiguity, 286; and
God, 102, 104, 105; and Hegel, 293;
and humanity, 107, 111; and influences
on Beauvoir, 9; and "Introduction to
an Ethics of Ambiguity," 281, 282,
285–87, 291–94; and "Moral Idealism
and Political Realism," 181, 188; and
philosophical novel as methodological alternative to absolutes and system building, 8; and philosophy as
way of life, 224; and *Pyrrhus and Cineas,* 83–86, 93, 102, 104, 105, 107,
111, 114–17, 122, 129, 130, 132,
135–38; of Sartre, 224, 291, 292; and
She Came to Stay, 39; and "What Is Existentialism?" 325
Beauvoir, Simone de: death of, 1; further
research on, 9–10; influence of, 1;
misunderstanding of works of, 1–6; organization of works of, 6–7; Simons
and Benjamin interview of (1979), 2,
34, 36; as student, 3, 16–17, 264
Beauvoir, Sylvie Le Bon de, 1
becoming, 101, 110, 111–12, 117
Being and Nothingness (Sartre): and ambiguity, 291; and Beauvoir's *Harper's
Bazaar* article about Sartre, 224, 229;
and Beauvoir's review of Merleau-
Ponty's *The Phenomenology of Perception,* 163; criticisms of, 197–98,
285; and existence, 292; failure in,
292; and "Introduction to an Ethics of
Ambiguity," 285, 291, 292; and phenomenology, 154; as philosophical
text, 39; and Sartre on being, 115; and
Sartre's relationship with Beauvoir,
2–3, 33, 34, 36; and subjectivity, 320;
and "What Is Existentialism?" 320
Being and Time (Heidegger), 199

Benjamin, Jessica: interview of Beauvoir
by, 2, 34, 36
Bergoffen, Debra B., 10, 79–81
Bergson, Henri-Louis, 7, 9, 105, 264, 265,
273
Bernanos, Georges, 119
Bernard, Claude, 7, 9, 10, 17, 19, 265. See
also *Introduction to the Study of Experimental Medicine* (Bernard)
biological determinism, 20
Blanchot, Maurice, 2, 139, 264, 266, 274
The Blood of Others (Beauvoir): and action, 200; ambiguity in, 8; and Beauvoir's commitment to philosophy, 3;
Beauvoir's early philosophical work as
context for, 7; criticisms of, 3, 264,
266; and "Existentialism and Popular
Wisdom," 197, 200; and "Literature and
Metaphysics," 266; and "Moral Idealism and Political Realism," 164–65,
168; and naming of existentialism,
320; and Nazi occupation, 200; as
popular and critical success, 263, 264;
publication of, 263; and *Pyrrhus and
Cineas,* 79; as "thesis novel," 264;
translation of, 266; violence in, 168
body: and Beauvoir's *Harper's Bazaar* article about Sartre, 225, 231–32; and
Beauvoir's review of *The Phenomenology of Perception* by Merleau-Ponty,
154, 160–61, 162, 163; and existential
ethics of Beauvoir, 226; and "An Existentialist Looks at Americans," 314;
and "Introduction to an Ethics of Ambiguity," 290; and "Moral Idealism
and Political Realism," 183, 184
Bonaparte, Napoleon, 111
Bossuet, Jacques-Bénigne, 205
Brasillach, Robert, 6–7, 8–9, 239, 240,
243, 252, 253, 254, 257. *See also* "An
Eye for an Eye" (Beauvoir)
The Brothers Karamazov (Dostoevsky), 275
Bude, Guillaume, 51, 53

Camus, Albert, 92, 93, 171, 208, 223–24,
239

197; and naming of existentialism, 320; and organization of Beauvoir's philosophical works, 6; and *Pyrrhus and Cineas,* 200; reasons for writing, 197; and Sartre, 200; and *The Second Sex,* 201

"An Existentialist Looks at Americans" (Beauvoir): and *America Day by Day,* 301, 305; by Beauvoir, 307–15; and *The Ethics of Ambiguity,* 303; and *The Force of Circumstance,* 304; Mussett introduction to, 301–5; and organization of Beauvoir's philosophical works, 7; and *Pyrrhus and Cineas,* 303, 304; and *The Second Sex,* 305

experience: and Beauvoir's review of *The Phenomenology of Perception* by Merleau-Ponty, 154–55, 160, 163; and existentialism, 35; Husserl's views about, 155; and "Introduction to an Ethics of Ambiguity," 282, 286; and "Literature and Metaphysics," 264, 270, 271, 273–74, 275; Merleau-Ponty's views about, 154–55; and phenomenology, 35; and theory, 9

experiment: definition of, 25. *See also* scientific experimentation

exteriority. *See* inside-outside

external world: Beauvoir's valuing of discovery of, 18–19, 20, 39

"An Eye for an Eye" (Beauvoir): ambiguities in, 8–9; Arp introduction to, 239–44; by Beauvoir, 245–60; and *The Ethics of Ambiguity,* 240–41, 243; and "Existentialism and Popular Wisdom," 243; and organization of Beauvoir's philosophical works, 6–7; as philosophical essay, 240; as response to Brasillach's treason trial, 6–7, 8–9, 239, 240, 243, 252, 253, 254, 257

Ezekiel (prophet-priest), 135

facts, 27–28, 258, 272

failure, 254, 258–59, 285, 287, 291–93

fascism, 185, 186

Faulkner, William, 310

Fear and Trembling (Kierkegaard), 105, 274

feminism, 19, 20, 67, 80. *See also specific work*

Ferdonnet, Paul, 246

Ferdousi, Shahnameh, 209

finite. *See* infinite/finite

Fink, Eugen, 154

Flaubert, Gustave, 102

The Flies (Sartre), 231, 232

Flight to Arras (Saint-Exupéry), 133

The Flight of the "Firecrest" (Gerbault), 116

The Force of Circumstance (Beauvoir autobiography): and Beauvoir's commitment to philosophy, 3–4; and Beauvoir's study of phenomenology, 154; and existential ethics, 226; and "Existentialism and Popular Wisdom," 197, 201; and "An Eye for an Eye," 240; and "Literature and Metaphysics," 265–66; money in, 304; and "Moral Idealism and Political Realism," 167, 170, 172; and naming of existentialism, 319; and *Pyrrhus and Cineas,* 80; and Sartre-Beauvoir relationship, 2, 227; and "What Is Existentialism?" 320

Foreign Lands (Arland), 98

Fouillée, Alfred, 9, 16

France/French: and Brasillach's trial, 239; characteristics of, 313; education of women in, 15–16; intellectuals in, 239, 324–25; literary realism in, 264–65; philosophy in, 324–25; political parties in, 184; realism and idealism in postwar, 170; Revolution of 1789 in, 184. *See also* Nazi occupation; *specific person*

Francis of Assisi, 103

Françoise (fictional character). See *She Came to Stay*

fraternity, 199, 200, 203, 204, 206, 213

freedom: and action, 135, 136–39; and Beauvoir's 1924 student essay on Bernard, 7, 18; and Beauvoir's *Harper's Bazaar* article about Sartre, 224, 225,

analysis of, 17–19, 20; Simons and Peters' introduction to Beauvoir's analysis of, 15–22
"inverted vision," 161
investigation. *See* observation; scientific experimentation
"The Invitation to the Voyage" (Baudelaire), 57

Janet, Pierre, 97
"Jean-Paul Sartre, Strictly Personal" (Beauvoir), 4, 7; purported manuscript of, 229–35; Vintges introduction for, 223–28
John of the Cross (saint), 116
journalism, 240
justice: and "An Eye for an Eye," 241, 243, 246–47, 249, 251, 252, 254, 258; and *Pyrrhus and Cineas,* 80, 85–86, 87

Kafka, Franz, 105, 139, 274
Kant, Immanuel: disillusionment with ideas of, 197; ethics of, 127, 131, 138, 177–78, 189; and "Existentialism and Popular Wisdom," 197, 198, 214; and "An Eye for an Eye," 257; and "Literature and Metaphysics," 269; and "Moral Idealism and Political Realism," 169, 177–78, 189; objectivity of, 258; and *Pyrrhus and Cineas,* 84, 125, 127, 128, 131, 138, 139; as system builder, 34; and "What Is Existentialism?" 321, 324
Kierkegaard, Søren, 81, 105, 114, 156, 274, 291, 319
knowledge, 282, 291, 294, 310
Kruks, Sonia, 164–73
Ku Klux Klan, 251

La Balue (French prelate), 250
La Fontaine, Jean de, 205, 208, 313
La force de l'âge (Beauvoir), 156
La Rochefoucauld, Duke de François, 198, 205, 211, 212
La structure du comportement (Merleau-Ponty), 153

Labiche, Eugéne, 204
Laforgue, Jules, 106
Lahr, Charles, 16, 18
language, 133, 141, 162, 163
Laurencin, Marie, 67
Laval, Pierre, 252, 253
Leibniz, Gottfried Wilhelm, 2, 7, 17, 274
Lenin, V. I., 180
Les bouffons (Zamacois), 44
Les Éditions Nagel, 239
Les temps modernes (journal): Beauvoir's writings in, 4, 6, 7, 154, 167, 197, 198, 239, 320; and desire for new world, 170; founding of, 164; and Merleau-Ponty, 4, 167–68; and naming of existentialism, 320; purpose of, 240; and Sartre, 4, 197, 199, 240
Letters to Sartre (Beauvoir), 5
Lévinas, Emmanuel, 154
life: and "An Existentialist Looks at Americans," 308, 314; and Hegel, 290; and "Introduction to an Ethics of Ambiguity," 284, 290–91; and "Literature and Metaphysics," 266; and *The Mandarins,* 266; philosophy as way of, 216–18, 223, 224–26, 227; "tragic sense" of, 314; and "What Is Existentialism?" 326. *See also* death
literature, 231, 264–65. *See also* "Literature and Metaphysics" (Beauvoir)
"Literature and Metaphysics" (Beauvoir): and *America Day by Day,* 265; and appearance, 275; by Beauvoir, 269–77; and Beauvoir's commitment to philosophy, 3; and Beauvoir's enthusiasm for scientific discovery, 19; and *The Blood of Others,* 266; as critical success, 266; as defense of metaphysical novel, 7, 264–68, 269–77; and influences on Beauvoir, 9; and *The Mandarins,* 266–67; and methodology, 8, 19, 265; and organization of Beauvoir's philosophical works, 7; and *Pyrrhus and Cineas,* 266–67; Simons introduction to, 263–68
logic: and Beauvoir as student, 16

Beauvoir of, 156–57; and morality, 156; and philosophy as way of life, 224; and *Pyrrhus and Cineas*, 81, 108, 109, 114; and *She Came to Stay*, 56, 59, 60, 63, 65, 68; and spirit of serious-mindedness, 309; and subjectivity, 156; and "What Is Existentialism?" 319

nihilism, 320

No Exit (Sartre), 232

nominalism, 10

nothing/nothingness: and Beauvoir's *Harper's Bazaar* article about Sartre, 224; and "Introduction to an Ethics of Ambiguity," 289, 294; and *Pyrrhus and Cineas*, 107, 114, 125, 130, 139, 140. See also *Being and Nothingness* (Sartre)

novels: as "adventure of the mind," 272, 275; as alternative to methodology of absolutes and system building, 9, 19; authentic, 265; "Literature and Metaphysics" as defense of metaphysical, 264–68, 269–77; and methodology of novelists, 35; psychological, 273, 275; as theme in Beauvoir's philosophical works, 8

object/objectivity: and "Existentialism and Popular Wisdom," 198; and "An Existentialist Looks at Americans," 302–3, 309, 310, 313; and "An Eye for an Eye," 255, 258; false, 99, 126, 139; and "Introduction to an Ethics of Ambiguity," 283, 290, 294; of Kant, 258; and "Literature and Metaphysics," 264, 265, 274, 275; and "Moral Idealism and Political Realism," 177, 178–79, 181, 188, 189; and *Pyrrhus and Cineas*, 99, 119, 126, 139; and *The Second Sex*, 321; and "What Is Existentialism?" 320, 325. See also subject/subjectivity

observation, 17, 23–28

Odile (saint), 65

Odyssey (Homer), 120

old age, 18

Other/others: ambiguities of, 8–9; Beauvoir's failure to win recognition for formulation of problem of, 4; and Beauvoir's *Harper's Bazaar* article about Sartre, 225–26; and Beauvoir's review of *The Phenomenology of Perception* by Merleau-Ponty, 162; and communication, 126–35; and devotion, 117–26; and *The Ethics of Ambiguity*, 285–86, 287; and existential ethics, 226; and "Existentialism and Popular Wisdom," 208, 212; and "An Eye for an Eye," 241; and freedom, 83, 86, 287; and "Introduction to an Ethics of Ambiguity," 283; and "Moral Idealism and Political Realism," 168, 183; and philosophy as way of life, 227; and *Pyrrhus and Cineas*, 8, 80, 83–87, 93, 97–98, 101, 108, 111, 116–35, 140, 141; Sartre credited with formulation of problem of, 4; and Sartre's influence on Beauvoir, 227; and *She Came to Stay*, 2, 39, 264; as theme in Beauvoir's works, 8; translation of, 5. See also *specific work*

outside. See inside-outside

pacifism, 169, 185

Palissy, Bernard, 204, 206

Paquis, Jean Hérold, 246

paradise, 98–99, 110, 124, 209, 312

Parain, Brice, 36

Parshley, H. M., 4–5

Pascal, Blaise, 97, 98–99, 183, 198, 205, 325

Pasteur, Louis, 28, 204

perception: and Beauvoir's review of *The Phenomenology of Perception* by Merleau-Ponty, 153–64

personality, 17, 27

Pétain, Philippe, 252, 253

Peters, Hélène N., 16–22

phenomenology: and *America Day by Day*, 265; and *America Day by Day* (Beauvoir), 265; Beauvoir's attempt to integrate science and, 19–20; and

Merleau-Ponty, 159; and differences between Sartre and Beauvoir, 201; and disillusionment with Kantian ideas, 197; and "Existentialism and Popular Wisdom," 200, 211; and "An Eye for an Eye," 251, 258; Flaubert's views about, 102; and humanity, 131; and "Literature and Metaphysics," 273; and "Moral Idealism and Political Realism," 169, 172, 177, 178; and *Pyrrhus and Cineas,* 83, 86, 101, 102, 104, 111–12, 113, 138; and Sartre, 199, 201
usefulness/uselessness, 292, 294
The Useless Mouths (Beauvoir), 7, 197, 199, 263–64
utilitarianism, 182, 205
utopianism, 87, 180

Valéry, Paul, 97, 98
values: and Beauvoir's review of *The Phenomenology of Perception* by Merleau-Ponty, 155; and *The Ethics of Ambiguity,* 155; and "Existentialism and Popular Wisdom," 197, 198, 203; and "An Existentialist Looks at Americans," 304, 309, 312; and "An Eye for an Eye," 245, 257, 258; and "Introduction to an Ethics of Ambiguity," 287, 294; and "Moral Idealism and Political Realism," 169, 170, 171, 172, 175, 181, 182, 183, 187, 188–89; and *Pyrrhus and Cineas,* 99, 119, 127, 140; source of, 155; and "What Is Existentialism?" 325
Van Gogh, Vincent, 62, 63, 67, 94, 208
vengeance. *See* revenge
Verlaine, 69
Vintges, Karen, 4, 223–28
violence: in *The Blood of Others,* 168; in *The Ethics of Ambiguity,* 86; and evil, 86, 87, 138; and existentialist ethics, 8; and "An Eye for an Eye," 241–42, 249, 251, 252, 255, 256; and further research on works of Beauvoir, 10; and "Moral Idealism and Political Realism," 168, 171, 179; in *Pyrrhus and Cineas,* 80, 86, 87, 124–25, 136, 138; in

The Second Sex, 86–87; as theme in Beauvoir's works, 8
virtue, 213–14
vitalism theory, 17
Voltaire, 308. *See also* Candide's garden

Walden (Thoreau), 116
The Wall (Sartre), 232
war, 290
"The War Has Taken Place" (Merleau-Ponty), 167–68
Warnock, Mary, 35
Weidmann, Eugene, 206
Weiss, Gail, 281–88
"What Is Existentialism?" (Beauvoir): Bauer introduction to, 319–22; by Beauvoir, 323–27; as defense of existentialism, 7; and influences on Beauvoir, 9; and organization of Beauvoir's philosophical works, 7; and *Pyrrhus and Cineas* (Beauvoir), 320; and *The Second Sex,* 321
When Things of the Spirit Come First (Beauvoir), 7, 19, 198
Wilson, Woodrow, 180
wisdom, 100
women: and differences between Sartre and Beauvoir, 200–201; education of, in France, 15–16; and existential ethics, 226–27; and "Existentialism and Popular Wisdom," 205. *See also* feminism
Woolf, Virginia, 157
world: and Beauvoir's review of *The Phenomenology of Perception* by Merleau-Ponty, 162–63; Beauvoir's valuing of discovery of external, 18–19, 20, 39
World War I, 180, 216
World War II, 180–81, 231. *See also* Nazi occupation; *specific person*
Wright, Richard, 264
writers: responsibility of, 240

Zamacois, Miguel, 44
Zeno of Elea, 100
Zimmermann, Jean-George, 24
Zola, Émile, 52

The University of Illinois Press
is a founding member of the
Association of American University Presses.

UNIVERSITY OF ILLINOIS PRESS
1325 South Oak Street   Champaign, IL 61820-6903
www.press.uillinois.edu